SAP BW Reporting and Analysis

PRESS

SAP PRESS is issued by
Bernhard Hochlehnert, SAP AG

SAP PRESS is a joint initiative of SAP and Galileo Press. The know-how offered by SAP specialists combined with the expertise of the publishing house Galileo Press offers the reader expert books in the field. SAP PRESS features first-hand information and expert advice, and provides useful skills for professional decision-making.

SAP PRESS offers a variety of books on technical and business related topics for the SAP user. For further information, please visit our website: *www.sap-press.com*.

Frank Forndron, Thilo Liebermann, Marc Thurner, Peter Widmayer
mySAP ERP Roadmap
2006, 293 pp., ISBN 1-59229-071-X

Norbert Egger, Jean-Marie R. Fiechter, Robert Salzmann,
Ralf Patrick Sawicki, Thomas Thielen
SAP BW Data Retrieval
2006, 552 pp., ISBN 1-59229-044-2

Steffen Karch, Loren Heilig et al.
SAP NetWeaver Roadmap
2005, 312 pp., ISBN 1-59229-041-8

Jens Stumpe, Joachim Orb
SAP Exchange Infrastructure
2005, 270 pp., ISBN 1-59229-037-X

Arnd Goebel, Dirk Ritthaler
SAP Enterprise Portal
Technology and programming
2005, 310 pp., ISBN 1-59229-018-3

Norbert Egger, Jean-Marie R. Fiechter,
Jens Rohlf, Jörg Rose, Oliver Schrüffer

SAP BW
Reporting and Analysis

SAP PRESS

Contents

3 Sample Scenario 87

4 The SAP Business Explorer Query Designer 99

5 The BEx Web 199

6   Information Broadcasting   365

7 SAP Business Content 423

A Abbreviations 445

B Queries 447

C   Formula Operators   473

D   Attributes and Values of BEx Web   479

E   Transaction Codes   505

F   Metadata Tables   509

G   Glossary   513

H   Literature   561

I   The Authors   563

Index   567

Preface

"I want to be kept informed of incoming sales orders and revenues on a daily basis, regardless of whether I'm at the office, and irrespective of the people who prepare and present these figures for me. Furthermore, I want to be able to retrieve those figures whenever I need them. I want to be informed ... especially if deviations and particular events occur."

This scenario isn't new. But, do you know of any executive board in which the automatic supply of up-to-date business information really works?

In addition to a consolidated periodic reporting, the timely, often daily information regarding the most important key figures of a company, or of a specific area of responsibility, represents a critical requirement for executives.

For well over a decade, data warehousing systems have been trying to master the quick, convenient, and secure supply of information for the decision-makers in companies. The comparison with the department store of data—where you can simply fetch the required information from the shelves—has become a standard analogy. For a long time, this notion has been hindered by IT systems that didn't meet the technical requirements, whereas today, complex business structures and processes, as well as a vast amount of information, pose the main obstacle.

With SAP Business Information Warehouse (SAP BW), SAP entered the data warehousing solutions market extraordinarily late. Based on the motto, "Rome wasn't built in a day," SAP BW excels because of a very sophisticated concept, and since Release 2, this concept has been fully implemented up to and including the area of reporting. As you will see, it is especially in the field of reporting that the Releases 3.0/3.1 and 3.5 have taken major steps toward achieving enhanced functionality, increased flexibility, and greater comfort.

In addition to the basic reporting functions of a data warehouse that must be a given, there are other often allegedly minor features and soft factors that affect user acceptance and the successful use of the solution:

▶ **The performance of the tool**
Although users had to wait hours and sometimes even days until they received the required information before a data warehouse was introduced in their company, today, one minute spent waiting in front of the computer screen is often regarded as unacceptable. The tolerance threshold is 10 to 15 seconds.

▶ **The time invested by the user**
In these fast moving times and with increasingly shorter product life-cycles, it is expected that even managers (who are not as familiar with data analysis tools as their assistants or controllers) can learn how to use and master a reporting tool within the smallest possible amount of time.

▶ **The use of a familiar IT environment**
An unpopular tool such as MS Excel often gains in popularity if it is to be replaced, for instance, by a web application. The decision as to which frontend tools are to be used for SAP BW must be thoroughly evaluated and consistently implemented. If you don't have a frontend strategy, you will most probably encounter a number of problems, which will undoubtedly generate additional costs.

▶ **The right combination of flexibility and functionality and easy usage**
Too many navigation options can lead to a very high degree of complexity and even obstruct their use; on the other hand, an insufficient range of functionalities can prohibit a flexible data analysis. It is therefore imperative that you find the right combination that is tailored to meet the specific requirements of users.

The further development of SAP BW is proceeding rapidly. It is a challenge for BW developers to keep up-to-date. Furthermore, it is always the latest details that are decisive, especially in reporting; however, many functions aren't used because they are simply unknown, or insufficiently documented.

To utilize the available but previously unused potentials of a release can be compared to leveraging the potential value of a small release update. The BW trainings that are currently available provide an introduction to the basic principles. But, to obtain a deep insight into the BW know-how and to be able to quickly implement projects, you must collaborate with experienced consultants and refer to the specific recommended literature.

This book is intended to help readers increase and enhance their SAP BW knowledge, and therefore make optimal use of this potential.

Heerbrugg (Switzerland), February 2006
Bernhard Fritz
Leica Geosystems

Foreword

SAP BW Library

When Wiebke Hübner, then an editor at SAP PRESS, asked me in December 2002 if I wanted to write a book on SAP BW, I waved her off. Such a book, I thought, would have to be too voluminous in order to offer an adequate presentation. I also believed that a viable market for such a book would not exist, so the effort would be of no value. Luckily, she was resolute, which resulted in our first book on SAP Business Information Warehouse, *SAP BW Professional*. I paid particular attention to the rapid development of the reporting functionality in SAP BW 3.x and other topics in that book.

Background

Besides the fact that writing the book proved to be enjoyable, the general interest that this work generated after its publication surprised me a great deal. That's why I'm so pleased to thank you, the readers, at the very beginning of this book for your great interest and the wonderful feedback that you've provided. You should note that a second edition of the first book has already been published in several languages.

Thanks to readers

I hope to contribute to companies to best help them meet the challenges of adequately mining and using information. That includes the successful use of business intelligence tools. In SAP BW, SAP has offered a very powerful tool for several years now. But, because implementations often fail to reach an appropriate standard, the question regarding the ability of such a product to function in real life often arises. Therefore, my hope is to increase knowledge about the options and functionality of business intelligence tools so that future implementations and the operation of these solutions are more successful and useful.

My vision

Based on the great interest shown in the first book, the rapid development of SAP Business Intelligence components, and the welcome growth of our company, the management of the CubeServ Group decided to approach the topic even more consistently in collaboration with SAP PRESS. Gradually, we happened upon the idea of offering a comprehensive compendium—a compendium that would describe the functionality of SAP BW in even greater detail.

The idea of a compendium

It became readily apparent that one book and one individual involved in the life of a project could not complete such a monumental task: The functionality (luckily) is too vast and such a book would be too comprehensive. We therefore needed to create a multivolume work that would

The SAP BW Library

focus on specific aspects, such as data modeling, extraction, transformation, and loading (ETL) processes, reporting, and planning. The idea of a new series, the *SAP BW Library*, began to take shape.

Because our wonderful CubeServ team consists of many highly motivated co-workers, we were quickly able to create a team of authors who were willing to split up the work and produce a book on each topic.

Volume 1: SAP BW Data Modeling
Volume 1 of the SAP BW Library, an introduction to data modeling using SAP BW, was published last year and, to our delight, met with a remarkable response.

Volume 2: SAP BW Data Retrieval
The second volume, an introduction to data retrieval using SAP BW, is also already available in bookshops. It supports readers in finding the right path to mapping ETL processes using SAP BW.

A look ahead
Because several authors are already working on the forthcoming volumes, I'm confident that, step-by-step, this series will offer you a comprehensive description of the functionality of SAP BW. Furthermore, if interest continues to remain high, additional books will appear after the first four volumes and address SAP Business Intelligence tools in even greater detail.

A Note on this Book

Volume 3: SAP BW Reporting and Analysis
It gives me great pleasure to be able to present the third volume of the *SAP BW Library* with an introduction to reporting and analysis with SAP BW.

The authors are all employees of the CubeServ Group and have been involved in implementation projects and the operation of data warehouses, particularly SAP BW, for many years. The focus of this book lies mainly with the description of the basic concept and a first set of functions. This is complemented by useful information on a selection of new functions that have been available since the introduction of SAP BW Release 3.5.

Jona (Switzerland), February 2006
Norbert Egger

Introduction and Overview

Data retrieval with reporting and analysis represents the most obvious step within the data warehousing process for the end user. In times where the successful information management has become a core competence in all companies, data retrieval becomes particularly important.

Introduction

This book is the third volume of a new series, the *SAP BW Library*[1]; all its authors are considered experts in business intelligence and work at CubeServ Group. This book examines the fundamentals of *reporting and analysis*; the other volumes of the SAP BW Library address other topics regarding both their basic principles and the details. The topics include *data modeling* and *data retrieval*.

Volume 3 of the SAP BW Library

To enable easy access to the complex subject matter of SAP Business Information Warehouse (SAP BW), we've decided to work as closely as possible to the actual implementation and with as many examples as necessary in all volumes of the *SAP BW Library*. Therefore, the foundation for our books is a uniform case study developed by the authors: a virtual company (CubeServ Engines). We will use this case study to present and communicate all the important requirements of business intelligence applications in a manner that reflects real life experience.

Comprehensive case study

The first goal of this book is to introduce the basic concepts of SAP BW, both in terms of data warehousing in general and specifically regarding the area of reporting and analysis. A second goal is to present the steps involved in implementing reporting and analysis processes in SAP BW systematically and step by step. Our case study will serve as an unbroken thread as you go through the material.

Goal of this book

The detailed description of the components and implementation steps will enable the various groups within a company that deal with SAP BW to comprehend the material even if they have no deeper understanding of IT. We hope to use this procedure to make SAP BW projects more successful so that employees of user and IT departments, application

---

1 You can find an overview of the volumes of the *SAP BW Library* in Appendix H of this book.

experts, and consultants can gain profound knowledge and reach a common foundation of knowledge and language.

Structure of the Book

Four topic areas: This book can be divided into four essential areas:

1. Background and theoretical basics of SAP BW reporting and analysis (Chapters 1 and 2).
2. Presentation of the case study (Chapter 3)
3. Detailed presentation of four major topic areas: "SAP BEx Query Designer," "SAP BEx Web," "Information Broadcasting," and "SAP Business Content" (Chapters 4–7)
4. Additional supporting information (Appendices)

Chapter 1: Data Warehousing and SAP BW

Chapter 1 gives you an overview of the basic concepts and architecture of data warehouse systems as well as an overall understanding of the functionality of SAP BW.

Chapter 2: Data Retrieval Concepts and SAP BW

Chapter 2 provides a complete overview of reporting and analysis concepts and their implementation with SAP Business Information Warehouse. You will develop an insight into data retrieval in the data warehouse environment and the data acquisition components of SAP Business Information Warehouse.

Chapter 3: Sample Scenario

Chapter 3 gives you an overview of the basic elements of the case study used in all volumes of the SAP BW Library. In light of the subject matter of this book, the chapter examines specific aspects of *reporting and analysis* in detail.

Chapter 4: The SAP BEx Query Designer

Queries represent the core of the reporting and analysis functionality in SAP BW. *Chapter 4* introduces the concepts of the major functions of an SAP BW query and the associated design tool and provides a series of examples that build upon each other.

Chapter 5: The BEx Web

SAP Business Explorer (BEx) Web comprises all BEx tools that can be used to create web-based applications or are themselves web applications. *Chapter 5* enables you to evaluate and use the web reporting functions provided in SAP BEx Web.

Chapter 6: Information Broadcasting

Chapter 6 describes the basic functionality of SAP BW Information Broadcasting and its integration with other SAP NetWeaver components. This enables you to provide users with business intelligence content that is specifically designed for the target group.

Chapter 7 describes the preconfigured solution, SAP Business Content, which SAP delivers with SAP BW. In particular, this chapter outlines the solution's strengths and weaknesses, and recommends ways in which you can leverage Business Content for reporting and analysis to meet your requirements.

Chapter 7: SAP Business Content

The *appendices* provide additional assistance for your daily work: overviews, documentation on the queries used in the sample scenario, and, in particular, a comprehensive glossary.

Appendices: Overviews and glossary

Working with This Book

The goal of this book is to offer users of SAP BW—from various areas and differing levels of knowledge—a strong foundation for modeling data with SAP BW.

This book is readily accessible to readers with varying levels of knowledge and individual information requirements.

What do you want to know?

▶ Readers who want to study SAP Business Information Warehouse starting from its conceptual design should begin by reading the theoretical approach in Chapter 1, *Data Warehousing and SAP BW*.

▶ Those readers who mainly want a quick overview of reporting and analysis with SAP BW should begin with Chapter 2, *Data Retrieval Concepts and Their Implementation in SAP BW*, and then, as needed, look at the details in the subsequent chapters.

▶ Readers interested in individual aspects, such as defining queries, using web items, publishing reports in SAP Enterprise Portal, and so on, can and should use this book as a reference guide. They can find information on specific topics by using the table of contents, the index, and the glossary.

To make it even easier for you to use this book, we have adopted special symbols to indicate information that might be particularly important to you.

Special symbols

▶ **Step by step**
An important component of this book is to introduce complex work with SAP BW step by step and explain it to you precisely. This icon points to the beginning of a step-by-step explanation.

▶ **Note**
Sections of text with this icon offer you helpful hints and detailed information in order to accelerate and simplify your work.

▶ **Recommendation**
This book offers tips and recommendations that have been proven in our daily consulting work. This icon indicates our practical suggestions.

▶ **Caution**
This icon indicates tasks or steps that require particular attention. The accompanying text indicates when you should exercise particular caution.

After You've Read the Book ...

Even after you've read the book, we'd like to continue to assist you if you need advice or help. We offer the following options:

▶ **SAP BW Forum**
Under the motto of "Meet the Experts!" you can use an Internet forum to send additional questions to the authors and share them with the business intelligence community.

Stop by for a visit: *www.bw-forum.com*. You will find exclusive materials for download here.

▶ **E-mail to CubeServ**
If you have additional questions, you're invited to send them to the authors directly by e-mail. See Appendix I, *The Authors*, for their e-mail addresses.

Acknowledgements

Books are never produced without the support and collaboration of many. That's why we'd like to express our special thanks to the following people for their collaboration, help, and patience:

Norbert Egger

Because various members of our CubeServ team are creating the SAP BW Library, I'd like to thank all the authors sincerely for their participation. Without them, work on this book would have been impossible, because it requires comprehensive and specialized knowledge. Acknowledgement is also due to all other colleagues in the CubeServ Group, especially since I had less time than usual for them and my own work as well, while working on this volume. On behalf of all the authors of this volume, I would especially like to thank Wiebke Hübner, who made this book possible thanks to her great dedication and immense creativity. I would also like to thank my publisher Galileo Press for their cooperation and patience.

Above all, I thank my family, especially my beloved wife. During the course of this project, she once again supported me by managing the entire family business and showing an endless amount of patience and care. My thanks also goes to our children, whose great tolerance, even on weekends or during their school vacation, made it possible for me to work on the SAP BW Library.

Jean-Marie R. Fiechter

This volume would not have been possible without various sources of help. Thanks are due to all those who helped me. I would especially like to thank my two sons Patrick and Oliver for their support and encouragement. I dedicate this work to my beloved wife Karin.

Jens Rohlf

Without the support of and feedback from all employees at the CubeServ Group, the creation of this book would have been impossible—many thanks. I'd especially like to thank my wife, Claudia, for the time and space she gave me as I worked on the book.

Jörg Rose

I'd like to say a special thanks to all the other authors for their cooperation while writing this book, and also thanks to all those who supported me in my work on this book. In particular, I'd like to thank them for their understanding since a large part of my time that was usually allocated to them went into the writing of this book.

Oliver Schrüffer

Many thanks to Wiebke Hübner and Jörg Rose, and, of course, to all those who participated in writing this book and supported me in my work. Thanks are also due to all customers who—with their interesting projects and ideas—have dramatically added to the enormous pool of knowledge that we have today. Thanks also to my friends, Simon and Andi, who haven't heard much from me during the course of this project. I would especially like to thank my wife, Daniela, who always provided me with help and advice, and who is probably the person most elated now that the book has been completed. During the course of writing this book, our daughter, Emma Lavinia, was born, and she was the most beautiful Christmas gift that I could have ever wished for.

Special Thanks

All of the authors would like to thank Bettina Kaehne and Daniela Schären who have produced the screenshots for this book with commitment and great care.

Jona (Switzerland) and Flörsheim am Main (Germany),
February 2006
Norbert Egger
Jean-Marie R. Fiechter
Jens Rohlf
Jörg Rose
Oliver Schrüffer

1　Data Warehousing and SAP BW

Data warehouse systems enable efficient access to data from heterogeneous sources of information, customized storage, and a convenient display of the information gathered for the end user. This chapter gives you an overview of the basic concepts and architecture of data warehouse systems.

1.1　Introduction

The structure of a data warehouse and the formatting of data in a format specific to and optimized for the end user serve one main goal: to provide information that supports decision-making and generates knowledge, and therefore enables actions beneficial to the business.

For several years, two terms have become preeminent in the area of information retrieval:

Data Warehouse and OLAP

▶ **Data Warehouse (DWH)**
 As a data pool to retrieve consolidated, historical, and consistent information

▶ **Online Analytical Processing (OLAP)**
 As a description for the multidimensional analysis concept

SAP Business Information Warehouse (SAP BW) is described as a comprehensive tool for analytical applications that contains all required data warehouse components.

In this chapter, we describe the main features of the concepts *Data Warehouse (DWH)* and *Online Analytical Processing (OLAP)* and how these concepts are implemented in SAP BW.[1] Our goal in doing so is to provide you with a sufficient introduction to the basics, which should act as a foundation on which to base your understanding of the analysis and reporting process of SAP BW.

1.2　The Data Warehouse Concept

The main benefit of a data warehouse system lies in its ability to derive required information from data, which, in operational systems, is available only in a form that is inappropriate for analysis.

Main benefit

---

[1]　You can find more detailed information on Data Warehousing and the theoretical principles in Volume 1 of the *SAP BW Library*: Egger, Fiechter, Rohlf, 2005, Chapter 1.

Such a system merges fragmented information from the most important systems across the whole value chain in a manner that enables quick and targeted decisions at all company levels. The data warehouse unifies information on vendors, products, production, warehouse stocks, partners, customers, and sales, for example, into a holistic view and does so independently of the data's source platform.

Example

The derivative of warehouse (that is, "Warenhaus" or department store) is an apt analogy. A data warehouse can also be described as a self-service store for information. In fact, many characteristics of a data warehouse are identical to those of a traditional department store. The data warehouse is the central storage point for data (which primarily offers read access) and guarantees the formatting and availability of all required information. As is the case in a self-service store, end users (customers) independently take a product, in this case information, from the shelves and put it into their shopping cart. The shelves are arranged by product; the supply of goods is customer-oriented. Similar goods from various sources are located next to each other.

Typical characteristics

According to Inmon,[2] the information in a data warehouse differs from the data in operational systems and exhibits the following characteristics:

▶ **Subject-orientation**
The data warehouse is organized according to the subjects to be analyzed, and not according to the operational application structure. Therefore, the data warehouse concept is based on the concentration of object and subject areas, such as products and customers. Operational data that is important only for running operational processes and is not involved in the process of supporting decision-making has no place in a data warehouse.

Example

If we return to the department store metaphor, this approach means that a buyer preselects goods and then places on the shelves only those goods for which demand likely exists. The buyer tries to avoid shelf-warmers.

▶ **Integration**
There are no syntactical and semantic data inconsistencies in the data warehouse. One of the central characteristics of a data warehouse is

---

2 Inmon, 2002.

that when data is collected from the operational systems, it is brought to a consistent level in terms of both syntax and semantics. This uniformity comprises completely different aspects and usually refers to the formats, units, and coding. In addition, designers must agree on the characteristics stored in the data warehouse, because the various operational systems often describe the same concept with different characteristics and various subject areas with the same characteristics.

The goal of this uniformity is to achieve a consistent set of data that represents "one source of the truth," even when the data sources are heterogeneous.

Example

In terms of the department store example, this means that the goods must undergo an inspection when they arrive. This control sorts out unusable goods from partial deliveries and then formats and standardizes the remaining goods.

▶ **Time variance**

To enable time-series analyses, the data warehouse stores information over longer periods. But this apparent deficit of the data warehouse approach results from the way it is used. Views of long- and mid-term periods (annual, monthly, or weekly examinations) are the focus of DWH reports. That's why information that might not be completely up-to-date is fully acceptable for these evaluations. The data warehouse is updated at defined intervals (hour, day, or month), depending on the requirements for timeliness. Once stored, information is not typically modified or removed from the data warehouse.

The time variance also means that data in the data warehouse is valid only at a specific time for a specific interval. This *validity period* is recorded as part of the key for all the relevant data in the data warehouse. Temporal analyses (historical views of the changes over a given period) are possible because the data that is already in the data warehouse is not modified; however, updated data is added to it with a new validity period.

Validity period

Example

The goal of our "department store" is not to follow the latest trends all the time, but to maintain an established supply of goods over the long term with periodic deliveries of goods. New models don't replace existing models; rather, they supplement existing models.

▶ **Non-volatility**

The storage of data over long periods requires well planned processes, tailored system landscapes, and optimized storage procedures to minimize the scope of the information to be stored and the runtime of individual analyses and reports. Alternatively, data of operational applications ultimately remains in those systems only until the processing of a specific transaction is completed. Then, the data is archived or deleted so that the performance of the system is improved and unacceptable response times are avoided.

The optimization of data access and the loading of data are important issues in modeling data warehouses. Updating data (modifying contents) is also not recommended, because the data of a data warehouse has a documentary character.

Example

In our example, the requirement of non-volatility would mean that the department store has an extensive storage capacity and ensures the availability of goods over the long term.

1.3   Basic Characteristics of a Data Warehouse Solution

Overall goal

The overall goal of a good data warehouse architecture should be to describe an integrated data warehouse environment that meets the requirements of a company and that can be implemented iteratively.

The integrated environment covers all aspects of the data warehousing process: data acquisition, data storage with detailed data, slightly and heavily aggregated data, and the provision of analyses and reports (see Figure 1.1). All layers provide administrative functions that are supported by a comprehensive and consistent metadata repository. The repository contains information on the data stored in the data warehouse.

Layers of the data warehouse architecture

A logical data warehouse architecture can be divided into three main layers.

▶ Data acquisition layer

▶ Data storage layer

▶ Data presentation layer

We will now describe these layers.

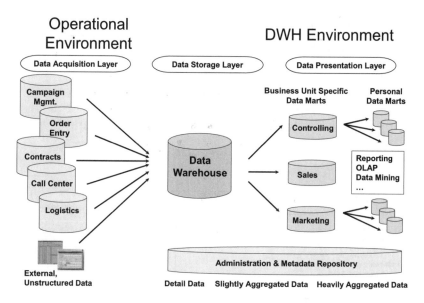

Figure 1.1 The Layers of an Integrated Data Warehouse Environment

1.3.1 Data Acquisition Layer

The function of the data acquisition layer is to extract data from various (operational) source systems through interfaces, to transform it, and to load it into the data warehouse.

The data acquisition layer (also called the *ETL* layer, for *Extraction*, *Transformation*, and *Loading*) is broken down into the following three process steps:

Three process steps

▶ **Extraction**
Filtering the required data from the operational data sources

▶ **Transformation (data cleansing)**
Syntactic and semantic data preparation

▶ **Loading**
Inserting data into the data warehouse

Scheduling and metadata management round out these functions (see Figure 1.2). The following sections describe these functions in more detail.

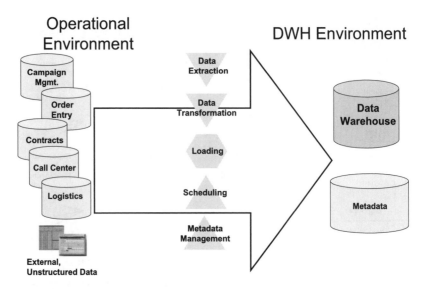

Operational Environment

Campaign Mgmt.

Order Entry

Contracts

Call Center

Logistics

External, Unstructured Data

Data Extraction

Data Transformation

Loading

Scheduling

Metadata Management

DWH Environment

Data Warehouse

Metadata

Figure 1.2 The ETL Process

Extraction from Source Systems

Extraction

In the extraction process step, the data needed by users is collected from the data sources so that it can then be stored in the data warehouse. After the initial data import (*initial load*), the data warehouse must be reloaded with new data according to user-defined requirements for timeliness and consistency.

Possible methods

Users have two methods for a reload:

▶ **Reloading, Full Load**
The complete reloading of all data.

▶ **Incremental Load, Delta Load**
The incremental data acquisition. Instead of deleting and reloading a section of the data in the data warehouse, during an incremental data acquisition only the changes to the operational data are loaded into the data warehouse.

The initial load, as well as the complete reload of the data, does not pose any specific data acquisition problems.

Obstacles to incremental loading

However, for an incremental data import, you must first extract the changes relevant to the data warehouse from the operational systems. Depending on the operational application, you have the following various options from which to choose:

▶ **Triggers**

If the operational database supports the use of SQL triggers, you can use them to retrieve the data. Triggers allow the definition of database operations that are executed automatically based on specific events. For the extraction of data, triggers are used that run at each modification of the operational data set and store the modifications in an appropriate modification table. The data records in the modification table can then be transferred to the data warehouse at regular intervals.

▶ **Log files**

You can often use the log files (*logs*) of the operational database systems for extraction. Most database systems support log files to recreate a consistent state for the database (*recovery*) after a system failure. Special programs can evaluate log files and extract the data manipulation operations contained therein. The data is then transferred into the data warehouse.

▶ **Monitor programs**

In some circumstances, neither triggers nor log files can be used to extract data, so that the only remaining option is access to the operational data set. In this case, you can use special monitor programs to extract the relevant modifications. Such programs periodically generate a snapshot of the data and then calculate the difference between the current snapshot and the previous one (*differential snapshot algorithm*).

▶ **Modification of the operational application systems**

If the operational system storing the data does not support triggers or log files, and you cannot use a monitor program; you must modify the operational system so that it logs every modification that it executes in a separate database. Then, you can transfer the relevant modifications into the data warehouse periodically. Some manufacturers of operational application systems have adjusted their software in order to enable the automatic transfer of differential data to specific data warehouse systems. One example is the integration of the Enterprise Resource Planning (ERP) application, SAP R/3, with SAP Business Information Warehouse (SAP BW).

In some circumstances, an update of the data warehouse requires both the filtering of the relevant modifications and the executing of queries and transformations on the operational data in order to reduce the number of data records to be transferred.

Data Cleansing

Transformation A unified data schema is set for the data warehouse during the development phase. The data from the various operational systems must then be transformed into the data warehouse format during loading. In addition, the heterogeneity of the data sources and the operational systems frequently leads to inconsistencies and even to erroneous data. For example, the following problems can occur: The use of different attribute values for the same attributes, missing values, different formatting of the data, and so on.

In order to create a clean and consistent data warehouse, these problems must be eliminated. The data cleansing tools on the market can be subdivided into the following groups:

▶ **Data migration tools**
This category of data cleansing tools permits the definition of simple transformation rules to transform the data from the source systems into the target format (for example, transformation of attribute value "male" to "m" or "1").

▶ **Data scrubbing and data cleansing tools**
Data scrubbing tools use area-specific knowledge to cleanse the data from the operational sources. For example, they might use a table of all postal codes, localities, and street names to check and correct addresses. In terms of technology, these tools frequently use fuzzy logic and neural networks.

▶ **Data auditing tools**
You can use data auditing tools to recognize rules and relationships between data. The tools then verify whether the rules have been violated. Since it is almost impossible to determine with absolute certainty whether an erroneous state exists, the tools simply notify you of possible errors, which you must then correct manually. Such tools can use statistical evaluations to determine that the discrepancies between specific values might indicate the presence of incorrect entries. This type of data analysis is usually based on data mining techniques.

Inserting Data in the Data Warehouse

Loading The actual inserting of the data into the data warehouse occurs after the extraction of the required data from the source systems and the subsequent data cleansing. Most systems also perform the following tasks concurrently:

- ▶ Checking the integrity constraints
- ▶ Calculating aggregations
- ▶ Generating indices

To reduce the load on the operational systems to a minimum, you can decouple the actual inserting of data into the data warehouse from the transmission of data from the operational systems. You would use *operational data stores (ODS)* to do so. An ODS stores data from the operational systems in an almost unmodified form until it can be inserted into the data warehouse. To reduce the length of the load process, you can execute data cleansing and aggregation operations within the ODS tables.

Operational data store

Data is loaded into the data warehouse based on user-defined timeliness and consistency requirements. To avoid inconsistent results from queries, you cannot access the data in the data warehouse during the update. However, a "query copy" of the data can be made available during the update. For this reason, most data warehouses are updated when few queries on the data occur, namely at night and on weekends. In addition to updating the actual data warehouse, you must also, while loading the data, update the data basis of the data mart system used. For relational data mart systems, this data basis is usually identical to the data warehouse. However, multidimensional data mart systems (OLAP systems) are based on specific multidimensional database systems that must also be brought up-to-date.[3]

Consistent query results

1.3.2 Metadata Management

In principle, metadata is data on data. It describes both technical and business-relevant characteristics of data. During the data acquisition phase, you must also consider the relevant metadata. This includes the management of all types of metadata (technical, administrative, business-relevant, and so on).

A central, integrated metadata repository enables the transparent and unified access from all components of the business intelligence solution to all data. In this way, changes in one process (for example, ETL) can be seamlessly passed along to all other processes (for example, to the end user analysis tools).

Purpose of the metadata repository

---

3 Volume 1, Chapter 1, of the *SAP BW Library* provides detailed information on the different OLAP technologies. See: Egger, Fiechter, Rohlf, 2005.

This is an essential capability for the IT department, as well as for the user departments.

▶ For IT, it allows a better understanding of the effects of changes in the data and in the data flow, as well as the development of consistent, analytical applications.

▶ It also provides the user departments with a transparent and seamless access to information, regardless of the analysis tools used.

Types of metadata In general, we differentiate between the following types of metadata:

Technical metadata

This type of metadata contains all the technical information required for the development, operation, and use of a data warehouse. This metadata can further be distinguished by the time of its creation:

▶ **Administrative metadata**
This type of metadata contains all the information created during the development and use of the data warehouse. Examples include:

   ▶ Definition of the data warehouse and OLAP schema with the corresponding key figures, characteristics, attributes, dimensions, and hierarchies

   ▶ Description of the data sources, time of data loading, data cleansing, and transformation rules

   ▶ Description of the indices and aggregates used

   ▶ Characteristics of predefined reports and queries

   ▶ User profiles and roles with the corresponding authorizations

▶ **Operational metadata**
Operational metadata is created during the operation of the data warehouse. Examples of this data include:

   ▶ Monitoring data for the ETL process (extractions, transformations, data cleansing, and data loading) and modifications of the source system

   ▶ The state of archiving and backup jobs and monitoring of memory usage

   ▶ User statistics and requests that contain errors

Business metadata

This type of metadata contains all the required information on the business environment in the company. It includes the following:

- ▶ Definition of field contents
- ▶ Nomenclature (synonyms and homonyms)
- ▶ Glossaries

It also stores the rules for semantic interpretation, derivations, and calculations.

1.3.3 Data Storage Layer

In simple terms, the data storage layer of a data warehouse consists only of the data and its relationships. The relationships are derived from the corresponding relationship in the source system and stored permanently. In terms of the database technology, *materialized views* are used to depict these relationships. Operational systems, however, usually use *virtual* (also called "normal") *views* that store only the definition of a query, so that the result must be recalculated at each new access.

Materialized versus virtual views

Materialized views mean that the results don't have to be recalculated for each query; they can be precalculated, resulting in a significant improvement in performance. However, the modified data from the affected relationships in the source systems must be loaded into the data warehouse at regular intervals. Because a data warehouse rarely uses *real-time data*, materialized views don't have to be updated every time the data in the source system is modified. A deferred update at regular intervals is usually satisfactory.

Materialized views

Because a data warehouse should also ensure seamless access to integrated and historical data, it must sometimes deal with huge volumes of data (several gigabytes up to tens of terabytes). Such large volumes of data require special techniques for the efficient processing of queries.

The following section looks at the two most common options for query optimization: the use of aggregates and special indexing procedures.

Query Optimization

In addition to materialized views, *aggregates* (also called *aggregation tables* or *pre-aggregations*) are built in the data warehouse to optimize queries. Such aggregates are simply materialized views that usually contain the data being used in a pre-aggregated form. These aggregates allow you to respond to user-defined queries directly from the pre-aggregated values instead of having to calculate them from the detailed data each time.

Aggregates

The only drawbacks of these aggregates are the increased need for memory and the additional effort involved during the loading of the data warehouse.

Using aggregates Two challenges arise from the use of aggregates:

1. The correct choice of the aggregates to be built (considering the need for memory and the effort required in an update) and the expected use of these aggregates to process queries. The need for additional memory and the effort involved in the update make it impossible to calculate all combinations of aggregates. In addition, only a few of these combinations are actually used. Good data warehouse systems offer tools to determine the optimal combinations of aggregates.

2. The automatic (transparent to the end user) use of the available aggregates (if appropriate). This option is also characteristic of a good data warehouse.

Figure 1.3 illustrates the inner structure of a data warehouse and the distinction between detail data and aggregated data.

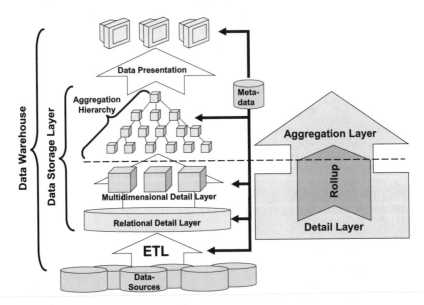

Figure 1.3 The Various Layers of a Data Warehouse

Relational detail data layer The materialized views fed directly from the source system are assigned to the *relational detail data layer* of the data warehouse. These tables serve as a consistent foundation for the other layers in the data warehouse. To prepare for future modifications that might be wanted and to contribute to the greater flexibility of the data warehouse, the relational detail data is often stored at a greater level of detail than is currently required.

The *multidimensional detail data layer* forms the basic layer for processing queries, while the aggregation layer above it contains aggregates for efficient processing of the queries.

Aggregation layer

Aggregation hierarchies are created when aggregates are built on the basis of other aggregates. The terms *upflow* or *rollup* are often used to describe the flow of information within such aggregate hierarchies.

Aggregation hierarchies

The division into a relational detail data layer and various multidimensional aggregation layers above it also allows you to meet simultaneous requirements for different types of updating, and it does so without compromising the consistency of the data warehouse.

Indexing Schemes

In addition to aggregates, indexing schemes are often used to accelerate the execution of queries. Studies of data warehouses over several years have shown that, besides the usual indices, two specific indexing schemes are particularly appropriate: the *bitmap index* and the *join index*.

Bitmap indices allow for a very efficient determination of the attribute properties of a data record. For example, a bitmap index for the four points of the compass would contain a two-bit vector with the following values: 00 for north, 01 for east, 10 for west, and 11 for south. The selection of all data records with the south attribute would therefore require a Boolean comparison with the value of 11. Such a task can be realized in a computer extremely efficiently. In addition, a bitmap index requires relatively little memory, because only bit vectors are stored. Furthermore, Boolean operators (AND, OR, and XOR) can calculate intersections and set unions of bitmap indices very efficiently.

Bitmap index

But there's also a downside to using bitmap indices, namely, they are only appropriate for attributes with a relatively small number of value properties (i.e., for attributes with a high cardinality).

A *join index*, however, maps the connection between relationships in terms of a common key; traditional index structures refer to a single table. To implement a join index, the references to all records (and the foreign key of the second table) are stored for each primary key of the first table.

Join index

This approach permits an extremely efficient calculation of joins between two tables.

Star index The literature also uses the term *star index* for the enhancement of the join index concept into a multidimensional model (star schema). A star index permits the storage of all relationships between a fact table and dimension tables that belong to it so that it can very efficiently determine the records that belong to one or more dimension table elements.

Data Modeling

To differentiate data modeling from data handling by transaction-oriented systems, we usually refer to *online analytical processing (OLAP)* in this context.

The OLAP model can best be described as a Rubik's cube.

Quantitative data (key figures)
▶ The quantitative data (*key figures*, such as sales and distribution, also described as *variables*, or *measures*) builds the cells inside the cube.

Qualitative data (characteristics)
▶ The desired approaches and aspects (*characteristics*, such as sales organization, products sold, time, that make up the qualitative data) are mapped on the dimensions (axes) of the cube.

The result is a multidimensional data structure, also called a *hypercube* or *data cube* (see Figure 1.4). Even if, strictly speaking, the metaphorical use of the cube is valid for only a three-dimensional model, we still speak of a cube, even with "n" dimensions.

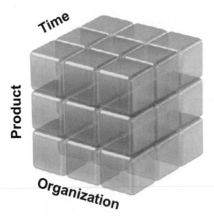

Figure 1.4 OLAP Data Model: Sample Cube

Fact tables Key figures are usually stored in *fact tables* in OLAP implementations. The fact tables form the foundation of an OLAP data structure.

Dimension Hierarchy

Another important function of a data warehouse is the storage of aggregate data. That's why you can aggregate dimension elements at multiple levels and create dimension hierarchies or *consolidation paths*.

Normally, a *total aggregation* forms the highest level within a dimension. In our example, it allows you to evaluate key figures by organization and time, independently of the product. | **Total aggregation**

The lowest characteristic level within a dimension provides the granularity of the data and thus also determines the data set stored in the cube. | **Granularity**

You define how aggregation is to occur individually for each key figure. In our day-to-day work, we often encounter key figures whose totals don't yield the desired results, or even lead to an incorrect result. For example, stock key figures (such as inventory stock) cannot be totaled. Totaling cumulative value key figures along certain dimensions (such as a data type dimension with plan, budget, and actual figures) is not very sensible. The system must offer alternate aggregation forms here: "last value," "average," "maximum," "no aggregation," and so on. | **Alternate aggregation forms**

1.3.4   Data Presentation Layer

In order to convert the data collected in a data warehouse into information that is relevant to the business, the data must be formatted accordingly before it can be presented properly to a target group. It is exactly this layer of the data warehousing process that this book is dedicated to. For this reason, we'll only briefly outline it at this point.

The extremely varied needs of users are the most important consideration here. Because of these differences, it is imperative that business-relevant information and facts that are necessary for decision-making be made available in diverse forms. The main categories include the following: | **Needs of users**

▶ Standard reporting

▶ Ad-hoc analyses

▶ Business planning and budgeting

▶ Data mining

Subsets (organizational, geographical, temporal, and so on) of data from the data warehouse are usually sufficient to mine the desired information. To accelerate and simplify the analysis and presentation tools, the required data is often extracted from the detail layer of the data warehouse and stored in a specific and optimal format for the target tool (data marts). | **Data marts**

Data marts are specific (often organizational or geographical) subsets of a data warehouse. They enable an iterative implementation of data warehouse systems. Data marts built on a central data warehouse enable the extraction of subject-specific data (from the underlying data warehouse) for individual groups of decision-makers (see Figure 1.5).

The data presentation layer usually consists of one or more data marts that provide the required (multidimensional and tabular) structures for frontend applications and presentation tools.

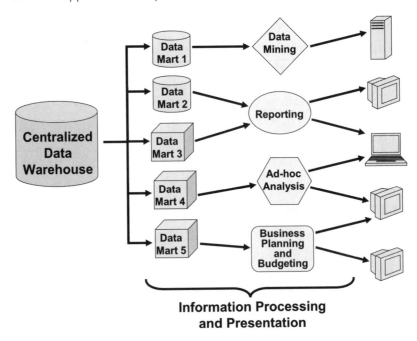

Figure 1.5 Various Target Groups and Their Influence on the Provision of Data

1.4 Architecture of SAP BW: Overview

A good example of an integrated DWH environment is the SAP Business Information Warehouse. SAP BW provides analytical applications as defined in the data warehouse and OLAP concepts; it also builds the core of the SAP NetWeaver Business Intelligence components.

Main components It contains all the components required for the data warehouse process. The following lists the core elements of SAP BW:

▶ **Functions for the ETL process**
Extraction of data from source systems and the corresponding data processing

▶ **Components for data storage**

For data storage and data provision there is a central management tool—the Administrator Workbench—which enables the structure, maintenance, and operation of the data warehouse.

▶ **Tools for analyses and reports**

SAP Business Explorer with the browser-based SAP Web reporting and the Excel-based Analyzer

In addition to these core elements, SAP BW offers the required additional components, with tools for customizing (to set up and configure customer-specific applications), for administration, monitoring, scheduling, performance optimization, open hub components, and so on. All elements of SAP BW are based on consistent metadata, and you can manage the metadata with the Administrator Workbench.

Additional components

The data warehouse components of SAP BW in the current Release 3.5 are shown in Figure 1.6.

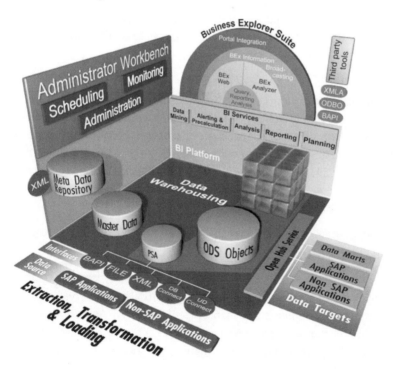

Figure 1.6 The Integrated Data Warehouse Architecture of SAP BW (Source: SAP AG)

The functionalities of SAP Business Information Warehouse shown above are those of the key processes of analytical applications: data acquisition, data storage, and data presentation. Numerous other components are also available, but addressing them here exceeds the scope of this introduction. We'd simply like mention the following additional components and functionalities:

▶ The powerful and mature basic functions available as part of SAP R/3 Basis technology: job control, role and printing functionality, user management, and so on

▶ SAP BW components such as SAP BW-specific functions to control authorizations, based on core functions in SAP R/3 or the integration of documents in the reporting

Metadata repository The core element of administration of a data warehouse is a central metadata repository. It contains all relevant information on the data stored in the data warehouse.

SAP BW Business Content With the SAP BW Business Content, SAP offers a variety of predefined analytical solutions directly supplied with SAP BW. These predefined models help to greatly reduce the time and effort required to set up and implement SAP BW, because they contain all the necessary components—from extraction to the data model to reports.

Thus, as part of a new SAP BW installation, Business Content allows for much shorter setup times, even if it is being used only as a template. However, you should not accept the predefined solution unquestioningly, even with all its benefits. This is because the solution frequently doesn't adequately fulfill the requirements of a real-world company. You should always check whether you can use the Business Content directly 'as is,' or whether it would be preferable to use it as a template for creating your own objects.

For additional tips and advice on this subject, see Chapter 7 of this book (*SAP Business Content*) as well as the relevant chapters of volumes 1 and 2 of the SAP BW Library.[4]

A look ahead In the following sections, we provide you with a brief overview of the most important elements and concepts of SAP BW. A more in-depth description of the data acquisition process (ETL) is provided in the chapters that follow. For additional information, we suggest that you refer to the other volumes of SAP BW Library.[5]

---

4   Volume 1: Egger, Fiechter, Rohlf, 2005, Chapter 7.
    Volume 2: Egger et al., 2005, Chapter 7.
5   See Appendix H, The *SAP BW Library*.

1.4.1 Data Acquisition in SAP BW

For the data acquisition for SAP BW, data from almost any source can be used (see Figure 1.7). You can differentiate between the following main groups of source systems:

Types of source systems

▶ **SAP systems**
Such as SAP R/3, SAP CRM, SAP APO, SAP SEM

▶ **Structured interface files**
So-called *flat files*

▶ **XML data (via standard SOAP protocol)**
You can use XML data to implement cross-system business processes directly, or by using SAP Exchange Infrastructure (SAP XI). Within the overall architecture of SAP NetWeaver, SAP XI handles the task of process integration.

▶ **Relational database systems**
Enable a connection via DB Connect

▶ **Universal Data Connect (UD Connect)**
Permits access to practically all relational and multidimensional data sources

▶ **Third-party systems**
Third-party systems can use *staging BAPIs* to load data and metadata into SAP BW (tools like Ascential Datastage and Informatica Power-Center).

In the end, the source systems just make the data available, usually through DataSources. Upon request, SAP BW starts to transfer the data. With source systems such as SAP systems, database systems (with UD Connect and DB Connect), and third-party systems (linked via BAPIs), the connection is highly integrated. SAP BW reads the data directly from the source system and then imports it according to the selected procedure.

DataSources

You can maintain Source Systems under Source Systems in the **Modeling** view of the Administrator Workbench, the SAP BW tool for the configuration, control, monitoring, and maintenance of all the processes involved in data acquisition, processing, and storage (see Figure 1.8).

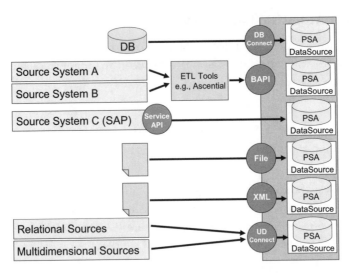

Figure 1.7 Integration of the ETL Process into the BW Architecture

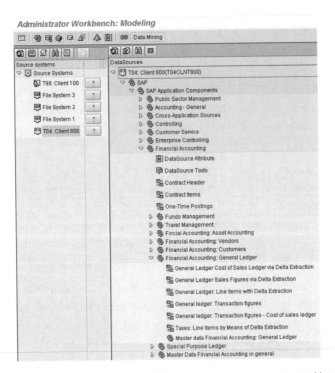

Figure 1.8 DataSources of SAP Systems in the Administrator Workbench

For each source system, the known DataSources can be displayed. You can use DataSources for all objects that contain data: master data (texts, attributes, and hierarchies for InfoObjects) and transaction data.

The structure for transferring data from a DataSource to SAP BW is called a **Transfer structure** *transfer structure*. If new DataSources are added later, they become available with a subsequent metadata upload. SAP R/3 systems provide a number of SAP Business Content DataSources that you can use immediately.

1.4.2 InfoSources

An *InfoSource* is a set of logically related information that is combined **Definition** into a unit.

You can maintain InfoSources under InfoSources in the **Modeling** view of the Administrator Workbench (see Figure 1.9). One or more DataSources for each selected source system is assigned specifically to an InfoSource. Each DataSource then makes its transfer structure available to the InfoSource.

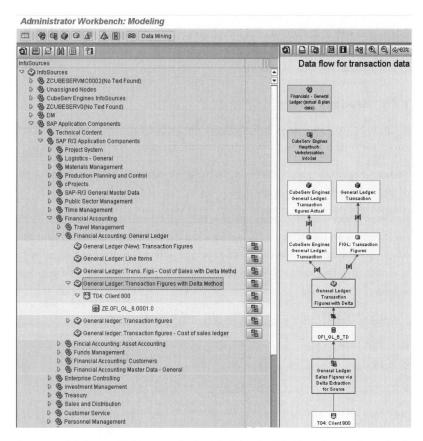

Figure 1.9 InfoSource Maintenance in the Administrator Workbench as an Example of Data Acquisition

The *communication structure* contains those InfoObjects into which an InfoSource is to transfer data (for master data, characteristic property, language key, and long texts, for example).

You use *transfer rules* to connect the data delivered in the transfer structure to the conversion of the data in a form appropriate to SAP BW in the communication structure. The transfer can occur in any of the following ways:

▶ Direct transfer (1:1 rule)

▶ Assignment of a constant value

▶ Routines (ABAP/4 program coding)

▶ Formulas

You can use the mechanisms described here to update master data directly in the InfoObjects. For InfoProviders (transaction data and, as an additional possibility as of SAP BW 3.0, also InfoObjects), posting occurs in a second step, the *update rules*.

1.4.3 Update Rules

In the update rules, you specify how the data from the communication structure of the assigned InfoSources is inserted in an InfoProvider.

You can maintain update rules under **InfoProviders** in the **Modeling** view of the Administrator Workbench.

Processing occurs differently for the various types of InfoProviders: You must define an update rule for every key figure and the related characteristics for InfoCubes. For ODS objects, the same requirement applies to the data and key fields; for InfoObjects, it applies to attributes and key fields.

The basic types of updates include the following:

▶ No update

▶ Addition, minimum, or maximum

▶ Overwrite (only for ODS objects)

You can set up the required rules for each key figure for key fields (or characteristics in InfoCubes). Here, too, you can use the following processing methods:

- ▶ Direct transfer (1:1 rule)
- ▶ Assignment of a constant
- ▶ Routines (ABAP/4 program coding)
- ▶ Formulas

In general, we recommend that you use the transfer rules to achieve adequate cleanliness of the data and the update rules to create logical transformations. Although SAP does not require that you adhere to this approach, it has the advantage of cleansing the data as soon as it "enters" SAP BW. It also allows you to dispense with (possibly) redundant cleansing functions and avoid the danger of not cleansing at all the required locations, which would result in inconsistent and incorrect data for reporting.

1.4.4 Requesting the Data Transfer and Monitoring

You use the scheduler to request that the date be transferred into SAP BW. Configuration occurs in *InfoPackages* that you maintain under **Info-Sources** in the **Modeling** view of the Administrator Workbench.

InfoPackage

InfoPackages define the selection, processing, and scheduling criteria for a DataSource assigned to an InfoSource. Customizing of the InfoPackages offers the settings required by the DataSources for various types of source systems:

- ▶ For interface files, you select the location of a flat file.
- ▶ For delta-capable SAP R/3 DataSources, you choose the full or delta upload option.
- ▶ For third-party tools, you select the parameters specific to the tool.

As of SAP BW 3.0, you can use process chains to configure complex processes (defining the sequence and criteria according to which data requests are to be processed).

Process chains

You can observe the load in progress with the monitor. The monitor offers an overview screen, as well as detailed information on the status and result of the load process.

Monitor

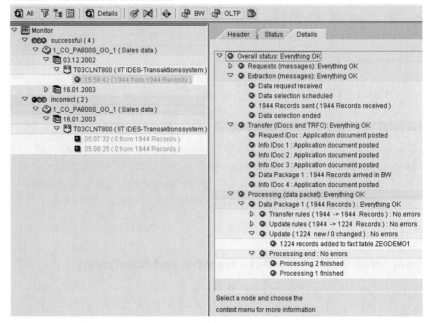

Figure 1.10 The Monitor Allows for Cross-System Monitoring of Data Acquisition and Supports Error Analysis.

1.4.5 Data Storage in SAP BW

InfoObjects

Definition   SAP refers to InfoObjects as *business evaluation objects*. InfoObjects provide the basis of the data model in SAP Business Information Warehouse.

You can edit InfoObjects under **InfoObjects** in the **Modeling** view of the Administrator Workbench (see Figure 1.11).

Figure 1.11 Maintaining InfoObjects in the Administrator Workbench

InfoObjects are divided into *key figures* and *characteristics*:

▶ Key figures provide the values (amounts, quantities, counters, dates, and time) to be analyzed.

Key figures

▶ Characteristics represent the business events and create relationships. SAP provides the following types of characteristics:

Characteristics

 ▷ Business characteristics (sold-to party, cost center, company code, and so on)

 ▷ Units (currency and quantity)

 ▷ Time characteristics (calendar day, calendar year, and fiscal year)

 ▷ Technical characteristics (number of a data load procedure, for example)

You can store master data, texts, and hierarchies for InfoObjects of the "characteristic" type. This data is then available for reporting on master and transaction data.

Master data and texts

SAP BW thus offers an opportunity to map very powerful key figures and characteristics. Examples include: non-cumulative key figures built by opening and supporting postings, complex, time-dependent texts (short and medium-length texts), attributes (profit center and person responsible, for example), and hierarchies-based characteristics and characteristics compounded to a controlling area.

Complex key figures and characteristics

InfoObjects are contained in *InfoObjectCatalogs*, which, in turn, are grouped by application area into InfoAreas.

InfoProviders

Definition All reportable objects (those that can be evaluated with *SAP Business Explorer*, the standard reporting tool of SAP BW) are called *InfoProviders*.

The SAP BW InfoProviders can be found under **InfoProviders** in the **Modeling** view of the Administrator Workbench (see Figure 1.12).

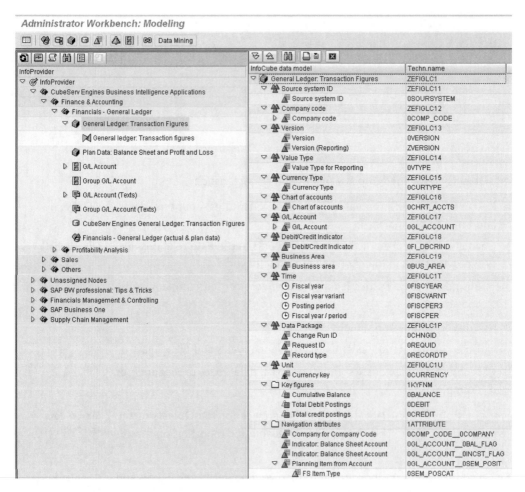

Figure 1.12 Maintaining InfoProviders in the Administrator Workbench; Example: InfoCubes

InfoProviders include the following objects:

Types of
InfoProviders

▶ **Objects that physically contain data**
SAP BW stores the data for these objects in the database tables that belong to them. The group of objects that physically contain data includes InfoCubes, operational data store (ODS) objects, and InfoObjects that contain master data.

▶ **Logical views**
Objects whose data is stored in another system (such as SAP R/3) or in another physical object. The group of logical views includes InfoSets, RemoteCubes, SAP RemoteCubes, virtual InfoCubes with services, and MultiProviders.

The basic InfoCubes that contain data consist of several relational tables that organize the InfoObjects they contain according to the enhanced star schema, which enables the mapping of complex data models.[6]

InfoCubes

Technically, ODS objects are simple tables that contain a number of key fields and a number of data fields.

ODS objects

Note the following (possible) limitations to this approach: The number of key fields is limited to a maximum of 16. The arrangement of all key and non-key characteristics with the key figures in one data record can lead to extremely long records. The options for optimizing performance are much more limited here than they are with InfoCubes.

Master-data-bearing characteristics as InfoProviders provide reporting with the master data tables of the attributes and texts of the particular characteristic involved.

InfoObjects as
InfoProviders

Additional InfoProviders, objects in SAP BW that do not contain data, include the following: *SAP RemoteCubes* (access to transaction data in other SAP systems, based on an InfoSource with flexible update rules), *RemoteCubes* (access to data from another system via BAPIs), and *virtual InfoCubes* (access to data from SAP and non-SAP data sources via a user-defined function module). All these InfoProviders enable flexible reporting.

SAP RemoteCube,
RemoteCube, and
virtual InfoCube

Like InfoObjectCatalogs, InfoProviders are grouped into *InfoAreas*.

InfoAreas

---

6 You can find further detailed information on this topic in Volume 1 of the *SAP BW Library*: Egger, Fiechter, Rohlf, 2005, Section 1.11.

MultiProviders

MultiProviders combine data from various InfoProviders. One possible use of a MultiProvider is the combination of an InfoCube with sales data with an additional InfoCube with headcount data. This approach would enable reports that calculate "per capita sales." Another possible use of a MultiProvider enables the combination of InfoCubes with sales with an InfoProvider type of InfoObject Material to display materials without sales (see also Figure 1.13).

Note that MultiProviders are not based on a join operation, but on a union operation (a union of the tables involved).

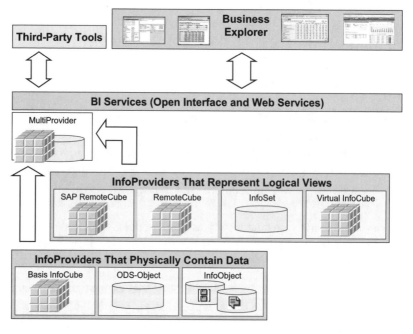

Figure 1.13 MultiProviders Make Objects That Physically Contain Data and Logical Views Available for Reporting

InfoSets

InfoSets form a semantic layer above the data sources, such as ODS objects and master data. With InfoSets, you can use all database techniques, including joins.

The ability to use this technology greatly increases your flexibility in SAP Business Explorer.

For all objects, however, note that storing data in other systems and remote access generally precludes you from influencing the system behavior, especially in terms of performance. Therefore, you should use these objects only after careful consideration.

One use that has been proven effective is for data checking: a SAP RemoteCube enables access to a source system; a MultiCube links the SAP RemoteCube to a BasicCube. A deviations analysis determines whether the data in the source system is consistent with the data in SAP BW.

Performance Optimization and Aggregates

You can use various functions to optimize performance. One of the main functions is the ability to model *aggregates*. Like InfoCubes, aggregates are modeled objects with a reduced volume of data or improved access options; SAP BW synchronizes aggregates automatically.

Modeling aggregates

1.4.6 Reporting and Analysis Tools

Various reporting and analysis tools can be used with SAP BW. Because these tools are the main subject of this book and will be described in detail in the subsequent chapters, we will only mention them briefly here. A basic differentiation exists between SAP tools and third-party tools.

The SAP BW standard reporting tool is the *SAP Business Explorer (BEx)*, which contains the following components:

SAP Business Explorer

▶ Query Designer
▶ Web Application Designer
▶ Web Applications
▶ Analyzer
▶ Information Broadcasting
▶ Additional functions

The functions of SAP Business Explorer are complemented by those of the *SAP Reporting Agent*. The reporting agent offers background and additional functions, such as

SAP Reporting Agent

▶ Evaluation of exceptions (exception conditions)

▶ Printing queries

▶ Precalculation of web templates

Integration These reporting functions can also be seamlessly integrated into the SAP Enterprise Portal (see Figure 1.14) without incurring a problem.

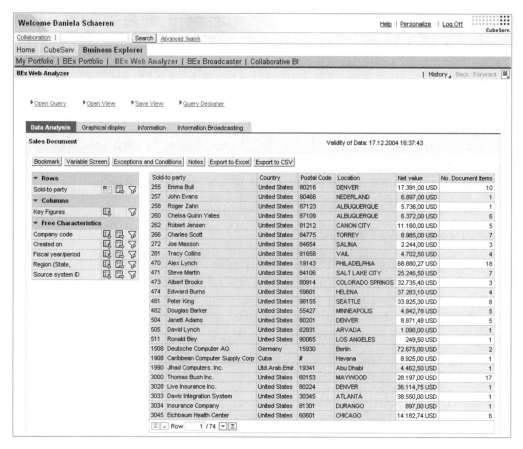

Figure 1.14 Integrating SAP Business Explorer with SAP Enterprise Portal 6.0; Example: BEx Web Analyzer

Third-party tools You can also use a variety of third-party tools to access data in SAP BW.

In Chapter 2, *Data Retrieval Concepts and Their Implementation in SAP BW*, we provide you with a detailed introduction to the field of reporting.

2 Data Retrieval Concepts and Their Implementation in SAP BW

This chapter will provide you with an overview of the most visible (to the end user), and thus most important step in the data warehousing process: data retrieval.[1] In addition to developing an insight into analysis and reporting concepts in the data warehouse environment, you'll be introduced to the relevant components of SAP Business Information Warehouse.

2.1 Introduction

Data retrieval, which consists of analyzing and modeling (as the primary activities) as well as of presenting and distributing information (as secondary activities) represents the second and third steps in a *closed-loop business analytics process*.

Closed-loop business analytics process

Typically, such a process consists of the following five steps (see Figure 2.1):

▶ Track

▶ Analyze

▶ Model

▶ Decide

▶ Adjust/Act

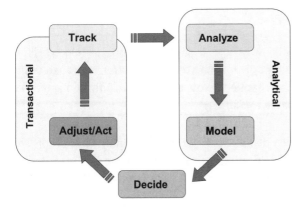

Figure 2.1 Closed-Loop Business Analytics Process (Source: IDC, 2003)

---

1 In this chapter, we will use the universally accepted term of Data Retrieval for this step of the Data Warehousing Process. Note that SAP generally uses the term Data Retrieval to describe the Data Acquisition (ETL) step of the same process.

The closed-loop business analytics process thus enables you to convert operational data into analyzable information from which you can then generate *actionable knowledge*, which you can use to influence the operational systems.

Once the data has been extracted from the operational systems, then transformed, cleansed, and loaded into the data warehouse (all of which corresponds to the first step in the closed-loop business analytics process, the "tracking"), it can finally be analyzed using business intelligence tools, which means that it is available for queries, reporting, and multidimensional analyses.

Traditional BI tools Traditional business intelligence tools enable decision-makers and information users to answer the following questions:

▶ What happened?

▶ How did it happen?

▶ When did it happen?

If one additional aspect could be added, it might be:

▶ Why did it happen?

However, the following questions are not even considered:

▶ Which alternate decisions are available?

▶ Which one is the ideal decision?

▶ What are the implications and possible consequences of this decision?

▶ What is going to happen?

 To run a company with just those traditional BI tools would be like driving a car and looking only into the rear-view mirror. Although you can see everything that happens, you don't see it until it has happened, which is probably too late.

Advanced analytics tools At that stage, the advanced analytics tools come into play. These tools are used to create rules, classifications, and additional models in order to support the decision-making process. In this context, the following means are used:

▶ Decision modeling

▶ Forecasting

- ▶ Simulation
- ▶ Optimization
- ▶ Risk analysis

Even though the illustration in Figure 2.1 leaves one with the impression that analyzing and modeling represent sequential steps, real life is different. It often happens that the results of an *Online Analytical Processing (OLAP)* analysis serve as the basis for the creation of a model, and conversely, forecasts and simulations often result in profound analyses, or the modeling results must be presented and distributed. Thus it is obvious that both steps are closely interrelated.

Problems in the procedure

But as the majority of business intelligence tools are not advanced analytics tools (and vice versa), this is where the problem begins: Incompatible tools are used that often have different databases, access different upstream systems, and are hardly able to exchange data with one another. As shown in Figure 2.2, this often results in a knowledge or learning gap that drastically disrupts and slows down the closed-loop process.

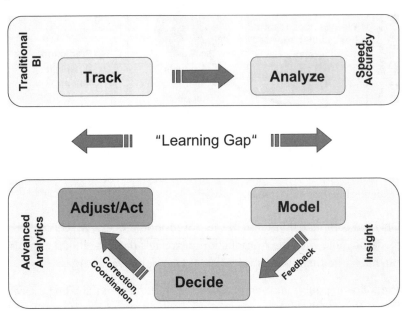

Figure 2.2 The Knowldege Gap ("Inconsistency Ditch") in the Closed-Loop Process (Source: IDC, 2003)

It is the objective of each organization to accelerate the process of "track, analyze, model, decide, adjust, and act" in order to attain a competitive advantage. However, speed without understanding can also result in faster but wrong decisions. Therefore, speed and precision must merge with understanding to produce a real competitive advantage.

Benefits of modern data warehouse systems

This is the point at which modern data warehousing systems such as SAP BW come into play. By providing a solid and consistent architecture as the foundation for the entire closed-loop process, they allow for faster, more precise and apt decisions and thus produce the necessary competitive advantage for the organization (see Figure 2.3).

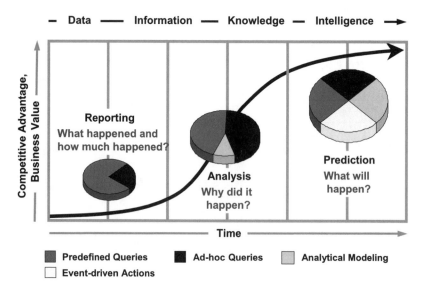

Figure 2.3 Evolution Path of Analytical Methods

Only the complete utilization of the closed-loop process, which has been made possible with the introduction of today's data warehousing tools, can maximize the business value and the competitive advantage.

The following quote also emphasizes the importance of creating a clean foundation for the data warehouse, particularly regarding data retrieval:

> *While the end user's needs and tools that support these needs differ, foundational components of business analytics software must be able to provide a unified architecture that supports all the user groups. End users should be able to view summary information and then drill down into*

detail that is specific to their business process. The underlying measures that enable this analysis must be consistent across the enterprise.[2]

To be able to really benefit from the use of a data warehouse, the closed-loop process must by no means end with the modeling step. It is vital that this step is followed by the additional steps, "decide" (based on solid information), and "act." This step ("act") represents the necessary feedback into the operational processes of the company.

Additional steps in the closed-loop process

In some cases, the feedback occurs automatically. If that happens, we speak of a *retraction*. In other cases, a decision-maker (or end user) obtains actionable knowledge; then, we speak of *manual feedback*.

Retraction and manual feedback

After this introduction to the closed-loop process, we'll now describe the two steps that are most relevant to us in this chapter: analysis and modeling.

2.1.1 Deductive versus Inductive Analyses

We can divide analyses into two main categories (in this context, modeling is often treated in the same way):

▶ **Deductive analyses**
These analyses refer to the past, are informative, and confirm what happened.
They provide answers to questions such as "What happened?," "How did it happen?," and "How much happened?"

▶ **Inductive analyses**
These analyses refer to the future, and have to do with searching and discovering the unknown. They provide answers to questions such as "Why did it happen?," and "What is going to happen?"

Table 2.1 contains an overview of analysis methods and their characteristics.

Analysis methods

Business analysis method	Area of use	Time reference	Predominant objective
Gap analysis	Corporate management	Past and future	Strategic planning
Empirical curves	Marketing, sales, production	Past and future	Strategic planning

Table 2.1 Examples of Typical Business Analysis Methods (Source: BARC)

---

2 Dan Vesset, Research Director, Analytics and Data Warehousing, IDC, 2003.

Business analysis method	Area of use	Time reference	Predominant objective
Lifecycle	Marketing, sales	Past and future	Strategic planning
Portfolio analysis	Corporate management, marketing, sales	Past	Strategic planning
Matrices	All areas	Past	Control
Deviation analysis	All areas	Past	Control
Time series analysis	All areas except finance	Past and future	Strategic planning, control
ABC/XYZ analysis	Marketing, sales, production	Past	Strategic planning
Break-even analysis	Financing, accounting, controlling	Future	Strategic planning
Financial statement analysis	Corporate management, accounting, controlling	Past	Strategic planning
Sensitivity analysis	Marketing, sales, financing	Future	Strategic planning
Risk analysis	Marketing, sales, financing	Future	Strategic planning
Analysis methods of multivariant statistics	All areas except corporate management	Past and future	Strategic planning, control

Table 2.1 Examples of Typical Business Analysis Methods (Source: BARC) (Cont'd.)

Now, after all this theory, let's return to real life and examine the process steps that take place in the data retrieval layer.

2.2 Process Steps Involved in Data Retrieval

2.2.1 Preparation

In order to convert the data collected in a data warehouse into information that is relevant to the business, the data must be prepared accordingly before it can be presented properly to a target group. The conversion entails not only the automated creation of standard reports, but also comprehensive (and complex) analytical modeling and processing of the data.

Subsets (organizational, geographical, temporal, and so on) of data from the data warehouse are usually sufficient to mine the desired information.

To accelerate and simplify the work of analysis and presentation tools, the required data is often extracted from the detail layer of the data warehouse and stored in a specific and optimal format for the target tool, the data marts (see Figure 2.4).

In rough terms, the following categories of tools can be differentiated:

Information
preparation tools

▶ **Simple reporting and query tools**
Programs that allow a user-friendly definition of reports and queries.

▶ **Multidimensional analysis tools**
To clarify the difference in data handling a transaction-oriented system, one also speaks of *online analytical processing (OLAP)* in this context.[3] Special requirements exist for analytical tasks with OLAP support, particularly in terms of the speed of information delivery, the analysis options in the system, and regarding the security and complexity of calculations and the amount of data to be processed.

▶ **Executive Information Systems (EIS) and Management Information Systems (MIS)**
EIS tools were originally defined as tools to support decision-making in upper management. However, the application area quickly expanded to include all levels of management (MIS). To clarify the difference between OLAP, MIS, and EIS tools, the manufacturers of tools have begun to call simpler, ready-made application systems with predefined reports for specific areas of companies (marketing, finances, purchasing, HR, and so on) MIS and EIS tools.

▶ **Data mining tools**
Data mining is the process of finding previously unknown relationships and trends in large data sets. Data mining uses mathematical and statistical techniques from artificial intelligence (AI): neural networks, fuzzy logic, clustering, associations, regressions, chaos theory, machine learning, and so on (see also Section 2.2.4).

▶ **Tools for application development**
This group of frontend tools includes all application systems created individually for information mining. Development of these applications requires application development tools that support access to data warehouse systems. Today, application development tools are already integrated into most data warehouse systems.

---

3 Volume 1 of the *SAP BW Library* provides detailed information on OLAP concepts. See: Egger, Fiechter, Rohlf, 2005, Chapters 1–3.

2.2.2 Presentation

The setup of a data warehouse and the preparation of data in a format specific to and optimized for the target tool serve one main purpose: to present information that is relevant to decision-making and thereby promote actions beneficial to the company.

The extremely varied needs of the very heterogeneous user groups are of paramount importance here. These groups include the following, for example:

▶ Executives

▶ Line of Business Managers (LOB)

▶ Business analysts

▶ Model developers, statistical experts

▶ Information users or consumers

▶ Application developers

▶ External stakeholders (suppliers, customers, shareholders, and so on)

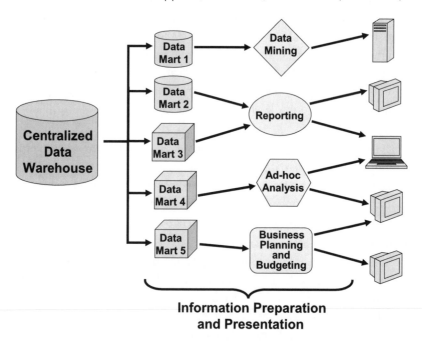

Figure 2.4 Various Target Groups and Their Influence on the Provision of Data

The different needs of those users demand that business-relevant information and facts oriented to decision-making be made available in various forms. In this context, we differentiate between the following main categories (see Figure 2.4):

▶ **Standard reporting**
Static or dynamic presentation of facts, often in a spreadsheet but increasingly in a multidimensional form—usually with comprehensive options for presentation and further distribution. Web servers, publish and subscribe processes, and portals (on the intranets, extranets, and on the Internet) enable simple, web-based access to information. This type of information presentation is suited primarily for executives, information consumers, and external stakeholders.

▶ **Ad-hoc analyses**
The dynamic display of information, usually from a multidimensional model; such analyses permit the user (often business analysts) to have a flexible and individual look at the data. Ad-hoc analyses can be implemented with either analysis tools or web frontends.

▶ **Business planning and budgeting**
Specific support for planning and budgeting processes with the availability of tools for data capture, quality assurance, workflow management, data distribution, forecasting, and simulation. Users of business planning and budgeting are often line of business managers (LOBs) and other managers who are involved in the budgeting process.

▶ **Data mining**
Complex and unsupervised analysis of very large quantities of data. The users here are highly qualified specialists who use various procedures—from statistics, machine learning, and artificial intelligence—to discover unknown structures and patterns. Data mining usually requires a specific data storage structure and a great deal of system resources.

2.2.3 Information Distribution

Once the data has been transformed into form information, this information must be distributed to the relevant recipients. In this context, it must be considered that each piece of information has a time-based dimension:

Time-based dimension of information

▶ Over time, information can lose its value and lead to misinterpretations.

▶ The timeliness of information must be known.

▶ A "high-value" piece of information must arrive or be present in the right place at the right time, and in the right form in order to be beneficial.

Proactive information distribution

Our experience shows that you shouldn't rely on the recipients alone to retrieve the relevant information. Proactive information distribution systems help to avoid the loss of information. Such systems are often referred to as *publish and subscribe* or *information broadcasting* systems (see Figure 2.5).

This technology facilitates the preparation and provision of data for an information producer. Only the information *channels* are defined through which specific information content is published (marketing, finance, management, HR, etc.).

Information producer

The *information producer* doesn't need to know exactly who is interested in his information or reports; he simply has to publish the information or reports in the corresponding channels.

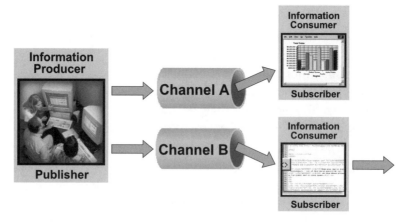

Figure 2.5 Proactive Information Distribution ("Information Broadcasting")

Information consumer

The *information consumer*, on the other hand, selects the most appropriate channels from a range of available channels that he is authorized to access and therefore decides on which information packages he wants to receive. This means that a consumer receives only the information that is relevant to him; however, this includes all the information from the chosen channels, irrespective of when it was published and by whom.

 You can compare this process to the publication of a magazine. The editor of a magazine knows his audience (the group of readers he writes for), but he doesn't know the readers personally. Alternatively, the magazine subscriber (the consumer or reader) doesn't know the editors. Nevertheless, the consumer obtains the information as soon as it is published, even if it is contained in a "special issue."

2.2.4 Data Mining and Advanced Analytics

Data mining is defined as a series of advanced methods used to explore data and establish relationships within large quantities of data. The term *data mining* describes a concept in which information that is relevant for decision-making is passed directly to the presentation phase after a problem definition and a data analysis. Even though data mining is basically just one variant of advanced analytics, it is often identified as the latter. **Definition**

Because there are numerous areas in which data mining solutions can be used, we can only mention a few examples at this stage: **Areas of use**

▶ Why do customers turn to the competition and how can they be won back?

▶ What is the best way to group customers by their buying behavior?

▶ Based on a customer's previous buying behavior, which product is that customer most likely to buy next?

▶ How will the demand for a specific service develop and how can this demand be optimally met?

▶ At what point can a credit card transaction or an insurance claim be regarded as fraudulent?

As the Gartner Group discovered in several research papers that were published between 1999 and 2004, data mining should not be thought of as an isolated analysis technique, but rather as a process in which different methods and techniques are used, depending on the type of exploration. Therefore, not only does a comprehensive data mining solution have to provide a complete range of data mining models and methods, but it also has to be an integral part of a modern data warehouse solution that contains the necessary tools for accessing data, converting it into a standardized form, and ultimately presenting the results. **Data mining as a process**

The typical unstructured problems that data mining tools are designed to solve require efficient methods when using these tools in a production environment. Figure 2.6 shows the stages into which a general data mining process chain can be divided.

In the following sections, we'll describe and explain the five most important steps in this chain.

▶ Sampling

▶ Data exploration

▶ Transformation or manipulation

▶ Modeling

▶ Assessment and deployment

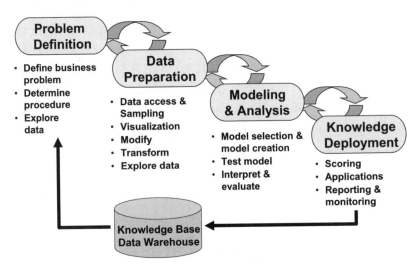

Figure 2.6 The Stages of the Data Mining Process (Data Mining Process Chain)

Sampling

Sampling Typically, data mining solutions have to cope with large data volumes (in the scope of gigabytes to terabytes). To be able to reduce the CPU time, a data mining solution must enable the user to draw representative samples, depending on the application. These samples range from simple random samples to multilayered samples for the correct recording of subgroups (for example, geographical areas, business areas, or parts of different manufacturing processes). The samples reflect the structure of the entire data record and can drastically reduce the CPU time and facilitate the development of calculation models.

Data Exploration ### Data Exploration

Once you have decided which data is to be analyzed, you must explore the data structure in order to identify obvious trends and anomalies. You can explore data in two ways: (1) Through direct visualization of the data in the form of tables and graphics, and (2) By using classical analysis and statistics techniques, such as factorization, cluster, or association analysis. The second option is preferable, if the data isn't suited for a visual exploration.

Transformation or Manipulation

After exploring the data, you might have to modify the data records. This may involve adding new information, forming customer groups, gathering information on the competition, and reducing the number of key figures used. This amount of data manipulation can result in a more targeted examination of the data that is located in the problem areas. The techniques used in this phase include the immediate creation and deletion of variables, and the integration of filtering and data transformation functions.

Manipulation

Modeling

Once the data has been carefully examined, it is ready for the analysis, that is, for the actual data mining. In this context, the data is (mostly) automatically searched for a combination of variables, and models are created that are used to forecast the result.

Modeling

We differentiate between the following six categories of methods:

▶ **Neural networks**

These networks learn from historical data and make predictions regarding future developments. The strength of neural networks lies in answering the question, "What happens, if …".

▶ **Decision trees (also referred to as induction methods)**

They map data into categorical (discontinuous) units. The mapping rules are derived through trainings on historical data for which the category mapping is already known. The strength of these models is the explicit determination of relevant variables, whereas irrelevant statements are eliminated.

▶ **Clustering**

Clustering is used to divide data into homogeneous groups. The model searches for a global structure of the data in order to partition the data into clusters.

▶ **Association analysis**

The association analysis can be used to identify cross-selling effects to uncover cross-selling opportunities, for example. In the search for associations, only those objects are considered whose scope of information can be compared with each other. Then statements are made in the form of rules about partial structures within the data. Contrary to the decision-tree classification, in clustering and in the association analysis, the models are determined on the basis of the data.

▶ **Scoring**

Scoring maps data to continuous units. A subsequent discretization enables you to subdivide the data into classes, if needed. The scoring function can be defined via weighted score tables or it can be determined as a linear or non-linear regression of a target variable via trainings on historical data.

▶ **ABC Classification**

Here, data that has been subdivided into the classes A, B, C and so on is displayed. The ABC classification uses threshold values and classification rules. The classified results are displayed in the form of an ABC chart or an ABC list.

Assessment and Deployment

Assess and deploy When different models have been developed, it is necessary to assess which is technically the best or most intuitive model. Moreover, at that stage, the selected model must be applied to the knowledge base in order to be analyzed. At this point, you must also determine whether there are any new or as yet unanswered questions.

2.3 The Data Retrieval Components of SAP BW

SAP BW provides great functionality and flexibility for the entire data retrieval process. SAP BW Release 3.5 provided additional innovations and enhancements for the analysis and modeling areas. Figure 2.7 gives an overview of the BW architecture for Release 3.5.

Innovations

As of SAP BW 3.0, reporting functionality provides significant enhancements and improvements. Here too, SAP can be viewed as a best-practice OLAP and data warehouse solution. Moreover, SAP BW 3.5 provides major advancements in the areas of data mining and advanced analytics.

Web reporting becomes main technology

Significant shifts have occurred among the reporting components provided by SAP. Up to SAP BW 1.2, SAP Business Explorer (BEx) Analyzer was the only standard tool that SAP provided for OLAP reporting. Even the appearance of web reporting with SAP BW 2.0 did not produce any significant shift. With SAP BW 3.0, however, web reporting clearly became the primary reporting technology in SAP BW.

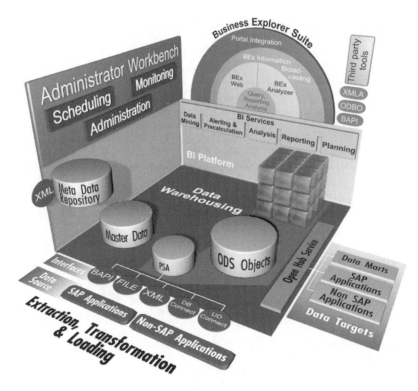

Figure 2.7 The Integrated Architecture of SAP Business Information Warehouse (Source: SAP AG)

The following points illustrate its predominant position:

▶ Default execution of queries in the HTML browser instead of MS Excel

▶ Significant enhancements in the reporting functionality of SAP BEx web applications, especially when compared to the Excel-based SAP BEx Analyzer

▶ Earlier significance of third-party frontend tools is declining

▶ Significantly greater functionality and extended options for web reporting

2.3.1 Overview

As we already mentioned in Section 1.4.6, you can use various reporting and analysis tools on the basis of SAP BW; however, there is a basic distinction between SAP tools and third-party tools.

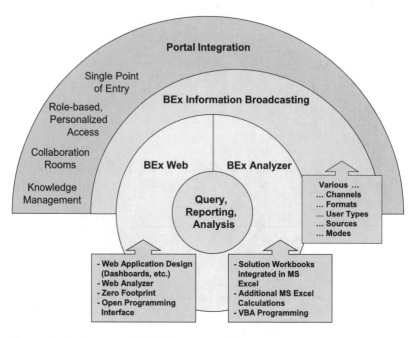

Figure 2.8 Architecture of SAP BW Reporting Components

With its different components, *SAP Business Explorer* (*BEx*) provides the SAP BW standard reporting and analysis tools. It consists of the following components that will be described in greater detail in the following sections:

▶ **Query Designer**
Tool to define queries on SAP BW InfoProviders

▶ **Web Application Designer**
Tool to create web-reporting applications

▶ **Web Applications**
The environment for running reports and analyses in an HTML browser

▶ **Analyzer**
The environment for running queries in MS Excel

▶ **Information Broadcasting**
The option to make objects with business-intelligence content available to a wide group of users

▶ **Additional Functions**
Personalization and mobile reporting components and functions to integrate SAP BEx web applications into SAP Enterprise Portal

SAP Reporting Agent supplements the functions of SAP Business Explorer. The reporting agent offers background and additional functions:

▶ Printing queries

▶ Precalculation of web templates and value sets for characteristic variables

▶ Managing bookmarks

▶ Evaluation of exceptions with alternate follow-up actions, such as "sending messages" (e-mail) or "creating entries in the alert monitor"

▶ Functions for third-party tools

SAP Reporting Agent

Moreover, the *Analysis Process Designer (APD)* and the *Data Mining Workbench* enable you to perform advanced analysis actions (see Section 2.3.7).

Advanced analytics

You can also use a variety of third-party tools to access data in SAP BW. Up to now, the primary means of doing so was to run an SAP Business Explorer query from a frontend tool supplied by a third party. Today you can also use various additional SAP interfaces to access queries:

Third-party tools

▶ The ODBO[4] interface

▶ The XMLA[5] interface

And, as before:

▶ The BAPI[6] interface

2.3.2 SAP Business Explorer Query Designer

The Query Designer enables you to define the components of an SAP BEx query:

Function

▶ General properties

▶ Filters

▶ Free characteristics

▶ Rows and columns

---

4 OLE DB for OLAP
5 XML for Analysis
6 Business Application Programming Interface

As of SAP BW 3.0, you can use the standalone tool, *Query Designer*, to define queries on SAP BW InfoProviders. With the addition of InfoObjects and their master data to the reporting-relevant objects (see Section 1.4.5), SAP now offers reporting on transaction data and the analysis of master data. Furthermore, as of SAP BW 3.0, you can use tabular reporting as a new functionality, in addition to the OLAP reporting available in earlier releases (see Figures 2.9 and 2.10).

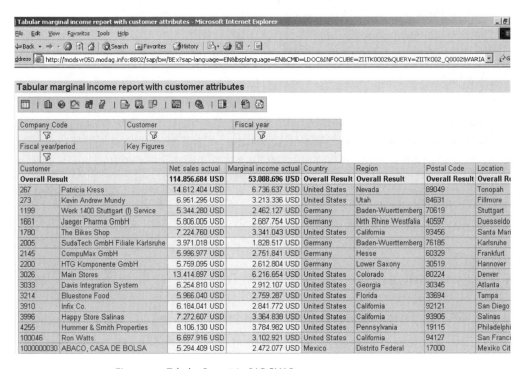

Figure 2.9 Tabular Report in SAP BW 3.x

You can select and organize the objects of an InfoProvider in many different ways. For example, you can output the characteristics of an InfoCube as a list or a group change criterion; you can also use them as a selection or free characteristics for slice-and-dice or to build complex structures. The key figures of an InfoCube can be used for display as well as to build formulas and reusable, calculated key figures. With combinations of characteristics and key figures, you can configure reusable, restricted key figures and structures (see Figure 2.11). In the query definitions, hierarchies can be flexibly displayed or used for a selection.

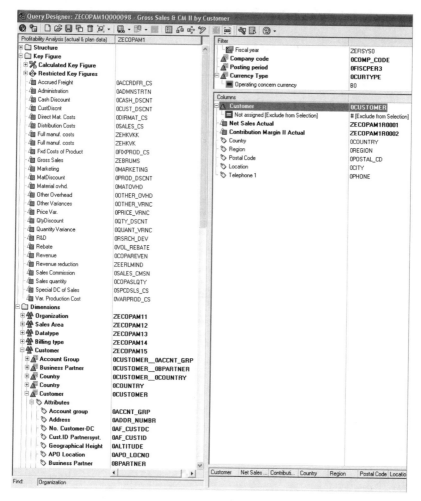

Figure 2.10 Creating Tabular Reports in the Query Designer

For an optimal selection, you can define variables that populate various query elements: You can use *Parameter Variables* (for selection of individual values), *Interval Variables*, or *Select Option Variables*, which support any selection on a characteristic, to select characteristic values.

Variables

You can select entire hierarchies (with *Hierarchy Variables*) or parts of hierarchies (with *Hierarchy Node Variables*) statically or dynamically. You can use *Formula Variables* for formula functions. *Text Variables* enable dynamic labeling of multilingual query elements, depending on the current selection, for example.

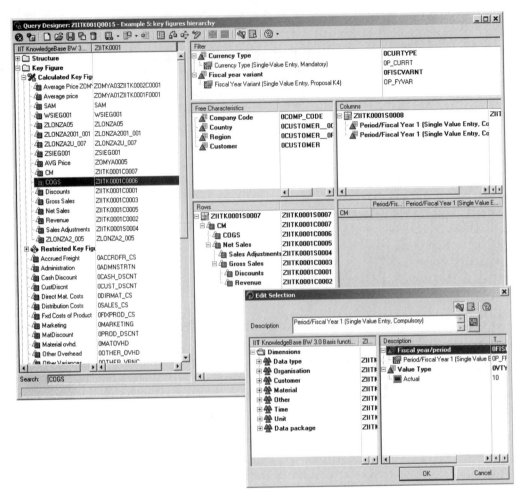

Figure 2.11 Definition of Query Elements: Key Figure Hierarchy, Variable Column Selection with Dynamic Texts and Variable Filtering

The processing of variables can occur in the following ways:

▶ Via manual entries with optional default values (selection of a company, for example)

▶ Via substitution paths (for example, a column header of **2003 Actual**, depending on the selection of the fiscal year and the value type **Actual**)

▶ Via SAP exit or customer exit (with ABAP/4 coding flow logic to determine the values)

▶ Via authorization (automatic population of variables with the authorizations of the user performing the task)

The Exception functionality of the Query Designer enables you to highlight critical situations in color. Examples include a negative deviation in sales between the current year and the previous year or the budget, or with a relative contribution margin lower than x %. You can use exceptions defined in the Query Designer in the reporting agent for the Alert Monitor (see Section 2.3.9).

Exceptions

The Query Designer also provides you with an option to define conditions. Conditions limit the results area with specific criteria. For example: Which customers have lower sales levels in the current year? SAP BW 3.0 vastly improved exception and condition functionality.

Conditions

You can run queries that have been defined in the Query Designer as soon as you have saved them. You can use the *Display query on the Web* button to start the query in a web browser (such as Microsoft Internet Explorer). Alternatively, you can also run queries in the SAP BEx Analyzer.

2.3.3 SAP Business Explorer Web Application Designer

The SAP Business Explorer (BEx) Web Application Designer is used to create web-reporting applications. The direct execution of queries uses a *Standard Web Template*. In this case, a systemwide template defines the functionality and layout of the query. This layout is usually only adequate for ad-hoc reports, which is why the Web Application Designer enables you to implement the layouts and reporting functionalities of your choice.

Function

The Web Application Designer supports all options—from creating OLAP reports according to targeted specifications to integrating a Business Intelligence Cockpit (BI cockpit) for management into the portal. All the required functions are supported, including professional navigation components, selection and presentation objects, and the entire range of layout options of the HTML technology. Such reports are stored in SAP BW as web templates in the form of HTML code. This feature also offers all the options of the web technology, such as standard HTML functionality and the use of formulas, style sheets, JavaScript, and so on.

Web templates and standard HTML functionality

The Web Application Designer will automatically insert all SAP BW objects as SAP-BW-specific object tags.[7] The tags represent control information for the following areas:

---

7 In HTML, the control code can be assigned in tags. For example, <a href ...> ... </a> defines a hyperlink to another document or a specific location within a document.

- Properties of web templates
- Data providers
- Web items

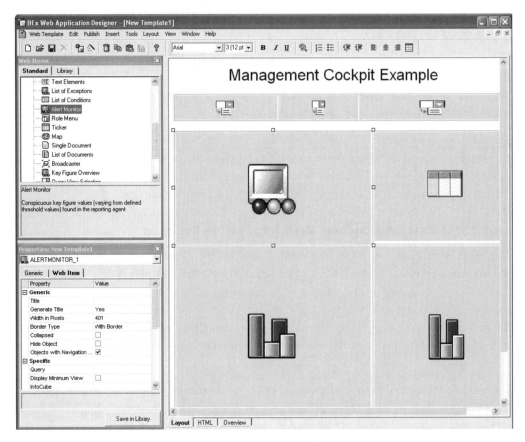

Figure 2.12 Web Templates Are Defined in the Web Application Designer of SAP BW

Data providers   Data providers make available the specific SAP BW information that serves queries or query views (stored navigational states of an SAP BW query) as the data source in each web template.

Web items   Web items are objects that display content that is specific to SAP BW, for example:

- **Tables**
  Display of the query results as tables

- **Charts**
  Display of the query results as navigable online graphics (bar charts, for example)

▶ **Dropdown boxes**
Objects for filtering characteristics

▶ **Text elements**
General query information, such as the timeliness of the data

▶ **Alert Monitor**
List of the exceptions calculated in the reporting agent

▶ **Role menu**
SAP menu tree with favorites and roles

▶ **Maps**
Map graphics populated with SAP BW data

The Web Application Designer also offers a number of additional functions (see also Chapter 5, *The BEx Web*): These functions range from universal resource identifiers (URLs) specific to SAP BW (to call other web templates or to insert language-dependent ABAP/4 text elements) and the Web Design Application Programming Interface (API), which provides support to ABAP/4 with changing the display and functionality of tables and navigation blocks.
Additional functions

As of SAP BW 3.0, the web templates created with the Web Application Designer are stored on the SAP Web Application Server (SAP Web AS). This feature is a significant improvement over earlier releases, because it makes obsolete the SAP Internet Transaction Server (SAP ITS) technology, which was not ideal for reporting. The technology of the SAP Web AS provides improved functions for SAP web reporting, especially in terms of interactivity.
Innovations

2.3.4 The SAP Business Explorer Web Applications

The SAP Business Explorer web applications make up the execution environment for reports and analyses in the HTML browser.
Function

After you have defined queries or query views, you can run them as web applications. As of SAP BW 3.0, you can store queries directly in SAP roles. Consequently, end users can run queries without performing additional tasks. The same holds true for web templates created with the Web Application Designer. After you assign these items to roles, you can start high-performance and complex reports from the role menu. When you start a report, the reporting data stored in the InfoProviders is presented online. You can navigate in the displayed results of a query by filtering, drilldown, and jumping to other reports, for example.
Running web reports

As of SAP BW 3.0, SAP web reporting functionality enables you to define ad-hoc queries at runtime. With the Ad-hoc Query Designer, you can do the following:

▶ Create queries through the arrangement of characteristics of an Info-Provider into the rows, columns, filters, and free characteristics and incorporate key figures of the InfoProvider into the key figure structure of the query.

▶ Restrict key figures and characteristics.

▶ Use predefined key figure structures and restricted or calculated key figures in the query.

▶ Set and change the properties of queries, key figures, and characteristics in the query.

▶ Create and change conditions and exceptions.

2.3.5 SAP Business Explorer Analyzer

The application that executes queries and views from Microsoft Excel is called *Business Explorer Analyzer* by SAP, an SAP BW add-on that enhances Excel. SAP BEx Analyzer provides two basic options:

▶ Upon opening, the tool provides a toolbar specific to SAP BW that enables starting SAP Business Explorer queries that have already been defined. As noted with web reporting, the query data is read from the InfoProviders online and is presented in Excel so that you can navigate through it.

▶ The second option is to open Excel workbooks that already contain embedded queries. This approach enables some report-specific formatting, linking graphics, and so on (see Figure 2.13). You can also assign these workbooks to role menus so that they are directly available to end users. *SAP Business Explorer Workbooks* represent an alternate option for the presentation of queries to end users. However, the functionality and layout options for this variant are limited when compared with SAP Business Explorer web applications.

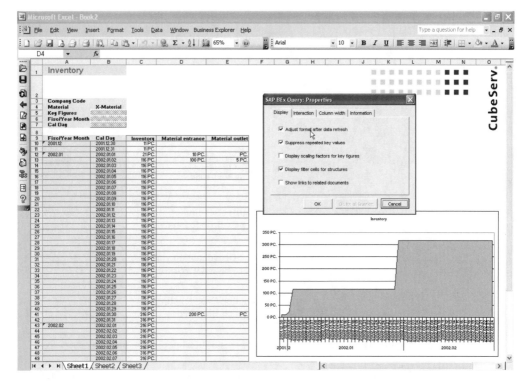

Figure 2.13 SAP Business Explorer Analyzer Combines Excel and OLAP Functionalities for Selected Tasks.

2.3.6 SAP Business Explorer Information Broadcasting

Innovations

BEx Information Broadcasting enables you to make objects with business-intelligence content available to a wide range of users according to the needs of customers. BEx Information Broadcasting is available in the various areas of SAP Business Explorer (BEx) (see Figure 2.14). It enables both the distribution of information to a large group of users and its consumption by these users.

With the BEx Broadcaster, you can precalculate BEx web applications, queries, and workbooks and then publish them in the SAP Enterprise Portal, or distribute them via e-mail. In addition to precalculated documents that contain historical data, you can also create online links to queries and web applications.

BEx Broadcaster

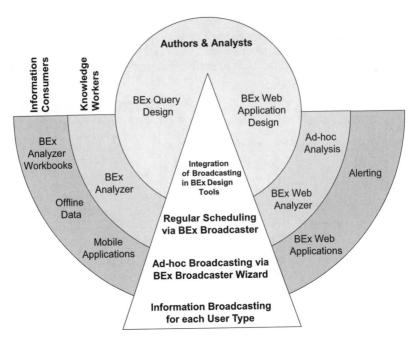

Figure 2.14 Overview of the Components of BEx Information Broadcasting

Call options You can call the BEx Broadcaster from the following areas of the Business Explorer:

▶ BEx Query Designer

▶ BEx Web Application Designer

▶ BEx Analyzer

▶ BEx web applications

▶ Ad-hoc Analysis and BEx Web Analyzer

You can also embed the BEx Broadcaster in any web application of your choice. Furthermore, you can publish queries and web templates to any SAP BW role or directly to the SAP Enterprise Portal from the design tools—*BEx Query Designer* and *BEx Web Application Designer*.

In the SAP Enterprise Portal, you would normally use a central entry point for business intelligence information (such as BEx Portfolio).

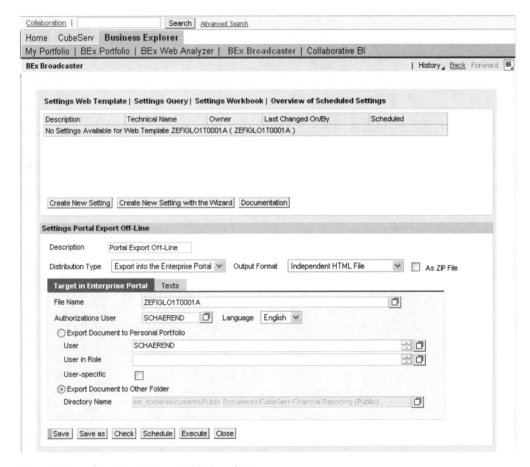

Figure 2.15 Configuration Options in BEx Broadcaster

2.3.7 Additional SAP BW Reporting Functions of SAP Business Explorer

SAP BW provides several additional functions for reporting.

The most important reporting function is personalization, which is available as of SAP BW 3.0. The personalization function enables a user-specific population of variables and the storage of user-specific start views of web applications. It also provides a user-specific history of the reporting objects opened last.

Personalization

You can use the functionality of BEx Mobile Intelligence to run web reports on mobile devices, such as mobile phones, or personal digital assistants (PDAs). The SAP BW server automatically recognizes the type of

Mobile reporting

end device and generates a device-specific page in HTML or Wireless Markup Language (WML).

Integration with SAP Enterprise Portal

The integration of SAP Business Explorer web applications into the SAP Enterprise Portal reflects the increasing importance of portals (see Figure 2.16).

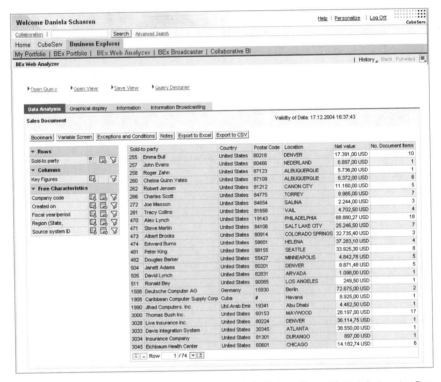

Figure 2.16 The Creation of Web Reports and the Integration with SAP Enterprise Portal Are Standard Functions of SAP BW.

Currently, when you create web templates, you can store them as an *iView*. An iView is a component of the portal solution that you can use to extract data from applications, documents, and the Internet and display it in the portal. These features enable you to use the web-reporting functionality with the options provided by the portal technology (Single Sign-On or SSO, and so on).

2.3.8 The Analysis Process Designer and the Data Mining Workbench

Additional information potential

As a data warehouse, SAP BW combines data from the different operational systems and databases in a company, and then consolidates the data and makes it available for analysis purposes. This data usually contains another valuable potential.

It contains entirely new information that is represented in the form of meaningful relationships between the data, but which is too complex or hidden to be uncovered by intuition or by simply viewing it. This information is analogous to the inconspicuous rough diamonds, which become glistening jewels only in the hands of a diamond cutter.

The *Analysis Process Designer (APD)* enables you to explore and identify these hidden or complex relationships between data in a simple way. Examples are the calculation of ABC classes, the determination of frequency distributions, the customer segmentation, and the determination of scoring information.

The APD

The Analysis Process Designer is a workbench with an intuitive, graphical user interface (GUI) that is used for the creation, execution, and monitoring of analysis processes (see Figure 2.17).

Workbench function

For this purpose, several data selection and data transformation methods are provided, such as statistical and mathematical calculations, data cleansing or structuring processes, and so forth. You can create analysis processes via Drag&Drop. The analysis results are stored in SAP BW data targets or in a CRM system. They are then available for all decision-making and operational application processes.[8]

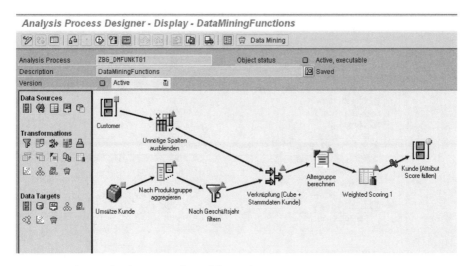

Figure 2.17 The Graphical User Interface of the Analysis Process Designer

---

8 This process also involves the final steps 4 and 5 of the closed-loop process described in Section 2.1.

Data Mining Integration

The Analysis Process Designer is the application environment for the SAP Data Mining solution. The following data mining functions are integrated in the APD:

Integrated functions

▶ Creating and changing data mining models

▶ Training data mining models with different types of BW data (data mining model as data target in the analysis process)

▶ Running data mining methods (e.g., prediction with decision tree and cluster model) and integrating third-party data mining models (data mining model as transformation in the analysis process)

▶ Displaying data mining models

The following SAP-proprietary data mining methods are available for which you can create your own models (see Figure 2.18):

Possible methods

▶ Decision trees

▶ Clustering

▶ Association analysis

▶ Scoring

▶ Weighted score tables

▶ ABC classification

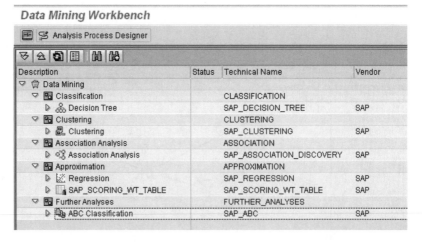

Figure 2.18 The Analysis Methods of the Data Mining Workbench and Its Integration with the APD

Moreover, there are comprehensive display options available in order to present the results in a significant manner (see Figure 2.19).

The detailed description of the areas of *APD and Data Mining* will be the subject of another volume of the SAP BW Library, which is why we won't go into further detail here.

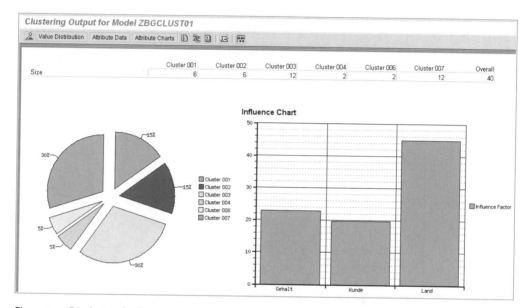

Figure 2.19 Displaying the Data Mining Results

2.3.9 The Reporting Agent

The options provided by the Reporting Agent enhance SAP BW with the following functions:

- ▶ Background functions
- ▶ Administrative functions
- ▶ Alert Monitor functions

The background functionality of the reporting agent provides the precalculation of query results. For example, these results are used when you run web reports that use the DATA_MODE=STORED mode. This approach significantly reduces the response time, because the query no longer has to access the often huge dataset of the InfoProviders involved. In addition, the Reporting Agent enables background printing of queries based on SAP Business Explorer Analyzer.

Background functions

The Reporting Agent stores and manages the bookmarks of all SAP BW users.

Exception reporting and *monitoring alerts* are particularly important. These components evaluate exceptions in the background to trigger follow-up actions that you can configure to meet your requirements. Follow-up actions can include messages (e-mail with information on the exception analysis) and alert-monitor entries (with traffic lights to display the entries and hyperlinks to the reports) (see Figure 2.20).

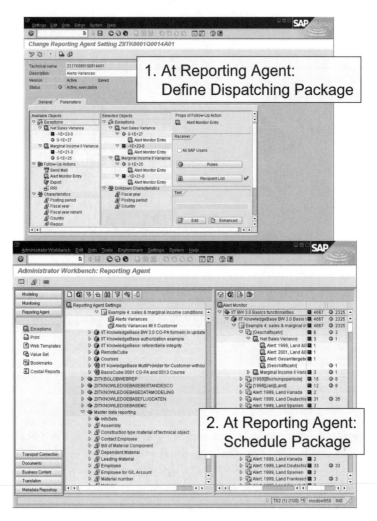

Figure 2.20 Information Distribution with the Alert Monitor in Web Reporting

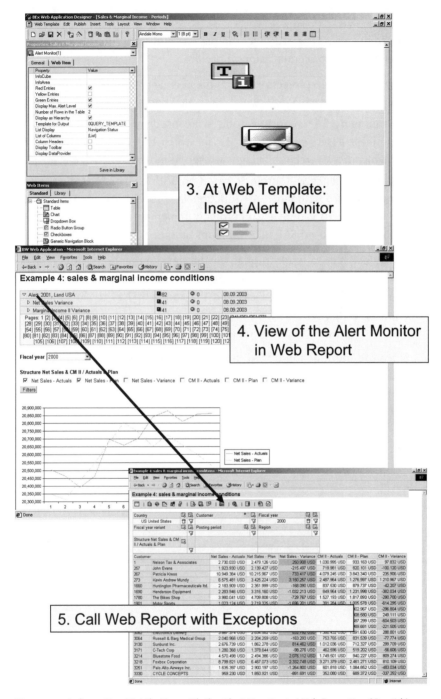

Figure 2.20 Information Distribution with the Alert Monitor in Web Reporting (Cont'd.)

2.3.10 Frontends for SAP BW

Decreasing use of third-party tools In earlier releases of SAP BW, the use of third-party frontend tools was integral to the implementation of projects.

Release 1.2B ▶ In 37 of the 40 projects in which the CubeServ Group[9] was involved—up to the release of SAP BW 1.2B—third-party frontends were used.

Release 2.x ▶ Proprietary SAP reporting tools were used in over 50% of the 60 projects based on SAP BW 2.x in which the CubeServ Group was involved. SAP web reporting was used in more than 10 projects.

Release 3.x ▶ Our experience with projects based on SAP 3.0 or 3.5 clearly shows a shift toward standard SAP functionality, specifically web reporting. More than 70% of over 100 projects implemented on the basis of SAP BW 3.x also used SAP BEx web applications.

Reasons for the change While SAP had to work through all the development steps of an OLAP frontend tool with SAP Business Explorer, the development of SAP BW had reached the limits of Excel and the company had to shift the paradigm to web technology. Simultaneously, other manufacturers already had mature products on the market.

Outlook Since the introduction of SAP BW 3.0, however, this situation has dramatically changed. We don't know any third-party tool that provides anything akin to the complete support afforded by the reporting functions of SAP BW. Consequently, the outlook for third-party frontend tools for SAP BW is very bleak.

---

9 The CubeServ Group specializes in business intelligence solutions (*www.cubeserv.com*). All authors of this book work at CubeServ Group.

3 Sample Scenario

This chapter introduces you to the case study that will be used throughout this book to illustrate typical scenarios that you might encounter in your everyday work. It describes the structure of CubeServ Engines, the model company, its analytical, reporting and planning requirements, and the SAP components included in the solution.

To help you understand the complex subject matter of SAP Business Information Warehouse (SAP BW), we've decided to work as closely to real-world situations and with as many examples as possible in all volumes of the *SAP BW Library*.[1]

Therefore, the basis for our books is a uniform case study developed by the authors: a virtual company (CubeServ Engines). We will use this case study to describe all the important requirements of business intelligence applications in a manner that reflects the everyday context of your work.

This chapter provides an overview of the basics of the case study. Because the focus of this book is on reporting and analysis, this chapter also contains a detailed description of the reporting requirements to be implemented.

3.1 The Model Company: "CubeServ Engines"

3.1.1 Company Structure

The model company, CubeServ Engines, operates internationally. It includes various subsidiaries as legal units. Subgroups combine the subsidiaries, and CubeServ Engines (Holding) runs the subgroups.

Businesses and subgroups

CubeServ Engines consists of the following subgroups (see Figure 3.1):

▶ The CubeServ Engines AMERICAS subgroup incorporates the American subsidiaries.

▶ The CubeServ Engines ASIA subgroup incorporates the Asian subsidiaries.

▶ The CubeServ Engines EUROPE subgroup incorporates the European subsidiaries.

---

1 See Appendix H, The *SAP BW Library*.

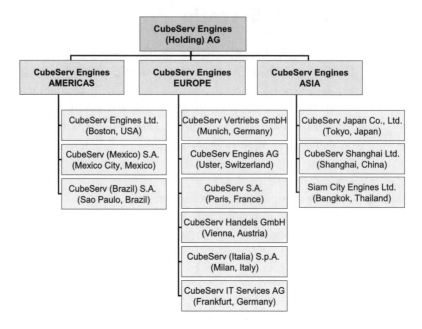

Figure 3.1 The Structure of the Model Company: CubeServ Engines

3.1.2 Infrastructure

Specializations   The various elements of the company are specialized:

► The following list contains companies involved only in sales:

- ► CubeServ Engines Ltd. (Boston, MA, USA)
- ► CubeServ (Brazil) S.A. (Sao Paulo, Brazil)
- ► CubeServ Vertriebs GmbH (Munich, Germany)
- ► CubeServ Handels GmbH (Vienna, Austria)
- ► CubeServ Japan Co., Ltd. (Tokyo, Japan)
- ► Siam City Engines Ltd. (Bangkok, Thailand)

► The following list shows the production companies that also perform sales tasks:

- ► CubeServ (Mexico) S.A. (Mexico City, Mexico)
- ► CubeServ Engines AG (Uster, Switzerland)
- ► CubeServ S.A. (Paris, France)
- ► CubeServ (Italia) S.p.A. (Milan, Italy)
- ► CubeServ Shanghai Ltd. (Shanghai, China)

- ▶ The following businesses provide shared services:
  - ▶ CubeServ Engines (Holding) AG
- ▶ CubeServ IT Services AG (Frankfurt, Germany)

The Euro is the group currency. The various company codes use the fol-   Currencies
lowing local currencies:

- ▶ **US dollar**
  CubeServ Engines Ltd. (Boston, MA, USA)
- ▶ **Mexican peso**
  CubeServ (Mexico) S.A. (Mexico City, Mexico)
- ▶ **Brazilian real**
  CubeServ (Brazil) S.A. (Sao Paulo, Brazil)
- ▶ **Euro**
  (CubeServ Vertriebs GmbH, Munich, Germany; CubeServ IT Services
  AG, Frankfurt, Germany, CubeServ Handels GmbH, Vienna, Austria,
  CubeServ S.A., Paris, France; and CubeServ (Italia) S.p.A., Milan, Italy)
- ▶ **Swiss franc**
  CubeServ Engines AG (Uster, Switzerland)
- ▶ **Japanese yen**
  CubeServ Japan Co., Ltd. (Tokyo, Japan)
- ▶ **Chinese renminbi (yuan)**
  CubeServ Shanghai Ltd. (Shanghai, China)
- ▶ **Thai baht**
  Siam City Engines Ltd. (Bangkok, Thailand)

The model company's fiscal year corresponds to the calendar year with   **Fiscal year variant**
four special periods.[2]

CubeServ Engines uses four different operational systems: It uses SAP R/3   **IT systems**
and the products of other software manufacturers for IT support of its
transactional processes.

3.2 Requirements of the Case Study

The existing analysis and planning applications used at CubeServ Engines
must be mapped by a uniform and professional IT solution based on SAP
NetWeaver, particularly SAP Business Information Warehouse (SAP BW)
and SAP Enterprise Portal (SAP EP). The transfer of data from legacy systems will occur via a file interface.

---

2 See also the descriptions on fiscal year variants in Egger, Fiechter, Rohlf, 2005.

The overriding need for analysis and planning at CubeServ Engines involves sales, profitability analysis, and financial reporting (general ledger accounting and consolidation). The company also requires that data from all the analytical applications be mapped for comprehensive management reporting. Such mapping demands integration with a link to aggregated information from sales and profitability analysis, along with financial key figures. Qualitative information in the form of documents must also be included in reporting.

3.2.1 Requirements of the Analytical Applications

Basic requirements The first step in implementing comprehensive business intelligence solutions includes mapping the analytical applications Sales & Distribution, Profitability Analysis, and Financial Reporting.

▶ For these applications, typical analyses such as comparisons with the previous year and periods, as well as time-series analyses are required.

▶ Both typese of analyses involve the use of hierarchies (characteristic and key figure hierarchies).

▶ A comprehensive consideration of the data requires currency translation.

▶ Both tabular and graphical presentations must be available.

Additional requirements The following special requirements apply to individual analytical applications:

▶ **Sales & Distribution**
Additional delivery status analysis (for late deliveries, for example)

▶ **Profitability Analysis and Financial Reporting**
Additional responsibility-based performance and structural analyses (the performance based on the structure portion of profitability analysis items per management task, for example)

▶ **Management Reporting**
Role-based navigation, geographical reporting (map graphics), information broadcasting, and publishing (publishing analyses in the SAP portal or automatic distribution via e-mail, for example)

Sales & distribution For the requirements from the Sales & Distribution area , the model company requires information from various sales documents (customer orders, deliveries, and invoices), as well as sales order stock.

Lists of customers and customer orders must be mapped first to meet this requirement. This process contains data from the customer order (sold-to party, for example), the customer order item (material, order quantity, and value, for example), and delivery scheduling (confirmed quantity and dates, for example) at the document level.

Other phases of the implementation will map the following additional information:

▶ **Deliveries**
Data on the delivery (ship-to party, for example) up to the delivery item (such as material and delivery quantity) at the document level

▶ **Invoices**
Billing data (such as payer) up to the invoice item (such as material, billed quantity, and value)

The following levels of detailed key figures must be mapped to meet the analytical requirements of profitability analysis:

Profitability analysis

▶ **Determining Net Revenue**
Revenues minus revenue reductions

▶ **Determining the Profit Margin II**
Net revenue minus full costs of production

▶ **Determining the Profit Margin III**
Profit margin II plus or minus price and quantity deviations

▶ **Determining the Profit Margin IV**
Profit margin III minus area fixed costs

▶ **Determining the Profit Margin V (= Operating Profit)**
Profit margin IV minus company fixed costs

The analyses of profit margins must be enabled as local solutions (the non-consolidated view of individual entities in the company) and as consolidated solutions (with the elimination of revenues and costs between subsidiary companies).

Information from general ledger accounting and consolidation is required to meet requirements in the area of financial reporting:

Financial reporting

ManagementreportingManagement reporting Managementreporting- Management reporting Data from all analytical applications is used to map comprehensive management reporting. The first step involves storing the complete data from the previous year and the periods of the current year. In the case study, this step includes the actual data of 2003 up to and including the data of September 2004.

Management reporting

3.2.2 Planning Requirements

Rolling planning requires the integration of sales, revenue, and profit margin planning with plan profitability analysis. The plan data of sales, revenue, and full cost of manufacturing planning must be transferred to plan profitability analysis.

Planning horizon Plan data is also available as of 2003. Planning involves September 2004 as the current planning point with plan data from October 2004 up to and including December 2005. Rolling planning occurs quarterly with a timeframe of 12 periods.

Planning functions The planning process adopts actual data (sales quantities) and extrapolates it to the entire year as an annual value. Distribution of data to the individual periods of the planning period is based on seasonal factors that you can enter. Variable, percentage-based revaluation is available for selected key figures. Revaluation of the sales quantities occurs on the basis of plan prices and plan cost rates; revenue reductions should be planned as devaluation percentages.

Key figures to be planned and granularity To meet the planning requirements, you must ensure that aggregated key figures are mapped:

- The key figures for sales, revenue, and the full cost of manufacturing must be mapped to the level of product hierarchy 2, customer country, company code, currency type, version, value type, transaction type, and period/year.

- Plan prices must be mapped to the level of product hierarchy 2, customer country, company code, currency type, version, value type, and period/year.

- Plan CGM/FC must be mapped as consolidated manufacturing costs at the level of product hierarchy 2, version, value type, and period/year.

- Plan profitability analysis must be mapped at the level of the company code, plan item, period/year, currency type, version, and value type.

3.3 Procedure and the SAP Components Involved

SAP R/3 upstream systems CubeServ Engines also requires coverage of the following SAP applications:

- **Profitability Analysis**
  SAP R/3 CO-PA (Controlling—Profitability Analysis)

- **Sales & Distribution**
    - SAP R/3 SD (Sales & Distribution)
    - SAP R/3 CO-PA (only incoming orders)
- **General Ledger Accounting**
    SAP R/3 FI-GL (Financial Accounting—General Ledger Accounting)

We will implement the analysis and reporting components for those applications in this book.

Whenever it made sense, the data modeling and Extraction, Transformation, and Loading (ETL) processes of our sample scenario used components of SAP Business Content. Alternatively, all required reporting components will be completely created from scratch (see also Chapter 7, *SAP Business Content*).

Use of SAP Business Content

Integrated data retrieval with extractors, business content extractors, and generic DataSources is used to link upstream SAP R/3 systems.

Extraction methods

Universal Data Connect (UD Connect) will link external systems. File uploads and XML interfaces retrieve additional data.

Linking external systems

In general, the reporting components in SAP BW use InfoCubes and MultiProviders. The planning applications write their data back to transactional InfoCubes. An operational data store (ODS) layer is used to store document data.

Use of SAP BW data targets

Business Explorer (BEx) web applications are used as the standard medium to map analytical requirements. The BEx Analyzer is used for specific requirements.

Reporting tools

The components to be implemented in this book consist of the following elements:

Specific components in this book

- **Queries**
    All reporting and analysis data is provided by using BEx queries. In addition to the raw data, these queries contain calculations, conditions, and exceptions.
- **Web Templates**
    The data of the queries is integrated in web templates so that it can be presented on the web. The presentation options available are tables and diagrams. Apart from standard web items, language-dependent texts and JavaScript enhancements are also used here.

▶ **Data Model Enhancements**

For specific requirements—such as the elimination of intercompany sales—the data model implemented in the previous volumes of the SAP BW Library will be enhanced, if necessary.

▶ **Documents**

The storage of additional qualitative information in the form of documents is carried out via the Business Document Service (BDS).

▶ **Information Broadcasting and Portal Integration**

Information broadcasting is used to distribute the generated web reports and queries via e-mail, or to publish them in the SAP Enterprise Portal. In this context, the publishing of information that is accessible both online and offline is implemented.

Planning interface Web interfaces are generally used as the standard medium to map planning requirements.

3.4 Details of Reporting Requirements

The main purpose of our sample scenario is to describe the basic SAP BW functionality. For this reason, we have to make some technical and contents-related compromises in this book with regard to detail requirements, which would not be made in a real-life application.

Regarding the content requirement in the analytical applications, our case studies focus on some core topics, which are understandably, far from comprehensive.

3.4.1 Queries and Query Components

Queries present the core of the analysis and reporting functionality. They are described in great detail in Chapter 4, *The SAP Business Explorer Query Designer*.

General requirements You should consider the following general requirements when implementing queries:

▶ Whenever it makes sense, you should use reusable query components for the queries, which optimizes the solution's modularity, prolongs its lifecycle, and increases its integrity. Moreover, this makes it easier to perform mass data changes and it reduces the risk of implementation errors and inconsistent data views.

▶ The queries should have a high level of flexibility, which enables you to map a high number of analysis requirements with a low number of queries.

Master Data Reporting

Application-specific requirements

▶ To map the reporting to the customer master data, we'll create a simple query for the InfoProvider of the Customer characteristic in Section 4.1.1.

▶ In Section 4.4.4, we'll describe the creation of a master data hierarchy for company codes.

Profitability Analysis

This book focuses primarily on implementing the profitability analysis. For this purpose, we'll develop the following detail solutions:

▶ Time series for sales analysis (Sections 4.1.1, 4.2.1, and 4.2.2)

▶ Monthly analysis of sales including a comparison with the previous year, different cumulations, and calculations (Sections 4.2.3, 4.2.4, 4.3.3, 4.4.1, 4.4.4, and 4.4.5)

▶ Time series for the structure of the local contribution margin (Sections 4.2.5, 4.4.3, and 4.7)

▶ Comparison with the local contribution margin structure of the previous year (Sections 4.3.1 and 4.3.2)

▶ Consolidated contribution margin (Section 4.3.2)

▶ Target achievement analysis for the management based on contribution margin data with exception reporting (Sections 4.3.4 and 4.6.2)

Sales & Distribution

The data for sales and distribution originates from both the Sales & Distribution module and the incoming orders in the profitability analysis. Here we'll develop the following detail solutions:

▶ Segment analysis for the sales order stock (Section 4.3.1)

▶ Sales analysis including details on the delivery status (Section 4.3.2)

▶ Delivery status analysis with conditions (Sections 4.5.4 and 4.6.1)

General Ledger Accounting

The presentation of the general ledger data and their consolidation is supported by the use of SAP BW master data hierarchies. The following detail solutions will be used for this presentation:

▶ Profit and loss accounting with currency translation (Section 4.3.5)

▶ Profit and loss performance benchmark (global/regional/local) with text variables of the **Customer exit** type (Sections 4.3.6 and 4.5.5)

3.4.2 Web Templates and Web Items

Web templates and web items are used for layout purposes and for navigating through the information available in queries. Moreover, you should use web templates and web items to enable reporting on documents of the Business Document Service. These components are the subject matter of Chapter 5, *The BEx Web*.

General requirements The following general requirements apply to the examples used in this book:

▶ Wherever possible, you should use reusable components to ensure the consistency and effectiveness of the web solutions. For example, a good solution here is to use style sheets, template items, and the web item library.

▶ Although NetWeaver 4 and SAP BW 3.5 provide experienced developers with almost boundless web reporting possibilities, the means that we want to use for mapping the requirements should be as simple as possible. Basically, we want to use the standard functionality of SAP BW web reporting.

Application-specific requirements The implementation of the web reporting examples is predominantly generic. Usually, the underlying data or queries are exchangeable. For example, for the implementation of a web template with the web item **table**, it's immaterial whether the query is based on data from SAP FI-GL or SAP CO-PA.

Therefore, the sample cases are based predominantly on the functionality. The most important elements are as follows:

▶ Web template with table (Section 5.1.1)

▶ Web template with chart (Section 5.1.6)

▶ Modification of the standard web template and personalization (Section 5.4.1)

▶ Language-dependent texts (Section 5.4.3)

▶ Using the Ad-hoc Query Designer (Section 5.5.15)

▶ Navigating with query view selection (Section 5.5.16)

▶ Geographical reporting, using the role menu and frames (Section 5.5.17)

▶ Document display (Section 5.5.18)

3.4.3 Information Broadcasting

The primary role of information broadcasting is to optimize the processes of information distribution or information access. This topic is described in greater detail in Chapter 6, *Information Broadcasting*.

Again the functionality is absolutely generic and independent of the reporting application so that the examples presented in this book are based predominantly on the functionality provided by SAP:

Process-specific requirements

▶ Sending reports as offline reports or as an online link via e-mail (Section 6.2)

▶ Publishing reports in the SAP Enterprise Portal (Section 6.3)

▶ Finding SAP Business Intelligence (BI) content in the SAP Enterprise Portal (Section 6.5)

4 The SAP Business Explorer Query Designer

Queries are the core of the reporting and analysis functionality in SAP BW. They provide a flexible and intuitive platform for data analysis that can be developed using the SAP Business Explorer (BEx) Query Designer. The following chapter will present all essential functionalities of an SAP BW query, as well as the corresponding design tools.

4.1 Data Analysis with SAP Business Information Warehouse—The Query Concept

Business intelligence tools are intended to support users in understanding the enterprise performance and to help users make appropriate decisions based on their understanding. One critical aspect here that you should note is the need to give all users an equal insight into the enterprise—an insight based on consistent data and standard analytical definitions. For consistent enterprise control, a unified view of information for all users is indispensable.

On the one hand, this is achieved by the SAP Business Information Warehouse (SAP BW) functionality for extraction and data warehousing via a consistent data basis. Conversely, queries can provide a unified and flexible analysis platform according to the *Single Point of Truth* concept. This means that within an enterprise, a piece of information (or a dataset) exists once as a reference and cannot be falsified by locally changed variants.

Essentially, a query is a database research action with interesting additional functionality like currency scenarios, complex calculation options, and analysis functions. However, analyses born out of queries can be applied flexibly to a multitude of areas in a multidimensional dataset of an SAP BW InfoProvider. This is enabled by combining analytical functionality with the provided drilldowns and filter options. Therefore, one query or few queries can often map an entire analytical application.

Within this chapter, all essential functionalities of an SAP BW query and the associated design tool are introduced, both in terms of their conceptual design and in examples that increasingly build on each other. The examples are analysis solutions for the data model that was already developed in the first two volumes of the SAP BW Library.[1]

4.1.1 Functional Overview of the BEx Query Designer

The Query Designer is a standalone tool that—to a great extent—can be handled intuitively. A look at the Query Designer's user interface helps to illustrate its functionality.

First Steps in the Query Designer

Open the Query Designer

Therefore, the first practical step should be to open the Query Designer in order to gain a quick overview of its different areas.

▶ You can start the Query Designer directly from the Windows program menu via **Business Explorer · Query Designer** (see Figure 4.1, Step 1).

▶ In the logon dialog, log onto your system (Step 2).

▶ Start by creating a query on the MultiProvider ZECOPAM1 Profitability Analysis (actual & plan data) (Steps 3 and 4).

The **Open** dialog (Step 4) allows you to display objects according to different perspectives. These can be recently opened objects, favorites, roles or InfoAreas. InfoAreas form the global folder structure, which is technically stored in the system. Additionally, roles and favorites can map individual folder structures.

Areas of the Query Designer

The Query Designer interface is divided into three main areas that are described in detail in the following sections:

▶ Available elements of the InfoProvider (see Figure 4.2, 1)

▶ Query definition (2)

▶ Toolbar (3)

---

1 See Chapter 3, *Sample Scenario*, and Appendix H, The *SAP BW Library*.

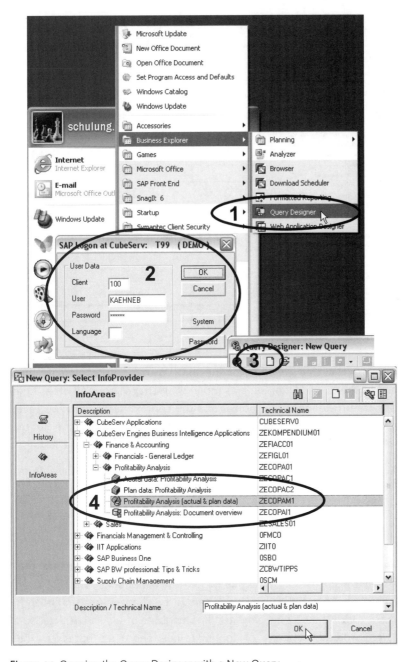

Figure 4.1 Opening the Query Designer with a New Query

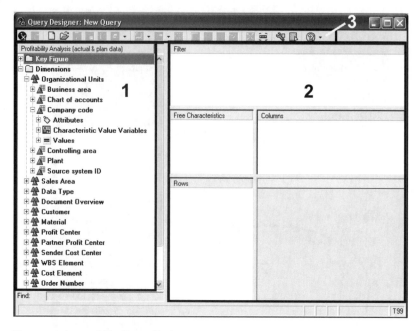

Figure 4.2 Areas of the Query Designer

From the available elements of the InfoProvider, you can create most parts of the query definition by simply using Drag&Drop. All other functions are provided via the toolbar and the context menu (which is called using the right mouse button). The standard functions of the context menu are highlighted in bold and can be executed by double-clicking.

Available elements of the InfoProvider

All characteristics, navigation attributes, and key figures of the InfoProvider are available for the query definition.

▶ *Characteristics* and *navigation attributes* include the master data (e.g., company codes, material).

Excursus

The essential difference between using a characteristic and using a navigation attribute is the modeling of time dependency. *Characteristic values* remain in the database and cannot be changed (frozen history). *Navigation attributes* are a master data attribute of such a characteristic (e.g., product hierarchy of the material). These attributes can be updated irrespective of the InfoProvider's transaction data and can also be presented in a time-dependent manner (rewrite history). Details can be found in Volume 1 of the SAP BW Library.[2]

---

2   Egger, Fiechter, Rohlf 2005.

▶ *Key figures* usually store value or quantity information. If global query elements have been created for the InfoProvider—for example, calculated or restricted key figures or structures—they can be included in the query definition as well.

Global query elements are those elements of data selection and calculation that are valid for the entire InfoProvider and simultaneously do not physically exist in the InfoProvider, but are determined only during the runtime of the OLAP processor.

The available characteristics are arranged in a hierarchical structure according to the dimensions of the InfoProvider. The available characteristic values and variables are then displayed beneath a characteristic.

The query definition contains the following areas:

Areas of the Query Definition and the target elements

▶ **Rows and Columns**

You can specify the details or granularity to be used for the first call of the query. If characteristics are entered here, they are presented in the report as dynamic drilldown. All characteristic values that exist as data in the InfoProvider and that are relevant to the current data selection are displayed.

You can also define fixed drilldowns in the form of structures. In this context, a separate data selection or formula can be defined for every structure element.

▶ **Free Characteristics**

You can specify characteristics that will be available during the query navigation for filtering and as drilldown. These characteristics are not displayed as drilldown when the query is called for the first time.

▶ **(Fixed) Filter**

You can specify characteristics that are restricted using filter values, but that are not to be used in the additional navigation. A drilldown using these characteristics is not possible.

In general, the available elements of the InfoProvider are included in the query definition per Drag&Drop. Within the query definition, all data definition and data presentation functions can be accessed via the context menu.

In addition to the query definition areas that are visible immediately, you can also separately define selections and formulas of single cells in a query. In this case, the definition of single cells of a two-dimensional structure matrix is controlled individually (see also Section 4.3.4).

Toolbar   The toolbar (see Figure 4.3) provides the functionality for managing and running the query. Additionally, you can specify settings that globally apply to the query and that determine the query's behavior, irrespective of the query areas mentioned above (see also Section 4.4.6). From here, you also access the definitions of the condition and exception analysis functions (see Section 4.7.1).

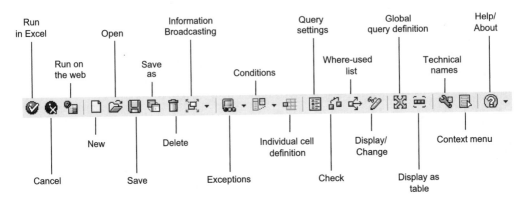

Figure 4.3 The Query Designer Toolbar

One important note before you will now create the first query. Particularly for flexible queries, it is advisable to limit the number of characteristics displayed in rows and columns for the initial call in order to enable an ideal performance. For this purpose, the characteristics released for navigation should be moved via Drag&Drop to the Free Characteristics and not to the Columns or Rows, wherever possible. For frequently used initial calls of queries, appropriate aggregates should be additionally provided.[3] This can help reduce the query runtime.

Create a Simple Query Based on CO-PA Data

In the first example, you will create two queries—a query of the gross revenues from CO-PA as well as a query for the master data reporting for customers.

▶ For CO-PA reporting, you can continue using the query you started on the ZECOPAM1 MultiProvider. There, set the display of technical names (see Figure 4.4, Step 1). Now Drag&Drop the **Revenue** key figure to the query definition, as shown in Figure 4.4 (Steps 2 and 3).

---

3 More information about aggregates can be found in Volume 1 of the *SAP BW Library*: Egger, Fiechter, Rohlf, 2005.

▶ The characteristics from the available elements will be placed in the different areas of the query definition (Steps 4 to 7).

▶ Set the view on your data by additionally limiting the characteristics in the filter area (Steps 7 to 8).

▶ The query can now be stored in your favorites or in a role (Step 9) as well as be executed on the web (Step 10).

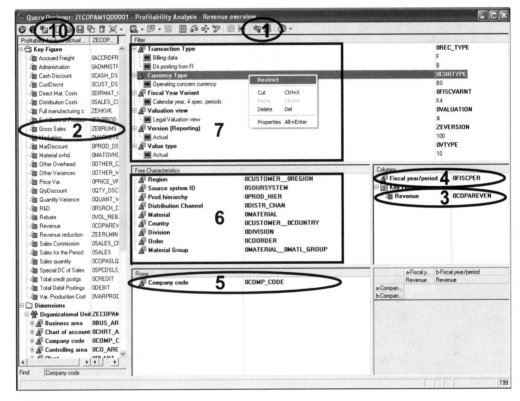

Figure 4.4 Simple Query: Revenue Reporting from CO-PA (Part 1)

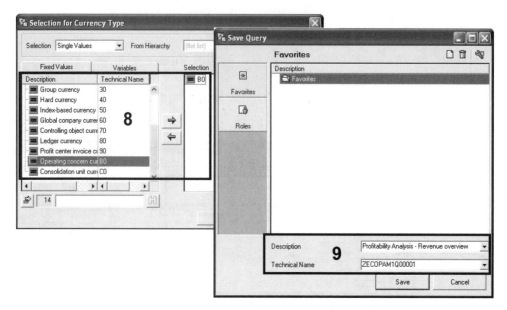

Figure 4.4 Simple Query: Revenue Reporting from CO-PA (Cont'd.)

If several variants of the data can be retrieved from the data model, like various internal management reporting views or views underlying external reporting guidelines, a correct data selection should already be ensured in the query definition. In this way, you can avoid using the query incorrectly at a later stage. In Figure 4.4, this was achieved using the global filters.

Create a Simple Query for Master Data Reporting of Customer Data

If a characteristic is released as an InfoProvider and thus released for master data reporting, queries can also be run directly against the master data tables of the respective characteristic:

▶ Create a query for the 0CUSTOMER characteristic (see Figure 4.5, Step 1).

▶ You can enter the name in the search field to avoid clicking through the InfoProvider structure (Step 2).

▶ Drag&Drop the attributes to be displayed immediately to the Rows field (Step 3) and the other available attributes to the Free Characteristics field (Step 4).

▶ You can now save the query as Customer master data report ZE0CUSTOMERQ00001 and start it (Step 5).

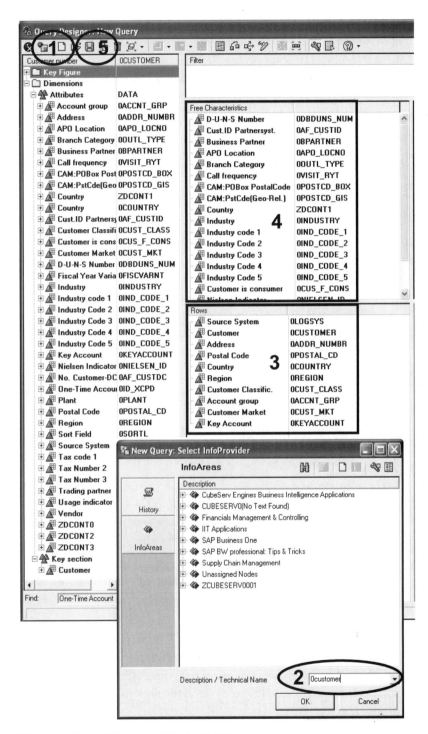

Figure 4.5 Query: "Customers" Master Data Report

The queries created here can still be substantially optimized, which is further explained in the following sections.

4.1.2 Overview of Query Elements

You can use different elements in the definition of a query. If these elements are visible, they are assigned a corresponding icon in the Query Designer (as illustrated in the figures of the following examples). Here is a short overview of the various elements:

▶ **Characteristics**
Characteristics define the available level of details (also called granularity) of the database. Therefore, you can filter data and define details for drilldowns.

▶ **Selections**
Selections usually query the value or quantity information of the database stored in key figures. Additionally, filter restrictions can be included for user-definable characteristic values so that the key figure value is issued for only these characteristic values. During the execution of the query, amounts can be converted using currency scenarios.

▶ **Formulas**
In formulas, further calculations can be carried out using the values determined by selections and other formulas. Several previously defined selections or formula results can be combined and included in the results of a formula.

▶ **Structures**
Every selection or formula is embedded in a structure as an element. From the user's perspective, these structures seem like characteristics that enable the selection of single structure elements. These structures often map the analytical functionality of the query.

▶ **Filter values**
The values of a characteristic that are available at query runtime can be determined in the query definition by using filter values.

▶ **Variables**
In most cases, characteristic variables are used to determine the characteristic values to be filtered before executing the query instead of specifying them already in the query definition. Additionally, text variables provide the possibility to dynamically determine the description of structure elements.

► **Hierarchies**

Characteristic values or structure elements can be displayed hierarchically during the execution of the query. It is also possible to navigate in hierarchies by displaying and filtering subtrees.

However, there might be elements in the query definition that are not immediately visible:

► **Data definition in cells**

If a query possesses two structures, single cells of the matrix formed by these structures can be defined separately. These can be either independent data selections or formulas that refer to other cells of the matrix.

► **Conditions**

The display of details can be controlled not only by selecting characteristics, but also depending on the value or quantity information in structures. For example, this enables typical top n analyses.

► **Exceptions**

Exceptions can be used to highlight data depending on the value or quantity information. Additionally, status information can be determined, which can be analyzed in separate exception reports.

The following sections discuss these elements in detail. They will then be integrated in the reporting solutions of the case study.

4.1.3 Global and Local Query Definition

Within the query definition, elements that are valid for all users can be distinguished from those elements that can be varied on demand. The latter can be changed both in the global and in the local query definitions. For the application of the query in Excel, for example, this is a significant advantage.

Open the Query Designer from Excel

The Query Designer can also be started from the BEx Analyzer in Excel. Open it via the Windows program menu by selecting **Business Explorer · Analyzer**.

► Using the Business Explorer menu in Excel, change to the global query definition. The functionality available here is identical to the functionality available when opening the Query Designer directly—in this case, however, the query can also be executed in Excel.

▶ Close the Query Designer and open the local view of the query (see Figure 4.6, Step 1).

▶ Exchange the elements **Fiscal year/period** and **Company code** (Step 2). In contrast to the navigation in Excel, this can be done via Drag&Drop for the local query definition in the Query Designer.

▶ The functionality is reduced to display and navigation settings in the local view (Step 3). In this view, you cannot filter characteristics or define formulas, as well as conditions or exceptions. But, you can change the layout easily using Drag&Drop functionality. Furthermore, you can define scaling factors and hierarchies in the local view.

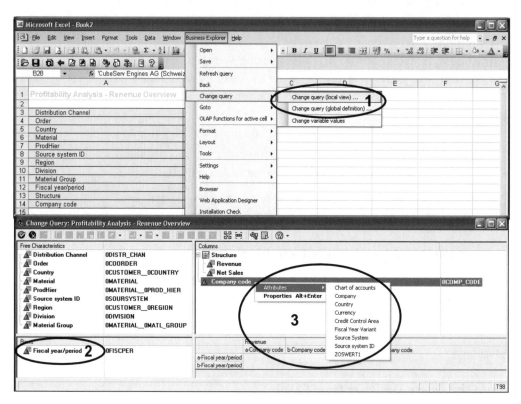

Figure 4.6 Calling the Local Query Definition in Excel

Centralized or decentralized control

Another important difference from the characteristics shown in the previous example is that all changes to the global query definition are stored on the server. Changes to the local view, however, are valid only for the currently selected query within the Excel workbook. Therefore, the query behavior can be controlled either in a centralized or a decentralized manner.

However, you can also store local views centrally on the server. As of BW Release 3.5, this can be on the web as well. Starting with BW 3.5, the navigational states stored in this way can be used for easily controlling flexible web cockpits.

This different validity area can be very useful for complex solutions, but also rather confusing at first. In simple solutions and at the beginning, it is therefore advisable to work with only the global query definition.

Another important aspect is the authorization for changing the two views. While changing the global view requires the authorization for changing the query definition on the server, changing the local view requires only the authorization for running the query. If a query is defined on the development system and transported to the production system, which is common practice, the aforementioned authorization aspect also applies to the change options of the query. All changes to the global view must take place on the development system. The local view, however, can be adapted as necessary on every system on which the query may be executed.

Authorization and Transport

4.2 Reusable Query Elements

To make the design of queries within reporting solutions efficient, you can modularize and reuse various query elements. You can use these elements across several queries. A one-time central change of the element immediately affects all queries using the respective element.

Modularization

This modularization option is a very effective means for centrally controlling the functionality of reporting solutions and for avoiding multiple development. But, clear guidelines for design and naming conventions—as well as the communication of requirements and responsibilities—are important prerequisites to ensure efficiency for several query developers.

In the following section, the special aspects of these elements are presented, in particular, regarding their reusability. The corresponding definition and presentation possibilities are discussed in detail in later sections.

4.2.1 Flexible Query Control with Variables

If a query was developed for particular analyses, its parameters should be controllable in a flexible way and without the necessity to change. In many cases, this is achieved using variables.

Variables are created globally per BW. Once a variable exists in the system, it can be used in all queries. Particularly in this context, it is recommended that you use naming conventions that are intuitive, that is, the name that you've assigned to the variable is synonymous with its function. Consequently, the obvious advantages of this principle can be used to their full extent, and all developers can work with the same variables.

You can find detailed background information about variables in Section 4.5. The following examples (up to Section 4.5) can be edited without having this information.

Include Variables in a Query

Now you'll create the restriction for fiscal period and other characteristics using variables for the ZECOPAM1Q00001 query that you just defined.

▶ For this purpose, open the global query definition. Using the context menu of the 0FISCPER characteristic, go to the filter menu (see Figure 4.7, Step 1).

▶ On the **Variables** tab (Step 2), select the 0I_FPER variable (Step 4). This variable of the "Interval" type is delivered by SAP as Business Content.

▶ To find the variable, you can first display technical names using the context menu (Step 3). You can also define variables.

▶ Restrict further characteristics of the query definition (Step 5).

▶ The variables now selected are marked as ready for input and will be displayed in a popup before the query is executed.

▶ You can specify the order of the variable query (Step 7) in the query properties (Step 6). For background information about the definition of user-defined variables and the available parameters, as well as an example of a variable popup, see Section 4.5.

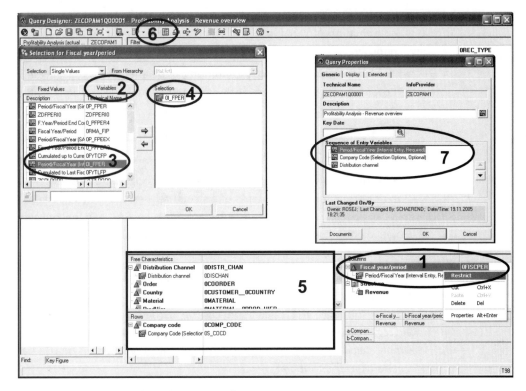

Figure 4.7 Inserting Variables in the Query Definition

4.2.2 Calculated Key Figures

Another group of reusable query elements are *restricted* and *calculated key figures*. You can globally define formula definitions per InfoProvider by using calculated key figures.

These key figures are unique per system (i.e., a specific technical name can be used once per system); however, they can only be reused within the InfoProvider for which they were created. This context calls for a viable naming convention as well.

Validity area

The creation of calculated key figures has several advantages:

▶ Effective mass changes can be carried out in the short term by changing one central element.

▶ Consistent data definitions can be easily enforced for even a multitude of queries and developers.

▶ The reuse of the same variables can be ensured. This allows for the combination of variable inputs when running several queries simultaneously.

▶ The largest part of the query definition can be effected by dragging and dropping predefined, frequently used selections, which simplifies the process considerably.

These arguments also apply to the restricted key figures and global structures described in the following section.

Available functions The formula definition in calculated key figures corresponds to the definition of normal formula elements of a structure. Besides the usual mathematical operators, further functions provided by SAP can be utilized. However, results-based calculations are not available (see also Section 4.3.2).[4]

Calculation time In general, formulas are analyzed after reading the data and its aggregation. This is advisable particularly for performance-related reasons. In simpler formulas, the calculation can be carried out even before the aggregation. As a prerequisite, only constants, basic key figures, or other simple calculated key figures with the same aggregation can be used as operands of the formula.

To avoid a loss of performance, as a solution alternative to mapping the reporting requirements, you should precalculate the value to be determined and, if possible, store it in the InfoProvider. If the data required for the calculation is stored as an attribute of a characteristic used in the report, you can also implement a formula using a formula variable with a substitution from the attribute data (see Section 4.6.4).

Create a Calculated Key Figure for Net Sales from CO-PA

In the following example, the sales analysis just created from the results calculation will be extended by the net sales and methodically optimized. For this purpose, you will extend the previously created ZECOPAM1Q00001 query by a calculated key figure for analyzing the net sales:

▶ Open the query and create a new calculated key figure for the net revenue via the key figures context menu (see Figure 4.8, Step 1).

---

4 An example of such a calculation is the percentage of a single characteristic value (e.g., "Sales of Material A") in the total of all characteristic values ("Sales of All Materials").

► In the formula editor displayed, the formula can be composed as usual, by double-clicking on the operands and functions or via Drag&Drop and keyboard input for basic functions (Steps 2 and 3).

► The result is determined by the key figures for:
Revenue (actual cube) + sales (plan cube) – several discounts (actual cube) – revenue reductions (plan cube).

► Since the CO-PA data model stores both revenues and expenses as positive numbers in the respective key figures, expenses must be subtracted from the revenues in the formula (Step 3, **Formula**).

► Indicate in the description that a restriction to specific views of the net sales hasn't been applied yet (Step 3, **Description**).

► After confirming your changes by clicking on OK, the formula properties are displayed. Assign a technical name and leave the other parameters unchanged for the present (Step 4).

► After saving the key figure to the InfoProvider, you can add it to the column definition via Drag&Drop (Step 5, **New Selection**).

► Since a restriction to the data view has already been effected in the query itself, the text of the already created structure element can be changed back to **Net sales** (Step 5, **Change description**). Thus, this change of the description is valid only within the query, and the global key figure still bears the required annotation.

You can also define exception aggregations in calculated key figures if the complexity of the formula is restricted to assigning a basic key figure. A typical example is the presentation of inventory key figures, for example, those of warehouse stocks. Naturally, when aggregating across several stock items, a total number must be used. When aggregating across time characteristics, though, the last available status is relevant rather than a summation. This can be achieved using an exception aggregation with regard to time characteristics.

Aggregation behavior

In a normal aggregation, the resulting values (usually totals) are always displayed in relation to the drilldown currently used in the query. In an exception aggregation, the results can be displayed in relation to another characteristic of the InfoProvider.

To enable exception aggregations for additional characteristics for a key figure, further key figures referencing the original key figure must be created.

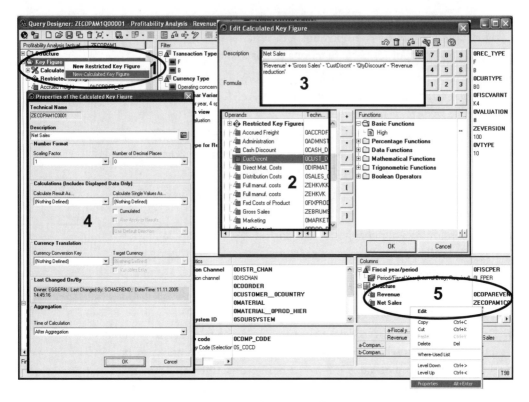

Figure 4.8 Net Sales Calculated Key Figure from CO-PA

Figure 4.9 shows the appropriate setting of the characteristic definition in the key figure definition of the Administrator Workbench.

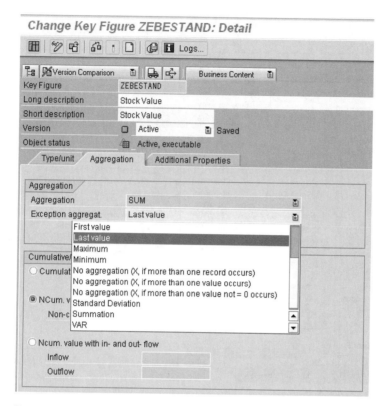

Figure 4.9 Definition of the Exception Aggregation of the Key Figure

4.2.3 Restricted Key Figures

As with calculated key figures, recurring selections for an InfoProvider can be created as a restricted key figure. Therefore, restricted key figures globally define a key figure and filter selection per InfoProvider.

The data selection in restricted key figures works like it does in normal structure elements. Even currency translation and scaling can be set in restricted key figures.

Create Restricted Key Figures as a Basis for a Comparison with the Previous Year in CO-PA

While the sales analysis query created up to now was very well suited for data retrieval and time series analysis, we will now create a query for a more detailed analysis of the sales performance during a specific period. This query provides data as a basis for the net sales comparison with the previous year, with monthly and cumulative values from the beginning of the fiscal year.

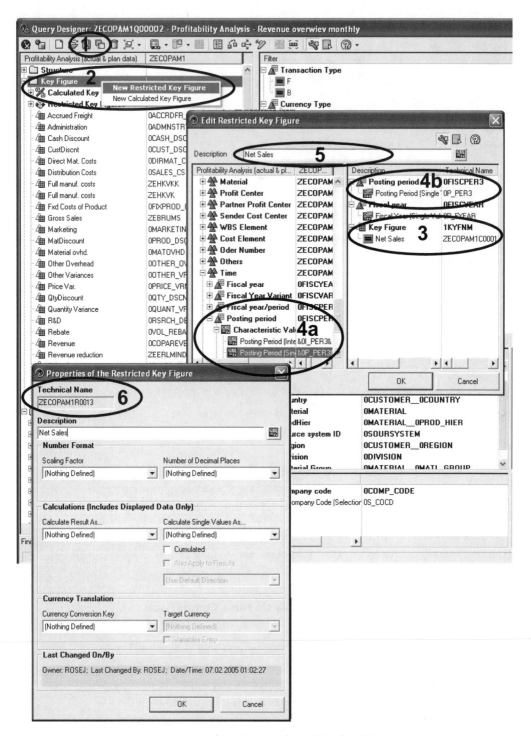

Figure 4.10 Restricted Key Figure: Selected Month MTH

▶ Save the ZECOPAM1Q00001 query as a copy under ZECOPAM1Q00002 **Profitability Analysis—Revenue overview monthly** (see Figure 4.10, Step 1).

▶ Create a restricted key figure for the monthly values (Step 2).

▶ In the selection editor, Drag&Drop the calculated net sales key figure created above to the definition (Step 3).

▶ The selection is further restricted by the characteristics 0FISCPER3 and 0FISCYEAR with the variables 0P_PER3 or 0P_FYEAR, respectively. In the list of available elements, you can browse directly to the variable (Step 4a) and transfer it via Drag&Drop (Step 4b).

▶ Enter a description (Step 5) and confirm your selection. A property window is displayed where you can simply enter the technical name for the time being (Step 6).

▶ For the key figure of the cumulative value for the previous year, proceed as described in Steps 2 to 4.

▶ Then the description needs to be adapted according to the definition (see Figure 4.11, Step 1).

▶ The selection for the fiscal year still needs to be edited in detail (Step 2).

▶ Specify a variable offset to set the filter value to the year before the entered variable value (Steps 3a and 3b).

▶ Additionally, the cumulation of the data must be stopped as of period 1. (Posting period 0 is not used in our data model.) Therefore, an interval of 1 up to the value of the 0P_FPER3 variable is defined in the detailed definition of the 0FISCPER3 characteristic (Step 4).

▶ For this purpose, first select the **Value Range** type (Step 5). Then, the 1 is moved via Drag&Drop from the fixed values to the definition to form the lower limit of the interval (Steps 6a, b, and c).

▶ Now the variable can be moved via Drag&Drop to the definition and then specifies the upper limit of the interval (Steps 7a, b, and c). Save the calculated key figure and give it a technical name.

▶ Then two other key figures must be created for MTH Y-1 and YTD values. The procedure is the same as the one described above.

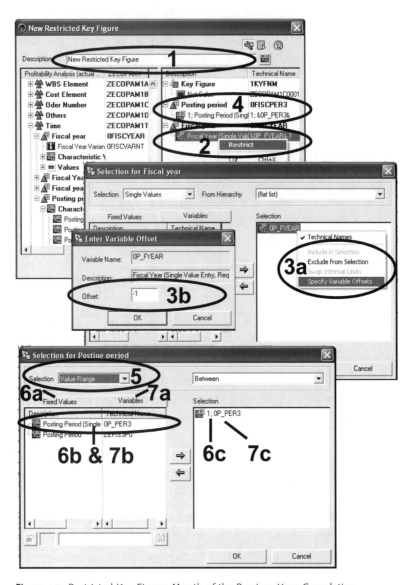

Figure 4.11 Restricted Key Figure: Month of the Previous Year, Cumulative

▶ Since you now have key figures that combine both time and key figure selection (see Figure 4.12, Step 1), you can remove the existing column definition.

▶ Then simply Drag&Drop the new key figures to the column definition to form a new structure (Step 2).

▶ In the query context, the key figures can be assigned more user-friendly names. Even line breaks are admissible (Step 3).

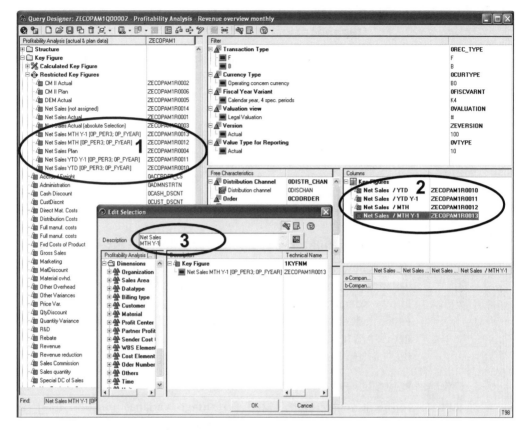

Figure 4.12 Query with Restricted Key Figures for CO-PA

 At this point, you may be thinking that this is too much effort for deriving these four scenarios; however, please consider that a Drag&Drop and the renaming of the structure element is all that is necessary for the next query to be defined. Additionally, if you do need to change the calculation method for net sales or to use different variables, this effort is only necessary once and in one place.

The current query has the disadvantage that the time selection is not visible in the column description. This can be solved by using text variables, which is described in detail in Section 4.6.3.

4.2.4 Restricted and Calculated Key Figures with Mutual Dependencies

Since BW 3.0, you can use restricted and calculated key figures in any combination. In the previous example, a calculated key figure was already used within a restricted key figure. Even more complex combinations are theoretically possible.

> This ability to nest one key figure within another key figure, in particular, allows for very flexible solution approaches. But, you should note that more complex nesting can negatively affect the performance of the OLAP processor.

Complex Calculated Key Figure for Sales Variance in CO-PA

In the following example, for the sales analysis based on CO-PA data, the variance percentage—as compared to the previous year—is stored on the InfoProvider using global key figures. In this way, these key figures can be easily added to other queries at a later stage. The query ZECOPAM1Q00002 Profitability Analysis—Revenue overview monthly that has just been created is then extended by these key figures:

▶ Create a new calculated key figure (see Figure 4.13, Step 1).

▶ The formula result is the **Percentage Variance** function (Step 2) between the Net Sales YTD operands of the current and the previous year (Step 3).

▶ The individual elements can be re-inserted using Drag&Drop or by double-clicking (Step 4).

▶ Save the calculated key figure. When saving, you should set the scaling factor in the properties; otherwise, the OLAP processor will return the numbers with the highest possible accuracy.

▶ Repeat this procedure to determine additional key figures for the monthly sales variance percentage—as compared to the previous year—as well as the monthly and the cumulative absolute variances (Step 5).

▶ You can now transfer the available key figures for the sales variance to the query structure using Drag&Drop functionality (Step 6).

▶ Figure 4.14 shows the result on the web. Here you have all the navigation options; for example, exchanging or adding drilldowns or sorting by sales growth.

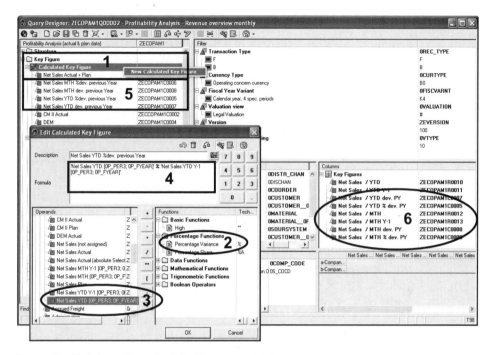

Figure 4.13 Global Key Figure for Sales Variance in CO-PA

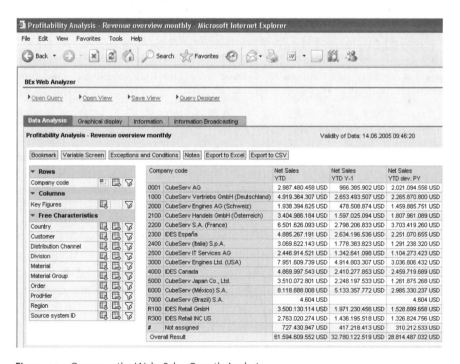

Figure 4.14 Query on the Web: Sales Growth Analysis

4.2.5 Global Structures

Frequently used combinations of different data selections or formulas can be created as a global structure. They have the same functionality, as do structures that are defined only within a specific query.

The following applies to the validity area: Like restricted and calculated key figures, global structures are created per InfoCube. They can be used in all queries for that particular InfoCube. The technical name of a global structure must be unique on the system.

All settings of the global structure are copied to all queries using that structure. In this context, it is significant that this applies to both data definitions and display settings. Contrary to restricted and calculated key figures, the display options in the query definition cannot be overridden. Hiding a structure element in one query, for example, will activate this behavior in all other queries using this global structure.

You can use a maximum of two structures within one query. If only one structure is used in the query, you can activate the tabular display as well. (see also Section 4.4.5.) When using two structures, you can define single cells (see Section 4.3.4). Within a query, only one structure can contain key figures of an InfoProvider.

Remove a reference If a query has been using a global structure that should be valid only locally within that query, you can remove the reference to the global structure. During this procedure, a copy of the global structure is created within the query definition.

Alternatively, a structure that exists only within one query can be made available as a global structure of the InfoProvider, as is illustrated in the following example.

Structure template You can also use global structures as templates for query definitions, provided that the definition of the query structure deviates slightly from the global structure. For this purpose, the global structure is transfered into the query via Drag&Drop, and the reference is then removed. All further changes to the structure within the query will no longer be transferred to the global structure.

When working with locally stored Excel workbooks, however, you must be careful when removing and creating global structure references. This process changes the (generated) technical name of the structure. If a workbook previously existed with a local view of this structure, this view is lost and the new structure will be displayed.

Create a Global Structure for Determining the Local Contribution Margin

The following example uses the full data range of CO-PA to create a contribution margin calculation. In our data model, this contribution margin calculation can be used for analyzing subsidiaries. It does not yet include any consolidated sales or expenses where the intercompany sales have been eliminated:

▶ Create a second copy of the query ZECOPAM1Q00001 as **Profitability Analysis—Contribution Margin Overview** with the technical name ZECOPAM1Q00003.

▶ Remove the key figure structure from the columns. Only the **Fiscal year/period** characteristic should be included (see Figure 4.15, Step 1).

▶ Drag&Drop the **Company code** characteristic from the Rows field to the Free Characteristics field (Step 2).

▶ In the Rows field, create a new structure to contain the contribution margin scheme (Step 3).

▶ Define the structure characteristics as shown in Table 4.1. Every row of this table contains a structure element and its definition.

  ▷ The first column describes the row number in the structure.

  ▷ Column 2 contains S for a selection and F for a formula. The row should be hidden if this column additionally contains the letter **H** (for Hide).

  ▷ Columns 3 and 4 contain the description and definition of the structure element.

Figure 4.15, Step 4, contains the example formula for contribution margin III (see table entry no. 23). For all other structure elements, you can proceed as shown in this example.

▶ The structure can now be saved globally as ZECOPAM1S00001 **Structure Contribution Margin I-V (local)** and then be used in other queries.

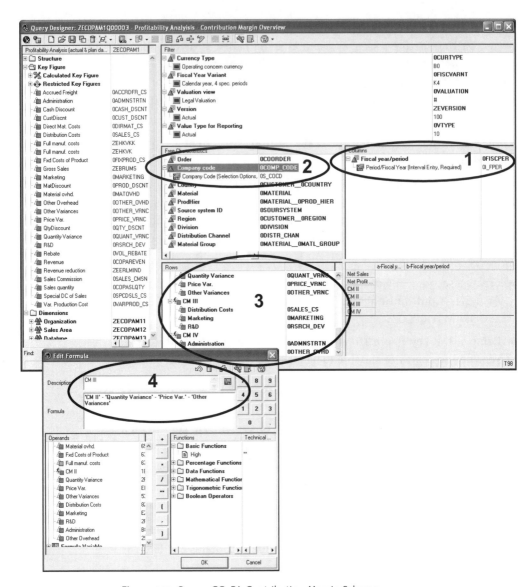

Figure 4.15 Query: CO-PA Contribution Margin Scheme

No.	FSH	Description	Selection/Formula
1	SH	Revenue	OCOPAREVEN
2	SH	Gross sales	ZEBRUMS
3	F	**Gross sales**	= (1) + (2)

Table 4.1 Local Contribution Margin Scheme of the Example

No.	FSH	Description	Selection/Formula
4	S	Customer discount	0CUST_DSCNT
5	S	Material discount	0PROD_DSCNT
6	S	Other revenue reductions	ZEERLMIND
7	F	**Net sales**	= (3) – (4) – (5) – (6)
8	S	Cash discount	0CASH_DSCNT
9	S	Volume rebate	0VOL_REBATE
10	S	Sales commission	0SALES_CMSN
11	S	Special direct costs of sales	0SPCDSLS_CS
12	S	Accrued freight costs	0ACCRDFR_CS
13	F	**Net sales revenue**	= (7) – (8 ... 12)
14	S	Direct material costs	0DIRMAT_CS
15	S	Variable production costs	0VARPROD_CS
16	S	Material overhead costs	0MATOVHD
17	S	Fixed production costs	0FIXPROD_CS
18	S	Full costs of production	ZEHKVK
19	F	**CM II**	= (13) – (14 ... 18)
20	S	Quantity variance	0QUANT_VRNC
21	S	Price variance	0PRICE_VRNC
22	S	Other variance	0OTHER_VRNC
23	F	**CM III**	= (19) – (20 ... 22)
24	S	Cost of sales	0SALES_CS
25	S	Marketing costs	0MARKETING
26	S	Research & development costs	0RSRCH_DEV
27	F	**CM IV**	= (23) – (24 ... 26)
27	S	Administration costs	0ADMNSTRTN
28	S	Other overhead costs	0OTHER_OVHD
29	F	**Operating profit**	= (23) – (27) – (28)

Table 4.1 Local Contribution Margin Scheme of the Example (Cont'd.)

4.3   Definition of Data

Several very powerful resources are available to provide the data required for the analysis from the InfoProvider data. This includes methods for filtering, further calculating, and presenting data in currency scenarios, which will be discussed in detail in this section.

Although a lot can be achieved with the functionality provided, it cannot always serve as a substitute for a data model that is optimized with regard to basic reporting requirements. In many cases, increased query complexity also means restricted flexibility and a higher maintenance effort. Depending on the requirements, the challenge here is to find an optimal balance between function and complexity of the data model and the queries.

4.3.1   Filtering Characteristics (Selections)

By filtering characteristics, the amount of data queried by the database can be restricted.

Performance aspects

The setting of filter values can have significant effects on the query performance:

▶ The more the query is restricted by filter values, the less data must be read in the database.

▶ Queries with restricting filter selections usually perform better than queries with the exclusion of characteristic values.

▶ Queries can be optimized to the required level of detail by pre-aggregating the data. To set the filter value, the corresponding characteristic must exist in the aggregate so that the aggregate can be included in the query.

The filter value is usually set in the filter editor (see also Figure 4.16). Here you can define the filter values (right-hand side) by dragging and dropping them from a list of available values (see Figure 4.16, left-hand side). Using the context menu of the filter value, you can determine whether this filter value works as a restricting or excluding element.

Single values and intervals

The filter type can be defined in the upper area of the filter selection. Here you can toggle between single values and interval selection. Within one characteristic, different single values and intervals can be used in any combination.

Additionally, you can store the filter values based on a master data hierarchy of the characteristic. In the upper area of the filter selection, you can select a hierarchy that should serve as a basis for filter values. After the selection, the available values show the hierarchy nodes of this hierarchy or available hierarchy node variables, respectively.

For hierarchy values, however, the selection is restricted to single characteristic nodes. Interval selections are possible only when the selected hierarchy node itself is defined as an interval within the hierarchy. When filtering hierarchy nodes, the excluding selection cannot be used.

The list of available values can be switched between the view of characteristic values or variables. If variables are included in the filter, you can also use values that deviate by a fixed integer amount from the original value instead of the values provided by the variable. This variable offset setting is called via the context menu of the variable.

The data selection within structure elements is also carried out like the filtering of characteristic values as described above. In this case, however, it is possible to filter any characteristics within a structure element. The structure elements created in this way can be provided as filter values during the query execution. Therefore, new data views can be defined very easily from different elements of the physically existing data set without changing it. This analytic view is eventually defined in the query.

If the query uses several structures, a specific characteristic may only be used in the filtered selections of one of the two structures. Overlapping filtered selections using one characteristic are therefore not possible.

You can also use variables to restrict structure selections. Variables that are determined from a precalculated value set, however, are not available for technical reasons.

Define Combined Filter Values for the Segment Analysis "Sales Order Stock"

In this example, a part segment analysis of the sales order stock is performed based on CO-PA data. A comparison with these part segments should be enabled for any selectable data:

▶ Create a new query on the InfoProvider ZEKDABC15[5] called ZEKDABC1Q00001 **Sales Order Stock—Part segment analysis**.

---

5 See Egger, Fiechter, Rohlf, 2005, Appendix D.6

▶ The global filters are restricted as shown in Figure 4.15 (see Figure 4.16, Step 1). The InfoCube for the sales order stock is populated from CO-PA as well, and therefore, requires a corresponding restriction of the data view.

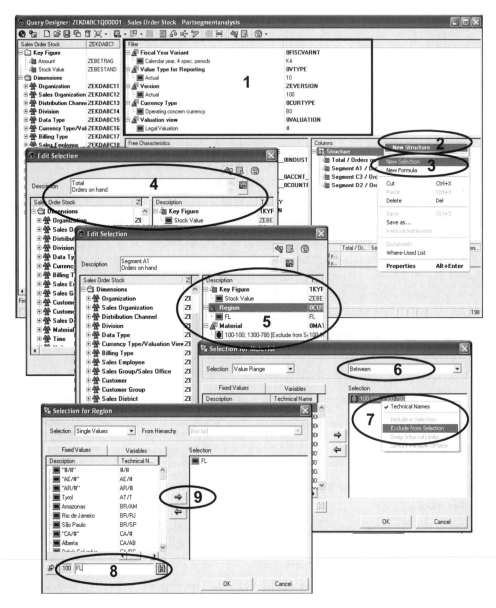

Figure 4.16 Part Segment Analysis "Sales Order Stock"

- The rows contain the 0FISCPER characteristic that is restricted via the 0I_FPER variable. In this case, you can proceed as shown in the example described in Section 4.2.1.
- In the columns, a new structure is defined (Step 2).
- A new selection can be created using the context menu (Step 3).
- It should contain all selected sales order stocks and thus only consists of the key figure ZEBESTAND (Step 4).
- The further selections contain additional restrictions to region and material that define the market segment (Step 5).
- In the detail editor for filter values, you can also specify intervals (Step 6) and excluding definitions (Step 7).
- If you want to restrict a characteristic, you can enter the filter value directly. For this purpose, the characteristic value must be entered in the lower left area in the internal format (Step 8).
- By clicking on the right arrow button, the value is taken over into the filter (Step 9).

Flexible Time Series for the Variance Percentage of the Contribution Margin Compared to the Average of the Previous Year

In the following example, you'll extend the query for the contribution margin scheme so that the structure allows for a variance percentage compared to the average of the previous year that is dynamic or depends on a variable entry, respectively. The analytic functionality for the data set of the profitability analysis is thus extended by another component.

- Create a copy of the query ZECOPAM1Q00003 from Section 4.2.5 as ZECOPAM1Q00004 **Profitability Analysis—Contribution Margin prev year compa**.
- From the columns, remove the characteristic 0FISCPER **Fiscal year/period** and replace it with 0FISCPER3 Posting period. This is restricted by the 0I_PER3 variable, which enables interval selections. This procedure is the same as the one in the example presented in Section 4.2.3.
- Underneath, you create a new structure for comparison with the previous year (see Figure 4.17, Step 1).
- A structure element with the selection on the current fiscal year must be created (Step 2). In the context of the query, this column shows the monthly amount of the current period.

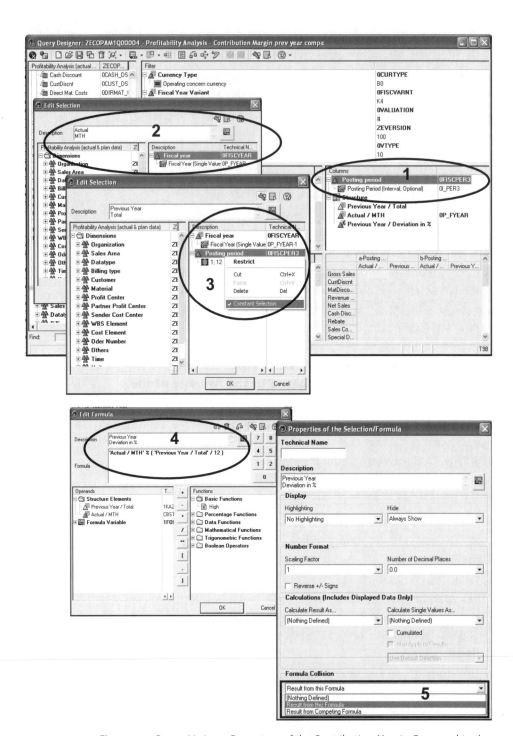

Figure 4.17 Query: Variance Percentage of the Contribution Margin Compared to the Average of the Previous Year

▶ Another selection is to provide the cumulative data of the previous year. In this context, several settings need to be made:

  ▷ The 0FISCYEAR characteristic is restricted by the 0P_FYEAR variable. This variable is reduced by a variable offset of −1.

  ▷ The posting period 0FISCPER3 is restricted to the interval January-December in order to provide the data for the entire year. This selection must be marked as a constant selection so that it isn't affected by the dynamic drilldown of the posting period (Step 3). (Here, we are anticipating Section 4.3.5, where this functionality will be discussed again in more detail.)

▶ The monthly average of the previous year is then determined by a formula, and the variance percentage of the selected period is calculated (Step 4).

▶ Since both the row and the column structures contain formulas, the order of the formula calculation must be set in the **Formula Collision Percentage Value Property** so that it is calculated last (Step 5). This and other details about formulas are explained in the next section.

▶ Now periods and other details like company codes can be flexibly compared and analyzed in the query (see Figure 4.18).

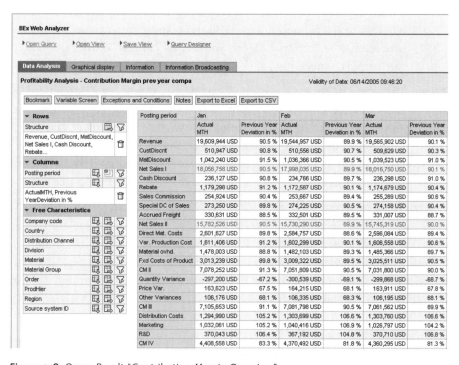

Figure 4.18 Query Result "Contribution Margin Overview"

4.3.2   Calculation in Formulas

Formulas can be stored in structures, calculated key figures, and single cell definitions as well. The formula editor used for this purpose is divided into the following areas:

▶ **Text field**
Contains the description of the formula. Text variables can be used here as well (see also Section 4.8.4).

▶ **Entry field**
Contains the formula definition. Numbers and mathematical basic operators can be entered manually. Functions and the operands are taken per Drag&Drop or by double-clicking from the following areas.

▶ **Operands**
Operands for the formula can be other structure elements of the structure, single cell definitions, or formula variables.

▶ **Functions**
Functions are available in addition to the mathematical basic operators. The function group predefined by SAP is divided into several categories.[6]

Similar to data selections, the properties of the formula can be set in addition to the formula contents. In this respect, you can set the display properties (see Section 4.4), but you can also influence the execution of the formula, if necessary.

The order of formula execution can be decisive for the correct result, especially for queries using two structures that both contain formulas. This is often the case, for example, when the row element contains a summation of various values, and the column element contains a percentage. For a correct calculation, the summation should be carried out before the calculation of the percentage. This precedence rule can be defined using the formula collision definition in the formula properties (see our example in Section 4.3.1).

The basic use of formulas was already explained in the previous examples. In the following section, you will be presented with some typical implementations of formulas that have a rather technical background but can be very helpful in daily use.

---

6 Appendix C provides an overview of the available functions and their typical usage. Their exact function can also be seen in the ABAP source code of the include LRRKOF10 Form LOC_RECHNEN.

Non-Defined Mathematical Operations

If you try to perform an inadmissible mathematical operation during the query execution (e.g., division by zero or the square root of a negative value), the system generates an error message. This behavior can be suppressed by using the functions NOERR() and NDIV0().

The presentation of the contribution margin overview query created above will be optimized in the following example:

▶ Open the query ZECOPAM1Q00004 for determining the variance of the contribution margin that was created in Section 4.3.1.

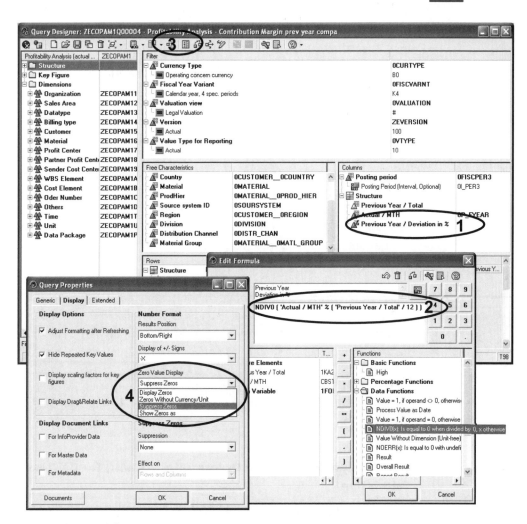

Figure 4.19 NDIV0() for Error Suppression

- The formula of the formula element for determining the variance percentage (see Figure 4.19, Step 1) must be executed within an error checking function. (In our example, you can use NDIV0(), see Step 2.)

- In the global query properties (Step 3), you can additionally suppress the display of zeros (Step 4).

- The error messages presented above will now be displayed as empty rows, which can improve the readability of the query.

Unit Precision of the Calculation

Another strong point of BW queries is the option to calculate with precise units. For example, when calculating the price from an amount and a quantity key figure, the price determined in the formula can be presented using the virtual unit "Currency per unit of measure."

Similarly, when totaling data, its unit is considered. However, the data records summed within the key figure (or the operators used in the formula) must have matching units.

While the attempt to divide monetary amounts (e.g., in EUR) by quantities (e.g., in kg) results in a new unit (in this case EUR/kg), the attempt to add them up produces an error. If this error can be detected during the query definition, the syntax check of the formula will fail. If the error is not detected before the execution, a corresponding error message might be shown in the cell. Both error messages, but also the display of the unit, can be suppressed using the NODIM() function for calculations without units.

The error messages created above can be configured using Transaction SPRO. For this purpose, several categories are available to specifically adapt the error message texts of the BW system. When using the aforementioned error-suppressing query functions, you should ensure that the content of the result produced in this way can be correctly interpreted. For example, the aggregation of amounts in different currencies wouldn't make much sense, whereas an error message in the report might be rather useful.

Sales Analysis of Incoming Orders with NODIM() for Unitless Calculation

In the following example, a sales analysis is performed based on the sales and distribution documents from Sales & Distribution (SAP SD). In addition, this query serves to demonstrate the NODIM() function. As already mentioned, the NODIM() function also causes the useful side effect of display formatting. This will be illustrated in the following example using a sales calculation based on incoming order data. In the corresponding query, a large amount of numbers is to be displayed within very little space; for this reason, units need to be suppressed:

▶ Create a new query based on the InfoProvider ZEVAHDM1[7] **Sales Document**, and save it as ZEVAHDM1Q00001 **Sales—Price analysis**.

▶ In the global filter, the data view of the query is restricted to actual values (see Figure 4.20, Step 1).

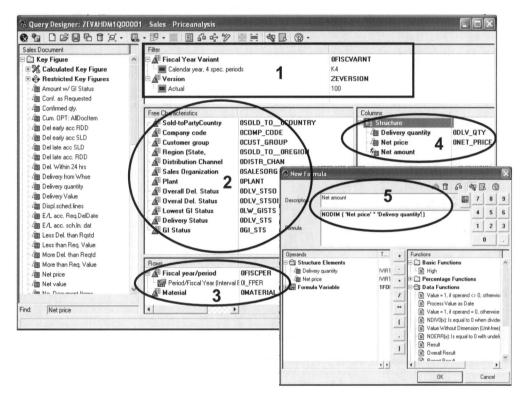

Figure 4.20 Query: Simple Price Analysis for Incoming Orders

▶ The free characteristics contain characteristics available for later navigation (Step 2).

▶ The rows contain the initial drilldown by material and fiscal year/period that is restricted by variables (Step 3).

---

7 See Egger, Fiechter, Rohlf, 2005, Appendix E.3.

▶ The columns contain a structure with the basic key figures **Delivery quantity** and **Net price**. Additionally, a formula is added that is to determine the achieved net sales (Step 4). This key figure could also be permanently stored in the InfoProvider. In this case, however, we want to calculate it so we can demonstrate the effect of including units.

▶ This simple formula is determined by the product of net price and delivery quantity. It will be called within a NODIM() function to suppress the unit of the price calculation (Step 5). Try creating this formula without NODIM() to see the result.

The presentation in the SAP standard version without unit suppression is shown in Figure 4.21. In the previous example, this was resolved in a more user-friendly way by using the NODIM() function.

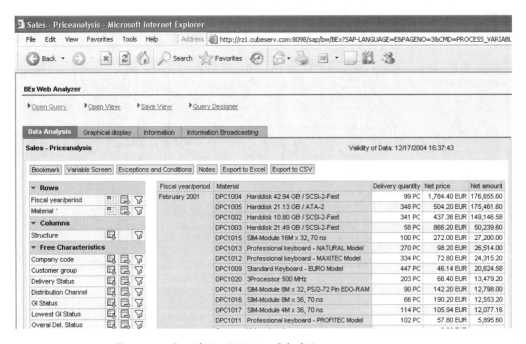

Figure 4.21 Considering Units in a Calculation

Logical Nesting

With another workaround, formulas can map a flow control as well, since by default, there is no direct possibility within the formula editor to control the formula execution depending on specific conditions. Fortunately, the available logical operators provide the possibility of a workaround for mapping if-then nesting.

Within the formula, logical relational operators like == or <= return the values zero for "false" and one for "true." This behavior can be used to dynamically display or hide values by simply multiplying the value with the result of the logical comparison. A simple condition of the format

IF (A>=B) THEN (C) ELSE (D)

can be presented as follows:

Result = (A >= B) × C + (A < B) × D

The letters A, B, C, and D represent any formula expressions—from numeric constants via structure or single cell definitions up to complex formulas. Provided the formula expression is correct, the result always returns C or D, because either the first or the second logical comparison of A and B produces a value of one (and the other produces a value of zero). The admissible nesting depth is restricted by a reduced readability of the formula rather than by technical constraints.

Consolidated Contribution Margin and If-Then Query

In the contribution margin overview discussed in Section 4.2.5, sales and manufacturing costs are only presented based on the local view of the companies (in particular, this applies to the data model based on Business Content that we use here). The sums of the sales and costs of the companies do not necessarily reflect the consolidated amounts of the group. The reason for this is that companies also include the amounts invoiced within the group in their contribution margin calculation. In a consolidated view, however, only the sales and costs regarding third parties should be considered. The example presented in this section is a bit more complex, because it also deals with the background of the elimination of IC sales and with the extension of the previous CO-PA data model. The example is divided into the following sections:

▶ Calculation example for illustrating the requirements

▶ Assumptions of our data model

▶ Extension of the data model in the Administrator Workbench

▶ Creation of the query in the Query Designer

If you are interested only in the functionality of the Query Designer, you can skip to the next section. However, this detailed example is very useful for illustrating the connections between reporting requirements, data modeling, and query design. In particular, users who have not yet delved into data modeling will certainly gain some helpful insight.

Background of the Elimination of Intercompany Sales

A simple example calculation for eliminating the intercompany sales is as follows:

▶ CubeServ Vertriebs GmbH in Germany sells a product to a customer and receives a monetary amount of 1000.

▶ For this product, Germany imports components from CubeServ Engines Switzerland for a monetary amount of 700 (which is usually determined based on a transfer price rule). These components are usually sold to customers as well by the Swiss company. The full manufacturing costs in Switzerland amount to 500; in Germany, they amount to another 100. The revenues from Germany and Switzerland are posted in the revenue key figure of the corresponding SAP R/3 systems, extracted to SAP BW, and therefore, they show up in the query.

▶ In the aggregated view of Germany and Switzerland, the sum 1000 + 700 = 1700 is shown as the revenue, which is reported by both companies for their local financial statement. But, the consolidated view may only display an amount of 1000, because this is the consolidated external sales of the group.

▶ The same applies to the costs. Suppose that Germany books the costs by default—as required for the local contribution margin—as full manufacturing costs. The aggregated view of Germany and Switzerland would amount to costs of 700 + 100 + 500 = 1300 although the costs of the group only amount to 100 + 500 = 600.

It is apparent that the consolidated view requires an elimination of the intercompany sales (or costs, respectively). SAP BW provides a standard solution for this purpose that can be applied under certain conditions. (For lack of space, the elimination of intercompany sales in SAP BW using the OLAP processor cannot be described here in detail.) But, the CO-PA model based on Business Content does not necessarily contain the information necessary for consolidating across company codes. The consolidation of profit centers is supported, however, if the required data has been stored in R/3.

Assumptions in the Data Model of the Example

To perform a consolidated contribution margin calculation based on the company code information, there are various alternatives in which specific assumptions need to be made for the data model. The following example explains some simple alternatives and their assumptions and maps them in the system:

▶ Suppose that the master data attribute 0PCOMPANY **Partner Company** contains a value for all customers acting within companies of the group. This field is not populated for all external customers. This attribute is activated as a navigation attribute to the customer and can thus be filtered in the query. Therefore, by filtering the value **#—Not assigned** within the navigation attribute, only the sales with third parties are shown.[8]

▶ In common models for determining consolidated costs, the assumption is made that the consolidated costs are determined based on the transferred amounts and the consolidated material costs that are valid throughout the group or are specific to the country. This assumption is made in our model as well, although we cannot completely illustrate its derivation within this chapter. This presentation confines itself to calling a corresponding function module to derive another key figure ZEHKVKK **Full manufacturing costs consolidated** that is stored in the InfoProvider.

▶ Thus, the group view can be shown by selecting the consolidated sales and cost key figures, and the local view can be called by selecting the unrestricted sales key figure and the originally extracted local cost key figure.

The Administrator Workbench: An Excursus

Figures 4.22 to 4.24 illustrate the necessary steps for extending the existing CO-PA data model at the reporting level. Note that not every step is indicated in these figures:

---

8 With regard to data modeling, this solution is not ideal: A separate additional attribute or characteristic would be more favorable. However, this is a typical restriction of the data model based on Business Content.

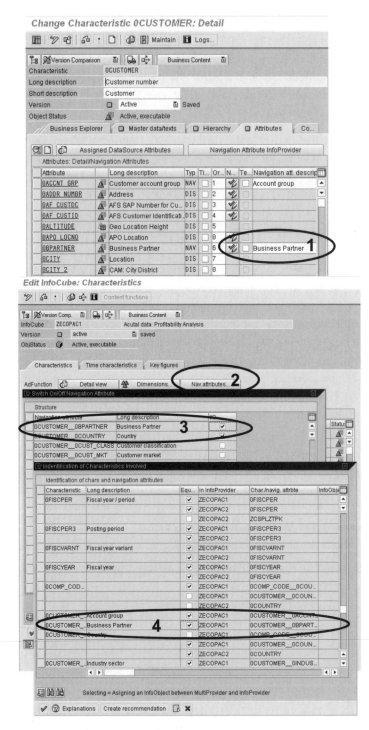

Figure 4.22 CO-PA Extension for the "Customer" Account Group

▶ The 0PCOMPANY attribute is activated as a navigation attribute in the InfoObject 0CUSTOMER (see Figure 4.22, Step 1), in the BasisCube ZECOPA01 (Steps 2 and 3), and in the MultiProvider ZECOPAM1 (like in ZECOPA01, not shown).

▶ Additionally, the mapping of characteristics needs to be adapted in the MultiProvider (Step 4) in order to determine the BasisCube characteristic or navigation attribute to be used for populating the MultiProvider field.

▶ A new key figure ZEHKVKK **Full manufacturing costs consolidated** is created as a copy of ZEHKVK (see Figure 4.23, Steps 1 to 3).

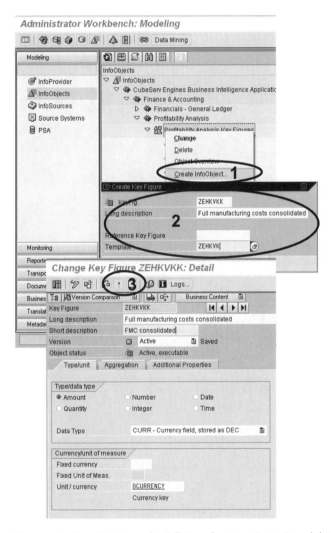

Figure 4.23 New Key Figure for Full Manufacturing Costs Consolidated

- ▶ This key figure is integrated in the BasisCube ZECOPA01 (see Figure 4.24, Steps 1 and 2) and the MultiProvider ZECOPAM1 (like in Basis-Cube, not shown). Again, the mapping of the key figures was automatically adjusted by the system.

- ▶ Additionally, the update rule for the InfoCube ZECOPA01 is adjusted in order to populate the newly created key figure. For this purpose, a simple ABAP routine is used for deriving the key figure (Step 3). In this routine, the relevant source fields for fixed costs and variable costs are updated in the new key figure based on the rule defined above (Step 4).

- ▶ After saving the routine (Step 5) and activating the update rule (Step 6), the extension of the data model is complete.

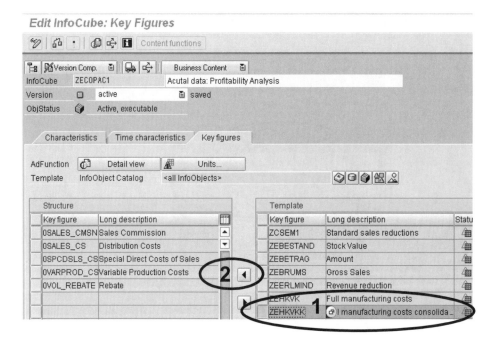

Figure 4.24 New Key Figure in InfoCube and Update Rule

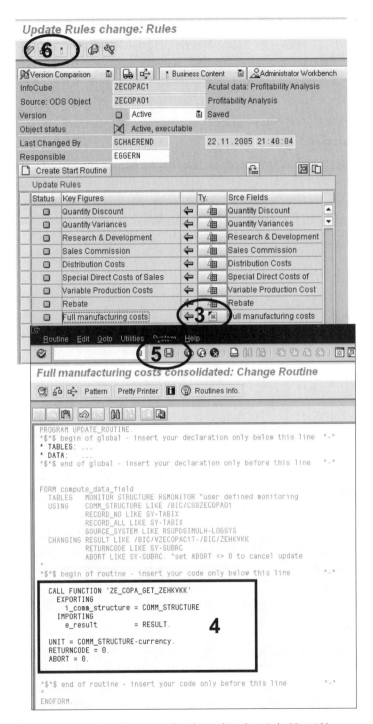

Figure 4.24 New Key Figure in InfoCube and Update Rule (Cont'd.)

Query for Local and Consolidated Contribution Margin

If this information is available in the data model, you can begin the implementation of the reporting solution. Here, a query should reflect both the local and the consolidated contribution margins of the company codes:

▶ Create a copy of the query ZECOPAM1Q00003 as ZECOPAM1Q00005 **Profitability Analysis—Contribution margin consolidated and local**.

▶ Drag&Drop the company code to the **Definition** column, and **Fiscal year/period** to the global filter. Remove the remaining characteristics from the Free Characteristics field. The reason for this is that the navigation across certain characteristics in this query can lead to incorrect results.

▶ To adjust the contribution margin structure without changing the other queries, the structure reference must be removed.

▶ On the InfoCube, a new restricted key figure ZECOPAM1R0014 is created for **Net Sales Cons. (not assigned)** (see Figure 4.25, Step 1). This key figure is based on the calculated key figure ZECOPAM1C0001 **Net Sales (not assigned)** that has already been created.

▶ Additionally, from the navigation attribute **Business partner**, the value **#—Not assigned** is added to the selection (Step 2).

▶ The new restricted key figure is copied into the contribution margin structure. The original formula for net sales is copied and saved as **Net Sales Local** (Step 3).

▶ The consolidated costs key figure created above is also copied into the structure (Step 4).

▶ When displaying single values (in this case: per company code), the new formula for net sales shows the local net sales. For results across all company codes, the consolidated net sales are shown. In this case, the flow control method with the aforementioned logical operators is used (Step 5).

▶ A new formula is created for calculating the local full manufacturing costs (Step 6).

▶ Additionally, a new formula for calculating the entire full manufacturing costs is required. This always includes the plan costs, because, according to the requirements, we do not differentiate between consolidated and local cost planning. With regard to the actual costs, the flow control is implemented just like the sales calculation (Step 7).

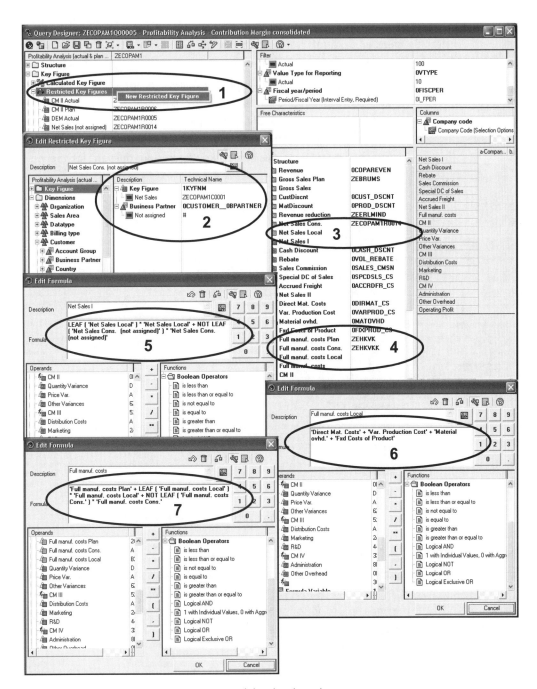

Figure 4.25 Query: Contribution Margin, Consolidated and Local

- ► For the purpose of clarification, inessential details for calculating net sales and manufacturing costs should be hidden via the properties of the relevant structure elements.

- ► Figure 4.26 shows hidden structure elements for local and consolidated costs separately to illustrate the different calculations for the results column and the individual company codes. While the local key figures are used to calculate the contribution margin for the individual company codes, the consolidated key figures are relevant for the view of the group.

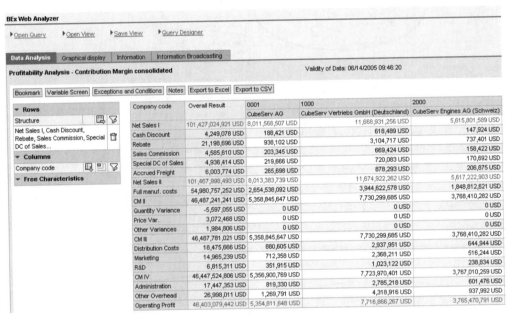

Figure 4.26 Report: Contribution Margin, Consolidated and Local

Thus, the choice of the key figure depends solely on whether the calculation is performed within a results column. This applies to all characteristics and cannot be limited to the company code. By restricting the navigation options for users, you can avoid a query of possibly wrong data.

The above example was well suited for illustrating a variety of interrelations of query design and data modeling. Nevertheless, you might have noticed that the flexibility of the reporting solution is clearly restricted for this requirement. The primary reason for this is that an ideal mapping of the reporting requirements must not only be supported by the query, but often by the reporting layer of the data model as well. Since the data model is widely based on Business Content for the purpose of simplicity, there are various limitations for consolidated presentations.

4.3.3 Calculation in the Display

Additionally to calculations within formulas, some calculations can be performed within the display as well. In a display calculation, you can toggle between the calculation methods—both in the local query definition and after executing the query using the context menu. This is the essential difference when compared to the calculation within formulas. Therefore, the user can configure his calculations in the query without changing the global query definition.

All calculations can be set per structure element. Within the structure element, various calculations for single values and result rows can be performed. Some calculations can be set per characteristic.

Note that when the data of the respective structure element is further used within the query, the basic values are often employed instead of the values calculated in the display. For example, if the **Ranking** display format is chosen for the display of a column with selling values of the current month, every exception or condition referring to the structure element is determined by the selling value, not by the ranking number.

You can specify the following settings per characteristic and for the single values per structure element:

▶ **Cumulation**
In a list of several values, the single values are shown cumulatively. In other words, instead of the second basic value, the second value is shown as the sum of the first value and the second basic value.

▶ **Standardization**
The percentage of the result is measured that is taken by the single value in the drilldown. Consequently, either the entire query result or the next result in the drilldown, or the one after that, can be used. When standardizing the query result, the filter settings made in the navigation are not even considered.

You can also combine both elements to present the cumulative portion of the result.

The following applies to the scope of use for these settings: If the settings mentioned above are specified in a characteristic, they affect all structure elements but only for this characteristic. In turn, if the setting is specified in a structure element, it only affects this structure element, but all of this element's characteristics are affected as well.

Therefore, the standardization or cumulation setting in the characteristic makes sense, particularly when only displaying specific characteristics is required.

Additional settings of structure elements for single cells and results are:

▶ **Minimum and maximum**
The lowest or highest value determined is displayed.

▶ **Count of all values or all values <> 0**
The number of values determined in the drilldown is counted. On demand, null values can be excluded from the count.

▶ **Average of all values or of all values <> 0**
The average of values in the drilldown is determined. Again, null values can be excluded from the calculation.

The following calculation method exists only for single cells:

▶ **Ranked List and Ranked List (Olympic)**
The values are sorted in a ranked list according to their amounts, where the highest value starts with one. In the normal variant, if several values rank in the same position, the next higher value obtains the next ranking number. In the olympic variant, the next ranking number of the ranked list is always the number of already ranked elements plus one.

The following calculation methods exist only for results:

▶ **Summation and Summation of rounded values**
The summation is the classical form of aggregation where the single values in the result are simply totaled. The "Summation of rounded values" variant sums up only the values presented (with regard to scaling factors and decimal places).

▶ **Standard deviation**
This setting determines the standard deviation of the single values.

▶ **Variance**
This setting determines the variance of the single values.

▶ **First value and Last value**
This setting copies the first or the last single value into the result.

Create Ranking and Normalized Values for an Extended Sales Analysis

This example extends the query ZECOPAM1Q00002 **Profitability Analysis—Revenue overview** for an overview of the share of sales and the contribution to the previous year's variance:

▶ Create a copy of the YTD selection (see Figure 4.27, Step 1) and set the cumulation of single values in the properties (Step 2).

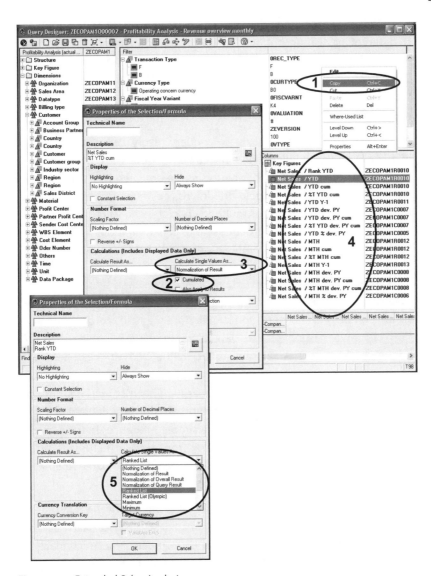

Figure 4.27 Extended Sales Analysis

- Now copy this selection and set the standardization of single values to the interim results (Step 3).

- Repeat this procedure for the column with the absolute YTD deviation, as well as for the columns with the MTH values and the absolute MTH deviation. Thus, with a few clicks and some copying, you receive a multitude of possibilities for analyzing the same data (Step 4).

- Create another copy of the YTDCHF column and determine the ranking of the corresponding values (Step 5).

- You can now open the query that you created on the web and apply the different navigation options. For example, you can hide unnecessary analysis scenarios. Data can also be sorted by one of the analysis scenarios in order to receive a list of the products that have changed the most.

4.3.4 Data Definition in Cells

As soon as two structures exist in a query, every cell of the resulting matrix can be separately defined in a cell definition. Thus, the cell definition always refers to the point of intersection between two structure elements. By using further flexible drilldowns, however, the cell defined in this way can also be used for multiple characteristic values of the query result. The definition of structures and cell definitions is repeatedly applied to every displayed combination of characteristic values.

Because transparency and maintainability can be easily affected, in particular, for complex definitions, we urge you to use this functionality with caution. Furthermore, you should note that a loss of performance can occur when using separate data selections in the cells, because separate database queries must be started by the OLAP processor.

Cell references Every defined cell can be used in formulas within structures and other cell definitions. This holds true irrespective of whether the defined cell is an independent calculation, selection or a simple reference. In the case of a simple reference, the cell of the matrix from both structures is simply given a name. Originally, a query does not include such name references. They must be created explicitly per cell.

Auxiliary cells If you want to define an additional cell that is outside of the matrix specified by the structures, you can create an auxiliary cell. Auxiliary cells can also contain their own data selections or formulas. The functionality of data selection and formulas is identical to the available functionality for structure elements.

Target Achievement Regarding Profitability with a Single Cell Definition

In the following example, a formula for the management performance is derived based on CO-PA contribution margin schemes that is to serve as a profitability monitor. There are company-wide targets for the share of the various contribution margin levels in net sales. The actual target deviations, however, are considered in the overall evaluation with different weighting factors for different functions:

▶ Create a copy of the query ZECOPAM1Q00003 as ZECOPAM1-Q00006 **Profitability Analysis—Contribution Margin Targeting**.

▶ Drag&Drop the time selection over the fiscal period to the free characteristics and remove all other characteristics, with the exception of the company code. They could produce misleading data when used in the navigation (see Figure 4.28, Step 1).

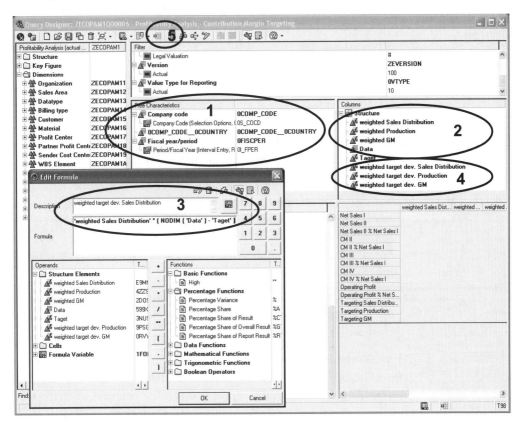

Figure 4.28 Query: Contribution Margin Target Achievement, Part 1

- In the columns, create a column, **Structure**, with formulas for specifying the weighting per management function as well as the company target. In their original formula definition, the value of these formulas is null. It will be specified later per row and column in the single cells (Step 2).

- You need to create another column, **Data**, as a selection. It is not further restricted and thus shows the data of the contribution margin scheme selected by the other elements (Step 2).

- In other formulas, the subtotal of the weighted deviations is calculated from the product of the weighting factor and the difference between the actual value and the target value (Steps 3 and 4).

- In the single cell definition (Step 5), you can now store the values for the weighting of deviations per management function (see Figure 4.29, Steps 1a and 1b) as well as the target values (Steps 2a and 2b) as amounts in a formula. The weighting indicates to what extent the target deviation per contribution margin scheme element should be considered for a management function. The target values are fixed percentages for the share of the contribution margin element in net sales.

- The single cell definition also provides the cells that contain the weighting subtotals as a cell reference for further use in the query (Step 3).

- Additionally, help cells are created that contain the total weighting per management function (Step 4a and 4b).

- In the row structure, new rows are now added per management function for the determined target achievement. (For this purpose, you must exit the window for defining single cells.) This is calculated by the sum of the subtotals divided by the total weight determined above. To format this value as a percentage, the percentage function is used in the formula (Step 5).

- In the row structure of the contribution margin scheme and in the column structure for calculating the weightings, all inessential elements can now be hidden.

In the illustration of the report, all columns for determining the weightings still exist in order to demonstrate the calculation (see Figure 4.30). You can navigate through this report as usual. For example, try to filter for the data column and one row with targeting values. By displaying company codes in the columns and months in the rows, you quickly receive a comprehensive performance overview.

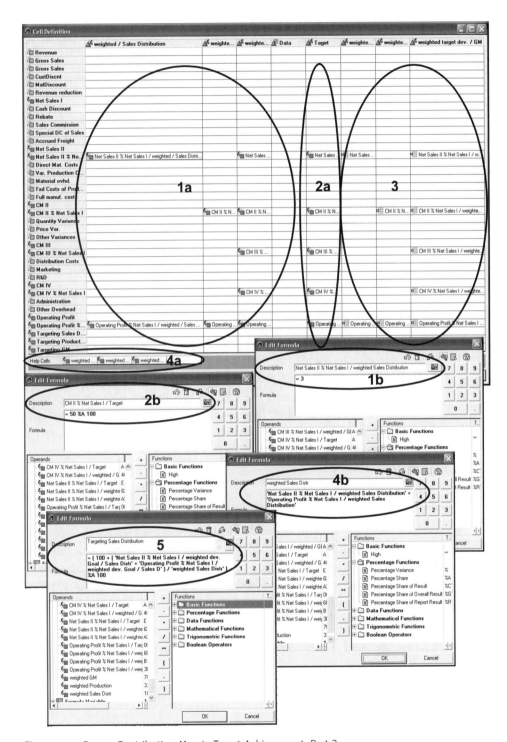

Figure 4.29 Query: Contribution Margin Target Achievement, Part 2

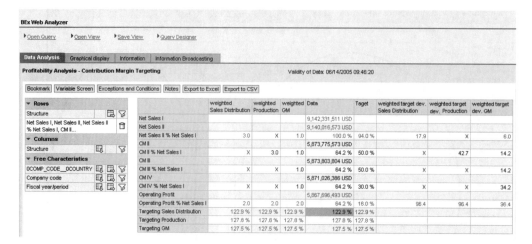

	weighted Sales Distribution	weighted Production	weighted GM	Data	Target	weighted target dev. Sales Distribution	weighted target dev. Production	weighted target dev. GM
Net Sales I				9,142,331,511 USD				
Net Sales II				9,140,016,573 USD				
Net Sales II % Net Sales I	3.0	X	1.0		100.0 %	94.0 %	17.9	X	6.0
CM II				5,873,775,573 USD				
CM II % Net Sales I	X	3.0	1.0		64.2 %	50.0 %	X	42.7	14.2
CM III				5,873,803,804 USD				
CM III % Net Sales I	X	X	1.0		64.2 %	50.0 %	X	X	14.2
CM IV				5,871,026,386 USD				
CM IV % Net Sales I	X	X	1.0		64.2 %	30.0 %	X	X	34.2
Operating Profit				5,867,696,493 USD				
Operating Profit % Net Sales I	2.0	2.0	2.0		64.2 %	16.0 %	96.4	96.4	96.4
Targeting Sales Distribution	122.9 %	122.9 %	122.9 %		122.9 %	122.9 %			
Targeting Production	127.8 %	127.8 %	127.8 %		127.8 %	127.8 %			
Targeting GM	127.5 %	127.5 %	127.5 %		127.5 %	127.5 %			

Figure 4.30 Report: Contribution Margin Target Achievement (Before Navigation, with Subtotals)

4.3.5 Currency Translation

SAP BW provides flexible and powerful possibilities for calculating currency scenarios during the execution of a query. This shortens the effort of precalculating and saving currency scenarios in the database and sometimes considerably extends the analysis possibilities. Within the Query Designer, you can assign different currency translation types to structure elements, and calculated and restricted key figures. These are created in SAP GUI using Transaction RRC1 and contain all the necessary parameters for the currency translation.

Currency translation types are another typical example of the modularization of Reporting elements. They are stored centrally in the system and can then be reused in different places. Essential benefits are the one-time implementation effort when creating them, as well as the consistent definition in later uses. At creation time, the essential parameters of currency translation types can be constantly defined, read from the current data record, or transferred by a variable.

In the simplest case, the exchange rate to be applied can be read directly from the data record. Otherwise, you might have to define the following parameters:

► **Exchange rate type**
For different currency scenarios or currency translation methods, you can store different exchange rate types in the system. These can be, for example, the official daily exchange rate, or buying or selling rates. Often, separate exchange rate types are stored for assumed or average rates.

The currency translation type can be selected as a fixed value or as a variable. When using a variable, the variable value is determined immediately before executing the query. The variables of the 0RTYPE InfoObject are available for this purpose.[9]

► **Source currency**
This specifies the source currency on which the exchange rate is based. It can be selected as a fixed value or read from the data record.

► **Target currency**
To define the target currency that the exchange rate is based on, you can store it as a fixed value, read it from the data record, or populate it using a variable. The variables of the 0CURRENCY InfoObject are available.

► **Date of translation**
Here you can define the time of the currency translation. For the determined date, the last exchange rate available is read from the system during currency translation. For example, if the determined date is 8/27/2005, and the last exchange rate loaded for the required combination of exchange rate type is source currency, and target currency was loaded on 1/1/2004, this exchange rate is used for currency translation.

You can store the date as a fixed value, determine it in a variable (created on 0CALDAY), or derive it from the data.

Deriving it from the data gives you the additional option of selecting any time characteristic that can be defined as well. The time information determined in this way can also be "rounded." For example, this means that the first or the last day of the month should be used for currency translation.

---

9 Because, as of SAP BW Release 3.0, variables can be created only in the Query Designer, an InfoProvider must exist in BW that contains the InfoObjects 0RTYPE and 0CALDAY in order to access the variable wizard. If this is not the case on your system, you can create a MiniCube that contains only the InfoObjects 0RTYPE, 0CALDAY, and 0AMOUNT.

After the currency translation type has been defined, it can be stored in structure elements with data selections, as well as global restricted and calculated key figures as a currency translation parameter. During query execution, the variables used herein are treated and populated just like any other query variables.

Creating Currency Translation Types With Variables

In the following example, currency translation types will be created and transferred to a query to determine consolidated plan and actual scenarios.[10] In our simple data model, we assume that the values that are saved monthly can be translated using a monthly translation rate and can then be summed. In more complex consolidation scenarios, however, YTD values are usually set against average YTD exchange rates. The annual result in a consolidated currency that is determined in this way is often more meaningful. However, the monthly values in a consolidated currency must be calculated based on the consolidated YTD values in order to produce correct values. In our examples, we will use the simpler alternative.

▶ In Transaction RRC1, create the new currency translation type ZECE01FIP **Monthly average ex rate of fiscal period**.

▶ Specify dynamic reading of exchange rates using exchange rate type CE01 **Monthly average rate** (see Figure 4.31, Step 1). The input help for available exchange rate types is displayed if you place the cursor in the **Exchange Rate Type** field and press F4 (Step 2).[11]

▶ In this example, the source currency for the currency translation is taken from the data record (Step 3), and the selection of the target currency is to take place in the definition or when calling the query (Step 4).

▶ The time of the currency translation should be variable based on the fiscal period of the data record (Step 5). The exact date is to be the last day of the period (Step 6).

---

10 If the exchange rate types used here do not exist on your system, you can use one of the existing ones, or create a new exchange rate type for testing purposes and populate it with exchange rates.

11 These exchange rates are probably loaded under a different technical key or don't even exist on your system. In the first case, you can use the existing exchange rates. Otherwise, you'll find the necessary exchange rate data and instructions for setting them up on your system in the Internet forum for this series of books under *www.bw-forum.com*.

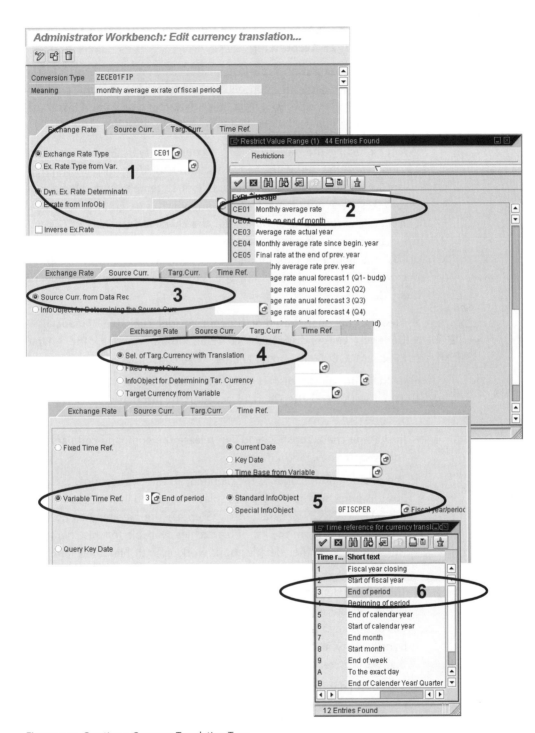

Figure 4.31 Creating a Currency Translation Type

Profit and Loss Statement with Currency Translation Based on General Ledger Accounting

The currency translation type just created can be used to enable the query to display values in a consolidated currency with dynamic currency translation. This is to be used for a presentation of a profit and loss statement based on general ledger data from SAP G/L accounting.

When extracting the data from G/L accounting, typically only the base accounts are extracted with the transaction data. The consolidation necessary for determining the profit and loss statement and the balance sheet takes place during query execution, which is based on a consolidation hierarchy for these accounts. For the characteristic OGL_ACCOUNT G/L account, the hierarchy is extracted from R/3. Although we cannot discuss the details of data modeling and extraction within the scope of this book, this information is important for understanding the following query design:

- ▶ Create a new query based on the InfoProvider ZEFIGLM1 **Financials— General Ledger (Actual & Plan data)** under the name ZEFIGLM1Q00001 **General Ledger—P+L consolidated**.

- ▶ In the global filter, restrict the data view to **Legal Valuation** of the actual values and the Chart of accounts to **International** (see Figure 4.32, Step 1).

- ▶ In the free characteristics, you can release the company code and the company for navigation (Step 2).

- ▶ The row definition contains the hierarchy of the G/L accounts (Step 3). For this purpose, the hierarchy display is activated in the properties of the OGL_ACCOUNT characteristic (Step 4). The hierarchy to be used can be selected from the list of hierarchies available for this characteristic (Step 5). Further details about working with hierarchies are discussed in Section 4.4.1.

- ▶ The column definition contains the selection of the fiscal period as well as the key figure OBALANCE **Cumulative Balance** (Step 6). The properties of this key figure define the currency translation with the currency translation type ZECE01FIP **Monthly average ex rate of fiscal period** that we just created.

- ▶ The consolidation currency for our scenario is Swiss Franc (Step 7). The key figure description can also be accordingly adjusted.

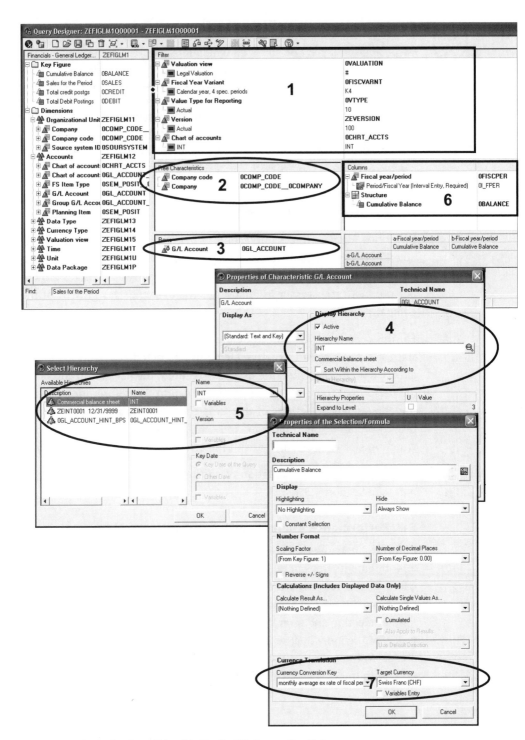

Figure 4.32 Query for Consolidated L+P with G/L Accounting Data

Especially in complex currency scenarios with different exchange rate types per data view or currency simulations, we recommend that you store the currency translation in a globally defined key figure so that changes to the requirements can be carried out in one central location.

If the reporting requirements are stable and if performance problems still occur due to the complexity of the underlying calculation, it is often advisable to store the precalculated consolidated values in the InfoProvider.

4.3.6 Constant Selections

In various situations, it is interesting to perform a comparison of selectable data with constant reference data. The selectable data should also provide a drilldown option. This could be, for example, the sales growth per product or customer in relation to the average sales growth of the company code.

For this requirement, you can define selections of characteristics as constant selections within structure elements, restricted key figures, and single cell definitions. When the query is executed, the navigation and filtering performed there do not affect the selection. Therefore, for example, the overlapping selections of the same characteristic are ignored if they result from a flexible drilldown. You can specify this setting for an entire structure element, or only parts of the selection of a structure element.

For an example implementation of constant selections based on CO-PA data, see Section 4.3.1.

P+L Performance Analysis with Constant Selections

In this example, we will create another query for analyzing the profit and loss statement. This query enables you to calculate the change rates compared to the year before for all items of the profit and loss statement based on cumulative annual values. These change rates are determined for the selection and reference data. In this case, the global values and the values of the individual regions America, Asia, and Europe serve as a reference. In the query, you can then compare the change rates of the selections with the change rates of the reference data:

- Create a copy of the query ZEFIGLM1Q00001 as ZEFIGLM1Q00002 **General Ledger—P/L Performance comp local/region/global**.

- Remove the fiscal year period as a characteristic from the columns and add the option of variable input for the company code (see Figure 4.33, Step 1).

- The column selection **Balance/CHF YTD** is extended with variables for the selection of the fiscal year and the posting period. In a copy of this selection as **Balance CHF/previous year YTD**, the corresponding previous year is queried via variable offsets, as explained in Section 4.3.1 (Step 2).

- Two formulas now calculate the deviation in percentage and absolute figures (Step 3).

- In a second structure in the columns, the data selections are defined for the segments to be analyzed. In our example, we use an existing master data hierarchy for mapping the regions of the company codes. From this, the single selections can be created per region and globally. In the single selections, the filters for the **Company code** characteristic are defined as constant (Steps 4 and 5).

- Another column, **Selection**, is created that does not contain any further restrictions (Step 5).

- In the single cell definition, all cells are now made available as a reference in which the deviation percentage compared to the previous year is determined (Step 6).

- In the structure for calculating the percentage, new formulas are added that are determined by the difference between the cell references that were just created. These formulas calculate the relative deviation of the selection in relation to the entire group or to a specific region (Steps 7 and 8).

- The elements of the structure with the organizational hierarchy can now be hidden, with the exception of the selection.

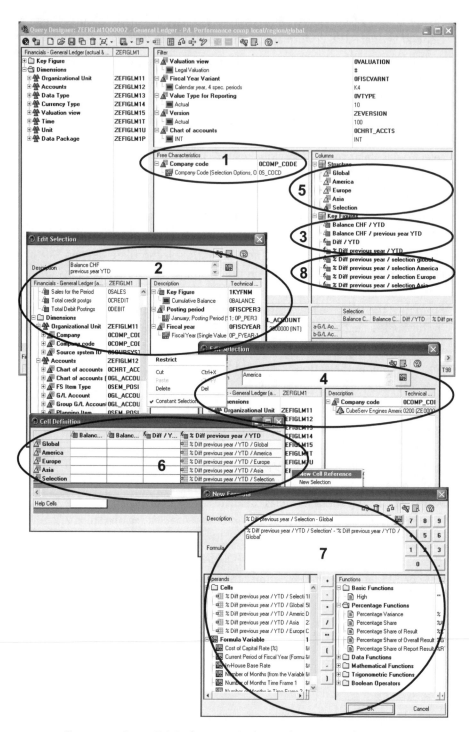

Figure 4.33 Query: P+L Performance Analysis with Constant Selections

| G/L Account | | Selection | | | | % Diff previous | % Diff previous year | % Diff previous year | % Diff previous year | % Diff previous year |
		Balance CHF YTD	Balance CHF previous year YTD	Diff YTD		year YTD	selection global	selection America	selection Europe	selection Asia
▾ Profit and loss stat	INT 3000000	203,076.55 CHF	-968,569,482.96 CHF	968,772,559.51 CHF		100.02097 %	0.00000 %	100.02097 %	-0.00000 %	100.02097 %
▸ Sales revenues	INT 3010000	203,076.55 CHF	-63,269,758.88 CHF	63,472,835.43 CHF		100.32097 %	0.00000 %	100.32097 %	-0.00447 %	100.32097 %
▸ Inventory changes	INT 3020000		5,855,799.78 CHF	-5,855,799.78 CHF		-100.00000 %	0.00000 %	-100.00000 %	0.00000 %	-100.00000 %
▸ Other operating inco	INT 3040000		-1,234,310.56 CHF	1,234,310.56 CHF		100.00000 %	0.00000 %	100.00000 %	0.00000 %	100.00000 %
▸ Raw materials and co	INT 3050000		-942,645,840.98 CHF	942,645,840.98 CHF		100.00000 %	0.00000 %	100.00000 %	0.00000 %	100.00000 %
▸ Staff costs	INT 3060000		14,903,510.92 CHF	-14,903,510.92 CHF		-100.00000 %	0.00000 %	-100.00000 %	0.00000 %	-100.00000 %
▸ Other operating char	INT 3080000		17,821,116.77 CHF	-17,821,116.77 CHF		-100.00000 %	0.00000 %	-100.00000 %	0.00000 %	-100.00000 %

Figure 4.34 Report: P+L Performance Analysis

4.4 Presentation and Formatting

Using the presentation and formatting options of the Query Designer, you can further process the data for analysis and reporting. These options include a flexible hierarchical presentation, sorting, scaling, the display of master data details, and others.

4.4.1 Hierarchies—an Overview

The possibilities of a hierarchical presentation with SAP BW are very powerful and consist of various technical options that can be combined and displayed in rows and columns. You can even navigate through the hierarchy during query execution.

In a classical master data hierarchy, the values of a characteristic are arranged in a hierarchical presentation. The lowest nodes of the hierarchy are always values of this characteristic. The superior nodes of the characteristic values are fixed and can be freely chosen. They can also be values of another characteristic or freely defined text nodes. The hierarchy is created as a master data hierarchy in the system for the characteristic. The hierarchy levels can be extended as necessary. Both symmetric and asymmetric hierarchies are admissible. A typical example is the mapping of organization chart-like structures that are based on only one characteristic (i.e., a management hierarchy for products or key accounts). Classical master data hierarchies are maintained in the SAP BW Administrator Workbench. The maintenance dialog is called via Transaction RSH1.

Classical master data hierarchy

In the dynamic master data hierarchy, the values of different characteristics are arranged hierarchically. Every characteristic is assigned to exactly one hierarchy level. Like drilldowns, the hierarchy levels can be changed during the analysis in the local view. The hierarchy is determined by the loaded transaction data. The hierarchies created are therefore always symmetric. This functionality is typical of attribute-controlled hierarchies like the material hierarchy of SAP R/3.

Dynamic master data hierarchies

Structure hierarchy A structure hierarchy is defined in the query. If you want, you can arrange the elements of a structure hierarchically. While the master data hierarchies display only those parts of the hierarchy that contain data, the structure hierarchy can display all nodes, if necessary. You should note, however, that if you do use structure hierarchies, you can only use the following two hierarchies in a query: symmetric and asymmetric.

Working with hierarchies When working with hierarchies, you should consider the following points:

▶ The navigational state of hierarchies can be stored in the local view and thus in the Excel workbook. It remains available when refreshing the query.

▶ The level up to which the hierarchy should be extended can be defined with a few clicks. In the global and the local view, the properties of the affected elements provide appropriate settings, which can be accessed quickly via using the context menu.

▶ You can assign master data hierarchies in the local view as well. This applies both to the selection and activation of the hierarchy and to their settings. The structure hierarchy display, however, can only be set in the global query definition. The local view permits only navigation.

Dynamic Master Data Hierarchy for Sales Analysis

The examples in the following sections illustrate the different properties of these variants. In Section 4.4.3, a structure hierarchy is demonstrated using an example. Section 4.4.4 explains the maintenance and implementation of a classical master data hierarchy.

The following example uses a dynamic master data hierarchy:

▶ From Excel, start the Query Designer for the local view of the query ZECOPAM1Q00002 **Profitability Analysis—Revenue overview monthly**.

▶ Define the drilldown for the rows with several characteristics (see Figure 4.35, Step 1) and activate the display of rows as a hierarchy. The relevant setting is available on the context menu of the row title (Step 2).

▶ Specify the level up to which the hierarchy should be opened when the query is first called.

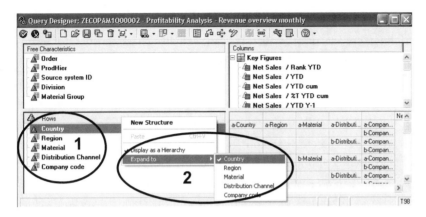

Figure 4.35 Query Definition: Dynamic Master Data Hierarchies

▶ After executing the query, the dynamically created hierarchy is available for further navigation. Since local calculations, like ranking and cumulative values, cannot be presented in a logical way anymore due to the hierarchical presentation, these structure elements should be removed from the display (see Figure 4.36).

	A	B	C	D	E
1	**Profitability Analysis - Revenue overview monthly**				
2					
8	Key Figures	Net Sales ☐YTD, Net Sales ☐YTD dev. PY, Net Sales ☐MTH...			
13	Company code				
22					
23	Country	Net Sales YTD	Net Sales YTD dev. PY	Net Sales MTH	Net Sales MTH dev. PY
24	Overall Result	104,439,108 USD	49,039,781 USD	8,802,087 USD	4,316,918 USD
25	▷ Canada	979,404 USD	-170,543 USD	84,084 USD	-13,944 USD
26	▽ Germany	35,833,388 USD	13,603,001 USD	3,089,091 USD	1,268,070 USD
27	▷ DE/Not assigned	228,446 USD	149,984 USD	16,168 USD	10,119 USD
28	▽ Hamburg	2,711,170 USD	1,694,190 USD	238,995 USD	155,952 USD
29	▷ C-1021	818,035 USD	93,720 USD	55,966 USD	3,205 USD
30	▽ CP-100	1,641,195 USD	1,586,118 USD	161,811 USD	156,933 USD
31	▷ GM store	1,641,195 USD	1,586,118 USD	161,811 USD	156,933 USD
32	▷ R100062	251,940 USD	14,353 USD	21,219 USD	-4,186 USD
33	▷ Lower Saxony	4,216,885 USD	2,845,943 USD	364,857 USD	250,259 USD
34	▷ Nrth Rhine Westfalia	4,804,098 USD	1,188,203 USD	445,499 USD	158,341 USD
35	▷ Hesse	6,409,519 USD	1,464,261 USD	544,867 USD	136,776 USD
36	▷ Baden-Wuerttemberg	5,370,560 USD	355,029 USD	463,802 USD	59,433 USD
37	▷ Bavaria	1,288,152 USD	1,223,909 USD	117,422 USD	111,340 USD
38	▷ Berlin	8,032,507 USD	2,979,778 USD	675,273 USD	274,570 USD
39	▷ Mecklenburg-Vorpomm.	1,509,278 USD	686,457 USD	110,770 USD	16,889 USD
40	▷ Saxony	1,262,774 USD	1,015,248 USD	111,438 USD	94,390 USD
41	▷ Spain	1,328,385 USD	856,280 USD	100,254 USD	63,430 USD
42	▷ France	2,792,549 USD	1,082,733 USD	236,167 USD	100,216 USD
43	▷ Great Britain	2,821,205 USD	1,947,885 USD	236,660 USD	172,403 USD
44	▷ Mexico	5,072,606 USD	3,415,493 USD	436,673 USD	297,903 USD
45	▷ Russian Fed.	744,558 USD	269,380 USD	62,679 USD	23,781 USD
46	▷ United States	54,867,014 USD	28,035,551 USD	4,556,479 USD	2,405,059 USD
47	▷ Not assigned	0 USD	0 USD	0 USD	0 USD

Figure 4.36 Sales Analysis with Dynamic Master Data Hierarchy in MS Excel

4.4.2 Presentation of the Structure

Structures in comparison with characteristics

In the query execution, structures can seem like characteristics; for example, their name can be freely chosen in the query definition. However, there are substantial differences:

▶ Structures cannot be aggregated. For characteristics, various aggregation types (usually the summation) can be set.

▶ Structure elements can contain complex definitions, whereas characteristics rely on the basic structure of the loaded files.

▶ The presentation of individual structure elements can be forced or suppressed, regardless of the loaded files. In the standard version, values are displayed for only those characteristics that have data in the Info-Provider.

Zero row and zero column suppression

For structures, you can set the suppression of individual structure elements as of SAP BW 3.5 if the values of the respective structure element are zero. This makes sense especially when using large structures (like in CO-PA) where only the details relevant to the currently selected data are to be shown.

This zero suppression is usually defined per query; however, it is only effective for structures if it is specified separately per row or column.

Structure presentation in external tools

To access the structure with external tools (e.g., via OLE DB), the technical name must be specified as a Unique Identification (UID). It is created automatically when the structure is saved for the first time. When the structure is saved globally for the first time or when the global reference of the structure is removed, this UID is changed. If the structure is already used in external tools, this change can lead to trouble with the link of the external tool to the BW query.

4.4.3 Presentation of Structure Elements

Description

The user can also define texts of the structure elements. In up to 60 characters, you can even use line breaks and text variables.

Language dependency

The texts are language-dependent and are saved in the logon language of the Query Designer. To be available in another language, the texts either have to be maintained in the Query Designer in another logon language, or created using the translation function of the Administrator Workbench.[12]

---

12 As is common practice in SAP solutions, the texts are stored separately from the technical attributes of the query elements. The majority of query element texts are located in RSZELTTXT.

Structure elements can be highlighted using an alternative formatting. To this end, an appropriate style is assigned in the target report (Excel or web). The format of the highlighted cells can be defined in this style.

Alternatively, structure elements can be prevented from being displayed. The following options are available:

▶ **Always Hide**

The elements are made completely unavailable to Reporting. This is particularly helpful for interim calculations as with this option activated the interim calculations cannot confuse the user of the query.

▶ **Hide (can be shown)**

The elements can be shown in the local view and in the cell for filtering the structure elements. This variant is recommended when only specific elements should be visible in the initial view of the query, but further details must be available on demand.

Scaling factors, number of decimal places, and plus/minus sign reversal can be configured in structure elements as well. Also, they can be changed in the local view of the query. If scaling and decimal places have not been specified, these settings are taken from the underlying global key figure or the InfoObject.

> If these settings are specified in two overlapping structure elements, the latest setting applies. This behavior can lead to undesirable effects, especially for large or complex structures or later changes. Therefore, you must ensure that scaling factors are set in one structure only, unless you explicitly want it to be different.[13]

The individual structure elements can be arranged hierarchically, as mentioned in Section 4.4.1. The superior nodes still maintain their original data definition, namely, that no special aggregation is performed. The hierarchy structure, however, can only be specified in the global query definition.

---

[13] This can cause problems frequently especially if you are using global structures. You can find details on this behaviour in SAP OSS Note 568630.

Structure Hierarchy for Navigation in the Contribution Margin Scheme

The navigation in the contribution margin scheme can be substantially simplified if the inferior elements are presented in a structure hierarchy, as demonstrated in the following example:

► Open the query definition for ZECOPAM1Q00003 **Profitability Analysis—Contribution Margin Overview**.

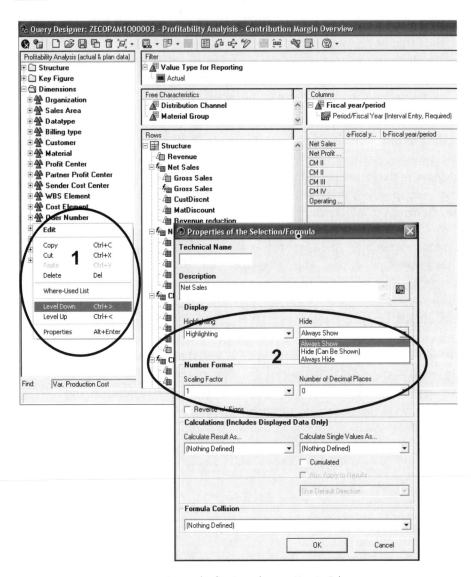

Figure 4.37 Structure Hierarchy for Contribution Margin Scheme

▶ Arrange the structure elements of the contribution margin scheme hierarchically. The corresponding functionality can be found on the context menu of the individual structure elements (see Figure 4.37, Step 1).

▶ Additionally, further display properties of the structure element can be changed, especially the highlighting or hiding options (Step 2).

4.4.4 Presentation of Characteristics

A multitude of display options can be set in the characteristic properties. These are described in detail in the following:

▶ **Description of the characteristic**
For characteristics, other descriptions than those of the underlying InfoObject can be used in the query as well. The InfoObject description is only intended as a suggestion. As soon as a query is saved, the description remains in the query and is not automatically adjusted when the description of the InfoObject is changed. In this way, when the same master data is used in a different application context, the contents might be easier to understand.

▶ **Name and key of master data**
You can specify whether the technical keys or any of the available descriptions of the characteristic values are displayed. Even a combination of both is possible.

▶ **Attributes in master data**
Characteristics can be enhanced with master data attributes. These can be flexibly displayed with key and description.

The data can be sorted by the master data contents. Available sorting criteria include the keys and the various names of the characteristic and those of the attributes. Displaying the attribute is not necessary. If nothing else is specified, sorting is carried out by the technical key.

Sorting by name, key, attribute

During the drilldown via one or more characteristics, you can display results and interim results. Per characteristic, you can define whether they should be displayed always, never, or only when at least one single value exists.

Result suppression

For a characteristic, the data loaded in the InfoProvider can be displayed based on a master data hierarchy (see Section 4.4.1). This hierarchy is stored in the system for the characteristic as a fixed value. When the query is executed, the single values are displayed from the InfoProvider as end nodes or nodes in the hierarchy. The values posted on these charac-

Classical master data hierarchies

teristic values are aggregated in their superior hierarchy nodes. For displaying the hierarchy, you can additionally define the following parameters:

▶ **Position of lower-level nodes**
Here you can specify the position of superior nodes in relation to lower-level nodes. If the lower-level nodes are up, the aggregated nodes are down and vice versa.

▶ **Values of posted nodes**
Suppose an account hierarchy is used for those values that are posted to base accounts and also those values posted directly to a totals account in the InfoProvider. Due to the hierarchy aggregation, the totals account has a value that is changed once more by the amount directly posted to the totals account. The details of this amount, which is posted directly to the totals account, can be shown separately or hidden. The total amount of the totals account remains unchanged in both cases.

▶ **Expand to level**
Specifies which hierarchy level the hierarchy should be opened up to when it is initially called.

▶ **Node with only one lower-level node**
If a summary node contains only one base node, the display of the summary node can be suppressed. This can enable a faster navigation to the details.

Classical Master Data Hierarchy for Mapping the Organizational Structure

The following example presents the organizational structure of the company codes in a hierarchy. For this purpose, the appropriate hierarchy is saved as master data information on the SAP BW server:

▶ In SAP GUI, start Transaction RSH1 (see Figure 4.38, Step 1).

▶ Create a new hierarchy for the InfoObject 0COMP_CODE (Steps 2 and 3).

▶ Assign a technical name and a description to the hierarchy (Step 4).

▶ Define the hierarchy structure. You can select the required nodes from the master data of the company code (Steps 5 and 6).

▶ The hierarchy can now be activated (Step 7) and is then available in Reporting.

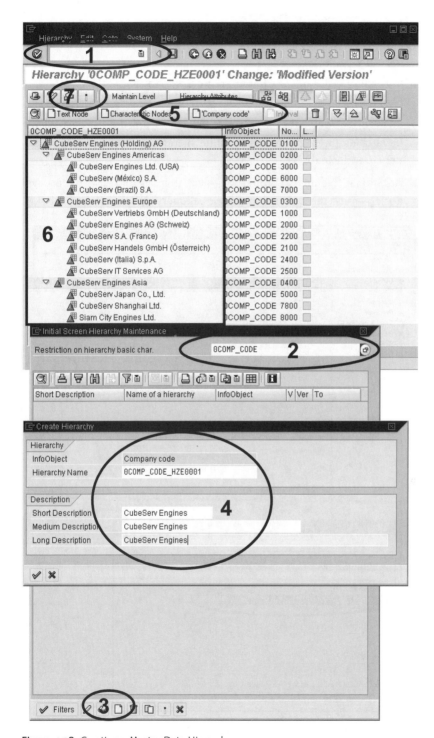

Figure 4.38 Creating a Master Data Hierarchy

- From Excel, start the Query Designer for the local view of the query ZECOPAM1Q00002 **Profitability Analysis—Revenue overview monthly**.

- In the Properties of the **Characteristic Company** code, the master data hierarchy can be configured (see Figure 4.39, Step 1).

- In the input help, the hierarchy is selected from the list of available hierarchies (Step 2). You can define hierarchy version, time dependency, and variables.

- Additional hierarchy properties—like the position of lower-level nodes—must be specified in the global query definition.

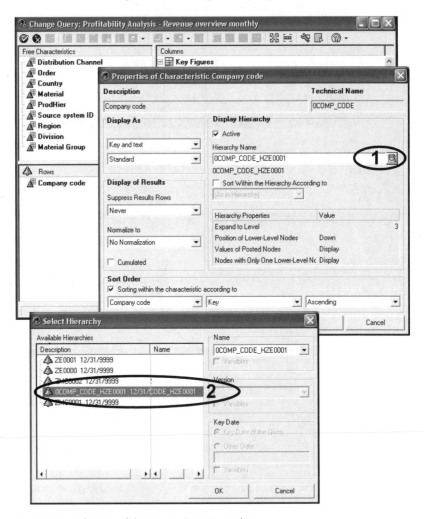

Figure 4.39 Selection of the Master Data Hierarchy

Figure 4.40 shows the report resulting from these settings.

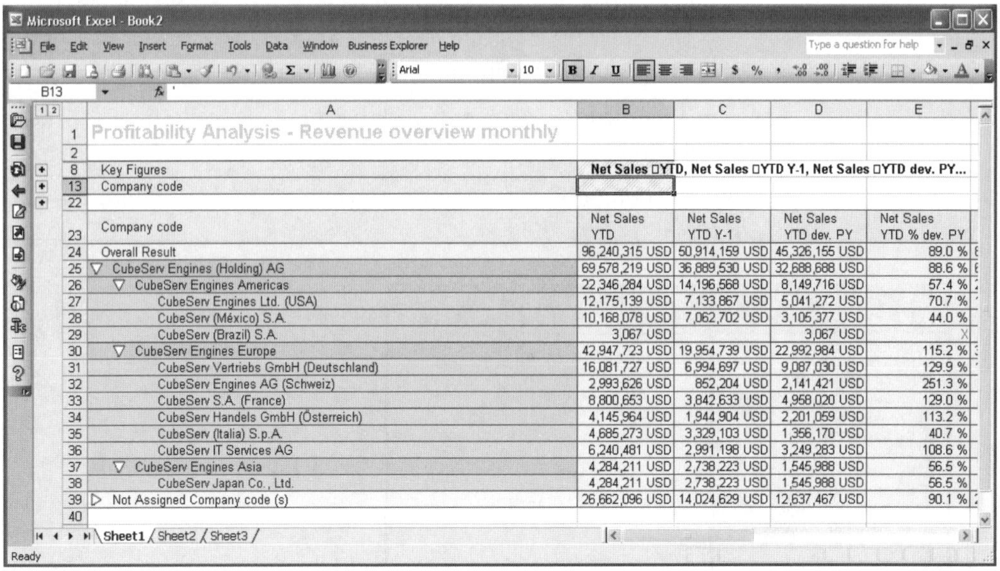

Figure 4.40 Profitability Analysis—Revenue Overview Monthly

4.4.5 Tabular Presentation

The presentation of the query can also be changed from the classical two-dimensional OLAP presentation to a one-dimensional tabular presentation. This setting can be specified if the query contains only one structure. It can also be changed in the local query view later on.

The columns can be freely arranged during the design phase. It is even possible to position a characteristic between two key figures or formulas. However, the navigation options in the tabular presentation are restricted. There are no free characteristics, which means that drilldowns cannot be exchanged or added.

This form of presentation is particularly well suited for formatted reporting, where the need for flexible arrangement is more important than navigation.

Sales Analysis in Tabular Presentation

In the following example, the Company code characteristic is placed between different structure elements to highlight the essential figures via this layout:

▶ From Excel, start the Query Designer for the local view of the query ZECOPAM1Q00002 **Profitability Analysis—Revenue overview monthly**.

▶ Change to the tabular presentation of the query (see Figure 4.41, Step 1).

▶ Arrange the structure elements and the company code characteristic as desired (Step 2).

▶ After executing the query, the new layout will be copied into the output (Step 3).

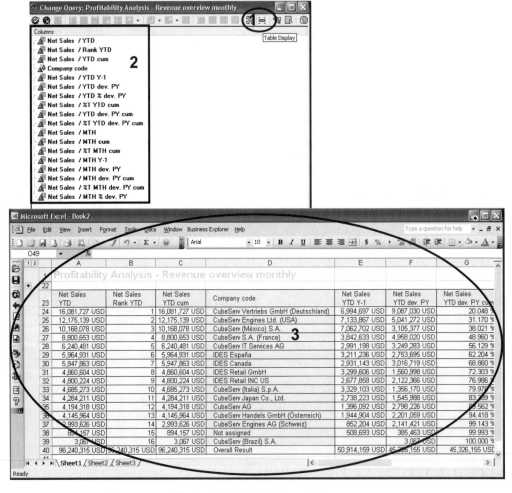

Figure 4.41 Sales Analysis in Tabular Presentation

4.4.6 Query Properties

The following properties apply to the entire query. In general, you can change these settings—even during navigation—after executing the query.

If time-dependent data is presented in queries, the underlying point in time can be controlled using the key date of the query. If no value or variable is defined here, the current date will be used as the key date.

Key date

The data to be presented can be reduced to those rows and columns that are not null. In this context, you can specify whether this check should apply to only result rows or to the single values as well.

Zero suppression

The presentation of zeros determined in the query result can be additionally configured. The relevant cells can display a zero, where the presentation of the determined unit can be suppressed. Alternatively, an empty cell or a user-defined character can be shown.

Zero presentation

Data with a negative sign can be displayed with a minus sign before or behind the value, or with the value enclosed in parentheses.

Presentation of plus/minus sign

Within the query, result rows can be arranged as needed, either at the top or bottom, or to the left or right, respectively.

Result position

The display of scaling factors can be suppressed, if necessary. When scaling factors are displayed separately, they also contain units or currencies if these can be clearly determined for the underlying data. If the scaling factors are not displayed separately, these units are presented within the data cells.

Display of scaling factors

If several characteristics are used in drilldowns, the repeated values are suppressed. This clarifies the visual presentation of the data structure. If the query data should be further processed in pivot tables, or used as a file to be loaded in third-party systems, the characteristic values can be presented in every cell.

Suppression of repeated keys

If native Excel formatting was used for presenting the query, the refreshment of the query formatting can be disabled. However, the formatting specified in Excel is not dynamically adjusted to changed output areas of the query during the refresh. Alternatively, this can be carried out either manually or using a VBA macro.

Adjust formatting after refresh

The order of the variables displayed in the popup can be user-defined as well.

Order of input variables

Links to documents For master data, transaction data, and metadata, the display of links to documents can be activated separately. This is effective both on the web and in Excel. Calling the link always loads the corresponding web page with a reference to the document contents.

Drag&Relate links On the web, you can display the appropriate links in the query if you use SAP Enterprise Portal and set up the Drag&Relate function. To use Drag&Relate, you also need to activate BW InfoObjects.

4.5   Variable Definitions in Detail

Variable types Variables for flexibly controlling query parameters can be used in different objects. The variable type is determined by the object for which the variable is to be used. The following sections discuss the available types of characteristic values, hierarchies or hierarchy nodes, text, and formulas.

Processing type The various ways for defining the variable values are determined by the processing type. The different variants are as follows:

▶ **Manual entry with default value**
Enables the user to enter values directly. You can specify a default value for the entry.

▶ **Substitution path**
For characteristic value variables, the filter values are derived from the result of a query. For formula and text variables, the values are derived from the characteristic value presented in the query results.

▶ **Precalculated value set**
In the Reporting Agent of the SAP BW server, several value sets per characteristic can be precalculated using queries and can then be provided for further analyses. Compared to the substitution path, this can improve the performance.

▶ **Customer exit**
Variable values are determined via an ABAP code. It can be freely defined and is run before the query is executed.

▶ **SAP exit**
This processing type is only available for specific variables defined within SAP Business Content. For user-defined variables, the customer exit should be used.

▶ **Authorization**
The values of variables are derived from the user's authorization.

In variables, the filter behavior of a characteristic can be activated or deactivated during query navigation. Therefore, you have several options for activating the filter and drilldown functionality during the navigation (see Table 4.2).

Change options during navigation

	Variable cannot be changed in navigation	Variable can be changed
Characteristic is contained in rows, columns, or free characteristics	Drilldowns using the characteristic can be performed; filter values can only be set in the popup.	Drilldowns using the characteristic can be performed; filter values can be set both in the popup and dynamically during navigation.
Characteristic is contained in global filter, structure element, or global restricted key figure	Drilldowns cannot be performed using the characteristic unless it was additionally used in rows, columns, or free characteristics. Filter values can only be set in the popup.	

Table 4.2 Change Options for Filter Values During Navigation

If a changeable variable cannot be changed during navigation for technical reasons (for example, within a structure element), the system handles it as unchangeable.

You can define default values for the values of a variable. These default values are then displayed in the popup before the query is executed, if the variable is marked as 'ready for input.' If it is not marked as 'ready for input,' the default values are copied directly when the query is executed.

Default values and ready for input status

If it is required that characteristic values are populated with default values for the execution of the query—while they should not be displayed in the popup, but should be changeable during navigation—you can create a variable that is changeable, but not ready for input and contains the relevant default values. If the values are stored as fixed values in the global query definition, they can no longer be removed during navigation.

As described below, the available processing types can be different, depending on the variable type. As to substitution paths, they even provide an entirely different functionality.

Variables can be edited and created using the variable wizard of the Query Designer. In a few steps, it guides the developer through all param-

Creating and editing variables

eters. The parameters provided depend on the settings specified before-hand.

Existing variables are edited using the variable editor. All parameters to be set are visible at a glance; however, after the variables have been saved for the first time, specific settings (particularly variable type and substitution path) can no longer be changed.

Variable maintenance is context-sensitive and available where the variable can be copied into the query definition. Characteristic variables, for example, can be created and edited in the filter definition of the characteristic, formula variables in the formula definition, and text variables in the description.

Input validation During the entry of variable values, the system carries out a validation of the correctness of master data to avoid input errors. But, this input validation checks only for the existence of master data, and not for the appropriate authorization.

Input help As an input help (see Figure 4.42, Step 1), there are search functions and an entry history, as well as the option to load input parameters from flat files and the clipboard (Step 2).

▶ Usually, the input help shows the personal value list from the entry history first (Step 3).

▶ To find all relevant values, you must switch to the global values (Step 4). For a large number of master data, the selection shown in this list is restricted as well.

▶ In the filter settings, this restriction can be eliminated (Step 5), or set to different criteria (Step 6), if desired. Depending on the variable type, different types of input are possible.

▶ In multiple selections, an extended input window can be opened for the variable (Steps 7 and 8).

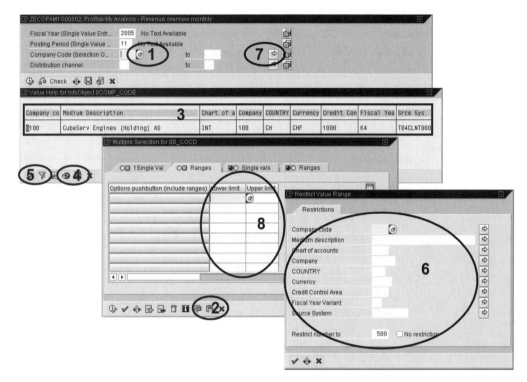

Figure 4.42 Input Help for Variables

4.5.1 Characteristic Value Variables

The most frequent implementation of variables is the dynamic filtering of characteristic values when executing or refreshing the query. If the variables are ready for input, an input window is displayed when refreshing the query data, in which the desired selection parameters can be specified.

For characteristic value variables, all processing types are available.

Processing types

In this case, the **Substitution path** processing type determines which values will be used for the filter from the result of another query. A popular example is filtering to the top n products depending on the revenue. This filter set can be used in any application that contains the **Product** InfoObject, for example, in InfoProvider queries with incoming orders, stock information, or costs. Nevertheless, the results thus determined can only be used as an including filter, and not as an excluding filter.

Substitution from query

In this processing method, two queries are executed in succession, which, depending on the query definition and the data model, can result in a noticeable loss of performance.

4.5.2 Hierarchy Variables and Hierarchy Node Variables

There are several options that can be combined for the dynamic selection of data using hierarchies. You can use variables for the selection of:

▶ Hierarchy
A complete hierarchy is selected for query execution.

▶ Hierarchy variant
Several variants can be stored for one selected hierarchy. This makes for more clarity, because only the variants belonging to a hierarchy are shown in the selection.

▶ Hierarchy time
Depending on time, the entire hierarchy or the definition of single nodes can be stored in the system. Here, you can define the validity time of the hierarchy.

▶ Hierarchy node
You can show only the subtrees or end nodes of a hierarchy. The top nodes, respectively, can be selected here.

Table 4.3 shows the basic combination of possibilities.

	Hierarchy node, fixed	Hierarchy node, variable
Hierarchy, time, version fixed	Fixed cost center, fixed hierarchy structure	Selectable cost center, fixed hierarchy structure
Hierarchy, time, version variable	Fixed cost center, selectable hierarchy structure	Selectable cost center, selectable hierarchy structure

Table 4.3 Variability of the Hierarchy Selection

Processing types   Manual entry and exits are always available for these variable types. Additionally, hierarchy nodes can be restricted with the authorization values of the user. In the input help for hierarchy nodes, the user can be selected from the tree structure of the respective hierarchy.

4.5.3 Text Variables

Using text variables, the descriptions of structure elements and query headings can be specified dynamically.

This is particularly interesting if the values in structure selection or formulas were selected dynamically using variables as well. The defined variable values are not available straightaway in the structure description, which can substantially reduce the informational value of a column or row description. This problem is solved by the use of text variables.

Text variables can be populated by manual entry, substitution path, and customer exit. For manual entry, however, there is no input help or validation available. **Processing types**

If the text variables are to be derived from a characteristic, this is enabled by the **Substitution path** processing type. Here, the variable value can be derived from the following elements: **Derivation from characteristic**

▶ **Key (internal or external presentation)**
The variable is populated with the key value of the underlying characteristic. The value can be copied from the internal or external presentation (e.g., in the case of 0FISCPER: internal = **2004001**, external = **001.2004**).

▶ **Description**
The description of the characteristic value can be copied into the text variable as well.

If it is not possible to derive the variable value from a characteristic, the derivation from another variable can often help. Technically, this is done with a customer exit, which is described in Section 4.6.5. **Derivation from other variables**

If only specific parts of the key or the description are to be copied, you can specify these partial sections by using the starting point and the length of an appropriate offset. **Partial sections (Offsets)**

If the selection of a characteristic contains an interval, the value to be replaced can be formed by the start value, the end value, or the difference between the two values. **Intervals**

The use of an appropriate naming convention should not be underestimated here. Because only the technical name of the variable is directly visible in the query definition, it can allow for more transparency.

4.5.4 Formula Variables

Formula variables enable the flexible parameterization of calculations in queries. They are usually implemented in formula elements of a structure, in global calculated key figures, or for controlling exceptions and conditions.

Units of formula variables In Section 4.3.2, we mentioned that the value units are considered when calculating formulas and, furthermore, that detectable errors can already be prevented when the query definition is checked. For this purpose and also for the input validation of variables, it is necessary to define the variable dimension for the unit precisely by using the variable type. The following types are available:

▶ **Number**
The value is considered to be a neutral number without a given dimension. This is the default setting.

▶ **Amount**
The corresponding dimension is of the **Currency** type (0CURRENCY InfoObject).

▶ **Quantity**
The corresponding dimension is of the **Unit** type (0UNIT InfoObject)

▶ **Price**
The corresponding dimension is a virtual type created from the quotient of currency and quantity.

▶ **Date**
The corresponding dimension is of the **Time** type (0CALDAY).

Processing types As with text variables, the processing types manual entry, substitution path, and SAP or customer exit are available for formula variables. Here again, no input help or value check is provided for manual entry.

Substitution path Using the substitution path, formula variables can be populated from the data of a characteristic that is used in the query details. The value of the characteristic must be clearly identifiable during the calculation of the formula. As with text variables, keys and texts can be derived from this value. Additionally, the following derivations are available:

▶ **Characteristic attribute**
In characteristics, both characteristics (e.g., a year) and key figures (e.g., a price) can be stored as attributes. If these attributes have a numeric format, they can be used to populate a formula.

- **Hierarchy attribute**

  In hierarchies with plus/minus sign reversal, this option is required to read the relevant attribute from the hierarchy. (It does not have any other effect in the SAP standard version). This value can be used in formulas to perform further calculations.

Existence check

When using the substitution path, either the determined value or the status can be used as a result, whether or not this value actually exists. In the second case, the result is null if the value does not exist, or if the corresponding substitution path returns a zero or a space.

Delivery Status Analysis with Formula Variables

In the following example, a simple delivery status report is created based on delivery of scheduling data from SD reporting in order to determine delivery delays. It demonstrates the use of formula variables with a substitution path from a characteristic in the query:

- Create a new query on the MultiProvider ZEVAHDM1 **Sales document**. This query can be saved as ZEVAHDM1Q00002 **Sales—Delivery date variance—quantities**.

- The global filter restricts to the data view and the InfoProvider in order to analyze only the data of the delivery schedule (see Figure 4.43, Step 1).

- All relevant characteristics for the analysis can be moved via Drag&Drop to the free characteristics. Company code, material and requested delivery date should be restricted with a variable (Step 2).

- In the columns, a structure is created that contains the key figures **Requested Deliv. qty.**, **Confirmed qty.**, and **Delivery quantity** (Step 3).

- The rows contain a drilldown by material, requested delivery date, confirmed delivery date, and most current goods issue date (Step 4).

- Additionally, this structure contains further formulas for determining the difference between requested date, confirmed date, and goods issue date. In these formulas, the difference is determined from two formula variables. The source for the values for these variables are the values of the corresponding date characteristics, which are used in the drilldown for the rows.

- You can create new formula variables by using the context menu of the formula editor (Step 5).

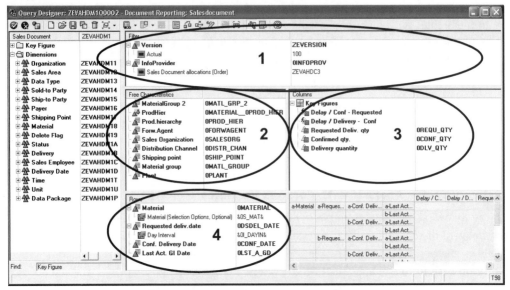

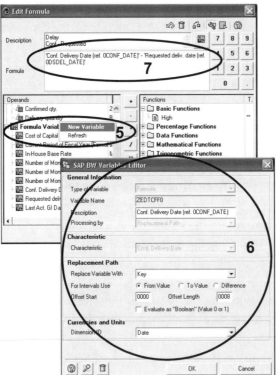

Figure 4.43 Query: Delivery Status Analysis with Formula Variables

- The available parameters should be set so that the date is read from 0CONF_DATE, 0DSDEL_DATE, or 0LST_A_GD depending on the variable (Step 6).

- Then, the formula can calculate the difference between two formula variables to determine the extent of the delivery variance (amount in days) (Step 7).

Figure 4.44 shows the report resulting from these settings.

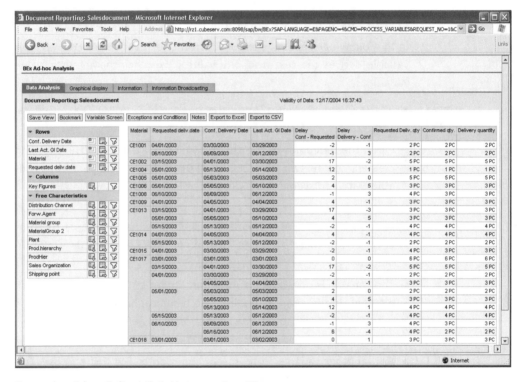

Figure 4.44 Sales—Delivery Date Variance—Quantities

4.5.5 SAP and Customer Exit Variables

To make the possibilities of data selection even more flexible, variables can also be populated with ABAP programming. This enables you to, for example, centrally control variable values, or derive them depending on other variables.

Some variables predefined by SAP already exist that can be activated from Business Content. Often, however, it is advisable to use user-defined variables so as to optimally map the desired behavior.

The source code for these customer exit variables is maintained centrally within the BW system. To avoid conflicts between several applications to be developed simultaneously, you should take technical measures, if necessary, to ensure independence between the individual applications. This can be achieved by using different name ranges for variables and by calling different independent function modules based on the variable name.

Create Customer Exit Variables

In the following example, a simple customer exit variable is created. This variable derives the text from the value of another characteristic value variable.

▶ In the Query Designer, open the query ZEFIGLM1Q00002 **General Ledger—P/L Performance comp local/region/global**.

▶ Open the definition of the structure element **Balance CHF YTD** and create a new text variable ZEFIYVT0 **OP_FYEAR Fiscal year from variable** with replacement by **Customer Exit** (see Figure 4.45, Steps 1 and 2).

▶ Set all parameters of the variable using the variable wizard. The processing type must be set to **Customer Exit**. The result is shown in Step 3.

▶ The variable is now added to the description of the affected structure element. In the query definition, the technical name of the variable is now shown in the structure element text. It is enclosed by an ampersand (&).

▶ Add another variable to represent the month. For this purpose, 0T_FPER **Text variable replaced by 0FISCPER3** can be used (Step 4). Contrary to the variable specified before, this variable reads the text from the selected characteristic value for 0FISCPER3. However, this is not always possible in every structure element.

▶ Then the query can be saved. If you ran the query now, the text of the customer exit variable would not yet be defined. The query result would return the technical name of the variable in the description of the structure element and in the Query Designer.

▶ Now the code of the variable is produced. For this purpose, call Transaction CMOD in SAP GUI.

▶ The ABAP code for customer exit variables can be found in the extension RSR00001 **BW: Extensions for global variables in Reporting**. This extension provides the include ZXRSRU01 that can be modified by the customer. In short, the extension cited must be included in a modification project. If such a project does not yet exist, you must create a new one on your system.

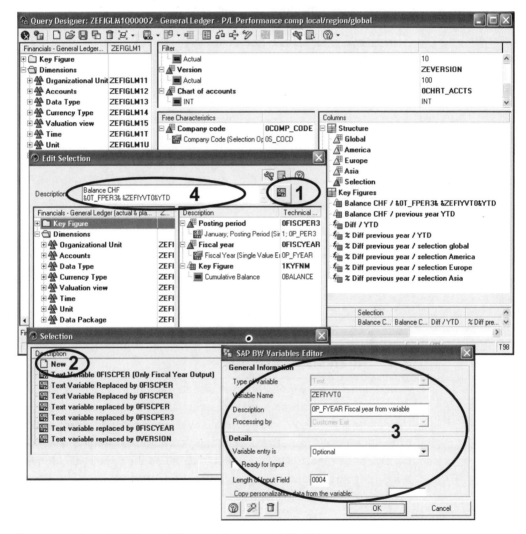

Figure 4.45 Query Definition with Text and Customer Exit Variables

▶ Store the coding that derives the value for our variable from the variables already populated in the query (see Figure 4.46).

- ▶ Activate the include, the function module, and the modification project.
- ▶ Execute the query. The text of the variable is now displayed in the structure element description. This dynamically created text is also shown when filtering the structure and in the local view of the query definition. You may need to log off from the server before the code takes effect in the Business Explorer.

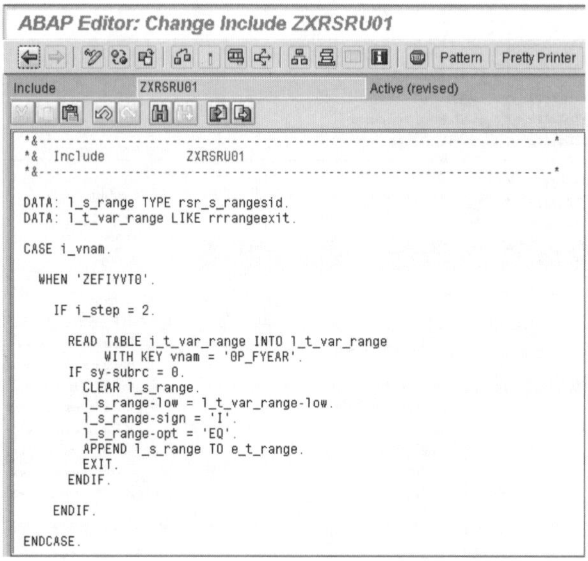

ABAP Editor: Change Include ZXRSRU01
Pattern
Pretty Printer
Include
ZXRSRU01
Active (revised)

```
*&---------------------------------------------------------------------*
*&  Include           ZXRSRU01
*&---------------------------------------------------------------------*

DATA: l_s_range TYPE rsr_s_rangesid.
DATA: l_t_var_range LIKE rrrangeexit.

CASE i_vnam.

  WHEN 'ZEFIYVT0'.

    IF i_step = 2.

      READ TABLE i_t_var_range INTO l_t_var_range
           WITH KEY vnam = '0P_FYEAR'.
      IF sy-subrc = 0.
        CLEAR l_s_range.
        l_s_range-low = l_t_var_range-low.
        l_s_range-sign = 'I'.
        l_s_range-opt = 'EQ'.
        APPEND l_s_range TO e_t_range.
        EXIT.
      ENDIF.

    ENDIF.

ENDCASE.
```


Figure 4.46 Code for Customer Exit for Variables

4.6 Analysis Functions

In addition to the various options of data definition and presentation, analytic functions can be used. These functions enable you to highlight the data found based on user-defined evaluation criteria (exceptions) or to exclude details from the presentation (conditions). Additionally, special exception reports can be generated based on the same evaluation criteria using the Reporting Agent. In these reports, the data is shown depending on the selected analysis criteria.

4.6.1 Conditions

Using conditions, the details to be presented in the query can be restricted based on user-defined criteria. Consequently, the output of the query can be efficiently limited to the relevant data in the analysis or in Reporting.

Conditions can be stored in the global query definition and created in the local view on the web. A definition of conditions in the local view in Excel is not yet supported.

To evaluate a condition, the data determined in the query is compared with a threshold value using one of the following analysis types:

Analysis types

▶ **Threshold**
A single value is displayed as soon as it fulfills the direct comparison with the given threshold.

▶ **List comparison**
The threshold to be used for the direct comparison is determined dynamically based on the query data. Several options are available for this purpose, like top n analyses. If the list comparison is activated, the output data is automatically sorted by the condition values.

The following is an overview of the options available for list comparisons. The input parameter used in the condition is represented by "X:"

▶ **Top X, Bottom X**
X details with the highest (or lowest) values are displayed.

▶ **Top X Percent, Bottom X Percent**
The details with the highest (or lowest) amounts are displayed, the cumulative amount of which contributes to the total result with a defined percentage of X. (Typical question: Which products or customers make up 80 % of the sales?)

▶ **Top X Total, Bottom X Total**
The details with the highest (or lowest) amounts are displayed, the cumulative amount of which exceeds a defined threshold of X. (Typical question: Which costs deviate from the budget by more than 10 %? The deviation percentage is defined as a structure element.)

The thresholds used in the conditions can be defined using variables as well. Formula variables are used in this case.

Variables

Conditions can be activated or deactivated during navigation. This does not affect the underlying data. Therefore, the values of the result rows and columns do not change when a condition is activated; only the output of specific details is suppressed in the display.

Calculation behavior

The data of a query is displayed only if all active conditions are met. Several conditions are therefore linked via a logical AND. Within one condition, several subconditions can be created, which are then linked via a

Several conditions

logical OR. Therefore, you can create a condition that displays both the top 10 and the bottom 10 products with regard to the change in sales.

Validity for structure elements The amount to be evaluated for the condition must be unique. For that reason, an appropriate structure element must be selected for every structure used in the query.

Validity for characteristics With regard to the characteristics of a query, you can activate the condition for all characteristics or for specific characteristic combinations only. This makes sense, for example, if the top n condition should be applied only to the display of products but not to the company codes if both are used as drilldowns in the query.

If a specific characteristic combination is given, the condition can only be activated if all characteristics are used in the query drilldown and displayed side by side in the rows or columns. The interim results of the given characteristic combination are hidden automatically. (If, for example, the top n incoming orders per salesperson should be presented, the interim results per order or per salesperson are no longer displayed. Instead, only the total result of all orders and salespersons is presented).

Scaling factors and local calculations When analyzing conditions, settings that can be made in the local view are not considered. In particular, this applies to the settings for scaling factors and local calculations (e.g., standardization and cumulation). In many requirements, however, the desired result can be determined by using a formula rather than a local calculation.

Conditions and master data hierarchies If a master data hierarchy is used in the drilldown, conditions based on a list comparison cannot be executed. The reason for this is that applying the condition to the basic values of the hierarchy does not make much sense, because the summary nodes are not correctly mapped if specific basic nodes are suppressed. With regard to contents, applying a list comparison to the summary nodes of the hierarchy only makes sense to a certain extent, and is therefore not supported.

Delivery Status Analysis with Conditions

In the following example, the query created above is extended by conditions to analyze the delivery status:

- In the Query Designer, open the query ZEVAHDM1Q00002 **Sales—Delivery date variance—quantities**.
- Via the toolbar, display an overview of the conditions created for that query (see Figure 4.47, Step 1).

▶ Create a new condition. It should be valid for all characteristics and be analyzed for the structure element **Delay Conf.—Requested** as soon as the threshold for the number of days reaches a value of 5 (Step 2).

The result of the report is illustrated in Figure 4.44.

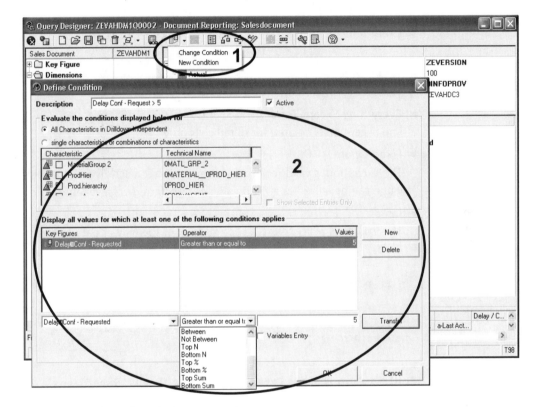

Figure 4.47 Condition for Delivery Status Analysis

4.6.2 Exceptions

Exceptions provide an analysis functionality comparable to conditions, although only details are highlighted depending on their contents.

In exceptions, you can define thresholds for up to nine levels. The values determined can be presented in the query using different formats—usually various shades of red, yellow, and green—but other formats are also supported.

For exceptions, too, you can define the structure elements to which they should apply. The validity can be restricted to a specific structure element, or the exception can be set to apply to all structure elements.

Validity for structure elements

For every exception, you can specify whether it should be applied to only the results or to the detail cells of the query as well.

Characteristic information can also be used to determine whether or not an exception should be created. Per query characteristic, the following options are available:

▶ **Everything**
There is no further restriction.

▶ **Totals Only**
The exception is created for results only.

▶ **Everything Except Total**
The exception is created for detail cells only.

▶ **Fixed Value**
The exception is valid for exactly one specific characteristic value. This value can be stored as a fixed value or transferred via a variable.

▶ **Level**
The validity is restricted to a specific level of the master data hierarchy used.

In an exception, several combinations of validity definitions can be stored. Per structure element, several rules can be stored for the validity of characteristics. Per characteristic, a maximum of one validity rule can be stored.

Contribution Margin Target Achievement with Exceptions

In the following example, the target achievement analysis of the contribution margin is extended by exceptions.

▶ In the query ZECOPAM1Q00006 **Profitability Analysis—Contribution Margin Targeting**, create a new exception (see Figure 4.48, Step 1).

▶ The exception is restricted to those structure elements that determine the target achievement (Step 2).

▶ The exception values must be assigned to the data values (Step 3).

▶ The general validity range is restricted (Step 4).

▶ Per characteristic, a special validity range can be defined, if necessary (Step 5).

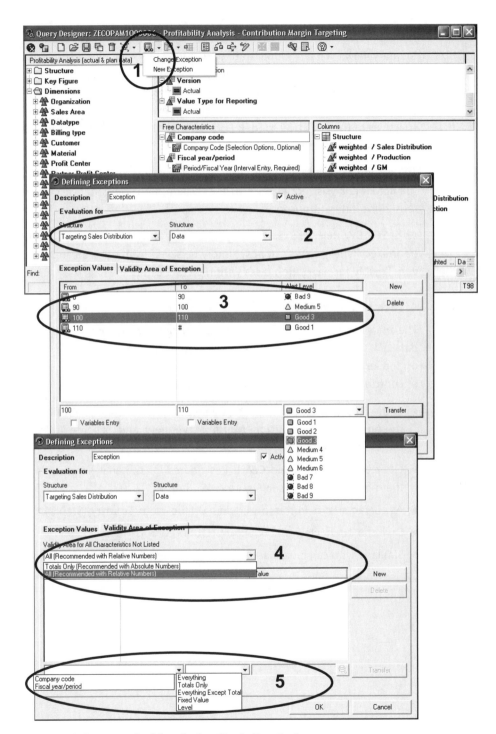

Figure 4.48 Exceptions for "Contribution Margin Targeting"

4.7 Query Views

In query views, a navigational state of the query is stored along with drill-downs, filters, variable values, hierarchy presentations, analysis functions, and other presentation options. If queries are regarded as a flexible analytical model for the underlying data, query views can map different perspectives of the analytical model. For example, the drilldown to products or customers can be mapped using a query.

The essential advantage of this approach is that you only need to create the actual analysis model once in the system, and thereafter, it can be reused for different purposes.

As of SAP BW Release 3.5, working with query views has been noticeably optimized. Query views can now simply be saved from the web and used very flexibly for navigation tasks within web cockpits.

Create a Query View

The analysis structure of the contribution margin scheme uses aggregated data of CO-PA. Their details are composed in different ways depending on the key figure. Using a query and different query views, detail queries of contribution margin components can be stored on the system.

- ▶ In the Query Designer, open the query ZECOPAM1Q00003 **Profitability Analysis—Contribution Margin Overview** and execute it from there on the web.
- ▶ Filter the **Net Sales** and **CM II** key figures for the analysis and place them in the columns (see Figure 4.49, Step 1).
- ▶ As characteristics in the rows, add a drilldown to **Country** (Step 2).
- ▶ Save the query view as ZECOPAM1Q00003V0001 (Step 3).
- ▶ Similarly, you can create additional detail queries based on the query.

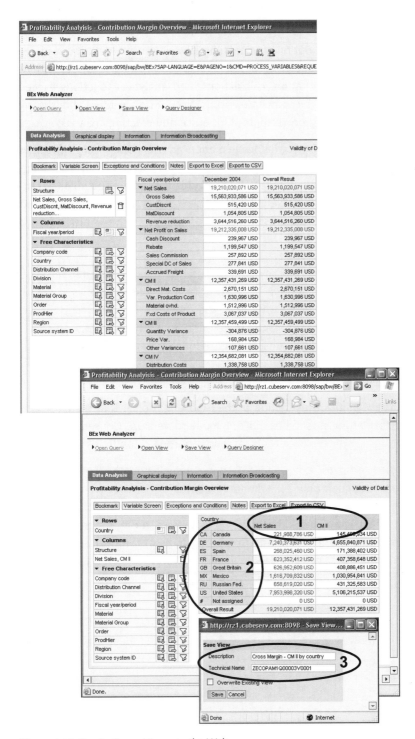

Figure 4.49 Create Query Views on the Web

4.8 Conclusion

Queries and their options for defining and presenting data requests are excellent tools for analyzing an SAP BW dataset. In particular, the options of hierarchy presentation, calculations, and analytical functions exceed the potential of many comparable tools. Users who are adept at designing queries have a very powerful tool for efficiently creating analyses.

But, practice has shown that less experienced users often have difficulties with some of the required topics that cannot be solved easily. For example, a controller with average IT knowledge will seldom be able to navigate through a formula definition regarding structure elements with text variables, even if the corresponding Excel equivalent looks rather simple in comparison.

Due to such restrictions in handling different details, it is often recommended that the editing of queries be limited to a group of well-trained power users. In any case, the query design should be made more efficient by implementing reusable query elements and, as appropriate, by providing a data model based on the reporting requirements.

Another significant restriction of the reporting tools is that there are limited formatting possibilities in the standard version. Consequently, you need to rely on separate tools for web reporting or on Excel workbooks.

In conclusion, less experienced users can benefit from the flexibility of the Query Designer only to a limited extent. Power users, however, can immediately benefit from a highly flexible and versatile tool. Therefore, it is a most gratifying development that even more progress can be expected with the analysis and reporting tools of the next SAP BW version, which, according to SAP, will be improved with regard to "advanced user experience" and "Adobe integration."

5   The BEx Web

SAP provides BEx Web as a composition of all BEx tools that can be used to create web-based applications, or are themselves web applications. This chapter introduces the individual components and explains more complex implementations using examples.

BEx Web contains various components that enable you to implement the very versatile requirements of individual users or user groups for Reporting in the web environment via web standard technologies and help elements that are predefined by SAP.

This volume of the SAP BW Library can only provide an overview of the manifold possibilities of BEx Web, since it would exceed the scope of this book to show you all the possible scenarios and settings in detail. Because the handling and function of individual BEx Web components, like the *BEx Web Application Designer* and the *BEx Web Analyzer*, are self-explanatory to a certain extent, we will discuss the individual BEx Web components. After reading this chapter, you will be able to classify and assess the functions provided by SAP BW within the scope of web reporting.

BEx Web comprises the following components:

Overview of components

▶ **BEx Web Application Designer**
The BEx Web Application Designer (WAD) is a standalone desktop application that you can use fairly easily to create your own web applications. In the BEx Web Application Designer, the individual web items provided by SAP BW are available for use in web applications. The majority of your web templates can be created by using the graphical user guidance, Drag&Drop, and simple formatting functions. The WAD also allows you to adopt a purely text mode so you can directly enter HTML code for your web template.

▶ **BEx Web Analyzer**
To view the queries that you created in the BEx Query Designer on the web without having created a separate web template, BEx Web provides the BEx Web Analyzer as a counterpart to the BEx Analyzer based on MS Excel. The BEx Web Analyzer is a standalone web application consisting of web templates that can also be opened and edited in the Web Application Designer (so that the web application is extensible as well). Using the BEx Web Analyzer, you can start your queries on the

web and a comprehensive online analysis application featuring many standard functions will be available for you to use.

► **Web Application Design**

For a generic Online Analytical Processing (OLAP) navigation in web applications and Business Intelligence cockpits to the data stored in SAP BW, Web Application Design provides numerous predefined presentation elements for visualizing your very complex reporting scenarios: The *web items* (e.g., **table**, **chart**, or **map**) are used for this purpose. Additionally, Web Application Design provides numerous functions that can arbitrarily extend and improve the interaction of web applications with the user via a comprehensive command set using command URLs.

► **Web Design API for tables**

To be able to give your web applications an even more individual design, or to provide additional functionalities not included in BEx Web, the Web Design Application Programming Interface (API) provides you with an interface that enables you to adjust the visualization (contents and formatting) of every single table cell in the web browser according to your needs. Additionally, you can generate special HTML and JavaScript code dynamically, depending on the navigational state.

► **BEx Mobile Intelligence**

BEx Web is not restricted to an Internet browser with an existing online connection to SAP BW Web Application Server. In fact, with BEx Mobile Intelligence, BEx Web provides another component that can extend your reporting environment and the associated functionalities considerably with little effort. For example, BEx Mobile Intelligence enables you to view web applications on very different kinds of presentation devices like mobile phones or digital palm pilots. You can precalculate entire HTML pages, including the BW-specific data, and download them—using the *BEx Download Scheduler*—to your local laptop or PC. Then, you can view these files on the go, without requiring a connection to SAP BW, in an Internet browser and also make selections using dropdown boxes.

5.1 The Web Framework of SAP: Terms and Functions

As of Release 2.0, SAP BW enables you to view queries created using the BEx Query Designer directly on the Internet via an Internet browser and to use the functions of generic OLAP navigation. Therefore, all the analysis options of the OLAP processor (drilldown functionality, slice-and-dice functionality, and many more) are available in the standard version. No further extensive programming is needed to provide these interactive functionalities in a frontend based on the Internet browser.

Additionally, SAP BW gives you numerous ways in which to create your own web applications and Business Intelligence cockpits for simple and highly individual scenarios. You aren't limited to the SAP BW range of services. In order to meet your demands, you can also use all traditional standard web technologies, for example, HTML, JavaScript, CSS, or XML.

The range of Web Framework functions has been widely extended in the current release. With the new web item **Web Template**, it is now possible to create modular web templates.

Functions of the Web Framework

This means that you can embed the HTML code of one or more templates in another web template. Consequently, the maintenance effort for your web templates, for example, when changing the layout, can be enormously reduced because the changes only need to be applied to selected central templates. For example, you could create one template for the header area and one for the footer area of your web applications and embed these header and footer templates in every one of your web templates. If you now make changes to the header and footer templates that you created, these changes are applied to all of your web applications.

BEx Web Application Design uses many specific terms (web items, data provider, web templates, and many more). In the following section, these terms are introduced and explained to provide a better insight into the Web Framework or SAP BW.

5.1.1 Web Items

The function of a web item is to present the data stored in SAP BW in an Internet browser. The various web items have different purposes and therefore have individual properties. Every web item sees the data to be displayed in an Internet browser in a different way. For example, the web item **Chart** produces a graphic from the underlying data, similar to the charts in Excel. The **Table** web item, on the other hand, uses the data to create structured information in the form of a table on the web, where every table cell provides a context-sensitive menu for additional functionality.

Most web items are populated by assigning a *data provider*; for example, a query or a query view. As was already mentioned, every web item has different properties, or attributes. Examples would include attributes like

Data sources for web Items

title, width, or border type.[1] Each of these properties can accept different values and thereby change the look and functionality of the web item in the browser.

Processing of web items

Web items are integrated in a web template as placeholders in the form of an *object tag*. At runtime, during the execution of the web template in a browser, web items are populated with BW contents by SAP BW and then converted into HTML source code for a web report. The value of attributes can be changed using *command URLs* even while the web report is run, for example, by using a hyperlink. In this way, very powerful web applications can be created. By using a hyperlink, you can change the size and the title of a web item, or the navigational state of the underlying data provider of a table.

There are virtually no limits. The number of web items provided by SAP has been increasing since Release 2.x and has greatly extended the functions of web reporting.

Example: Creating a Simple Web Template for Presenting the Profit and Loss Statement in a Table

Case study: Requirements

Our model company, CubeServ Engines, wants to present selected queries in a Business Intelligence cockpit on the web by using all of the BEx Web components. Additionally, BEx Web should be set up as the primary reporting frontend. The settings already made in Chapter 4, *The SAP Business Explorer Query Designer*, are adopted and further developed.

Requirements

The query for the profit and loss statement, which was created in Section 4.3.2, will be presented on the web for easier access by the management team of our model company, CubeServ Engines. For this purpose, a simple web template has been created using the Table web item. The presentation of the layout, however, will not be considered further.

▶ Open the Web Application Designer via **Start · All programs · Business Explorer · Web Application Designer**.

▶ Look at the different areas. From left to right, the following areas are visible:

  ▶ **Web Items** window (see Figure 5.1, 1)

  ▶ **Layout** window (2)

  ▶ **Properties of the Selected Element** window (3)

---

1 The individual web items and their properties, possible values, and effects are described in great detail in Section 5.5.

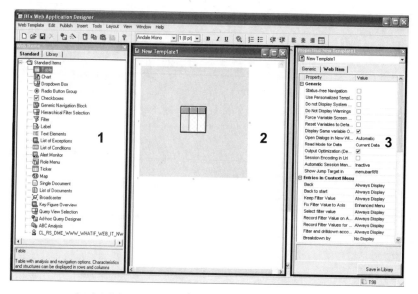

Figure 5.1 Web Application Designer

▶ From the left window **Web Items**, move the **Table** web item to the **Layout** window by Drag&Drop.

▶ The right window **Properties** now provides several attributes of the selected **Table** web item.

▶ Depending on the setting, the browser shows a different type of table.

▶ For a result to be visible in the browser, you must assign a data provider to the **Table** web item (see Figure 5.2). In this case, use the query ZECOPAM1Q00005 **Profitability Analysis—Contribution Margin cons. and local** that was created in Section 4.3.2

▶ This is done in the **Properties** window on the **Generic** tab. A detailed description of this function can be found in the example presented in Section 5.4.5.

▶ Figure 5.3 illustrates the generated web report with profit and loss statement in table format.

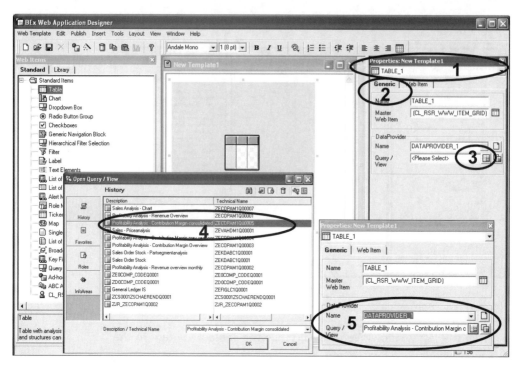

Figure 5.2 Properties Window for the Selected Web Item, Assigning a Data Provider

BW Web Application - Microsoft Internet Explorer

File Edit View Favorites Tools Help

▼ Profitability Analysis - Contribution Margin cons. and local

Company code	Overall Result	0001 CubeServ AG	1000 CubeServ Vertriebs GmbH (Deutschland)	2000 CubeServ Engines AG (Schweiz)	2100 CubeServ Handels GmbH (Österreich)
Net Sales I	18.625.320 USD	786.569 USD	2.740.817 USD	711.199 USD	727.848 USD
Cash Discount	239.967 USD	10.237 USD	35.492 USD	9.204 USD	9.592 USD
Rebate	1.199.547 USD	49.153 USD	181.027 USD	46.509 USD	46.671 USD
Sales Commission	257.892 USD	10.734 USD	38.104 USD	9.546 USD	10.241 USD
Special DC of Sales	277.841 USD	11.936 USD	41.075 USD	10.166 USD	10.967 USD
Accrued Freight	339.691 USD	13.848 USD	50.573 USD	13.205 USD	13.028 USD
Net Sales II	20.940.257 USD	882.475 USD	3.087.088 USD	799.830 USD	818.348 USD
Full manuf. costs Local	8.881.180 USD	379.259 USD	1.326.063 USD	332.600 USD	348.335 USD
CM II	12.059.078 USD	503.217 USD	1.761.026 USD	467.229 USD	470.012 USD
Quantity Variance	-304.876 USD	0 USD	0 USD	0 USD	0 USD
Price Var.	168.984 USD	0 USD	0 USD	0 USD	0 USD
Other Variances	107.661 USD	0 USD	0 USD	0 USD	0 USD
CM III	12.087.308 USD	503.217 USD	1.761.026 USD	467.229 USD	470.012 USD
Distribution Costs	1.338.758 USD	57.037 USD	221.591 USD	44.734 USD	72.993 USD
Marketing	1.057.938 USD	45.312 USD	176.770 USD	32.890 USD	59.371 USD
R&D	380.723 USD	16.827 USD	62.940 USD	13.137 USD	20.204 USD
CM IV	9.309.890 USD	384.041 USD	1.299.724 USD	376.468 USD	317.444 USD
Administration	1.294.137 USD	55.722 USD	210.874 USD	42.597 USD	69.473 USD
Other Overhead	2.035.756 USD	81.787 USD	337.076 USD	66.768 USD	109.120 USD
Operating Profit	5.979.998 USD	246.533 USD	751.773 USD	267.103 USD	138.852 USD

Figure 5.3 Simple Web Report in MS Internet Explorer, Example of Table Web Item

5.1.2 Data Provider

A *data provider* provides the data stored in SAP BW to the individual web items via a query or a query view. Within the web template, it is created as a logical object with a reference to the data source and with a unique name. The initial view of a data provider is then either the query view or a query at the time of its call. The navigational state of the data provider can be changed by navigating in the web application. Data providers are discussed in more detail in Section 5.4.5.

5.1.3 Web Templates and Web Applications

The web template is created in or via the Web Application Designer and contains the individual web items in the form of placeholders for the BW-specific data and the defined data providers that are assigned to the individual web items. Per web template, you can use any number of web items. For reasons of performance, though, you should ensure that you don't define too many web items or too many different data providers in one web template.

Additionally, you must specify all layout-specific settings and formatting for the later display in an Internet browser, as well as the behavior of the web application itself (e.g., deactivating or activating personalization functions) in the web template. The structure of the future web application is thus determined in the web template by defining which data provider will present the specific BW data in which way, that is, using which web items, and which additional operations can be carried out using command URLs.

According to SAP, the HTML document with the BW-specific placeholders is called *web template*, and the HTML page displayed in the Internet browser is called *web application*.

Naming conventions

If a request is sent from a web application; for example, from an Internet browser, to SAP Web Application Server, the structure of the requested web template is analyzed. At first, the properties of the template are processed; for example, whether the web template should access precalculated data or even precalculated HTML pages. Then, the embedded data providers are processed, the data of which can be used to populate the individual web items. Finally, all command URLs, for example, language-dependent texts of the web application, are translated into HTML-compliant code. The HTML code produced is then returned to the browser, processed, and displayed as a generated web application.

5.1.4 Web Report

The HTML page displayed in the Internet browser is called a *web report*. A web report is therefore the same as a web application. The term *web reporting* was introduced in BW 2.x and is no longer used in the current SAP documentation of Release 3.5. Instead, the current documentation uses the term *web applications*.

5.1.5 Object Tags

The individual BEx Web-specific objects of a web template, like the template properties, the data providers, and the individual web items, are created in the HTML code of the web template by using *object tags*. When calling a web template from a web browser, SAP BW converts the individual object tags to HTML code and sends this code back to the browser. Object tags are discussed in more detail in Section 5.4.2.

5.1.6 Query versus Query Views

Determine requirements Either a query or a query view is used as a data basis of the individual web items (or for defining a data provider). Which one of these is eventually used depends on the requirement:

▶ Queries are easier to maintain and are directly created in the Query Designer. They are stored hierarchically under the corresponding Info-Provider and can be saved directly to a role.

▶ The query view is stored hierarchically under the query and is created, for example, from the Web Application Designer on the web or in BEx Analyzer. A *query view* is a saved view of a query and therefore contains all drilldowns, filter values, and variable values of the executed query.

Usage in Templates and Role Menu The only reason for deciding against query views as a data provider is because of their complex maintenance. Still, the most dissimilar kinds of requirements can be excellently solved using query views, without having to create unnecessary, only marginally different queries. Some requirements can be comfortably solved using one query view only.

Like queries, query views can be called directly from the Role menu in BEx Web Analyzer or from any other web template stored in Customizing. A group-wide reporting, using a web frontend, can mean a lot of effort with respect to providing the most different queries or query views each in a separate web template. For normal reporting, queries and query views can be executed and analyzed very well from the Role menu on the web, or from the SAP Easy Access menu using a universal web template, like BEx Web Analyzer. For special requirements, single specific templates can be additionally generated. While queries can be saved to a role directly from the Query Designer, query views must be manually entered in the respective role via the role maintenance transaction (Transaction PFCG) for a better organization.

Example: Creating a Graphical Sales Analysis Using a Chart

For the Business Intelligence cockpit of our model company, CubeServ Engines, which is to be created later on, the key figures of a selected query should be presented graphically per company code across a time series using the **Chart** web item. Only one key figure at a time should be shown in the chart. The individual key figures and company codes should be selectable via a dropdown box. The initial call of the report on the web should first show the **Sales** key figure.

Requirements

▶ Create a new query ZECOPAM1Q00007 **Sales Analysis—Chart** on the InfoProvider ZECOPAM1 **Profitability Analysis (Actual & plan data)**.

▶ This query contains the key figures **Net Sales Actual, Sales quantity**, and **CM II Actual** in the rows and **Posting period** in the columns. **Fiscal year** and **Company code** are placed in the free characteristics (see Figure 5.4).

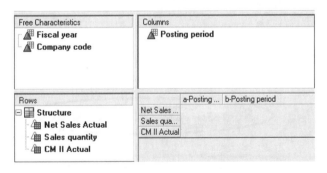

Figure 5.4 Example Query for Working with Query Views

▶ Now create a new web template (ZKOMP3T0001 **Sales Analysis— Chart**, see Figure 5.5, Step 1).

▶ Then add the **Chart** web item (Step 2) and two **Dropdown Box** web items (Step 3) to this template—one dropdown box for the key figures, the other for the company code.

▶ From the Web Application Designer, select the entry **View Definition • Based on a Query** from the **Tools** menu (Step 4).

▶ The **BEx Open** dialog is displayed. Select your query and confirm with **OK** (Steps 5 and 6).

▶ The web browser now starts the BEx Web Analyzer or the view-editing template stored in Customizing, respectively. In the Key Figures structure, now select the **Sales** key figure using the navigation block (see Figure 5.6, Steps 1 to 3).

▶ Then select **Save View** (Step 4), and assign a description and a technical name to the view (Step 5).

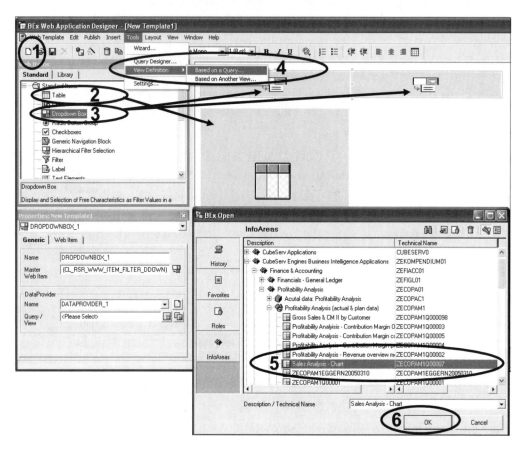

Figure 5.5 Selecting the Query to Serve as a Template for the Query View

Practice has shown that for the purpose of clarification, you should assign the same technical name to the query view that you used for the query, followed by the suffix **V** and a consecutive 3-digit number (example: ZECOPAM1Q00007V0001). Additionally, it can prove beneficial to use the technical name of the view as the description of the query views used on the web as well, because whenever you want to make changes to the view, you need to manually re-enter the description and the technical name. It is recommended that you create an additional maintenance list of the individual views for quick access to descriptions and technical names and for a better overview, for example, on the intranet or in the Business Document Service of SAP BW.

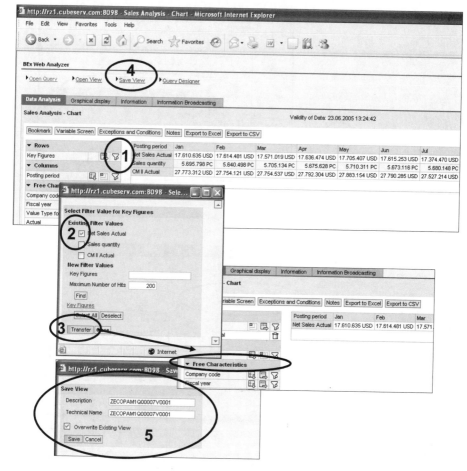

Figure 5.6 Creating a Query View from the Web

▶ Now assign the query view to the data provider used in the web template (see Figure 5.7, Steps 1 to 4).

▶ For the dropdown boxes, select the appropriate characteristic or the key figure structure, respectively, and save your web template (see Figure 5.8, Steps 1 to 4).

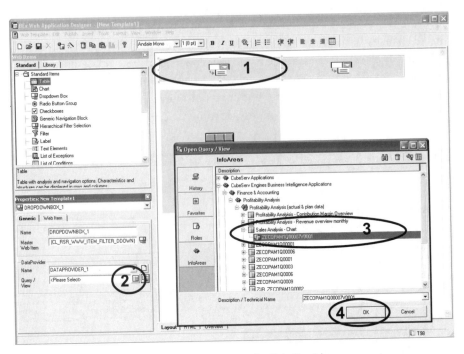

Figure 5.7 Assigning the Query Views to the Data Provider

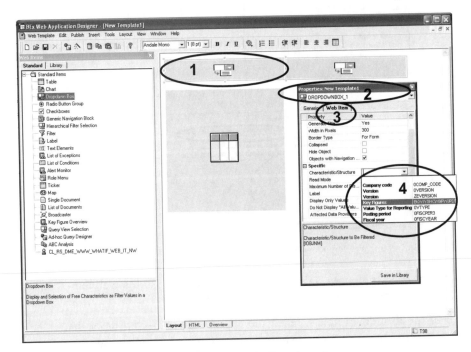

Figure 5.8 Assigning a Characteristic to the Dropdown Box

▶ If the web template is now executed in the web browser, only the **Sales** key figure is shown in the chart at first, and the corresponding dropdown box is preset to this value (see Figure 5.9).

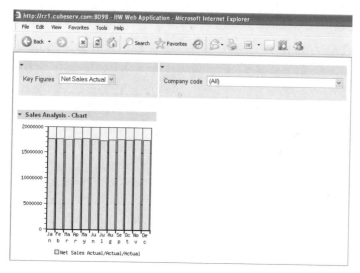

Figure 5.9 Preassignment with Query Views: Result in the Web Browser

5.1.7 Command URLs

Using command URLs, various commands can be applied online to the individual data providers, the web items, or the web template itself. For example, using a command URL, you can filter the **Country** characteristic by the value **Germany** and, at the same time, place the **Sold-to Party** characteristic vertically into the drilldown and change the title of the **Table** web item to **Sold-to parties in Germany**.

Via the URL using a text hyperlink, the individual commands are sent to the web server where they are processed. The web server then creates new HTML code and sends it back to the browser.

5.1.8 Cascading Style Sheets

Cascading Style Sheets (CSS) are an immediate extension of HTML.[2] They are a description language for the format properties, which can be used

Description language

---

2 Like HTML, CSS is also standardized by the W3 consortium. This means that CSS is a company-independent, openly documented, and freely usable standard. As is the case for HTML, the W3 consortium has installed a team that is responsible for CSS and the further development of the language. In doing so, this team acknowledges the rules for the creation of *recommendations* of the W3 consortium. You can find more information on this subject at *www.w3.org/Style/*.

to define individual HTML elements. For example, using style sheets, you can determine that the contents of an HTML table cell will be displayed with a font size of 10 points in green font and with a distance of 5 pixels to the cell border. You can also assign position specifications to individual elements that are exact, right down to the pixel.

Using CSS, you can note central formats in the header of an HTML file. For example, you can define a central format for a type of table cells. This format is then assigned to the table cell using the attribute `class="CentralCSSFormat"`. All relevant table cells of the HTML file then contain the centrally defined formatting properties.

Style sheet files   SAP BW uses different CSS formats for the most varied kinds of table cell types (e.g., data cell, title cell, characteristic value cell, etc.). For example, a table title of characteristics or attributes is assigned the format `SAPBEXchaText`. You can even note your style sheet definitions in separate files. The style sheet files can then reference any number of HTML files. In this way, you can design consistent layouts for large projects, or define your company-specific layout in a central file and respond to possible changes with very little effort. With a few small changes in a central style sheet file, you can thus achieve a different look in any number of HTML files.

BWReports.css   In the standard version of the SAP BW web template, the central CSS file, *BWReports.css,* which defines all formats used by SAP BW, is created. But, you should note that SAP delivers various CSS files with different layout definitions, which can be used as an idea for your own layouts or as an alternative presentation.

Print style sheets   The possibilities of CSS aren't limited to screen presentation. Additional options are available for defining page layout and text flow control for print layouts. For example, you can define the position in the document where a page break (new page) should be inserted.

Link to style sheet files   CSS files are integrated in an HTML document using the HTML `<link>` tag (logical relationship). The `<link>` tag has various attributes that can be used to further specify the relationship. Using the `href` attribute, the path to the CSS file is identified. The `type` attribute contains the MIME type of the file to be integrated, and `rel` specifies the logical relationship:

```
<link href="MIME/BEx/StyleSheets/BWReports.css"
  type="text/css" rel="stylesheet">
```

The individual CSS files are stored in the MIME Repository within SAP BW. The MIME Repository can be accessed directly using Transaction SO2_MIME_REPOSITORY or Transaction SE80.

Storage of style sheets

Browser-Dependent style sheets

Since the various web browsers handle HTML and CSS formats differently, SAP BW allows you to store different style sheets for each browser and its various release versions. In the MIME Repository, for the style sheets delivered by SAP, you will always find one style sheet without a suffix and four style sheets with the suffixes _ie5 (for Internet Explorer 5), _ie6 (for Internet Explorer 6), _n6x (for Netscape Navigator 6.x), and _n7x (for Netscape Navigator 7.x).

These style sheets are browser-optimized and are integrated when starting a web application of the respective browser. If there is no style sheet with the relevant suffix, the style sheet without a suffix is embedded in the generated HTML document. If a style sheet with the suffix _n6x exists, it will be used when you start the web application in Netscape Navigator 6.x. If there is no style sheet with the suffix _n6x, the style sheet without a suffix will be used.

Style sheet without suffix

For changed style sheets, this is only important if you are using several browser types. You can optimize the style sheet for every browser. If you are using only one browser type, optimize the style sheet without a suffix for that specific browser. For this purpose, use the style sheet with the browser-specific suffix as a template.

Print Style sheet

As is the case for the screen display style sheet, you can also integrate your own style sheet for print output in your web template. This makes sense in most cases in order to adjust the font size for printing (usually a little smaller), for example, or hide specific display elements from the printout. If no special style sheet is stored for printing, the screen display style sheet will be used for printing. The printing style sheet is a separate style sheet that is integrated in the HTML document and identified by another syntax in the HTML document:

```
<link href="MIME/BEx/StyleSheets/BWReports_print.css"
  type="text/css" rel="stylesheet" media="print">
```

The printing style sheet can also be integrated in the Web Application Designer via the **Insert** menu. This is discussed in more detail in Section 5.2.1.

CSS formats

The CSS formats used by SAP BW are illustrated in Figure 5.10, using the example of the **Table** web item (probably the most common web item). Because the used CSS format is not always apparent, depending on the cell type, this figure should also be regarded as a reference.

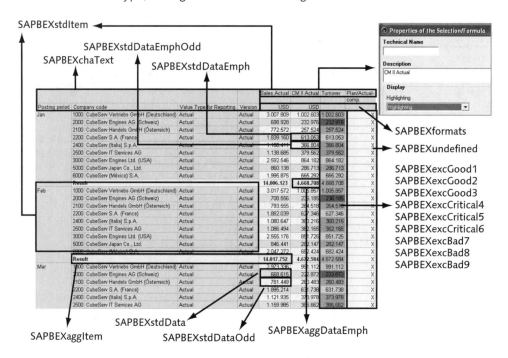

Figure 5.10 Used Style Sheet Classes in the Table Web Item

5.1.9 JavaScript

Independent programming language

JavaScript is an independent programming language that was introduced and licensed by Netscape in 1995. It was intended to be a supplement to HTML and allow for more interaction with the user. With JavaScript, it became possible to handle and process user events (e.g., mouse clicks). URLs can therefore be generated dynamically at runtime, depending on the user. It also became possible to validate entry fields before transferring them to the web server.

The Web Application Designer generates special JavaScript code for the individual web applications, without which the various functions would not be feasible. The context menu of the table, for example, is completely implemented using JavaScript. Although certain functions can also be implemented via pure HTML, the usability of these web applications is often inadequate.

Special JavaScript code

The Web Application Designer also generates various JavaScript variables and arrays that store values about the web application. The JavaScript array SAPBWTemplateProp[], for example, stores information about the current web application, such as whether a personalized web application or the web template itself was executed. This value can then be read via another JavaScript function and presented to the end user graphically, using various icons or via specific text. Another implementation option involves controlling frames and their contents via JavaScript.

SAP BW additionally provides numerous predefined JavaScript functions that can be used for creating complex web applications. For example, a daily calendar in JavaScript is integrated in the output web application, which can be called with parameters using the relevant command, and then applies the selection to a previously defined time characteristic and a specific data provider (see Figure 5.11).

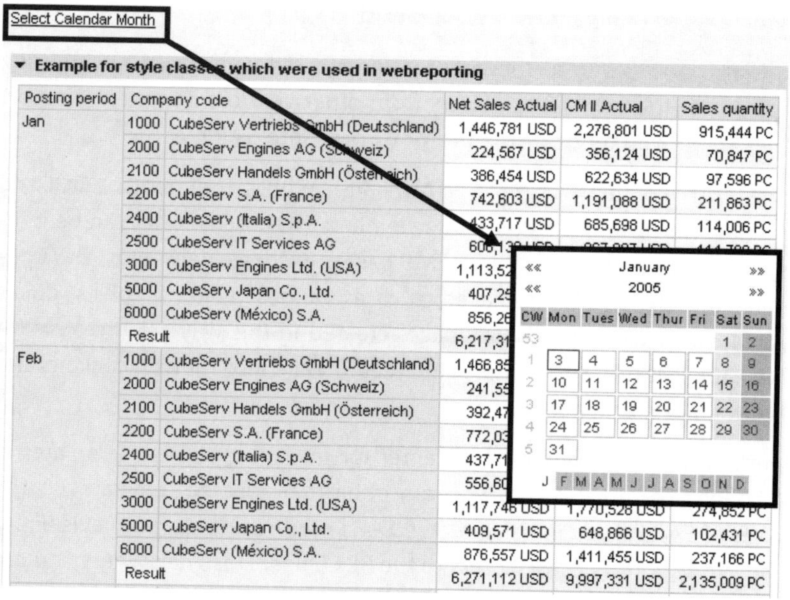

Predefined JavaScript functions

Figure 5.11 JavaScript Daily Calendar for Filtering by Time Characteristics

In addition, several JavaScript functions are available that determine the specified properties of the used web items and the defined data providers, or of the web template, and make them available for further processing.

5.2   The BEx Web Application Designer

Using the BEx Web Application Designer (WAD), you can easily create web reports or web applications with various functions and display elements. The WAD is the essential tool for creating and managing web applications. Using this tool, the functions provided by SAP in the standard version can be easily learned and implemented.

Web template wizard

The Web Application Designer also includes a web template wizard that guides you step by step through the creation of a web template, and provides explanations for all the settings of the template and the individual web items. Because the Web template wizard can be used intuitively, it is not described further in this book.

Need of additional knowledge

For more complex web applications or for those applications that require more layout work, basic HTML knowledge should exist because WYSIWYG ("What you see is what you get") is possible only to a limited extent. Depending on the complexity of the web applications, additional knowledge of JavaScript or VBScript—and perhaps of ABAP and Business Server Pages (BSP) as well—should exist.

External HTML editors

It is also possible to further process the created web templates by using more user-friendly HTML editors from other vendors and then reimport the edited web template via the WAD back into SAP BW.

Using the Web Application Designer

The WAD contains a simple HTML editor with a rudimentary GUI and also provides various BW-specific elements (web items) that can be integrated and parameterized in HTML pages. In these web items, BW-specific contents can be displayed, such as various tables, graphics, documents, and maps. The HTML pages created in this way are the basis for web applications with complex interactions and also for web cockpits and iViews of the SAP portal.

Web template administration

Furthermore, the WAD is the center for managing all web templates in SAP BW. From the WAD, you can publish all created templates to the roles of SAP BW, or in a connected SAP Enterprise Portal as iViews. From the WAD, you also have access to the BEx Query Designer, where you can create query views of queries.

Unfortunately, in our opinion, the WAD still has some weak spots and could be improved in various areas. For example, the WAD does not allow you to undo an inadvertent editing step in the layout mode, for example, the deletion of text. Several special techniques in the HTML mode—a JavaScript area within the `<select>` and `</select>` tags, for example—result in the written code having to be deleted completely when switching from HTML mode to layout mode.

The WAD is made up of the following areas:

Areas of the Web Application Designer

▶ Menu bar

▶ Application toolbar

▶ **Web Items** window

▶ **Template** window

▶ **Properties** window

To optimize the potential of the Web Application Designer, you should first specify the global settings and store company logos, and style sheets, if any, in the MIME Repository. This enables the initial transfer of the default settings to all newly created web templates. We will now take a closer look at these functions that can be found in the menus of the menu bar. In this context, we will also specify the necessary settings for the web applications of our model company CubeServ Engines.

5.2.1 The Menu Bar

The menu bar contains the most different kinds of functions for working with the Web Application Designer. Since most of the menu options (like **Open**, **Save**, **Search**, etc.) are self-explanatory, we will only provide you with a short explanation of selected menu options here.

Settings

In the Web Application Designer or in the Web Application Wizard, you can specify and save general settings. One way of calling the **Settings** menu option is via the **Tools** menu. There, you can select the style sheet to be used for creating a new web template using default values, as well as specify the path for the web browser[3] and an HTML editor for the external editing of web templates.

---

3 Contrary to the information provided in the SAP documentation, it hasn't been possible to change the preset Internet Explorer up to and including Release 6.40 Beta.

Please note that the style sheet selection list offers only those style sheets that are stored on the SAP BW server. Note also that you can delete the cache that stores some of the metadata information during a session in the Web Application Designer.[4] If other users change the data provider in the meantime, these changes might not be visible immediately in the Web Application Designer. In particular, this affects:

▶ Changes to query views from the web application

▶ Changes to the query implemented by other users

For example, if the underlying structure in a used query changes within a session, this information is not updated for you in the Web Application Designer. Instead of terminating and restarting the WAD, you can empty the cache; the structures are then read again.

Expert mode Additionally, you can switch to the **Expert Mode**[5] and activate and deactivate the **Translate into HTML entities**[6] function (see Figure 5.12). In the Expert Mode, you are provided with additional web items such as **Data Providers (XML), Object Catalog of the Web Application (XML)** and the **Web Template** item. For the additional items to be shown, you must set the flag for the expert mode and quit and restart the Web Application Designer (see Figure 5.12).

HTML entities For a smooth presentation of a web application—depending on the specified coding of the used Internet browser—we recommend that you select the checkbox **Translate into HTML entities**. Most web pages contain information that tells the browser which language code to use (language and character set).

The generated HTML code of the web report created from SAP BW also contains a note to the browser about the character set to be chosen for a clean presentation of all characters; otherwise, any special characters might not be displayed properly. For example, if the HTML entities function is disabled, the Euro symbol (€) can be used as a special character in the web template, but the Internet browser that is eventually used might not be able to display the Euro symbol depending on its setting, for example, Greek coding (ISO). By using the function **Translate into HTML**

---

4 OSS Note 629065 provides further information on this function.
5 OSS Note 720009 povides further information on the Expert Mode.
6 OSS Note 666388 provides further information on HTML entities.

entities, the Euro symbol is converted to HTML code and can then be presented in any coding.

If you want to save the generic settings you made, select the corresponding checkbox in the **Settings** dialog (see Figure 5.12).

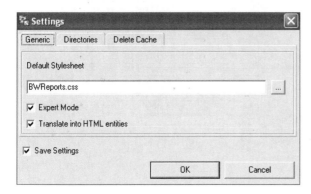

Figure 5.12 Settings Dialog in the WAD

Print Stylesheet ...

We already discussed style sheets and the option of manually integrating print style sheets in Section 5.1.8. Using the **Print Stylesheet ...** function from the **Insert** menu, a style sheet optimized for printing can be inserted from the MIME Repository into the web template.

The **Choose Stylesheet** dialog displayed in a new window (see Figure 5.13) lets you select style sheets from a list (left pane) and see a preview (right pane) of the various formats. In the bottom area, you can enter the absolute path of a style sheet that is, for example, stored on your homepage, and integrate it into your web template.

To view the print style sheets in the list, all style sheets within the MIME Repository (see Figure 5.14) below the *BEx* directory with the suffix *_print.css*, or with the respective browser-specific suffix *_print_ ie6.css*, *_print_ns7.css*, and so on, need to be displayed. To see the correctly formatted preview, however, you need to store a browser-specific style sheet in the MIME Repository, as shown in Figure 5.13. For all style sheets without a browser-specific suffix, no formatted preview is displayed at the moment.

Storage of style sheets

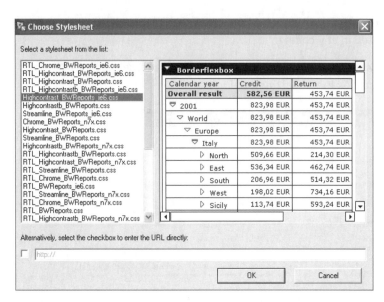

Figure 5.13 WAD Dialog for Selecting a Print Style Sheet

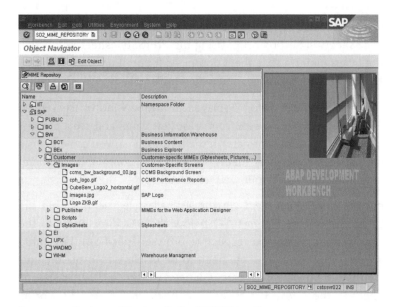

Figure 5.14 Customer Directory in the MIME Repository

Picture

Using this function, you can insert images, for example, company logos, in your web template. If you select this function from the **Insert** menu, the **Choose Screen** dialog is displayed in a new window (see Figure 5.15). From the list displayed in the left pane, you can select an image and view a preview of the selected entry in the right pane. If you need other images that are not stored in the MIME Repository and are thus not presented in the list, you can also enter the direct path of the image, for example, a logo from your homepage, in the bottom area of the window.

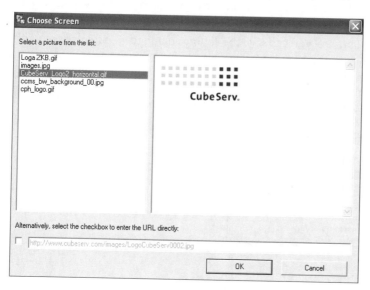

Figure 5.15 Choose Screen WAD Dialog

▶ The entries presented are read from the MIME Repository (Transaction: SO2_MIME_REPOSITORY) within the customer directory (see Figure 5.14). The complete path within the MIME Repository is: **SAP · BW · Customer · Images**.

▶ To store additional MIME objects, like graphics, for example, in the customer directory within the MIME Repository, mark the *Images* directory and press the right mouse button.

▶ From the context menu that appears, select the entry **Import MIME Object**.

5.2.2 The "Web Items" Window

Web Items are integral to web reporting, because they display the data of the defined data providers in the web browser. The **Web Items** window contains a list of all web items of SAP BW that are provided to you for designing your web application, and therefore, for presenting the data. Since every web item provides special functionalities, we will introduce them to you separately in Section 5.5. This is only an overview of the functions of the **Web Items** window.

As you can see in Figure 5.16, the **Web Items** window contains two tabs:

▶ On the **Standard** tab (1), there is a list of all web items delivered by SAP, which can be drawn to the layout area using Drag&Drop.

▶ On the **Library** tab (2), you can create your own libraries, that is, your own collections or groups of web items, and open them from there. Using libraries, you can save the settings made to web items as *reusable templates* or *master web items*.

In the lower area of both tabs (3), there is a text field that provides a more detailed description of your web item selection.

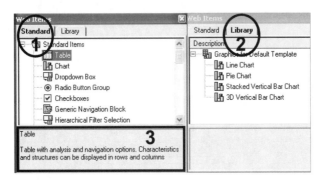

Figure 5.16 The "Web Items" Window with Its Two Tabs "Standard" and "Library"

5.2.3 The "Template" Window

The **Template** window contains the web templates that you edit in the course of the design process and that form the basis for the individual web applications. A web template is the HTML page where you specify the structure of the web application.

Footer of the "Template" window

The footer of the **Template** window (see Figure 5.17, 1) contains three tabs that you can use to toggle between the different template views, as in common HTML editors:

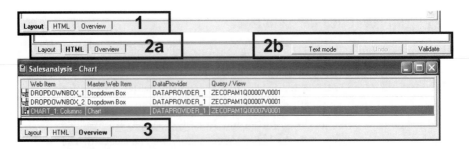

Figure 5.17 Footer of the "Template" Window

▶ **"Layout" tab**

The layout view lets you specify the layout of the web application. Per Drag&Drop, you can draw the web items provided in the **Web Items** window to the template (via Drag&Drop), author texts, create HTML tables for structuring the contents of your web application and carry out many more design-specific steps. The layout area represents your drawing area, so to speak.

▶ **"HTML" tab**

The HTML view shows the HTML code corresponding to the layout view. The elements created in the layout view are converted to HTML and can be edited here as you would do in a text editor. Word-processing functions like search and replace are available. The undo function, which lets you undo steps that you carried out inadvertently, is also supported. However, this function discards all changes you made after switching from layout to HTML mode. Optionally, you can edit the HTML code in an external HTML editor by saving the created web template locally on your computer using the **Export to File...** function. The HTML syntax in the HTML mode is colored and is divided into several areas, as shown in the following table.

Syntax element	Color
String constants (normal text)	Black
HTML	Blue
BW-specific contents like SAP BW object tags, SAP BW URLs and SAP BW texts	Red
Comments	Gray

Table 5.1 Coloring of the Individual Syntax Elements in HTML Mode

There are other tabs within the HTML mode (see Figure 5.17, 2 and 3):

More tabs

▶ **"Text mode" tab**

The text mode is an editing mode of the BEx Web Application Designer. In text mode, you can edit the web template as pure text and use the functions from the Web API, which cannot be supported in the layout view. From the HTML view, you can change to text mode via **Text mode** (Figure 5.17, 2b) and edit the following web templates:

▶ Web templates containing frame sets

▶ Web templates with objects that are only completely defined in context with the execution of command URLs. This includes web templates where, for example, the ITEM_ID or ITEM_CLASS parameters are missing.

▷ Web template fragments used in combination with the **Web Template** web item

Some functions of the Web Application Designer are not available in text mode, though:

▷ Change to the layout or HTML view

▷ Properties dialog for web items

▷ Inserting and editing charts

Please note that you cannot change back to HTML or layout mode from the text mode. You might be able to reopen it in another mode— only if you close the template— because when opening a saved web template, the system checks in which mode the web template can be edited, and then opens it either in layout or in text mode:

▶ If the web template can be edited in layout view, it will be opened in layout view.

▶ If the web template contains frame sets or template fragments, it is directly opened in text mode. Thus, by using appropriate comments, for example, you can ensure that a web template is immediately opened in text mode.[7] For example, the following comment in the HTML source code results in your being able to automatically open the web template in text mode: `<!-- texteditonly -->`.

▶ If the web template is not editable in layout view or text mode, it is opened in HTML view. From the HTML view, you can change to text mode.

▶ **"Overview" tab**
The **Overview** tab (Figure 5.17, 3) lists all web items with information about the master web item, the data provider, the query or the query view, respectively.

5.2.4 The "Properties" Window

The **Properties** window lets you define the properties of web templates and web items. From here, you create data providers for your web appli-

---

7 You can find further information on this subject in Note 668666 of SAP Service Marketplace. Go to *service.sap.com/notes*.

cation and assign them to the individual web items of your web template. You change the properties of your web items or of your web template and assign every created object a unique name by which you can address it via a command URL, for example, and override its attributes.

The **Properties** window is divided into three areas.

Structure of the window

▶ In Figure 5.18, the first area highlighted (1) displays a dropdown box where the web template and all web items contained therein are available for selection. Here, you select the element whose properties you want to define.

▶ In the second area highlighted (2), you specify the properties of web templates or specific web items, depending on the settings of the dropdown box. Two tabs are available for this task—**Generic** and **Web Item**.

Figure 5.18 The "Properties" Window

▶ On the **Generic** tab (see Figure 5.19, 1), assign a unique name (2) to every web item within a web template. If the name has been used, the Web Application Designer automatically truncates it by the last character. By assigning a unique name, you can address every web item in *command URLs* and change commands such as the number of rows to be displayed in a table.

▶ Also on the Generic tab, but in the DataProviders area (3), create new data providers or select an existing data provider from the dropdown box and assign it to the web item. Every data provider is assigned a unique name as well, by which it can be addressed using command URLs. In this way, you can transfer specific selection criteria, for example, to the data provider and change the drilldown of the current navigational state in the web application. As a data provider, you can either select a query or a query view.

▶ On the **Web Item** tab (4), the properties belonging to the individual objects are on hand and can be set according to your needs.

▶ A context-sensitive help function is available (5). An explanation is displayed for every property of a web item.

▶ If you want to reuse the settings that you specified for web items, you can store the created web item in a library (6).

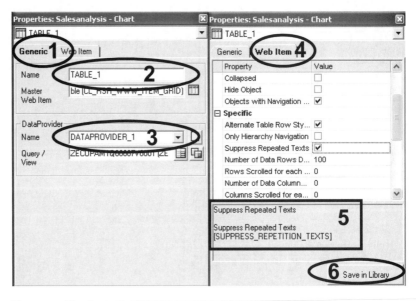

Figure 5.19 The Contents of the "Generic" and "Web Item" Tabs

5.3 The BEx Web Analyzer

Like the Excel-based BEx Analyzer, the BEx Web Analyzer is a web-based frontend tool provided by SAP, which you can use to present your queries and query views and further analyze your data.

Because most of the *BEx Web Analyzer* functions are similar to those of the *SAP BEx Analyzer*, we have chosen not to describe them here; instead, please refer to the corresponding discussions in Chapter *4, The SAP Business Explorer Query Designer*.

The BEx Web Analyzer (see Figure 5.20) is a standalone web application that was created in the BEx Web Application Designer and can be called via a URL by specifying the template ID 0ANALYZER. Moreover, you can call the BEx Web Analyzer as an iView in the SAP Enterprise Portal. However, the BEx Web Analyzer is only available as of SAP BW Release 3.5, because it uses web items that are supported only with this release.

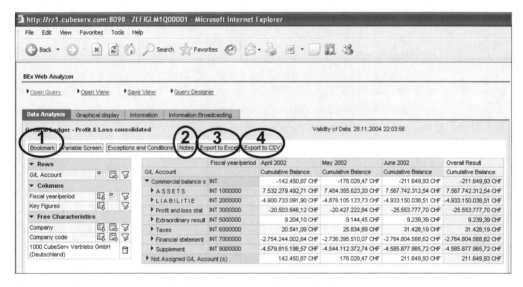

Figure 5.20 The Structure of the BEx Web Analyzer with Some of Its Various Functions

In the following sections, we'll describe some web functionalities that are also provided by the BEx Web Analyzer.

Bookmark

You can set a bookmark (see Figure 5.20, 1) to retrieve a specific navigational state of the query at a later stage. The system creates a bookmark-enabled URL that is shown in the address line of your web browser (see Figure 5.21). To be able to access the bookmarks, you can save the relevant URL in the favorites of your Internet browsers, or by using copy and paste in other files. You can also copy the URL to your e-mail program and send it via e-mail. The recipient can call the link in his or her browser and the navigational state that you saved is then displayed to that user.

 The viewed data, however, is not saved with the URL; instead, it is redetermined with every call. Therefore, if the data that has been set has changed during the time that the the bookmark is created and the next time it is called, you will see the current data displayed.

Figure 5.21 Bookmark-Enabled URL

Notes

Calling this function (see Figure 5.20, 2) brings you to the BW Document Browser (see Figure 5.22). This browser is displayed in a new Internet browser window that lets you create documents on the navigational state, or change or delete existing documents.

Therefore, you can leave notes to all users or a group of users, depending on their authorization. For example, you can create a note regarding why customer xyz, who usually accounts for the highest sales, has achieved a much lower volume in this month as compared to the previous months. To make full use of the documents on the navigational state at the characteristic value and key figure level, the individual characteristics to be used must be assigned the attribute **Characteristic is document property** in the InfoObject maintenance (Transaction RSD1).

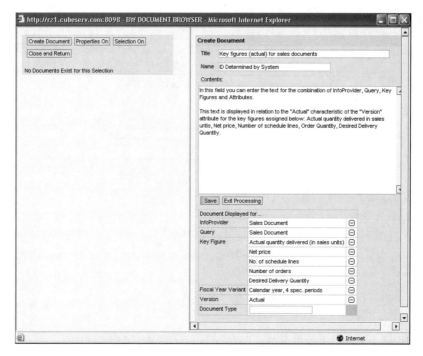

Figure 5.22 The Document Browser from the Web Analyzer

Export to MS Excel 2000

You can export the query data to MS Excel 2000 (see Figure 5.20, 3). The query data is displayed like queries in the BEx Analyzer: You can see the restrictions of the filter and the data in the table. As on the web, exceptions here are highlighted in color. You can further process the query using MS Excel functions, but will not have the opportunity for further navigation in MS Excel for the time being. To navigate, you must have started the BEx Analyzer before calling the **Export to Excel** function. Now refresh the report that you imported in Excel using the OLAP function. After the refresh, all OLAP functions are available in Excel as usual (see Figure 5.23). The export function only includes the data of the navigational state in the BEx Web Analyzer.

Export to CSV

You can also export the query data to a CSV (Comma Separated Value) file (see Figure 5.20, 4). Contrary to the export to MS Excel 2000, the context of the numbers is not visible and the filter information is not available in this format; however, you can import the exported data into a local database like MS Access and continue processing it there.

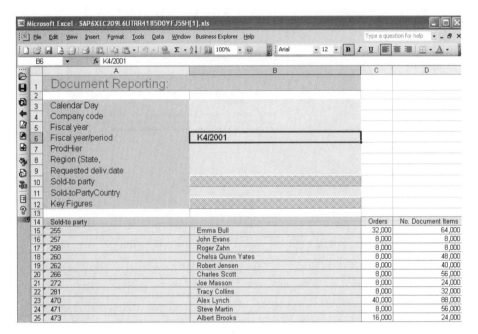

Figure 5.23 Report in MS Excel After Export from the Web Analyzer

The exported data is not restricted to the number of data shown at a time in the BEx Web Analyzer. For several reasons, the standard version of the Web Analyzer only displays 25 rows of the selected data set at a time with the option to scroll. If you use the export functions **Export to Excel** and **Export to CSV**, all data records are exported.

Information

The downside of the presentation of the set variable values and the static filter values is the mere display of the description of the selected value. The key is not shown. In Figure 5.24, the **Static Filter** and **Variable Values** sections only display the description of the selected value, which is not shown. Depending on the property of the respective characteristic in the query, the dynamic filters show the following information:

▶ Key and text

▶ Text and key

▶ Key or text

Depending on the display behavior setting of the characteristic, the information of the set filter is then displayed as well. Changing the display behavior, however, affects only the dynamic filter information, the display in the navigation block and in the tabular presentation; the static filter values and the variable values are not affected.

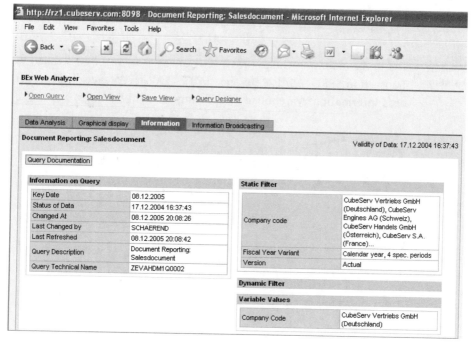

Figure 5.24 The Information Area in the Web Analyzer

5.4 The BEx Web Application Design

The BEx Web Application Design is composed of the most different kinds of parameterizable components and objects. The term *BEx Web Application Design* represents the Customizing-enabled processing logic for web applications.

In the following, we will discuss some of the individual components very explicitly, because you need to understand these objects and properties, as well as the interaction of the components, in order to make optimal use of your numerous options.

5.4.1 Customizing Settings for Web Reporting

For the reporting of SAP BW in general, and also for BEx Web in particular, the Implementation Guide of SAP BW (Transaction SPRO) provides some globally applicable settings that affect the behavior and control of BEx Web. Additionally, there are settings that provide additional functionalities for individual web items.

In general, we recommend that you look at the individual Customizing functions of SAP BW, because BW stores some interesting and important controlling functions (and in most cases, a detailed documentation as well).

Reporting-relevant settings

The Implementation Guide (IMG) (Customizing) of SAP BW is called via Transaction SPRO · **SAP Reference IMG** · **SAP NetWeaver** · **SAP Business Information Warehouse** · **Reporting-relevant Settings**.

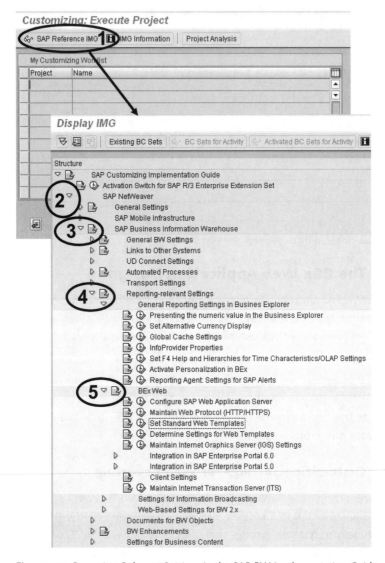

Figure 5.25 Reporting-Relevant Settings in the SAP BW Implementation Guide

Example: Modification of the Standard Web Template and Personalization

Instead of the standard template 0ADHOC, our model company CubeServ Engines wants to use the similar BEx Web Analyzer template 0ANALYZER for ad-hoc reporting on the web. This template is to be extended by the company logo. By exchanging the standard template with the BEx Web Analyzer template, the end user gains new possibilities. For example, it is now possible to open another query and query views on the web, and to navigate in them.

Requirements

In addition, personalization will be activated for end users. They should be allowed to personalize variable values for specific characteristics. The variable is then automatically populated with the saved value when a web application is called.

For now, we will look at the Customizing options for storing alternative templates.

Under **BEx Web · Set Standard Web Templates**, you can store user-defined templates for most of the different BEx Web areas or applications. At the moment, four areas (web applications) are available in which you can replace the web templates predefined by SAP with your own templates. If no entry is stored for the respective web application, the standard template provided by SAP is used instead. The technical name of the SAP BW standard template can be retrieved via the F1 help (place cursor in the field and press **F1**) of the relevant field.

Set standard web templates

The delivered standard web templates can be changed and tailored to meet your own requirements in the current version, just like any other Business Content object. However, we suggest that you create a copy of the standard template and store it here in Customizing.

For the web applications listed in Table 5.2, you can store a user-defined web template.

Template for ad-hoc analysis

Web Application	SAP Standard Template
Ad-hoc analysis	0ADHOC
Broadcasting	0BROADCASTING_TEMPLATE

Table 5.2 For these applications, the SAP standard template can be replaced with a company-specific template.

Web Application	SAP Standard Template
Query precalculation	0QUERY_TEMPLATE_BROADCASTING
Document browser	0DOC_TEMPLATE2

Table 5.2 For these applications, the SAP standard template can be replaced with a company-specific template. (Cont'd.)

Figure 5.26 Set Standard Web Templates

The template for the ad-hoc analysis is retrieved from the Query Designer or the BEx Analyzer when the query is called. It is also retrieved when queries stored in roles or favorites are called, if the entry in the role or the favorites has not been changed manually for another template.

The following steps adjust the standard web template to meet the requirements of our model company CubeServ Engines:

▶ Save the logo to be used in the MIME Repository, if this has not already been done. As with cascading style sheets, you gain access to the MIME Repository via Transaction SO2_MIME_REPOSITORY or Transaction SE80 (see Figure 5.27, Steps 1 to 4).

▶ The web template 0ANALYZER is opened in the Web Application Designer and extended by the company-specific logo (see Figure 5.28, Steps 1 to 6).

Figure 5.27 Storing the Company-Specific Logo in the MIME Repository

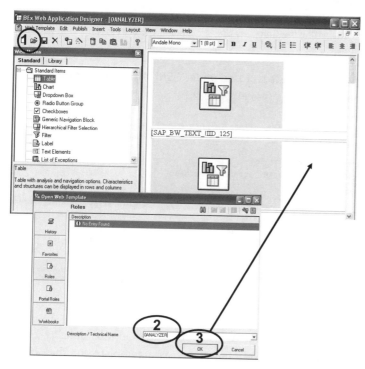

Figure 5.28 Integrating the Company-Specific Logo in the 0ANALYZER Template

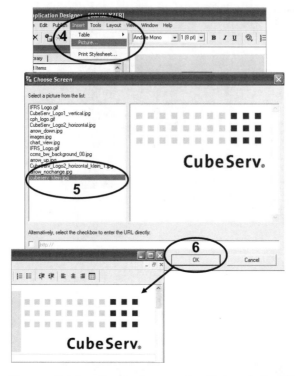

Figure 5.28 Integrating the Company-Specific Logo in the 0ANALYZER Template (Cont'd.)

▶ The modified template is stored under CSANALYZER0 **CubeServ Standard Web Templates** (see Figure 5.29).

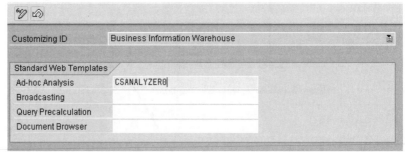

Figure 5.29 Storing the Modified Company-Specific Standard Template

▶ The newly created template is then stored in Customizing under **Change Settings for Web Templates** as a template for the ad-hoc analysis (see Figure 5.30).

Under **Change Settings for Web Templates**, you get to the window shown in Figure 5.31.

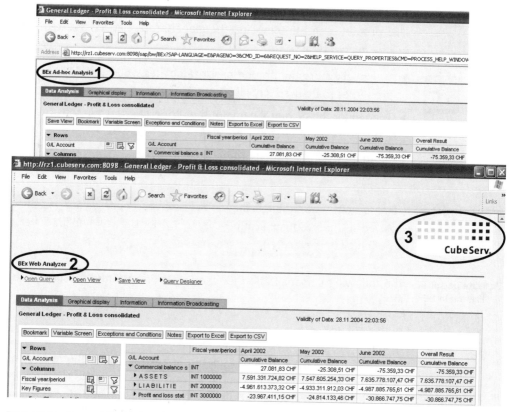

Figure 5.30 Query Call with Standard Template 0ADHOC and Query Call with Modified Template Based on 0ANALYZER and Logo

Figure 5.31 Customizing Setting "Change Settings for Web Templates"

Here you can store a style sheet to be used whenever the template called in the web browser is not assigned a style sheet. You also can store the template properties globally. In this way, you can enforce, for example, that warnings are suppressed in every template, or that every template will rely on precalculated data. However, you still have the option to locally assign specific properties to every template. If you define user-specific properties in the template, the global properties for that template will be overwritten.

▶ To globally store the properties for templates, you must first save the properties to be used globally in the library.

▶ Then enter the technical name of the properties saved in the library in the field **Template Attributes**, as shown in Figure 5.31.

▶ From now on, the stored properties will be used whenever a template is called.

Please note that although the globally stored properties are not displayed in the Web Application Designer, they are still applied when the template is executed.

Activate personalization in BEx

The following personalization functions can be activated irrespective of each other:

▶ **BEx History**
The workbooks, queries, views, or templates that were last executed by the user are saved and displayed as suggestions in the next open dialog. The created personalization data is stored in the ODS object OPERS_BOD—**Personalization data for the BEx Open dialog**.

▶ **Variables**
Variables selected by the user are stored per user with values that are copied into the query without further inquiry when the report is executed. The saved values are stored in the ODS object OPERS_VAR—**Personalization data for variable replacement**. Via a separate InfoSource with flat file connection, mass data for personalization can be loaded into the BW system as well.

▶ **Web Applications**
The drilldown of a report can be saved per user and template, if desired. The saved values are stored in the ODS object OPERS_WTE—**Personalization data for web template drilldown**. The personalization for web templates uses the bookmark technology.

> Please note that once activated, the personalization can no longer be deactivated; however, you can delete the ODS objects in order to disable the personalization option.

In the following example, the personalization option for the SAP BW system of our model company is activated:

▶ Open the personalization options in Customizing via the path **Transaction SPRO · SAP Reference IMG · SAP NetWeaver · SAP Business Information Warehouse · Reporting-relevant Settings · General Reporting Settings in Business Explorer**.

▶ Enable all three personalization options.

▶ All necessary ODS objects and programs are set up.

5.4.2 Object Tags

Basically, a web template is like a text document with HTML tags and JavaScript-specific code that can be interpreted, processed, and presented by a browser. The individual web items with their special attributes and the corresponding values, as well as the defined data providers and the properties of the web template itself, are objects and are integrated in the web template as HTML code using so-called *object tags*. These object tags define the properties of the web templates, the data providers, and the web items.

If a web item is dragged from the list of web items in the **Web Items** window to the layout area of the Web Application Designer, the Web Application Designer automatically converts the web item to object tags in the background (see Figure 5.32).

If a web template is called in a browser, the content of the template is first processed by the underlying SAP BW logic. If the SAP BW logic encounters an object tag, it searches for the owner of the object who is specified under the OWNER attribute within the object. With SAP BW objects, like web items, data providers and web template properties, the OWNER is filled with the value SAP_BW. The SAP BW logic recognizes that this is its own object, processes the information of the object, and converts it to HTML code, which, in turn, can be interpreted by the Internet browser.

Object Tags

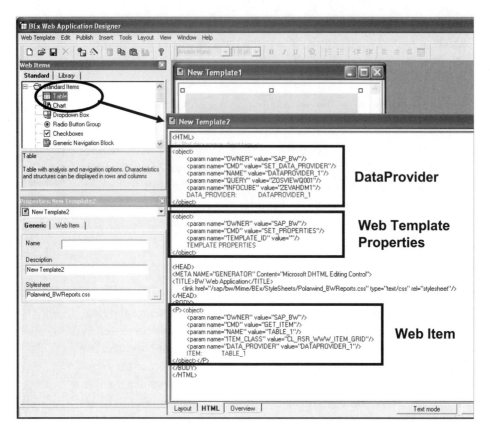

Figure 5.32 The Object Tags in the HTML Mode of the WAD

By changing the properties of a web item, a web template or a data provider in the **Properties** window of the Web Application Designer, the Web Application Designer automatically changes the relevant object tags in the background. An object tag consists of an opening (⟨object⟩) and a closing (⟨/object⟩) tag. Since the ⟨object⟩ tag is not a SAP BW-specific tag, but belongs to the HTML specification, it can be used in any HTML document. For the SAP BW-specific object tags to be recognized by the Web Application Designer as well, they must contain the OWNER attribute and the appropriate value SAP_BW. When the web template is executed in the browser, only these object tags are replaced with BW-specific contents. The other objects are transferred unchanged to the Internet browser and are processed there.

Two different syntaxes are available for the tag ⟨object⟩:

Syntax 1 ▶ For the BW object tags, the attributes should be set within the object tag in the form of parameter tags, as follows:

```
<object>
    <param name='OWNER' value='SAP_BW'>
    <param name='WIDTH' value='350'>
    ...
</object>
```

▶ Although in text mode, the attributes can be set in the object tag at the beginning: Syntax 2

```
<object WIDTH='350' HEIGHT='234' owner='SAP_BW' ..>
</object>
```

This notation is not recommended by SAP, because it is not supported in the Web Application Designer.

If you edit your web template with an HTML editor, the object tags are partially shown in the non-HTML code mode. Depending on the used HTML editor, there are several options for editing the individual objects. For example, you can edit the size and maintain the attributes of the object tag.

▶ If you use an HTML editor to open a web template, for example, Microsoft FrontPage or Dreamweaver, the SAP BW object tags are displayed as very small icons when you open the template for the first time (see Figure 5.33, Step 1).

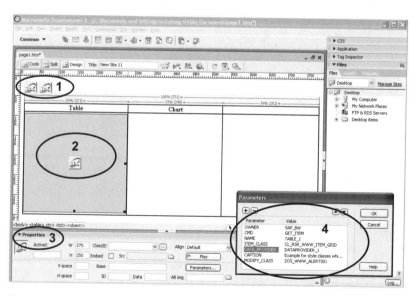

Figure 5.33 Microsoft FrontPage and SAP BW Objects

- You now can place and size the graphical icons per Drag&Drop (Step 2). The size of an object can be controlled only to a limited extent, because, in most cases, the actual size depends on the contents of the SAP BW object.

- Using the context menu, the properties of the SAP BW object can be called via the entry **Properties: ActiveX Control** (Steps 3 and 4). Here, you can change the values of existing attributes, or add other attributes that are supported by SAP BW.

The structure of object tags is always the same. Only the corresponding attributes and their values change, depending on the object.

Important object tags

The following object tags play an important role in BEx web applications:

- Object tag for the properties of web templates

```
<object>
    <param name='OWNER' value='SAP_BW'>
    <param name='CMD' value='SET_PROPERTIES'>
    <param name='TEMPLATE_ID'
    value='technical name of the template'>
    ...
</object>
```

- Object tag for data providers by query

```
<object>
    <param name='OWNER' value='SAP_BW'>
    <param name='CMD' value='SET_DATA_PROVIDER'>
    <param name='NAME' value='freely selectable name'>
    <param name='QUERY' value='technical name of the query'>
    <param name='INFOCUBE' value='technical name of the
                                  query InfoCube'>
    ...
</object>
```

- Object tag for data providers by query view

```
<object>
    <param name='OWNER' value='SAP_BW'>
    <param name='CMD' value='SET_DATA_PROVIDER'>
    <param name='NAME' value='freely selectable name'>
    <param name=' DATA_PROVIDER_ID' value='technical
```

```
   name of the query view'>
      ...
</object>
```

► Object tag for web items

```
<object>
   <param name='OWNER' value='SAP_BW'>
   <param name='CMD' value='GET_ITEM'>
   <param name='NAME' value='freely selectable name'>
   <param name='ITEM_CLASS' value='Item type'>
   <param name='DATA_
PROVIDER' value='Name of the data provider to be assigned'>
      ...
</object>
```

5.4.3 Language Dependency of Web Applications

SAP BW allows you to design all templates (and thus the generated web applications) as language-dependent. When calling the web template in the web browser, all texts are displayed in the logon language, if possible.

In the Administrator Workbench, the texts of the BW objects—like characteristics, key figures, query elements, and variables, for example—are translated into the desired languages using the translation function of the SAP BW. The description of the individual characteristic values is provided in the relevant language from the underlying source system.

In many web applications, however, there are texts (e.g., titles of web items or user-defined text in the web template) that are not stored in SAP BW, and therefore, cannot be translated. SAP BW provides a solution for that as well: In order to be able to use language-dependent elements, a standard ABAP program first needs to be created in the system. This ABAP program does not contain any code. You just access the text elements of this program. In the web template, a placeholder for texts is created using a special syntax. When the template is executed in the web browser, the runtime environment exchanges the placeholder with the appropriate text in the current logon language.

Non-translatable texts

Please note that no text is displayed if the placeholder text does not exist in the current logon language. Unfortunately, the language-dependency concept of SAP BW does not allow for a standard language for text elements that cannot be determined.

Example: Profit and Loss Statement with Language-Dependent Texts

Requirement The Business Intelligence cockpit of our model company CubeServ Engines is to be used by all companies worldwide in the languages German and English. Since they do not want to create a separate template for each language, they decided to use language-dependent texts on the web. Additionally, this variant allows for a later extension to other languages, without having to modify the individual web templates. The end user can therefore log on using his or her preferred language and will be provided with the Business Intelligence cockpit in that same language.

In the following example, the implementation of language-dependent texts is demonstrated using the profit and loss statement discussed in Section 5.1.1.

▶ In Transaction SE38 (ABAP Editor: **Initial Screen**) or SE80 (ABAP Workbench), create an ABAP program (see Figure 5.34). You need a developer key in the respective system to be able to create a program.

  ▷ Assign a technical name to the program and click on **Create**.

  ▷ Assign a text (description) to your program and select the type **Executable program**. Select **Save**, and assign the program to a package, if one exists, or save it as a local object.

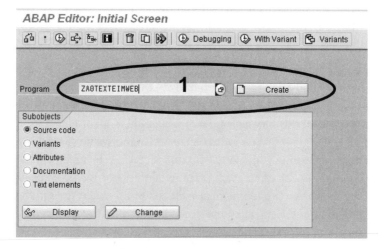

Figure 5.34 Creating an ABAP Program in Transaction SE38 for Language-Dependent Texts in Web Applications

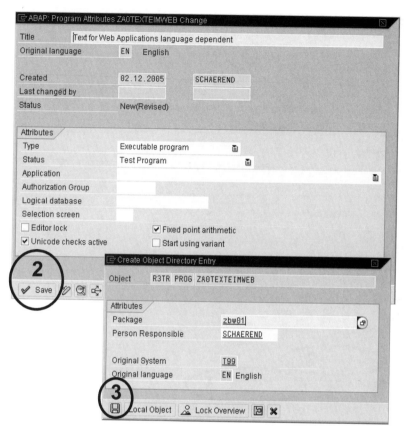

Figure 5.34 Creating an ABAP Program in Transaction SE38 for Language-Dependent Texts in Web Applications (Cont'd.)

▶ The screen shown in Figure 5.35 is displayed. Activate the program you just created (Steps 1 and 2), and go back one step using **F3**.

▶ Under **Subobjects**, select the **Text elements** option and click on **Change** (Steps 3 and 4).

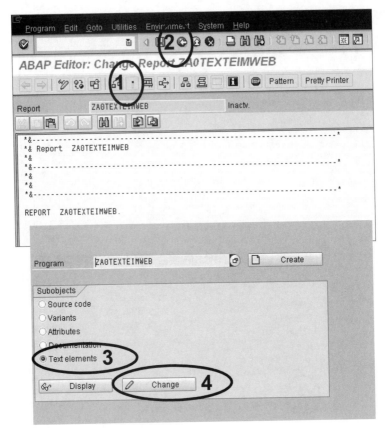

Figure 5.35 The Simple ABAP Program for Language-Dependent Texts in Web Applications Must Now Be Activated.

▶ The screen shown in Figure 5.36 is displayed. Assign a three-digit key for every text element and enter your text (Step 1).

 It is advisable to use three-digit numeric keys. Start at 000 and increase by one (000, 001, 002, 003, etc.).

▶ First save your entries and then activate the text elements.

▶ Via the menu option **Goto · Translation** (Step 2), you can now translate your created text elements into various target languages (Step 3).

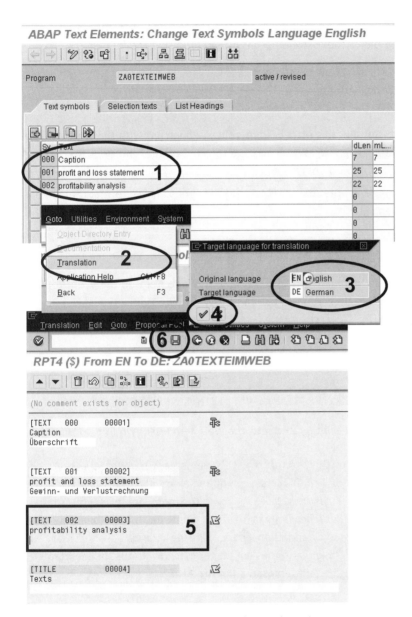

Figure 5.36 Text Elements for Language-Dependent Web Applications

Now that we have created the individual text elements and translated them to the desired target language, we can now integrate them in our web templates as well. You can use the text element as user-defined text in the web template, or as a title in a web item. Depending on the type of use, a different syntax needs to be applied:

▶ In the Web Application Designer, change to the HTML mode of the template. The text element is integrated using the following syntax:

```
<SAP_BW_TEXT PROGRAM='<Techn. prg. name >' KEY='
<Text element key>'>
<SAP_BW_TEXT PROGRAM='ZAOTEXTEIMWEB2' KEY='011'>
```

At runtime, this placeholder is then exchanged with the stored text in the appropriate logon language (e.g., "Gewinn- und Verlustrechnung" or "Profit and Loss Statement").

▶ Using the potential of HTML and CSS, you can also format the text element:

```
<span style="color:#ff000;">
<SAP_BW_TEXT PROGRAM="ZAOTEXTEIMWEB2" KEY="001"></span>
```

▶ To use text elements in the title of the web items in the Web Application Designer, you can use the following two syntax types:

```
SAP_BW_TEXT?PROGRAM=<Techn. prg. name>&
KEY=<Text element key>
```

or

```
SAP_BW_TEXT?PROGRAM=ZAOTEXTEIMWEB2&KEY=001
```

The syntax is integrated into the web item as shown in Figure 5.37.

In addition to the texts of the web elements, the metadata (e.g., the description of InfoObjects and query elements) must exist in the desired languages as well. To maintain the metadata texts, you can log on to the Query Designer or to the Administrator Workbench in the desired language, and then change the descriptions, if necessary. If master data is highlighted as language-relevant, it must be maintained or loaded in the text tables in all desired languages.

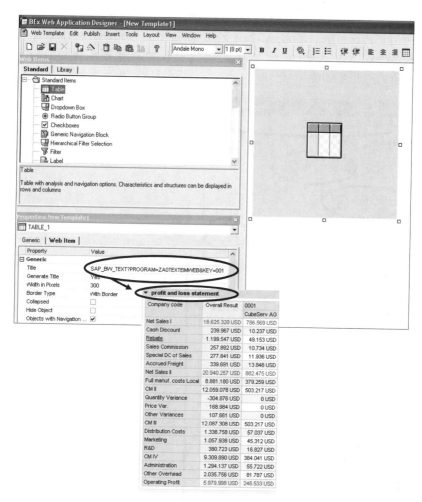

Figure 5.37 Placeholders for Language-Dependent Text Elements in Web Items

5.4.4 The Properties of the Web Template

Every web template has various properties that can be set in the **Properties** window of the Web Application Designer, or entered and edited directly in the associated object tag in HTML mode. One of the web template properties is the context menu of the web application to be created.

You can tailor the context menu of your web application according to your particular needs. If you want a restricted scope of functionality for your web application, for example, so as not to confuse the end users, you can prevent any navigation in the context menu.

First, however, you should become familiar with the individual elements of the **Properties** window. In Figure 5.38, the **Properties** window is shown with the **Generic** tab active on the left, and the **Web Item** tab (5) active on the right.

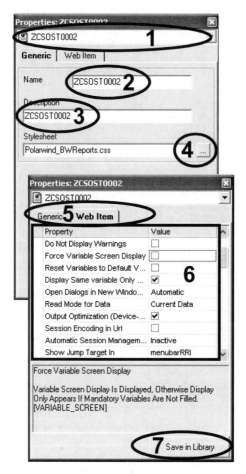

Figure 5.38 Possible Settings for a Web Template

▶ The web template and all the web items integrated in the web template are available for selection in the dropdown box (1). Depending on the selected type (**Template** or **Web Item**), the information and the presentation of the **Generic** tab changes.

▶ The technical name (2) of the web template is filled in only after you saved the template in SAP BW.

▶ You can assign a description (3) to your web template.

- The pushbutton (4) is for selecting and assigning a style sheet to your web template. The assigned style sheet contains formatting information for the browser of the individual defined formats in the web application.

- You can change between the two tabs (5).

- All the properties (6) of the web template or web item (in our case, all attributes of the template) are shown. Many of the properties can be enabled and disabled by marking them; others provide several values for selection in a dropdown box, and still others let you enter user-defined text.

- Eventually, your settings can be saved in a library (7) for later use, for further web templates, or for storing them as global template settings in the Customizing of SAP BW (mark 7).

In the following, the individual properties of a web template are described. We will also describe the technical name belonging to the property under which the property is to be used in the HTML code within the object tag of the web template properties or under which you can change the property via an URL.

Web template properties

Name of the Web Template
Every template has a unique technical name under which it can be accessed directly, and under which the web template was stored in the Web Application Designer (see Figure 5.38, 2).

Use Personalized Web Template, if Available
As of Release 3.0, SAP BW enables you to personalize every web template according to your needs. If a user is presented, for example, with the **Personalize Web Page** entry via the context menu provided in the web application, he or she can decide whether to personalize the navigational state of the web application.

This scenario is likely if only a few web applications are made available to many end users. Because every user has different demands on the data view, but does not want to navigate to the desired view every time the web application is called, you can offer the option of personalization. If you want the personalized state to be opened whenever a specific user opens the web application, you must set a value of X for the web template property USE_PERSONALIZATION. If no user-specific personalization is available when the web application is called, the actual navigational state of the assigned data provider is presented.

Path to a Style Sheet

Under this property, you enter the path of the style sheet to be used for screen presentation. Possibly, the style sheet has already been assigned by the Web Application Designer and is therefore overwritten.

Using JavaScript

Using this property, you can enable or disable the use of JavaScript for your web applications. By using JavaScript, the end user is given more interaction possibilities.

If you disable JavaScript, for example, the context menu can no longer be used and therefore the interaction of users is restricted. The functions of the individual web items are then implemented with standard HTML options. If you create a web application, for example, where little or no navigation is required, you can disable JavaScript for this web template. Less code to be transferred to the browser will be generated on the server-side, which improves the performance (web browser, server, and line). If you don't set or include this property, the use of JavaScript will automatically be enabled for the web browsers MS Internet Explorer and Netscape with a version number >=4.0.

Reloading Modified Page Components

In order not to transfer all data or the complete HTML code to the browser with every single navigation step, SAP BW gives you the option of flicker-free navigation. The communication with the SAP BW system is implemented via a delta technique based on JavaScript. The delta technique is optimized to such an extent that only the changes of the page are transferred, and the page is built without continuously reloading the entire views. But, because this makes higher demands on the web browser, this functionality might not be compatible with all web browsers. If web applications are started with current web browsers (e.g., IE >= 5), they are optimized for a flicker-free screen change. From a certain page size, however, it is more efficient to completely rebuild the web page. Therefore, SAP BW checks this automatically and rebuilds the page, if necessary.

Stateless Navigation

In every end user session, the data of the opened web templates is cached for achieving a quicker response time for more navigation. To optimally use the resources on the application server, the web template property **Stateless Navigation** provides a resource handling of the application server for different reporting scenarios. If you enable the stateless navigation, you are in *stateful mode*. If you do not enable this property, you are using the *stateless mode*.

Web applications in stateful mode are intended for scenarios where very complex and dense query states must be displayed and analyzed. For the users, it is imperative that they receive a quick response time from the web application. The data already requested is cached on the application server and retrieved for further navigation.

Stateful mode

Web applications in stateless mode are particularly suited for mass scenarios; for example, in the Portal environment or in different web cockpits where the users have mainly one view of the data. Here, it is essential to release any resources on the application server as quickly as possible in order to support a large number of simultaneous users. In contrast to the stateful mode, longer wait times can be acceptable in this case.

Stateless mode

Automatic Session Management

You can use the template property **Automatic Session Management** (USE_PAGE_WRAPPER) to optimize the management of system resources on the application server.[8] For example, you can use this function if executing a web application requires a lot of memory, or, if you anticipate a large number of users working simultaneously. As long as a session is valid for a specific user, it occupies memory on the application server. A server does not always recognize when a session is terminated, and therefore, reserves memory for it until the maximum timeout value set on the server is reached.

Open Dialogs in New Windows

Via the **Open dialogs in new windows** property, the display behavior of dialogs can be controlled. For example, the dialogs for selecting filters are presented in a new browser window.

Force Variable Screen Display

If you use queries for the data providers in your web template that contain variables, you can use this attribute to force the display of the variable screen when the web template is called. If you disable this property, only the attempt to suppress the display is made. If, for example, you're using mandatory variables in your queries, which are ready for input and aren't populated at the time the web template is called, the variable screen will still be displayed.

---

8 OSS Note 589272 provides further information on this subject.

Display Same Variable Only Once

If you're using several data providers with different queries containing variables in your web template, an entry field is created for every variable included in the query when the web template is called. Although, if a variable (e.g., for the fiscal year) were the same in all queries, you would also have to enter a value for every variable of a query.

This might make sense, because you can use a query giving you the current year and another query giving you the previous year in another context. But if the fiscal year were to be the same for all queries of a web template, it would be very cumbersome and confusing to enter the same value several times. Therefore, to ensure that you have to enter the same variables for this scenario only once, set the value of this property to **merge**. If queries with variables from different InfoProviders are used, the possible entries are read automatically from the master data table.

Reset Variables to Default Values

If you use a query view for a data provider that contains variables, the variable values saved in the query view that are offered to you in the variable screen can be reset to the originally defined values of the respective variable by means of this attribute.

Do Not Display Warnings

Enable this property if you want to suppress the display of warnings.

Do Not Display System Messages

If you want to suppress the display of system messages in your web application, you can control this using this property. If you want to display a system message only once per day and user, you can select the value 'CONDITIONAL'.

Read Mode for Data

As soon as you call a web template in a web browser, the underlying data is determined by the OLAP processor. This can take a very long time. For example, if you defined reports that return a large result set, or if you use several queries in a web cockpit, you can precalculate the corresponding data and the entire HTML page. But, your options for navigating through the displayed data are very limited.

Use of precalculated data

The following scenarios are likely:

▶ **NEW**
Current data is read from the database via the OLAP processor. If you're using the OLAP cache the data might be read from this cache.

- ▶ **STORED**

  Only precalculated data is used for generating the web application. The complete HTML code for the output is generated at runtime. If there is no precalculated data, an error message is displayed. This could serve as a control; however, it is not suitable for end users, because they cannot further execute the desired web application.

- ▶ **HYBRID**

  Precalculated data should be used and if there is none, the current data is requested from the database. This option does not cause an error message if no precalculated data exists.

- ▶ **STATIC**

  Precalculated HTML pages should be used. The web application has already been stored in the Business Document Service (BDS) of SAP BW as a final HTML document with all associated MIME objects. These HTML pages can be downloaded to the local computer via the BEx Download Scheduler or via WebDav folders and, depending on the configuration, even provide the option of selecting filter values in the precalculated report using one or more dropdown boxes in the web template. If no precalculated HTML pages exist, an error message is issued and the end user cannot execute the desired web application.

- ▶ **STATIC_HYBRID**

  Precalculated HTML pages should be used. If these are missing, the program searches for precalculated data. If this is missing as well, the current data is requested from the database. This is the safest option, but it requires the most resources.

Working with precalculated data or templates significantly shortens the response time of the request to the server, because it is not necessary to search for the data in a potentially large dataset in the database. In the Reporting Agent of the Administrator Workbench, you can precalculate web templates or their data.

Depending on the desired result, several options are available. Precalculated templates or data are particularly suited for Business Intelligence cockpits with restricted navigation options. Managing and calling the individual precalculated data can be very complex, however, because the control logic stored for this purpose requires calling the templates with special URL parameters. In this case, it is recommended that you implement a part of the cockpits as a BSP application. In this way, you can, for example, implement a separate role menu via a BSP application that adopts the task of calling the individual precalculated templates. Depend-

Options

ing on the global selection value, for example, the desired fiscal year period, the correct URL is generated by the BSP application and requests the precalculated template or data without generating an error message.

Only very little effort is necessary for creating BSP applications using the standard BEx Web Framework. Very complex Business Intelligence cockpits can be implemented within just a few days, which would hardly be possible with JavaScript, HTML, and the BEx Web only.

Output Optimization (Device-Dependent)

The web frontend of SAP BW provides functions for the most different kinds of presentation devices. For example, you can call the URL of a web application via a PDA. Since the presentations and functions vary, depending on the end user device, SAP BW automatically recognizes the relevant presentation device and optimizes the HTML output of the web application according to the setting of this attribute. You can also create specific web templates for different kinds of presentation devices that are then executed automatically, depending on the requesting presentation device. See Section 5.9 for more information.

Session Encoding in URL

After you called a web template in the web browser, you had to log on once to the SAP Web Application Server (SAP Web AS). On the one hand, the purpose of this logon was for checking if you had the necessary authorizations; on the other hand, a new session was opened. Under this session, all relevant data is saved for the communication of the SAP Web AS with your Internet browser.

Cookie In order for the Web Application Server to reuse the previously used data for another navigation step in a stateful web application, it needs to know with which session it is dealing. For this purpose, the required information is stored in a cookie on the user computer. The cookie information is then transferred to the Web Application Server with every new request.

Under certain conditions, however, the session handling using cookies can cause problems. In this case, you can implement the session encoding in the URL using this property. However, no session bundling is then available for different web applications, as you would have with a cookie, so that every web application (requested web template) requires a separate session on the server. For example, if you integrate a BEx Web Application in a stateless BSP application (BC-BSP), the session cookie of the BEx Web Application will be sent along to the BSP application. Due to the stateless property of the BSP application, however, the session is ended and the BEx Web Application terminates with a timeout. If, instead of the session cookie, the session encoding is carried out via the URL, the BSP application does not receive any session information.

Show Jump Target In

Since Release 3.0, web applications also allow you to use the report-to-report interface and thus to jump to other reports. The possible jump targets are provided via the context menu. In the standard version, the target reports are always displayed in a new window. Using this property, you can control where, that is, in which window, the target report should be displayed.

Don't make an entry if the jump target should be presented in a new window. To present it in a frame, enter the name of the frame. You can also call the target report in an existing browser window. For this purpose, enter the name of the window. The name of the window is specified via a JavaScript call. You can then use this name to access the window.

```
window.open(url,name of the window,window properties);
```
JavaScript syntax

If you enter a window name that does not exist, a new window will still be opened.

5.4.5 Data Providers

In Section 5.1.2, we alluded to data providers. In the following, the functionality of data providers will be illustrated in more detail.

Creating a Data Provider in the Web Application Designer

In the examples provided in the previous sections, we frequently mentioned assigning a data provider. This means the following:

▶ After you have dragged a web item to the layout area of the Web Application Designer, the **Generic** tab of the **Properties** window contains the **Data Provider** area (see Figure 5.39, Steps 1 and 2).

▶ You now have the option to create a new data provider by clicking on the appropriate button (Step 3).

▶ The Web Application Designer automatically assigns the logical name DATAPROVIDER_n, where n represents a consecutive unique number. Every time the button is used (Step 3), the Web Application Designer adds a new data provider to the template (visible only in HTML mode) and assigns a logical name with a consecutive number. The created data providers are then available for selection in a dropdown box.

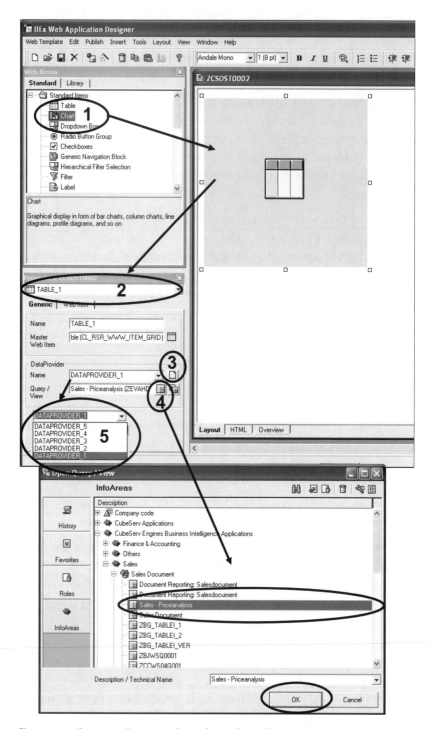

Figure 5.39 Creating a Data Provider in the Web Application Designer

- Until now, the data providers were defined only in the web template. In order to use the data provider effectively, though, it must be assigned a data source. This is done using the corresponding buttons (Step 4): If the data provider is to be based on a query, click on the left button. If it is to be based on a query view, click on the right button.

- An **Open** dialog is displayed (see Figure 5.39). Select the desired query or query view, and click on **OK** to confirm.

- Now you can assign the data provider a specific name, which can be used to access it via command URLs and to apply various commands. As shown under Step 5, click on the suggested name (DATAPROVIDER_n) of the Web Application Designer and simply overwrite it. You can now assign the data provider to every web item of your web template.

Creating a Data Provider in HTML Mode

The data provider can also be created manually in HTML code using object tags. The parameters or attributes listed in Table 5.3 are indispensable for defining a data provider.

You can also append additional commands to the data provider definition, which we'll discuss later in this book. For example, when defining the data provider, you can immediately filter via the value of a characteristic.

Attribute	Description
DATA_PROVIDER	Logical name of the data provider
DATA_PROVIDER_ID	Key for a query view
QUERY	Technical name of a query
INFOCUBE	Technical name of the InfoProvider
VARIANT	Name of the variant for populating variables
HOME_FRAME	Name of the main frame

Table 5.3 Possible Object Tag Attributes for Creating a Data Provider

To identify that a data provider is being created, the 'CMD' parameter must be assigned the value 'SET_DATA_PROVIDER'.

Examples of a query as the basis of a data provider can be found in Section 5.4.2.

Examples

5.5 Web Items in Detail

Web items are integrated in a web template as placeholders. When the web template is called in an Internet browser while SAP BW is running, they are converted to HTML code from the existing underlying data of the assigned data provider, and are therefore made visible in the created web application. Every web item has different properties that determine the functionalities and the look of the web application. Every attribute of a web item has a technical name that is used for saving a value. For example, the **Title** attribute that exists in every web item has the technical name CAPTION. The value, that is, the title, is saved under this ID and can be changed at runtime via a command URL.

However, not every web item requires a data provider in order to be used and presented in a web application. Some web items use the contents of several data providers, or are for administering the most different kinds of data providers. These include the following web items:

- ▶ Role menu
- ▶ Object catalog of the web application
- ▶ Web template, broadcaster
- ▶ Alert monitor
- ▶ Key figures overview
- ▶ Ad-hoc Query Designer
- ▶ ABC analysis
- ▶ Simulation prediction

Master web items   *Master web items* are all web items that are provided by SAP BW on the **Standard** tab of the **Web Items** window in the Web Application Designer, as well as all web items that were saved in libraries.

Every web item has different attributes (properties), some of which are predefined with default values.

- ▶ For example, the attribute **Number of rows displayed together** of the **Table** master web item (see Figure 5.40, Step 1) is predefined with a value of 100.
- ▶ After a master web item has been added to the layout area of a web template (Step 2), the web item is assigned a data provider (Step 3).
- ▶ From then on, you can change the attributes of the web item that was added to the web template. In this way, you are creating your own

user-defined web item, which you can save as a master web item in libraries for later use.

In the following, the individual web items are presented with their generic and specific attributes. You can specify the individual settings of the web items in the Web Application Designer in the **Properties** window of the respective web item, or completed and edited in the HTML code in the corresponding object tag. Table 5.4 gives you an overview of the web items provided in the Web Application Designer.

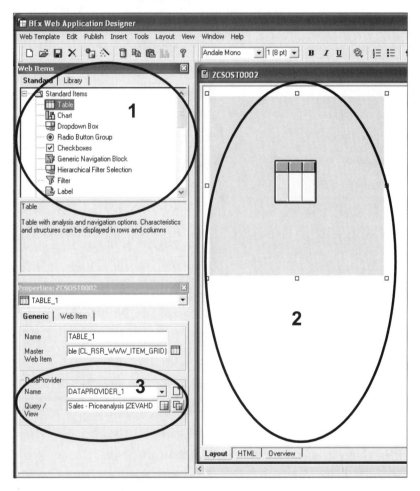

Figure 5.40 Master Web Items

Web Item	Item Class
Table	CL_RSR_WWW_ITEM_GRID
Chart	CL_RSR_WWW_ITEM_CHART
Dropdown box	CL_RSR_WWW_ITEM_FILTER_DDOWN
Radio button group	CL_RSR_WWW_ITEM_FILTER_RADIO
Checkboxes	CL_RSR_WWW_ITEM_FILTER_CHECKBOX
Generic navigation block	CL_RSR_WWW_ITEM_NAV_BLOCK
Hierarchical filter selection	CL_RSR_WWW_ITEM_FILTER_HIERDD
Filter	CL_RSR_WWW_ITEM_FILTER
Label	CL_RSR_WWW_ITEM_LABEL
Text elements	CL_RSR_WWW_ITEM_TEXT_ELEMENTS
List of exceptions	CL_RSR_WWW_ITEM_EXCEPTION
List of conditions	CL_RSR_WWW_ITEM_CONDITION
Alert monitor	CL_RSR_WWW_ITEM_ALERT_MONITOR
Role menu	CL_RSR_WWW_ITEM_MENU
Ticker	CL_RSR_WWW_ITEM_TICKER
Map	CL_RSR_WWW_ITEM_WEBMAP CL_RSR_WWW_ITEM_MAPLAYER
Individual document	CL_RSR_WWW_ITEM_DOC
List of documents	CL_RSR_WWW_ITEM_DOC_LIST
Data provider information	CL_RSR_WWW_ITEM_XML_QUERYVIEW
Object catalog of the web application	CL_RSR_WWW_ITEM_XML_CATALOG
Web template	CL_RSR_WWW_ITEM_TEMPLATE
Broadcasters	CL_RSRD_WWW_ITEM_BROADCASTER
Key figures overview	CL_RSR_WWW_ITEM_KYF_WATCHLIST
Query View Selection	CL_RSR_WWW_ITEM_VIEW_DROP_DOWN
Ad-hoc Query Designer	CL_RSR_WWW_ITEM_QUERY_DEF
ABC classification	CL_RS_DME_ABC_WEB_WWW_ITEM_ABC
Simulation prediction	CL_RS_DME_WWW_WHATIF_WEB_IT_NW

Table 5.4 List of All Web Items and the Corresponding ABAP OO Processing Classes

Generic Attributes

Since every web item fulfills a different task, the individual web items possess different attributes. Some of these attributes are the same for all web items, however, and are therefore contained in at least one web item.

These attributes are called **generic attributes** and are presented as such in the Web Application Designer (see Figure 5.41, Step 3). The specific web item attributes are offered under **Specific** in the **Properties** window (Step 4).

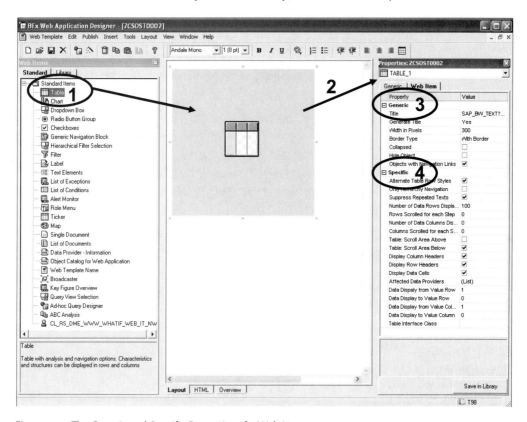

Figure 5.41 The Generic and Specific Properties of a Web Item

In the following, you are first presented the generic web item attributes.

Logical Name of a Web Item

Because every web item can be used several times in a web template and several web items can occur in general, every web item in a web template must be assigned a unique logical name. This logical name can then be used to address the web item using command URLs. Thus, you can, for example, populate the individual properties of a web item with new values at runtime.

SAP recommends that you adhere to the naming conventions that are also supported by the Web Application Designer: The name should contain a maximum of 30 characters and consist of the characters A-Z, 0-9 and the underscore "_", while it should not begin or end with "_". Adhering to these conventions simplifies the upgrade to future SAP releases.

Key of a Web Item

If a web item from a library is used, the ITEM_ID attribute is generated in the corresponding object tag of the HTML code and the relevant value is populated with the technical name of the web item from the library.

Example of the corresponding object tag

```
<object>
    <param name="OWNER" value="SAP_BW">
    <param name="CMD" value="GET_ITEM">
    <param name="NAME" value="TABLE_1">
    <param name="ITEM_ID" value="ZOSTABLE001">
    <param name="DATA_PROVIDER" value="DATAPROVIDER_1">
    ITEM:TABLE_1
</object>
```

Class Name of the Web Item Class

If a standard web item is used in the web template, the ITEM_CLASS attribute is generated in the corresponding object tag of the HTML code and the relevant value is populated with the ABAP Objects class that generates the output. The class name for the table is, for example, CL_RSR_WWW_ITEM_GRID.

Example of the corresponding object tag

```
<object>
    <param name="OWNER" value="SAP_BW">
    <param name="CMD" value="GET_ITEM">
    <param name="NAME" value="TABLE_1">
    <param name="ITEM_CLASS" value="CL_RSR_WWW_ITEM_GRID">
    <param name="DATA_PROVIDER" value="DATAPROVIDER_1">
    ITEM:TABLE_1
</object>
```

Logical Name of the Data Provider for the Web Item

As is the case with web items, every data provider of a web template requires a unique logical name. This logical name can then be used to specifically address the data provider using a command URL. In that way, you can, for example, apply filter commands to exactly one or several data providers. The recommendation for the naming convention applies here as well.

Title

Every web item can be assigned a title that is also displayed in the generated web application. If the attribute is not populated, the processing logic tries to determine a good default value. For example, the description of the underlying query is used as a title. If you enter the title as user-defined text, it is always displayed, regardless of the logon language. The title can also be assigned, however, depending on the language. In this case, instead of the text, a text element from an ABAP program needs to be stored. The following syntax is required for this purpose:

```
SAP_BW_TEXT?PROGRAM=<Techn. prg. name>&
   KEY=<Text element key>
SAP_BW_TEXT?PROGRAM=ZAOTEXTEIMWEB&KEY=001
```

Syntax

Depending on the logon language, the text element is used in the relevant language (if maintained). If the text element is not maintained in the logon language, the text to be displayed remains empty. Please refer to Section 5.4.3 for more information on using and maintaining language-dependent texts. You should note that the title is displayed in the web application only if the attribute **Generate title** is active.

Generate Title

In order to be able to present the value entered under the **Title** attribute in the web application, the **Generate title** property must be active. In addition to the possible settings for activating or deactivating, you can enclose the web item in a border without generating another row for the title (see Figure 5.43). In this way, you can implement all border types that are available for selection under the **Border type** attribute (BORDER_STYLE) without generating a title row. For the title, the SAPBEXTable-Caption style is used that is predefined in the delivered style sheet files.

Width in Pixels

For all web items, you can predefine a minimum width. Per default, all web items are predefined with a width of 300 points. If the contents of the web item exceed the specified width, the browser increases the width automatically. Therefore, you can only set the width to a certain extent. The specified width is definitely used for graphics and maps. If you want to design the width of a web item dynamically, depending on its contents, set the value to 0. The browser then determines the width.

Border Type

Depending on the setting, a border is created for the web item. The following types are available for the web item:

▶ **No Frames**

No border is generated. If the **Generate title** attribute is set to **Yes** (GENERATE_CAPTION=X), the following CSS-defined format is used for the non-existing frame:
SAPBEXBorderlessFlexBox.

▶ **Web Item with Border**

A border is created for the web item; however, it will only be displayed if the **Generate title** attribute is set to **Yes** or BORDER (GENERATE_CAP-TION=X or GENERATE_CAPTION=BORDER). For this border, the CSS-defined format SAPBEXBorderFlexBox is used.

▶ **For Form**

The contents of the web item is displayed with a blue background if the following standard-defined CSS format is used for this setting:
SAPBEXFlexBoxFormBg

▼ No Frames					Sales Actual	CM II Actual
Posting period	Company code		Value Type for Reporting	Version	USD	USD
Jan	1000 CubeServ Vertriebs GmbH (Deutschland)	Actual		Actual	3.007.809	1.002.603
	2000 CubeServ Engines AG (Schweiz)	Actual		Actual	698.928	232.976

▼ Web Item with Border					Sales Actual	CM II Actual
Posting period	Company code		Value Type for Reporting	Version	USD	USD
Jan	1000 CubeServ Vertriebs GmbH (Deutschland)	Actual		Actual	3.007.809	1.002.603
	2000 CubeServ Engines AG (Schweiz)	Actual		Actual	698.928	232.976
	2100 CubeServ Handels GmbH (Österreich)	Actual		Actual	772.572	257.524

▼ For Form					Sales Actual	CM II Actual
Posting period	Company code		Value Type for Reporting	Version	USD	USD
Jan	1000 CubeServ Vertriebs GmbH (Deutschland)	Actual		Actual	3.007.809	1.002.603
	2000 CubeServ Engines AG (Schweiz)	Actual		Actual	698.928	232.976
	2100 CubeServ Handels GmbH (Österreich)	Actual		Actual	772.572	257.524
	2200 CubeServ S.A. (France)	Actual		Actual	1.839.160	613.053
	2400 CubeServ (Italia) S.p.A.	Actual		Actual	1.100.411	366.804
	2500 CubeServ IT Services AG	Actual		Actual	1.138.685	379.562
	3000 CubeServ Engines Ltd. (USA)	Actual		Actual	2.592.546	864.182
	5000 CubeServ Japan Co., Ltd.	Actual		Actual	860.138	286.713
	6000 CubeServ (México) S.A.	Actual		Actual	1.995.875	665.292

Figure 5.42 The Different Border Types for a Web Item

Collapsed

Every web item can be generated in a collapsed state (CLOSED='X'). In this case, only the title row and the expand/collapse icon are displayed. The actual contents of the web item are not presented in the web browser for the time being (see Figure 5.43). The width of the web item in collapsed state is determined by the value of the **Width** attribute (WIDTH). In the expanded state, the set width might be exceeded, because the width depends on the contents of the web item and is not truncated by the browser.

Still, there are some more dependencies on other attributes:

▶ For the web item to be shown as collapsed, the **Generate title** attribute (GENERATE_CAPTION='X') must be activated; otherwise, this setting is not effective and the web item is presented as expanded.

▶ To provide the expand/collapse icon, the **Objects with navigation links** attribute (GENERATE_LINKS='X') must be activated as well; otherwise, only the title of the collapsed web item is shown.

▶ If the object is collapsed, the HTML code for this web item is not generated.

▸ Caption of Web Item Attribute

▾ Caption of Web Item Attribute

				Sales Actual	CM II Actual
Posting period	Company code	Value Type for Reporting	Version	USD	USD
Jan	1000 CubeServ Vertriebs GmbH (Deutschland)	Actual	Actual	3.007.809	1.002.603
	2000 CubeServ Engines AG (Schweiz)	Actual	Actual	698.928	232.976
	2100 CubeServ Handels GmbH (Österreich)	Actual	Actual	772.572	257.524
	2200 CubeServ S.A. (France)	Actual	Actual	1.839.160	613.053

Figure 5.43 The Expand/Collapse Function of the Generated Web Item

Hide Object

The individual web items can be added to a web application in a hidden state as well. The web item is then known to the web application and can be addressed via its logical name, but its content is not returned. Using a command URL, for example, you can hide a web item (e.g., a table), and simultaneously unhide another web item (e.g., a chart). Then, the HTML code of the hidden web item is not generated.

Objects with Navigation Links

In the default setting, every web item is generated with navigation links. Depending on the web item, this setting has different effects. In general, it controls the provided navigation options. For example, the **Table** web item with active navigation links also provides the context menu. Without navigation links, the context menu is not available.

You can effectively implement this property if you want to use, for example, specific web templates for printing, or for presenting overview information in a Business Intelligence cockpit (i.e., a simple navigation with buttons will be used). The processing in SAP BW can therefore be accelerated, because less HTML and JavaScript code needs to be generated. The expand/collapse icon in the title row is displayed only if navigation links are created; however, displaying the expand/collapse icon also requires a title. Therefore, you need to set the value of the **Generate title** attribute (GENERATE_CAPTION='X') to **Yes**.

Affected Data Providers

If you're using the context menu of the table for navigating and filtering, for example, the used commands are sent and applied to the data provider assigned to the table. This data provider might have been assigned to a chart as well. If you now set a filter for a characteristic within the table, not only the table but also the chart is restricted to the selected filter value. If the chart is also populated with data from a second logical data provider, the filter commands of the table will only apply to the table.

If you want the filtering and navigation of the table to be applied to other data providers as well (provided the other data providers contain the same elements), you can select the affected data providers in a list (see Figure 5.44). All data providers of the web template are included in this list. The commands of the table are then applied to all data providers listed.

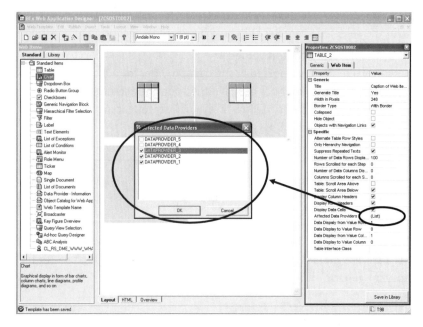

Figure 5.44 List of Affected Data Providers

Master Data Read Mode

Using this attribute, you can control the read mode and therefore, the provided characteristic values of the web items. The following settings are available:

▶ **M: All values from the master data table**

All characteristic values from the master data table are available for selection. With this setting, values might be displayed that don't occur in the data provider under the current filter conditions, and that return the result **No applicable data found** when filtering this value. Under specific conditions, however, this is the most expedient method, because only the values from the master data table need to be read.

▶ **D: Values from the dimension table of the InfoProvider**

This setting provides all values of the characteristic that are posted in the underlying InfoProvider. In this read mode, all entries are determined from the dimension table of the underlying InfoProvider. This read mode might return the result **No applicable data found** when filtering a value, because the current drilldown state is not fully taken into account. This mode is also a means by which the relevant values and the read performance can be displayed. The dimension table of the InfoProvider is read. Because a dimension table only contains the surrogate IDs (SIDs) of the characteristic values, the master data table of the selected characteristic must be read in a second reading step.

▶ **Q: Display only posted values**
Only values that are posted in the data provider for the currently applicable filter conditions are displayed. All currently set filter and variable values are considered, which is why this mode can take very long under certain conditions.

If you choose this mode, the end user cannot make a wrong selection, that is, the result set will never be empty, regardless of the values that are selected from the checkboxes provided.

The following code illustrates the definition of a standard web item (in this case the **Table** web item) in HTML code, using the object tags and all relevant generic attributes:

Example code
```
<object>
    <param name="OWNER" value="SAP_BW">
    <param name="CMD" value="GET_ITEM">
    <param name="NAME" value="TABLE_1">
    <param name="ITEM_CLASS" value="CL_RSR_WWW_ITEM_GRID">
    <param name="DATA_PROVIDER" value="DATAPROVIDER_1">
    <param name="CAPTION" value="Table title">
    <param name="GENERATE_CAPTION" value="X">
    <param name="CLOSED" value=" ">
    <param name="HIDDEN" value=" ">
    <param name="GENERATE_LINKS" value="X">
    <param name="BORDER_STYLE" value="BORDER">
    <param name="WIDTH" value="500">
    ITEM:TABLE_1
</object>
```

The Specific Attributes of the Individual Web Items

In addition to the generic attributes, every web item has specific properties. It would exceed the scope of this book to discuss every single attribute of the individual web items. Most of the attributes are self-explanatory, which is why we won't discuss every single web item.[9]

---

9 The SAP BW online help provides an adequate description of the individual specific attributes. Go to *help.sap.com*.

Appendix D contains a list of all attributes and their technical names for the object tags, with possible values for every web item.

Those web items that require special handling, or are more complicated to implement, are discussed in more detail in the following sections.

5.5.1 Table

Using the **Table** web item, the data of a data provider can be presented in the form of a table, as with the Excel-based BEx Analyzer, on the web. The output table is implemented purely by using HTML. Every field of a table displayed in MS Excel corresponds to a cell in the HTML table on the web (see Figure 5.45).

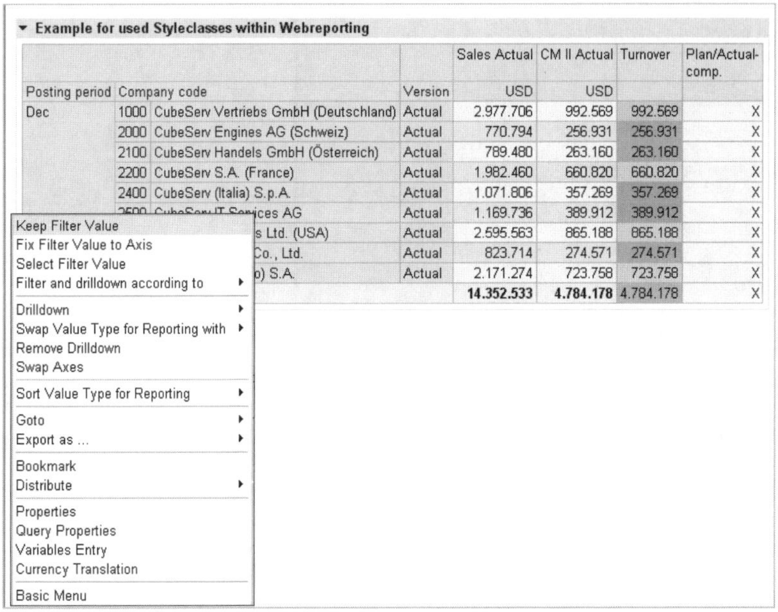

Figure 5.45 Table Web Item with Context Menu in the Browser

Additionally, a hyperlink (reference) to a JavaScript function is generated for the contents of every table cell on the web. Via this hyperlink, a context-sensitive menu (like in BEx Analyzer) is provided for further navigation and for additional functions on the underlying data providers. Depending on the cell type (data cell, characteristic cell, key figure structure cell, etc.), the context menu provides different options. The **Table** web item has special properties that can affect the presentation and function of the generated HTML table. These properties or attributes are described in more detail in the following.

Alternate Table Row Styles

The **Alternate Table Row Styles** property can be disabled or enabled via a checkbox in the Web Application Designer. In the corresponding object tag, the value is either initial or populated with an X. If you activate this property, a different style sheet format will be used for the key figure cells of every other table row (see Figure 5.46).

▼ **Example for used Styleclasses within Webreporting**

Posting period	Company code		Value Type for Reporting	Version	Sales Actual USD	CM II Actual USD	Plan/Actual-comp.
Jan	1000	CubeServ Vertriebs GmbH (Deutschland)	Actual	Actual	3.007.809	1.002.603	X
	2000	CubeServ Engines AG (Schweiz)	Actual	Actual	698.928	232.976	X
	2100	CubeServ Handels GmbH (Österreich)	Actual	Actual	772.572	257.524	X
	2200	CubeServ S.A. (France)	Actual	Actual	1.839.160	613.053	X
	2400	CubeServ (Italia) S.p.A.	Actual	Actual	1.100.411	366.804	X
	2500	CubeServ IT Services AG	Actual	Actual	1.138.685	379.562	X
	3000	CubeServ Engines Ltd. (USA)	Actual	Actual	2.592.546	864.182	X
	5000	CubeServ Japan Co., Ltd.	Actual	Actual	860.138	286.713	X
	6000	CubeServ (México) S.A.	Actual	Actual	1.995.875	665.292	X
Overall Result					**14.006.123**	**4.668.708**	X

▼ **Example for used Styleclasses within Webreporting**

Posting period	Company code		Value Type for Reporting	Version	Sales Actual USD	CM II Actual USD	Plan/Actual-comp.
Jan	1000	CubeServ Vertriebs GmbH (Deutschland)	Actual	Actual	3.007.809	1.002.603	X
	2000	CubeServ Engines AG (Schweiz)	Actual	Actual	698.928	232.976	X
	2100	CubeServ Handels GmbH (Österreich)	Actual	Actual	772.572	257.524	X
	2200	CubeServ S.A. (France)	Actual	Actual	1.839.160	613.053	X
	2400	CubeServ (Italia) S.p.A.	Actual	Actual	1.100.411	366.804	X
	2500	CubeServ IT Services AG	Actual	Actual	1.138.685	379.562	X
	3000	CubeServ Engines Ltd. (USA)	Actual	Actual	2.592.546	864.182	X
	5000	CubeServ Japan Co., Ltd.	Actual	Actual	860.138	286.713	X
	6000	CubeServ (México) S.A.	Actual	Actual	1.995.875	665.292	X
Overall Result					**14.006.123**	**4.668.708**	X

Figure 5.46 Alternate Table Row Styles

Only Hierarchy Navigation

Using the **Only Hierarchy Navigation** attribute, you can control the table navigation options that are provided on the web. If you enable this property, the end user no longer has a context menu for the individual table cells. Instead, he or she can only perform limited expand/collapse operations for an active hierarchy in drilldown state (see Figure 5.47). If no active hierarchy is included in a drilldown of the data provider, when the template is executed, the web application does not provide any navigation function for the generated table.

Country: Ship-To Pty		Orders No.	No. Doc. Items	Displ. sched.lines	Requested Deliv. qty	Delivery qty	Requested Deliv. qty per Order	Confirmed qty.	Net price	Net price per sched.line
Overall Result		6,376	13,944	109	*	2,904 PC				*
▼ WORLD	WORLD	6,376	13,944	109	*	2,904 PC	*	*	*	*
▶ AMERICAS	AMERICAS								199,853.64 USD	X
▼ EUROPE	EUROPE								*	X
▶ WESTEUROPE	WESTEUROPE								*	X
▶ OTHER	OTHER	6,376	13,944	109	*	2,904 PC	*	*		0
▶ N~~ Hierarchy Node Collapsed~~To Pty (s)									*	X

Figure 5.47 Only Hierarchy Navigation for the Table

Suppress Repeated Texts

By activating the **Suppress Repeated Texts** property, the individual cells of the lead columns in the drilldown are merged with the repeating values in the rows to one cell. The texts and keys are therefore not repeated (see Figure 5.48).

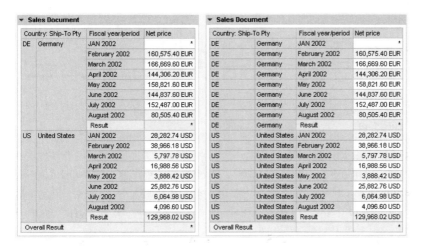

Figure 5.48 Suppress Repeated Values Yes/No

Number of Rows and Columns Displayed at a Time

Contrary to the BEx Analyzer, you can separately define the number of rows and columns displayed at a time for tables on the web. If the result set returns more data rows or columns than are specified in this attribute, an additional area is generated that provides a function for scrolling through the result set (see Figure 5.49). The scroll area is only inserted if one of the attributes **Table: Scroll Area Above** or **Table: Scroll Area Below** is activated. To display all data rows of the result set, the value must be set to 0. The value of this attribute indirectly affects the performance, because, in any case, the complete result set of the query has been selected for processing the web item. The output of several thousand rows at a time, however, can generate HTML code of several Megabytes that, in a worst-case scenario, needs to be transferred via a modem line, and therefore, causes long waiting times for the end user. The web browser or an outdated PC can lead to frustration as well, because they might require more time for processing the HTML code.

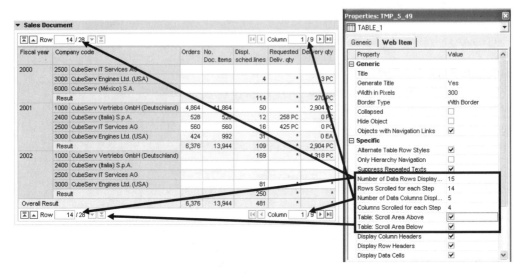

Figure 5.49 Different Settings for Scrolling

Scroll Area Above or Below

These attributes control whether a scroll area (see Figure 5.49) should be displayed at the beginning or at the end of the table. The scroll area is only shown if more rows or columns exist than can be displayed according to the restricted settings.

Display Column Headers

This attribute controls the display of the labels above the data. If this attribute is set to **No** (' '), no column headers will be generated for the table. By combining the attributes **Display Row Headers** and **Display Data Cells**, you can create individual presentations (see Figure 5.50).

Display Row Headers

This attribute controls the display of the labels to the left of the data. If this attribute is set to **No** (' '), no row headers will be created for the table. "Row headers" refers to the lead columns of the data. By combining the attributes **Display Column Headers** and **Display Data Cells**, you can create individual presentations (see Figure 5.50).

Display Data Cells

Using the **Display Data Cells** attribute, you can control whether or not the data cells will be displayed. In the default setting, all data cells are displayed. By combining the attributes **Display Row Headers** and **Display Column Headers**, you can create individual presentations (see Figure 5.50).

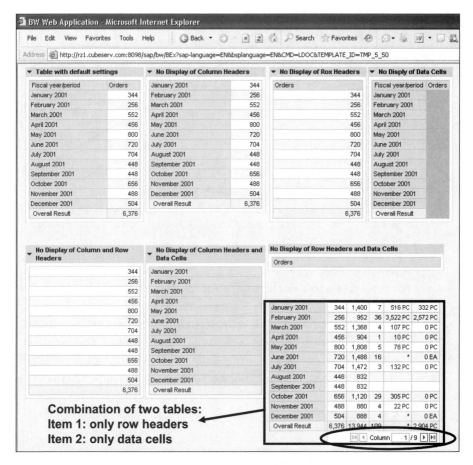

Figure 5.50 Different Settings Using the Attributes "Display Row Headers," "Display Column Headers," and "Display Data Cells"

Data Display from and to Value Row and Column

These attributes tell the table from which row (or up to which row) the content is to be presented. In combination with the following attributes, you can systematically present individual cells, columns, or rows in the web application. However, there are some dependencies on other attributes. If the value of the **Number of rows displayed together** attribute ($BLOCK\_SIZE$) is not null, and the scroll area is provided by the relevant attributes, the data will be displayed starting with the row that is set in this attribute. You can also scroll up to display the skipped rows. If no scroll area is provided, the table is displayed starting with the set row, without the option of displaying the skipped rows.

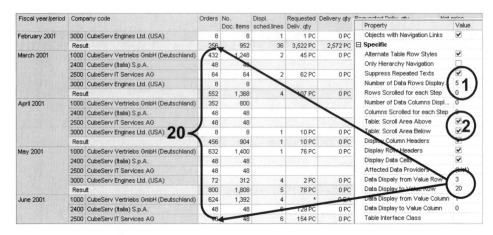

Figure 5.51 Display Behavior of the Affected Table via the Attributes "Data Display from and to Value Row"

Alternative ABAP Class

For the **Table** and **Generic navigation block** web items, via ABAP, SAP BW enables you to retrieve the data—already determined for the output of the HTML table—before it is transferred to the browser, and edit it as necessary. For this purpose, a separate ABAP Objects class is implemented that allows you to manipulate the contents of each table cell. Section 5.8 provides further information on Web Design for API Tables.

5.5.2 Chart

Using the **Chart** web item, you can graphically present the data of the data provider on the web. The generated graphics also allows for further context-sensitive navigation. For this purpose, another context menu is provided. Up to Release 3.1, it was necessary to install the Graphic Interface Server (GIS) on a Windows computer to process the individual charts; as of Release 3.5, the GIS is integrated in the SAP kernel, and therefore does not require any additional hardware. The charts can only be created and edited in the Web Application Designer.

Edit Chart: Chart Designer

After you have dragged the **Chart** web item to the layout area of the template (see Figure 5.52), you have two options for editing the chart. Using the **...** button (see Figure 5.52, 3) or the **Edit chart** icon on the application toolbar (4), the Chart Wizard is opened (5).

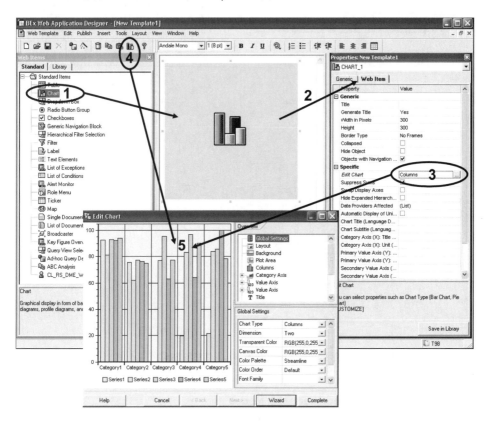

Figure 5.52 Edit Chart in the Web Application Designer

Suppress Sums

If the data provider assigned to the chart contains totals for rows or columns, they are displayed as independent values in the chart. In most cases, however, you would end up with many characteristic values that are close to the X axis, but are basically a mass without significance.

This property enables you to hide all totals for rows and columns of the data provider, especially for the chart (see Figure 5.53).

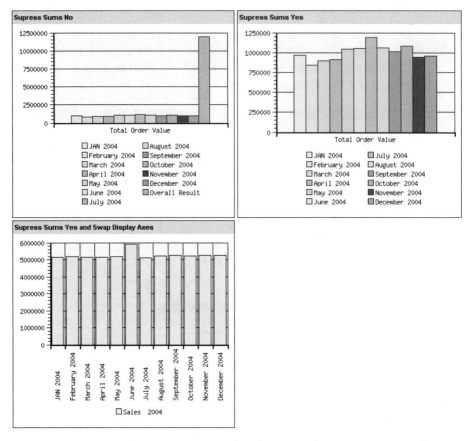

Figure 5.53 Presentation Variations for Charts Using the "Suppress Sums" and "Swap Display Axes" Attributes

Hide Expanded Hierarchy Nodes

If the underlying data provider contains an active expanded hierarchy, the individual sum nodes are presented as an independent value in the chart. This can lead to an unfavorable presentation however, because the actual values close to the axes can hardly be recognized. On the other hand, the sum of all values presented would be higher than the actual total of the top node. Using this attribute, the sum nodes of the presentation hierarchy are excluded from the presentation in the chart, and the sum of the displayed values is equal to the total.

Automatic Display of Units and Currencies

If the presented values in the chart represent only *one* currency or *one* unit, this currency or unit can be presented automatically in the chart (see Figure 5.54). But, if the query result returns different units or currencies, the function has no effect. In the Chart Designer, you can also set the display of units and currencies if you want.

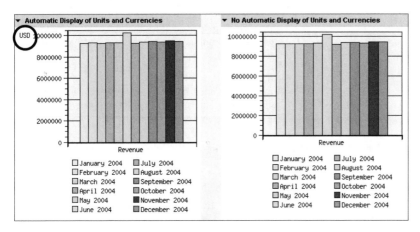

Figure 5.54 Automatic Display of Units and Currencies

Language-Dependent Texts in the Chart

A chart contains the most different kinds of axes where key figures and characteristics can be arranged. In addition, every chart contains a title and a subtitle. To customize the chart, you can enter your own descriptive text, since all of these descriptions have their own attributes. For the attributes listed in Table 5.5, you can enter the texts, depending on the language.

Attribute as Technical Name	Description of the Attribute
TITLE	Chart title
SUBTITLE	Chart subtitle
TITLE_CATEGORIES	Category axis (X): title
UNIT_CATEGORIES	Category axis (X): unit
TITLE_VALUES	Primary value axis (Y): title
UNIT_VALUES	Primary value axis (Y): unit
TITLE_SEC_VALUES	Secondary value axis (Y): title
UNIT_SEC_VALUES	Secondary value axis (Y): unit

Table 5.5 List of All Language-Dependent Attributes of the Chart

Attribute as Technical Name	Description of the Attribute
TITLE_SEC_CATEGORIES	Additional axis: title Language-dependent text for the title of an additional axis. This attribute is used for specific chart types only, such as histograms or scatter diagrams.
UNIT_SEC_CATEGORIES	Additional axis: unit Language-dependent text for the unit of an additional axis. This attribute is used for specific chart types only, such as histograms or scatter diagrams.

Table 5.5 List of All Language-Dependent Attributes of the Chart (Cont'd.)

For the language-dependent texts, SAP BW uses the text elements of an ABAP program. To be able to use language-dependent texts, you must first create an ABAP program. This program does not contain any code; only its text elements are required.

To present a language-dependent text in the chart, you must use the following syntax:

```
SAP_BW_TEXT?PROGRAM=<Techn. prg. name>&
   KEY=<Text element key>
SAP_BW_TEXT?PROGRAM=ZA0TEXTEIMWEB&KEY=001
```

The special chart attribute **Chart Title** (TITLE) generates a title within the chart itself, while the **Title** attribute (CAPTION) of the generic chart attributes generates a title above the chart and is displayed only if the generic chart attribute **Generate title** (GENERATE_CAPTION) is set to **Yes**.

Figure 5.55 shows some of the labeling possibilities of the **Chart** web item that are presented here. The labels in the example chart are the titles of the attributes.

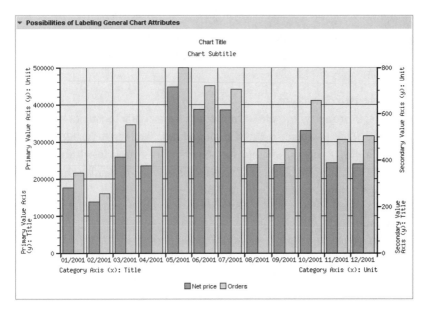

Figure 5.55 Some of the Labeling Options for a Chart

Automatic Labeling of Axes for Simple Charts

For very simple charts like vertical bar charts, bar charts, line charts, or profile charts, a label for the chart axes can be generated automatically. The underlying data provider must not contain more than one key figure and no second structure. The following functions are then implemented:

▶ If a key figure is used, its label is presented along the Y axis. The interaction options normally available are not provided in this case.

▶ Along the X axis, the names of the used characteristics are presented.

For a correct function, the axes might need to be swapped.

5.5.3 Dropdown Box

You can make the values of a characteristic or the individual structural components available for selection in a dropdown box. In this context, whether the latter is a key figure structure or a characteristic structure is irrelevant. If the dropdown box contains the values of a characteristic, you can define the values to be displayed for selection using the read mode, which has already been described under the generic attributes.

Objects with Navigation Links

The **Objects with Navigation Links** property from the generic attributes has a special effect on the dropdown box. If this attribute is disabled

(`GENERATE_LINKS=`), only the **All** entry is generated. The individual values or characteristic values are not generated, nor are they available for selection in the dropdown box. In this case, the dropdown box has no function.

Characteristic/Structure

Under this property, the technical name of the characteristic or structure is stored. Thus, you can make the individual characteristic values or, for example, key figures, available for selection in a dropdown box. If the characteristic is not included in the query, the web application terminates with an error message (see Figure 5.56).

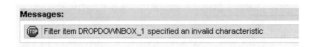

Figure 5.56 Error Message When the Characteristic or the Structure of the Dropdown Box Is Not Included in the Query or the Query View

Maximum Number of Characteristic Attributes in the Dropdown Box

To keep the values in the dropdown box concise, we recommend that you use a small value, depending on the requirement of the web application. If the value is set to 0, all existing values are displayed in the dropdown box.

Label

The long text of the characteristic is displayed as the label of the dropdown box. The label is pure text. It does not provide a hyperlink with a context menu.

Figure 5.57 Example of a Label in the Dropdown Box

Display Values Only

In the default setting, SAP BW generates the HTML form tag belonging to the dropdown box and sends the filter request directly to the Web Application Server, as soon as a new filter value has been selected from the dropdown box. To circumvent this default behavior, you can have only the relevant entries (`<option>` tag and content) of the dropdown box generated. In this case, the corresponding HTML form is not generated. Instead, it must be created manually in HTML mode, which can result in a more flexible use of the dropdown box because several dropdown boxes can be combined (see Figure 5.58).

The requirement to execute the value selected in the dropdown box using a Submit button might be implemented by deactivating JavaScript in the template properties. For a correct function, the value of the **Generate title** attribute (GENERATE_CAPTION) needs to be set to **No** (' '), and the value of the **Objects with navigation links** attribute (GENERATE_LINKS) must be set to **Yes** ('X').

Example of the ONLY_VALUES=X Attribute

```
<form name="CSForm01" method="post" action="<SAP_BW_
URL DATA_PROVIDER="DATAPROVIDER_1" FILTER_IONJM_
1="0FISCPER">">
<select name=FILTER_VALUE_1>
<object>
<param name="OWNER" value="SAP_BW">
<param name="CMD" value="GET_ITEM">
<param name="NAME" value="DROPDOWNBOX_3">
<param name="ITEM_CLASS" value="CL_RSR_WWW_ITEM_FILTER_
DDOWN">
<param name="DATA_PROVIDER" value="DATAPROVIDER_1">
<param name="GENERATE_CAPTION" value="">
<param name="GENERATE_LINKS" value="X">
<param name="IOBJNM" value="0FISCYEAR">
<param name="BOOKED_VALUES" value="M">
<param name="ONLY_VALUES" value="X">
ITEM:DROPDOWNBOX_1
</object>
</select>
<input type="submit" value="Filter">
</form>
```

Don't Display "All Values" Item

If, for example, the values of the **Company code** characteristic are to be presented in the dropdown box, and if the **Company code** characteristic is already restricted to a value when the web template is called using a query view, the set filter value is shown in the dropdown box. To remove the filter via the dropdown box, you need the **All** entry; otherwise, you can select only one company code at a time.

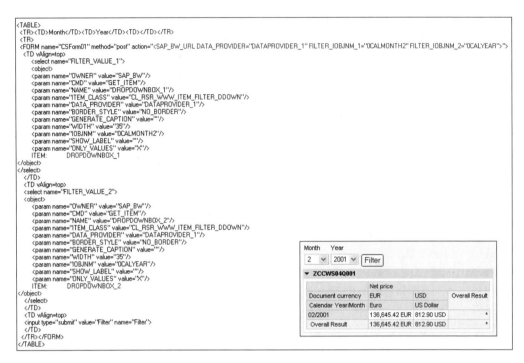

Figure 5.58 Code for Dropdown Boxes with Self-Generated Form and Submit Button

5.5.4 Generic Navigation Block

The generic navigation block provides all of the characteristics existing in the data provider sorted by groups and clearly arranged for fast navigation and for selecting filter values. Compared to Release 3.0, the options for the navigation block have been considerably extended so that a simple and clear navigation area can now be implemented in a web application.

Since most properties are self-explanatory, we will only discuss a few selected attributes here. A list of all properties and their corresponding values can be found in the Appendix D.

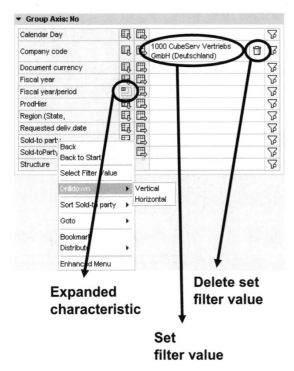

**Expanded
characteristic**

**Delete set
filter value**

**Set
filter value**

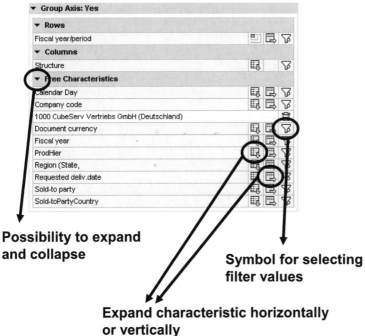

**Possibility to expand
and collapse**

**Symbol for selecting
filter values**

**Expand characteristic horizontally
or vertically**

Figure 5.59 The "Navigation Block" Web Item

Frame Name for the Input Help

For this attribute, enter the name of the frame in which the input help should be displayed. If this property is used, the HOME_FRAME attribute of the underlying data provider must be populated with the name of the calling frame, or with the name of the frame in which the output should appear (see Figure 5.60).

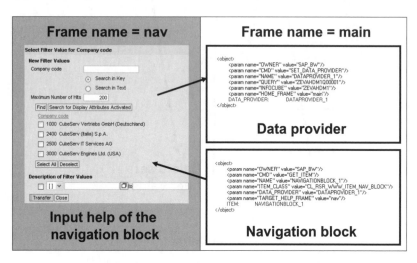

Figure 5.60 Presentation of the Input Help of a Characteristic of the Navigation Block in a Different Frame

Table Interface Class

Similar to the **Table** web item, the navigation block web item also allows you to use a separate table interface class for processing the output. You should assign the technical name of the created ABAP Objects class to this property. By using a separate class, you can change the contents of every cell, for example, as well as configure every cell of a table individually by assigning specific formatting properties. You can integrate additional complex navigation options in the individual cells of the navigation block. The use of the table interface class requires some ABAP knowledge.

List of Navigation Block Items

For every generic navigation block used, you can define which characteristics and structures should be contained and in which order. If no special list is specified, all characteristics and structures of the underlying data provider are displayed in the navigation block. The selection list also provides the **Read mode** attribute of the filter value selection for every characteristic. Thus, you can individually specify for each characteristic how to determine the available filter values. For example, for characteristics with many characteristic values, like the sold-to party, it would make sense to have the values read from the master data table instead of choosing the read mode **booked values**, because determining the values can take a very long time and end users might therefore not accept this web application.

If you populate this attribute yourself, using the object tags in the HTML code, you can use the `BOOKED_VALUES_n` attribute for the read mode of the associated navigation block entry `ITEM_NAV_BLOCK_IOBJNM_n`.

```
<param name="ITEM_NAV_BLOCK_IOBJNM_1" value="0CALMONTH"/>
<param name="BOOKED_VALUES_1" value="D"/>
<param name="ITEM_NAV_BLOCK_IOBJNM_2" value="0DISTR_CHAN"/>
<param name="BOOKED_VALUES_2" value="Q"/>
<param name="ITEM_NAV_BLOCK_IOBJNM_3" value="0SOLD_TO"/>
<param name="BOOKED_VALUES_3" value="M"/>
<param name="ITEM_NAV_BLOCK_IOBJNM_4" value="0COMP_CODE"/>
<param name="BOOKED_VALUES_4" value="Q"/>
```

Example code in object tags

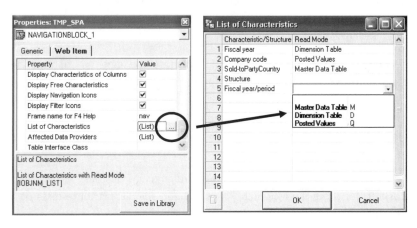

Figure 5.61 Possibility for Restricting the Presented Characteristics and Structures in the Navigation Block

5.5.5 Label

The web item **Label** provides a convenient way in which to create your own navigation areas in web applications. Depending on the settings, the label is generated as a hyperlink in the web application. If you click on the hyperlink, a context menu opens to support you in your further navigation. You can also simply use the label to display character names in order to integrate language-dependent text fragments into the web application.

For example, by combining the web items, **Label**, **Filter**, **Text element**, and **Dropdown box**, you can create a navigation area that meets your own specific requirements.

Context Menu
This property enables you to define whether or not the character label should have a context menu. If you disable this attribute, only the name of the characteristic or of the structure is displayed. The web item **Label** does not provide any other functionality. As an example of when you might want to disable this attribute, it may prove useful if you need a language-dependent characteristic name in one of your web applications.

Characteristic/Structure
This attribute must be provided with the technical name of the characteristic or structure, the language-dependent description of which should be displayed in the web application.

Structural Component
If you have specified a structure in the **Characteristic/Structure** (IOBJNM) attribute, you can further restrict the structure to a structural component whose text or context menu is displayed.

Attribute Name
Technical name of the characteristic attribute specified in **Characteristic/Structure** (IOBJNM) whose header is displayed as a label.

> Note that no context menu is available, if you choose a characteristic attribute as a label.

You can use this functionality for a multilanguage business intelligence cockpit, for example, in which you also need specific attribute texts of a characteristic.

Display Values Only
If you activate this attribute, the system only generates the string of the link to the context menu. Since the call of the context menu for a characteristic or structure is a JavaScript function, the system generates a text that calls a JavaScript function, which contains all parameters required for the respective characteristic. For example, for **Sold-To Party** (technical name: 0SOLD_TO), SAP BW would generate the following text string:

```
SAPBWM(event,9,2,'0SOLD_TO','','','',0,0);
```

This JavaScript function call can be applied to a graphic. Suppose that you want to use a globe symbol for the **Country** characteristic (0COUNTRY), and that globe is intended to be a hyperlink in the web application and provide the context menu for the **Country** characteristic.

The corresponding code would look as follows:

```
<a href="javascript:;" onclick="
<object>
<param name="OWNER" value="SAP_BW"/>
<param name="CMD" value="GET_ITEM"/>
<param name="NAME" value="LABEL_1"/>
<param name="ITEM_CLASS" value="CL_RSR_WWW_ITEM_LABEL"/>
<param name="DATA_PROVIDER" value="DATAPROVIDER_1"/>
<param name="GENERATE_CAPTION" value=""/>
<param name="IOBJNM" value="0COUNTRY"/>
<param name="ONLY_VALUES" value="X"/>
ITEM: LABEL_1
</object>
"><img src="/sap/bw/Mime/BEx/Icons/imo_geo_
full.gif" border="0" width="16" height="15"></a>
```

Figure 5.62 Options Provided by the Web Item "Label"

To use the attribute **Display Values Only** (ONLY_VALUES) correctly, do not generate a header or frame. This would result in additional HTML code for the header or frame, which would prevent you from using individual values for your own customized HTML dropdown box.

5.5.6 Alert Monitor

The alerts that have been scheduled and determined during the background processing of the Reporting Agent can be displayed using this web item. You can navigate to the underlying detailed report for each alert. The contents of the Alert Monitor are user-dependent and are controlled via the Reporting Agent. You cannot change the contents of the Alert Monitor via variables at web application runtime. For each user, the system displays all, or all relevant alerts of a specific area (query, InfoProvider, InfoArea, etc.). At this point, we won't describe all the individual properties of the Alert Monitor, as many of them are self-explanatory. Appendix D contains a comprehensive list of the properties.

Display Minimum View

If you set this attribute to **No**, all key figure columns defined in the query will be displayed when you navigate to the details. If you set this attribute to **Yes**, only those key figure columns—for which exceptions can occur—are displayed when you navigate to the details. If you don't specify this parameter, the system displays all key figures.

Template for the Output

You can use any template to output the detail view. Specify the technical name of the web template that you want to use as the basis for the detail view for this attribute. If you don't specify a template, the template for the ad-hoc analysis stored in Customizing will be used.

List of Columns with Captions

You can format the structure of the Alert Monitor to meet your requirements by adding and arranging predefined column types, and by assigning any caption you like to the individual columns. Select the column type for COLUMN_NAME_n, and assign the required column caption for the same index of the COLUMN_CAPTION_n attribute. The assigned column captions, however, are only displayed if you set the attribute **Display Column Captions** (DISPLAY_COLUMN_CAPTION=X) to the value **Yes**.

The following column types are available:

▶ TEXT: text

▶ ACTION: action

▶ VALUE: value for individual cells

▶ DOCUMENT: display of documents

▶ MAX_LEVEL: display highest alert level

▶ RED: number of red exceptions

▶ YELLOW: number of yellow exceptions

▶ GREEN: number of green exceptions

▶ DATE: creation date

▶ TIME: creation time

In the Reporting Agent, you can specify that the relevant Alert Monitor items should be assigned a URL. This stored URL is displayed in the **Action** column (COLUMN_NAME_1=ACTION) of the Alert Monitor, if the **List Display** (LIST_FOCUS_LEVEL=CELL) attribute is set to **Individual Cell** (CELL) or, if you drill the hierarchical display down to the deepest level of detail. Otherwise, the URL will not be displayed in the **Action** column.

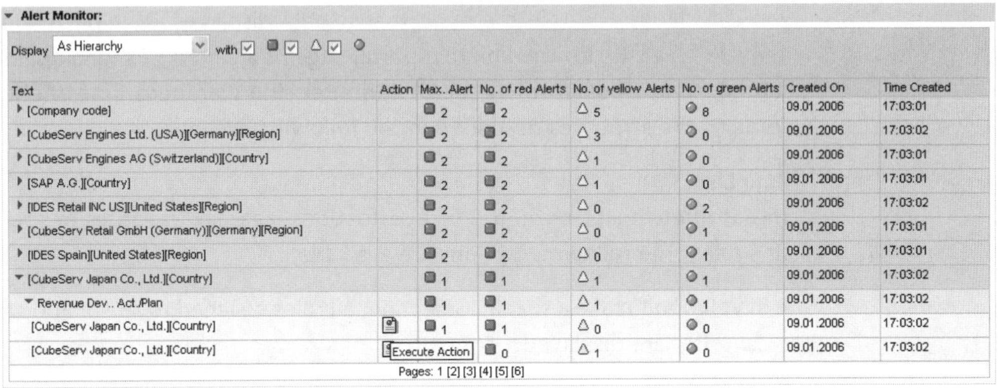

Figure 5.63 Example of the Alert Monitor Display

Display Data Provider

Suppose you have a web template that contains the web items **Alert Monitor** and **Table**. The web item **Table** is assigned a data provider with the logical name DP_1. Specify the logical name (DP_1) of the data provider for this attribute (DISPLAY_DATA_PROVIDER). If you want to navigate from the Alert Monitor to the detail view of the alert, the detail view of the data provider DP_1 is used in the same template, and the table displays the detail data of the alert.

Present in

"Present in" is the name of the frame for the detail view. If you don't specify a detail frame, the detail view is displayed in the same window, as was the pure HTML code (parameter JAVASCRIPT= in the URL when calling the template on the web, or JavaScript was disabled in the template properties), while a separate window opens, if JavaScript is enabled. Otherwise, you should specify the name of the frame in which you want to display the detail view of the exceptions. This is particularly useful when used in combination with the **Template for the Output** attribute

(TARGET_TEMPLATE_ID), as in this case, a specifically designed template can control the output of the individual exceptions in a frame.

5.5.7 Role Menu

The web item **Role Menu** enables you to provide a user with the assigned roles and with his or her favorites for the report selection on the web. The only precondition is that the roles have been maintained and assigned to the users. For the role menu on the web, you can even provide only certain types, such as web templates, queries, URLs, and so on. For example, you can define the role menu so that it only displays URL type menu items (e.g., a URL for the link to a portal page or a stored BEx web application). In addition to the general attributes, the web item **Role Menu** contains the attributes described in the following sections.

Role List

This attribute enables you to make restrictions regarding favorites or specific roles. The following options are available:

▶ If you don't make a specific selection, all roles assigned to a user and all favorites are displayed.

▶ Otherwise, the technical name of each role that is to be displayed must be specified. Then, an end user can see a role, only if he has been assigned to it.

▶ If you want to provide only certain items in the role menu, you can display the favorites with ROLE_n=SAP_BW__FAVORITES_ (using two underscores between SAP_BW and FAVORITES).

In the following example of the role menu ⟨object⟩ tag, we want to display the favorites and other roles.

Example code
```
⟨object⟩
    ⟨param name="OWNER" value="SAP_BW"/⟩
    ⟨param name="CMD" value="GET_ITEM"/⟩
    ⟨param name="NAME" value="ROLEMENU_1"/⟩
    ⟨param name="ITEM_CLASS" value="CL_RSR_WWW_ITEM_MENU"/⟩
    ⟨param name="ROLE_1" value="SAP_BW__FAVORITES_"/⟩
    ⟨param name="ROLE_2" value="SAP_BWC_SALES_COCKPIT"/⟩
    ⟨param name="IFRAME" value="X"/⟩
    ⟨param name="IFRAME_STYLE" value="X"/⟩
    ITEM:  ROLEMENU_1
⟨/object⟩
```

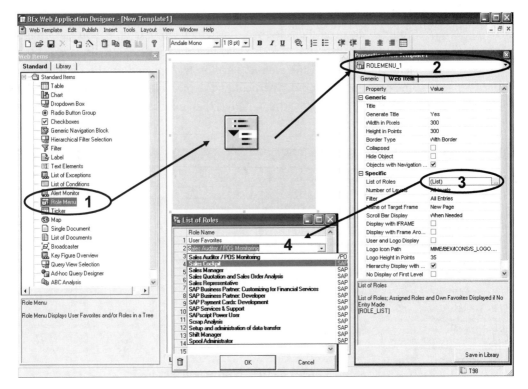

Figure 5.64 Selecting Specific Roles to Display in the Role Menu in Web Application Designer

Filter

The individual menu items of the role menu can be divided according to types. This attribute enables you to set one or more filters for the types. The following types are available for display in the role menu:

▶ 'U' = URLs

▶ 'P' = web templates

▶ 'Y' = queries

▶ 'R' = Crystal Reports

▶ 'A' = BSP applications

If, for instance, you enter the filter value 'P' for this attribute, only the web templates will be available in the role menu. You can also combine different filter values. The filter values are then displayed in sequential order in the role menu. For example, the filter 'UY' displays all URLs and queries of the selected roles. If you don't specify any restrictions, all available items will be displayed.

Name of Target Frame

You can also use the role menu in frames. For example, you can design the window structure in such a way that the role menu is displayed in the left-hand area and the web application is displayed on the right. Assign the name of the frame for executing the menu items to this attribute. The underlying URL for the menu item is then executed in the specified frame (see Figure 5.65).

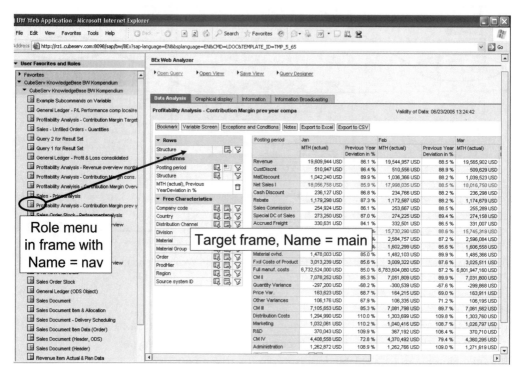

Figure 5.65 Role Menu in a Frame and Target Frame for Displaying the Menu Items

Display with IFrame

A frameset is generated for the role menu in the default setting. The role menu displayed on the web is loaded in a frame. The items and the complex JavaScript functions necessary to control the role menu on the web are loaded in a separate hidden frame. This entails several restrictions for using other web items in the same web template, since those web items won't be displayed in the web browser.

However, if you want to display these web items in the web browser, you can display the role menu in an IFrame. For example, by using an IFrame, you can display the role menu, a navigation block, and a table collectively in a web application. Unfortunately, use of the IFrame function is not supported by Netscape 4.7 and PDAs. The use of IFrames gives you more freedom for designing the page around the role menu. The role menu in the frameset (without IFrame) is created generically and cannot be manipulated externally. For technical reasons, you can only display one role menu per web template in the standard version. Similarly, the IFrame property allows for only one role menu per web application. However, you can create your own IFrames to display more than one role menu in the web template: Per IFrame, a web template that contains a role menu is loaded.

Display of User and Logo

Here you can display the name of the logged-on user and a logo above the role menu. The display of the welcome text and the name of the user can be controlled using the style sheet class SAPBEXMenuLogo. In addition to the output of the user name, the system generates a small graphic that looks like an arrowhead. The graphic contains a hyperlink that brings you to the top-level window of a frame hierarchy into which it loads the template of the role menu.

This hidden functionality is quite useful if the role menu is called in a small frame on the intranet when there's not much space available and the functionality or navigation options of the intranet are no longer needed. The logo to be displayed and its height or size can be adjusted using the following two attributes.

Path of the Logo Icon

In this attribute, you must store the path of the icon in the MIME Repository, which is to be displayed as a logo (image). You can enter the path as a relative or absolute path. This attribute can only be used in combination with DISPLAY_USER. As an example, we'll use the following as the default path: *BEx/Icons/s_logo.gif.*

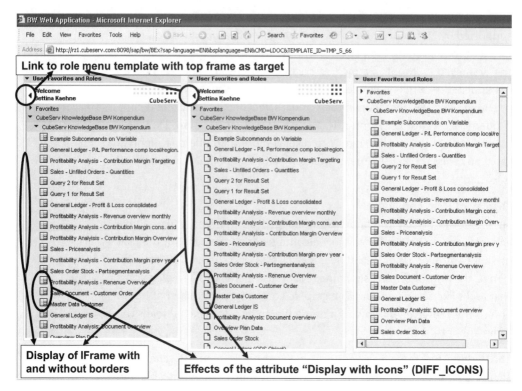

Figure 5.66 Display Variants of the Role Menu in an IFrame

5.5.8 Ticker

Tickers are frequently used to display current stock-exchange prices; however, they can be used for many other purposes as well. Because a ticker is created using a JavaScript function, a web browser with active JavaScript is a prerequisite for using tickers.

Figure 5.67 Web Item "Ticker" in the Browser

Creating a Hidden Form

If you activate this attribute (ONLY_VALUES='X'), a hidden form is generated for the further processing of the ticker text—that is to say, the ticker text is always output in a hidden form—whereas the JavaScript code that calls the JavaScript function for activating the ticker is not generated.

You cannot address the form by using a specific name, since its name is dynamic and is generated by SAP BW as follows: SAPBW_TICKER_nnnn (nnnn stands for a consecutive number, e.g. 0001).

Separator
For this attribute, you can specify any freely selectable character or character string as a separator that is displayed between two ticker lines. Separators are output between two lines of the result set.

Speed in Milliseconds
Time is displayed in milliseconds that elapse between two movements of the ticker.

Width of Ticker Text in Characters
This attribute controls the width of the display area for the ticker text in terms of characters. The specified width (WIDTH) of the general attributes can be overruled with this attribute.

Place Caption to the Beginning of the Ticker Text
This attribute enables you to define whether you want to place the value of the general attribute **Caption** (CAPTION) at the beginning of the ticker text.

Delay in Milliseconds
Specify a value in milliseconds for this attribute. The value represents the time period after which the ticker text should be started, once it has been loaded into the browser.

5.5.9 Object Catalog of the Web Application

The Object catalog of the web application web item enables you to generate the entire information on current web template properties, data providers, and the web items used in the web template in XML format. The XML code is also transferred to the browser, but it won't be displayed. However, you can view the generated XML code in the source text of the web application. For example, all attributes of a web item in use, including their values, are output in XML format. That enables you to access this information, for example, by using JavaScript to integrate it into your own customized functions of the web application. Moreover, you can also display the information in the web application by using a JavaScript function. Apart from the general attributes, which aren't important here, since nothing is displayed and XML is generated instead of HTML, this web item contains the specific attributes described in the following sections.

Output Web Template Properties

You can use this attribute to output the web template properties in XML format in the source text of the web application. To do that, set the value to **Yes** (PROPERTIES='X'). You should note that, however, the structure of the context menu, which is a component of the web template properties in Web Application Designer, is not output in this context. Rather, it is only the properties of the web template that are generated as XML code.

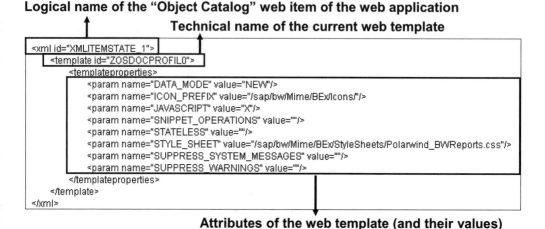

Figure 5.68 Structure of the XML Code for the Web Template Properties in the Source Text of the Web Application

Output List of Data Providers

A list of all defined data providers is output in XML format in the source text of the web application. This list is not very helpful, however, since only the logical names of the existing data providers are generated without any further information. Currently, SAP is not planning to develop this attribute further.

Output List of Web Items

If you need a list of all web items used in the web template, including the associated attributes in XML format, you should use this attribute.

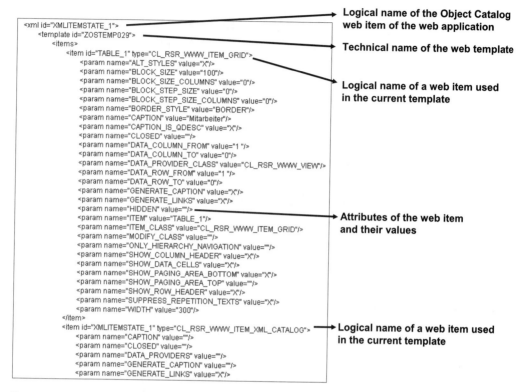

Figure 5.69 XML Output of Used Web Items for the Web Item "Object Catalog of the Web Application" in the Source Text of the Web Application

5.5.10 Data Providers — Information

This web item enables you to generate the query result data (or the data of the navigation status of a query) in XML format. The XML code is also transferred to the browser, but it won't be displayed.[10] However, you can view the generated XML code in the source text of the web application. For example, all attributes of a web item in use, including their values, are output in XML format. That enables you to access this information by using JavaScript, for example, to integrate it into your own customized functions of the web application. Moreover, you can also display the information in the web application by using a JavaScript function. Apart from the general attributes, which aren't important for this item because nothing is displayed and XML is generated instead of HTML, the web item **Object catalog of the web application** contains only specific attributes.

---

10 Depending on the browser you use, the results can be different. Microsoft's Internet Explorer does not display XML code, whereas the Firefox browser displays the entire text that is contained within XML tags, in other words, all data.

The result set of a query or the current navigation status on the web can also be exported via a command URL in XML format. In this case the data provider command 'EXPORT' is used.[11] Unlike the Excel and CSV export functions, the XML export function is not available in the context menu. You can integrate it as a hyperlink, however, by using the following syntax in the HTML code of the web template:

```
<a href='<SAP_BW_URL DATA_PROVIDER='
<logical name of the data provider>'
CMD='EXPORT' FORMAT='XML'>'>Export as XML</a>
```

5.5.11 Individual Document

You can create individual documents in the Administrator Workbench or in master data maintenance that refer to the individual values of a characteristic. Furthermore, you can also create documents as characteristic value combinations that refer to transaction data. These documents can be of different types, which means they can be available in different formats (e.g., MS Excel, plain text, HTML, etc.). This web item enables you to display and generate those documents in the web application.

For example, if in the web application the **Company code** characteristic is restricted to the value **CubeServ Engines Holding AG**, and if a document exists for this value in the Business Document Service (BDS), this document will be displayed on the web.

Document Class
You can use the **Document Class** attribute to define whether a document for a characteristic value of master data or for InfoProvider data (transaction data) will be displayed on the web.

Document Type
This attribute is used to specify a restriction to a specific document type. Each document in the BDS contains specific attributes. One of those attributes is the **Document Type**, which is specifically used for handling documents in web applications. The document type supports the logical or semantic grouping of documents and is freely selectable. You can specify a freely definable text of up to 20 characters for this attribute in the BDS for any document. In this way, you can create several different document types for each value of a characteristic.

---

11 If Support Package 05 for SAP BW 3.5 is not yet installed, functionality errors may still occur. Please refer to OSS Notes 751680 and 738563 for more information.

For example, you could create different documents for a value of the characteristic **Employee** (0EMPLOYEE); in other words, for an employee. First, you create a document of the self-defined document type PICTURE, which contains a picture of the employee. Then, you create another document of the self-defined document type PROFILE, which contains the employee's resume. Therefore, you can display several documents that refer to the values of a characteristic in a web application.

▶ To do that, use this web item (**Individual document**) once in your web application and restrict it to the document type PICTURE in order to display the picture of the employee. Then, use another web item **Individual document** and restrict that item to the document type PROFILE to present the profile of the selected employee.

▶ If you maintain this attribute in the Web Application Designer, a list of all document types that exist at a given point in time in the BDS will be made available to you.

▶ If you don't enter any information for this web item attribute, the processing logic assumes that exactly one document exists for each value of the selected characteristic.

▶ If, however, several document types exist for a characteristic value in the BDS, the system displays a corresponding notification message in the web browser when you run the web application, and no document will be displayed for the selected characteristic value.

This notification message can look as follows:

▶ No document found

▶ The document is not unique (several documents available)

Characteristic
If you select the value MAST for the **Document class** (DOCUMENT_CLASS) attribute, that is to say, if you want to display a document referring to master data on the web, you must use the technical name of the characteristic for this property.

Frame for the Display
You can use this attribute to assign the name of the HTML frame that should be used for outputting the document. IFrames are also possible here. Some documents, such as MS Word, Excel or PDF documents, cannot be displayed within the web item in the web application. These documents must be loaded in a separate frame, as a specific browser plug-in must be used for displaying them.

The following data types can currently be displayed by the web item in the web browser, without the help of frames:

▶ Images: image/jpeg, image/gif
▶ Text: text/plain
▶ HTML: text/html

All other types of data should be displayed in a frame.

In addition to unique frame names, you can also use the following values for this attribute:

▶ _self = current frame, frame of the web item
▶ _top = top-level frame in the current window or the entire page
▶ _blank = new page or window
▶ _parent = superordinate frame

Nesting Depth of the Frame

If you use framesets and the **Target Frame** attribute (TARGET_FRAME), you must also use the **Nesting depth of the frame** attribute to inform the processing logic about the level—at which the frame that was specified with the unique name in the **Target Frame** attribute is located—for displaying the documents. Enter the value 0, if you use IFrames that are used in the same web template or on the same HTML page.

Display in the Same Browser Window

The document can be displayed in the same browser window, or a hyperlink is generated that opens the document in a new browser window. You can display documents only of the following types in the same browser window:

▶ Images: image/jpeg, image/gif
▶ Text: text/plain
▶ HTML: text/html

For all other documents, a hyperlink is generated automatically, if the TARGET_FRAME attribute is not used.

Links for Document Display

Instead of displaying the contents of a document directly in the web application, you can also generate a hyperlink to jump to the document. When you click on the generated hyperlink, a list of all documents that meet the current selection criteria is displayed in a separate browser window. This means that you can also use this web item if several documents exist for a specific characteristic value, because, in that case, a hyperlink that takes you to all the relevant documents is created instead of an error message.

Default Picture
Here you can specify the absolute or relative URL that points to an image, which will be displayed in the web item whenever no document could be found, or when a document is not unique.

5.5.12 Web Template

This web item enables you to integrate other existing web templates in your web template. In other words, this web item enables you to assemble web applications as you would do with a construction kit. For instance, you can use one web template (see Figure 5.70) to create the header area including the logo and company name, while another template can be used to create a separate footer area with specific non-changeable contents. Those two web templates can be integrated as includes into any other web template by using the web item **Web Template**. If changes to the layout become necessary at a later stage, simply maintain the templates for the header and footer areas. The changes will be adopted by all other web applications that contain the two templates. Depending on the settings, only the HTML code within the ⟨BODY⟩ and ⟨/BODY⟩ tags of the web template, embedded by this web item, is integrated into the activated template at runtime. In contrast to the HTML frame technology, the system does not generate a new page at this stage, which reduces the workload of the web browser.

Only <body> Tag
You can use this attribute to define whether you want to integrate only the contents of the ⟨BODY⟩ tag into the embedded template, or whether the complete HTML code including the ⟨HTML⟩ and ⟨/HTML⟩ tags should be output as well. The default setting (default value) for this attribute specifies that only the contents of the ⟨BODY⟩ tags should be output.

Prefix for the Logical Names
If the same logical names were used for the objects (such as web items or data providers) in the main template and in the template to be embedded, the names would no longer be unique and could not longer be addressed. If that is the case, you can assign a prefix to all logical names of objects contained in the templates to be embedded. This attribute defines a string of characters, which is to be used as a prefix and therefore, make all objects unique again.

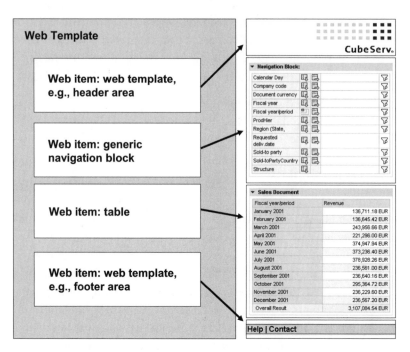

Figure 5.70 Purpose and Use of the Web Item "Web Template"

If the logical names in the individual templates are different, it isn't necessary to use prefixes. For example, if you use a data provider with the logical name DATAPROV1 in the main template, and this data provider delivers data from a query with sales key figures, and the template to be embedded also contains a data provider called DATAPROV1, which provides data from a query used in the controlling area, the queries for the sales key figures will be displayed in the running web application for all web items that are assigned the data provider DATAPROV1. To avoid this confusion, all objects of the template to be embedded are assigned a prefix. For example, this can be the prefix TEMP1. Hence, the data provider of the template to be embedded is assigned the logical name TEMP1.DATAPROV1, and all relevant web items are automatically assigned this name as well.

Additional Attributes

There are additional attributes available for the web item **Web template** that are not provided by the Web Application Designer. Instead, they must be maintained in the relevant ⟨OBJECT⟩ tags in the HTML code of the web template. These attributes are re-initialization functions. The web items and data providers that are already contained in the web templates to be embedded can be assigned these attributes.

Overwrite the Web Item Initialization

This attribute enables you to re-initialize the web items that are contained in the web templates to be embedded. If, for instance, you want to embed a web template that contains a table, but you want to use a chart instead of the table, you can use this attribute to re-initialize and therefore redefine these web items. You can do that via the logical name that must be assigned to each web item (Example: TABLE_1).

Overwrite the Data Provider Initialization

Here you can overwrite the initial data provider settings in the web template to be embedded. Suppose you use a web template containing a table, and a data provider that provides revenue data. When you embed the template that you want, the embedded data provider provides sales data instead of revenue data. Consequently, you may want to use this attribute to re-initialize the data provider.

5.5.13 Query View Selection

The web item **Query View Selection** enables you to use a dropdown box or pushbuttons to toggle between different queries and query views, and to define different types of display for each item in the dropdown list or for each pushbutton.[12] For example, you can display the data for the **Regional sales** item in a table, while the data for the **Sales in the by-product group** item is displayed in a chart. This web item enables you to create complex navigation scenarios easily, which would otherwise have required a great deal of JavaScript code. As already mentioned, you can toggle between the different queries and query views by using a dropdown box or certain pushbuttons. The web item must first be assigned an initial web item that is responsible for the display. The end user can also create local query views, which can be included in the selection. To use this web item, you must make some specific settings. At the end of this description, you'll find a simple example containing step-by-step instructions for using the web item.

Affected Web Item

The web item **Query View Selection** expects an entry in this attribute. Here you enter the logical name of a web item that exists in the same web template. This web item is used for initially displaying the data provider that is assigned to the web item; it is also used for displaying all query views that haven't been explicitly assigned to a different web item.

---

12 The following OSS Notes provide help in case of errors related to the **Query View Selection** web item: 778714, 747827, 694500, and 757952.

List of Query Views

Here you maintain the individual query views that are listed in the drop-down box, or can be displayed using the pushbuttons. But first, you should assign a data provider to this web item (**Query View Selection**); otherwise, the execution of the web template in the web browser might abort.

The same data provider must also be assigned to the web item that is responsible for the display. The web item used for displaying the queries and query views appears with the data of the initial data provider during the execution of the web template in a web browser. For that reason, you should enter the data provider into the list; then, the web API will attempt to find the data provider in the list and display it in the **Query View Selection** dropdown box. If the web API doesn't find the data provider in the list, the first item of the list is displayed in the dropdown box. This can result in misinterpretations, as the provided data of the web item for the display doesn't match the entry in the dropdown box. When maintaining this attribute via the Web Application Designer (see Figure 5.71), an input list in the form of a table is made available to you. But, if you want to make these entries directly in the HTML code for the associated ⟨object⟩ tag, an attribute is available for each column.

Each line of the list shown in Figure 5.71 represents an item in the dropdown box. For each item, you must or can make different entries, such as the following:

▶ **Description for the item in the dropdown box**
For each item in the dropdown box, you must specify a description in this field. (Example: VIEW_DD_DESCRIPTION_1='Revenues by company code'.)

▶ **Name of Query**
Here you can enter the technical name of the query that you want to display. This entry is optional. You cannot select the query using provided input help. Instead, you must enter the technical name of the query manually, or copy and paste it into the field. If you want to use a query view instead of a query, you can skip this column or omit this parameter in the ⟨object⟩ tag. (Example: VIEW_DD_QUERY_SELECTION_1='ZOSA0SDC01Q001'.)

▶ **Query View Name**
As in the **Column/Name** attribute of the query, you should enter the technical name of the query view here. You can select a query view from an input help. This entry is optional as well. If you don't want to enter

anything here, you can simply leave this column or the corresponding attribute in the associated ⟨object⟩ tag blank. However, it is mandatory that you specify either a query or a query view per line. (Example: VIEW_DD_DATA_PROVIDER_ID_1='ZOSA0SDC01Q0 01V01'.)

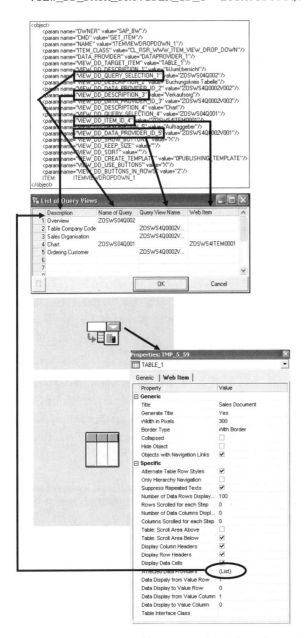

Figure 5.71 Maintenance Table or List in the Web Application Designer for the Query View List Attributes and the Associated Object Tag in HTML Code

Technical name of the web item

If you want to use a different web item—than the one that has been set as the initial web item—to display the data, you must enter the technical name of a web item from a library here. You cannot enter the logical name of a web item from the web template in this field, as this would result in the web application terminating the execution in the web browser and returning an error message. However, entering a value here is not mandatory. If you don't enter a value, the web item that was specified in the **Affected Web Item** attribute will be used to display the data.

Display Create/Delete Button

The user of a web application, which contains a **Query View Selection** web item, can define new user-specific items for the dropdown box and delete them, provided that this function has been specified by using the **Display Create/Delete Button** attribute of the web item.

If this property is displayed, a **Create/Delete** button is provided next to the dropdown box. The underlying functionality for the **Create/Delete** button is called by a standard SAP BW display template. If you want to use a web template that you created for displaying or creating query views, you must specify it in the **Web template** attribute (VIEW_DD_ CREATE_TEMPLATE). Note however, that the self-defined template should provide the same functionality as the standard template with regard to creating and saving views.

Maintain Filter Values for Query Views

If, for example, you're currently looking at the query view **Revenues by company code** and use a navigation block to filter the current month, the set filter value is maintained when you change to a different item in the dropdown box, and, if possible, it is even applied (i.e., if the characteristic exists in the query).

Maintain Settings of Affected Web Item

If the list of query views contains additional web items, this attribute enables you to control whether the properties (width, size, number of data rows and so on) of the mandatory web item, which has been specified in the **Affected Web Item** attribute, should be transferred in the event of a change to another web item.

Use All Query Views of a Query

You should use this attribute, if all existing query views of the data provider assigned to this web item should automatically be used in the dropdown box. If entries have already been made in the attributes of the **List** of **Query Views**, those entries won't be considered. In that case, the query views can be displayed only by using the web item specified in the **Affected Web Item** attribute of the web template.

Sort Query Views in Alphabetical Order
If you select this attribute, the query views in the dropdown box are sorted alphabetically. Otherwise, the query views are displayed in the order of the items listed in the **List of Query Views**.

Web Template for the Creation of New Items for the Dropdown Box
Here you should specify the technical name of the web template that is to be called to create new items for the dropdown box using the **Create** button. You should select this attribute only if you want to display the **Create/Delete** button (**Display Create/Delete button** attribute). If you specify a template that you have created, you must ensure that your template provides the necessary functionality for creating and saving query views; otherwise, the user can't use this function. For the exact coding of the required functionality, it is helpful to analyze and use the generated source text of the standard template called.

Generate Buttons
Instead of a dropdown box, you can also have the system generate the selection of individual query views as buttons. For this reason, you must set the attribute to **Yes** (VIEW_DD_USE_BUTTONS='X').

Number of Buttons per Row
If you have set the **Generate buttons** attribute to **Yes** (VIEW_DD_USE_BUTTONS='X'), you can use the **Number of Buttons per Row** attribute to define how many buttons should be displayed per row.

5.5.14 Ad-hoc Query Designer

The **Ad-hoc Query Designer** web item is a simple tool contained in a web application that is used for creating and modifying queries. Regarding its functionality however, this web-based query designer is rather limited. The Ad-hoc Query Designer is not intended to replace the standalone BEx Query Designer. Instead, it should viewed as a complementary tool for the user. Thus, you can provide a simple tool in your web applications that enables the user to create easy individual ad-hoc reporting queries.

Name of the InfoProvider
Enter the technical name of the InfoProvider here that is used to launch the Ad-hoc Query Designer. The Ad-hoc Query Designer is then dis-

played, along with the key figures and characteristics of the assigned Info-Provider, in the web application, which is generated in the web browser.

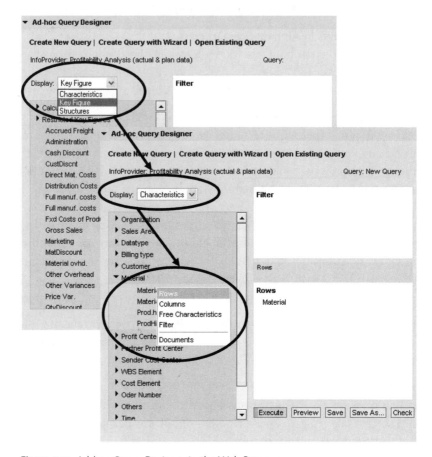

Figure 5.72 Ad-hoc Query Designer in the Web Browser

Name of the Query
Enter the technical name of the query here that is used to launch the Ad-hoc Query Designer.

Template for the Output
You must name the web template to be used for displaying the query results. When you run the generated queries, they're opened in a new window using the web template specified here. The Web Application Designer provides an input help for this attribute. There, you can select the web template from your history, favorites, or role, or from the list of workbooks. If you don't specify a web template, the system automatically uses the standard web template.

Frame for Outputting the Query

The **Frame for Outputting the Query** attribute is used to specify the name of the frame in which the query output is displayed at runtime. If you specify a frame here, the output of the query is directed into this frame. Otherwise, the query output is displayed in a new browser window.

Action on Execute

You can use this attribute to define what happens to the **Ad-hoc Query Designer** web item in the web application, if you click on the **Execute** button in the Ad-hoc Query Designer. This attribute is particularly useful, if you use the options provided by the **Display data provider** attribute (DISPLAY_DATA_PROVIDER). You can then run the queries of this web item in the same web template and control the display of the item.

The following options are available:

▶ **Web Item not changed**

The query is run with the specified web template in a new browser window, and the **Ad-hoc Query Designer** web item remains unchanged.

▶ **Web Item hidden**

The Ad-hoc Query Designer is hidden during the execution of the query. If you want to unhide the Ad-hoc Query Designer, click on the toolbar link in the standard web template. Then the Ad-hoc Query Designer is opened in another new window. If you use a different web template, you must manually integrate the option for unhiding the Ad-hoc Query Designer into that template.

▶ **Web Item collapses**

The Ad-hoc-Query Designer is collapsed during the execution of the query. You can see the web item with arrow and title collapsed. If you want to expand the Ad-hoc Query Designer, click on the arrow.

Action on Close

You can use this attribute to define what happens to the **Ad-hoc Query Designer** web item in the web application, if you click on the **Close** button in the Ad-hoc Query Designer. This attribute is particularly useful, if you use the options provided by the **Display data provider** attribute (DISPLAY_DATA_PROVIDER). You can then run the queries of this web item in the same web template and control the display of the item.

The following options are available:

▶ **Web Item not changed**
On closing, the query in the Ad-hoc Query Designer is closed. The individual fields—such as rows, columns, filters, or free characteristics—then remain empty. The web item itself does not change.

▶ **Web Item hidden**
The Ad-hoc-Query Designer is hidden upon closing. If you want to unhide it, click on the corresponding link in the toolbar of the standard web template. If you use a different web template, you must manually integrate the option for unhiding the Ad-hoc Query Designer into that template.

▶ **Web Item collapses**
The Ad-hoc Query Designer is collapsed upon closing. You can see the web item with arrow and title collapsed. If you want to expand the Ad-hoc Query Designer, click on the arrow.

Display Data Provider
Here you can specify the logical name of a data provider from the current template with whose query the Ad-hoc Query Designer is initially to be displayed in the web template. If you then open a query in the Ad-hoc Query Designer, or create and run a new query, this query can be executed in the same web template and applied to the data provider specified here, depending on the settings of the other attributes. The query from the Ad-hoc Query Designer is then applied to all web items contained in this web template, which receive their data from the specified data provider. For this attribute, the Web Application Designer provides a dropdown box with a list of all data providers contained or defined in the web template.

The following list describes the dependencies with other attributes of this item:

▶ If you specify a DISPLAY_DATA_PROVIDER but no TARGET_FRAME nor TARGET_TEMPLATE_ID, the specified DISPLAY_DATA_PROVIDER will be replaced in the current web template during the execution of the query.

▶ If you don't specify the optional attributes DISPLAY_DATA_PROVIDER, TARGET_FRAME, and TARGET_TEMPLATE_ID, the query results will be displayed in a new browser window in the standard web template for ad-hoc analyses.

▶ If you specify a value for the `DISPLAY_DATA_PROVIDER` and `TARGET_TEMPLATE_ID` attributes, the query of this item will be run in the specified template.

Example: Using the Ad-hoc Query Designer

The following requirement is used as an example to demonstrate the **Ad-hoc Query Designer** web item: You want to provide the user with an option for creating his or her own queries, or for opening existing queries to apply them to the web item **Table**. The chart is supposed to always display the same data. Moreover, you want to collapse the **Ad-hoc Query Designer** web item after running a query.

Requirements

▶ First, you must create a web template containing the web items **Table**, **Chart**, and **Ad-hoc Query Designer**.

▶ Create two data providers called DP1 and DP2 for the web items **Table** and **Chart** respectively.

▶ Then enter the logical name of the data provider for the table (DP1) into the **Display data provider** attribute of the **Ad-hoc Query Designer** web item (see Figure 5.73). The **Action on Close** attribute is assigned the value **Item collapses**. All other attributes keep their initial values.

▶ Save the web template and run it in the web browser.

▶ Select your new query and click on the **Execute** button (see Figure 5.74, Steps 1 through 4).

▶ The selected query is then displayed in the web item **Table**. The data contained in the web item **Chart** remains the same as when the template was initially called, and the **Ad-hoc Query Designer** web item is displayed as collapsed (see Figure 5.75).

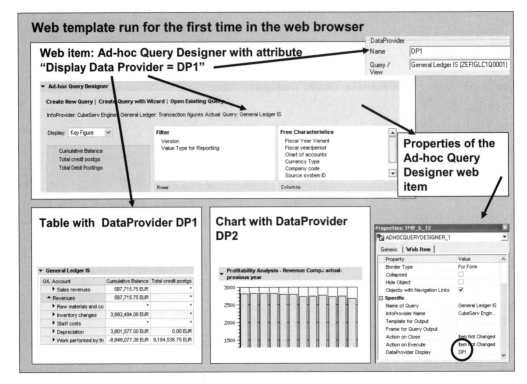

Figure 5.73 Possible Structure of a Web Template Containing the Ad-hoc Query Designer Web Item and Using the Display Data Provider Attribute

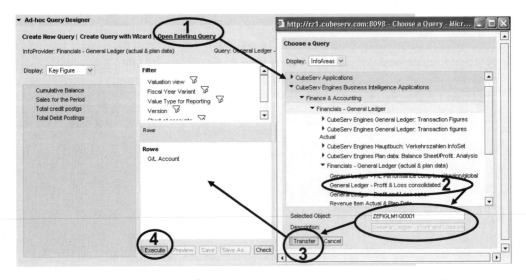

Figure 5.74 Selecting and Running a New Query in the Ad-hoc Query Designer Web Item

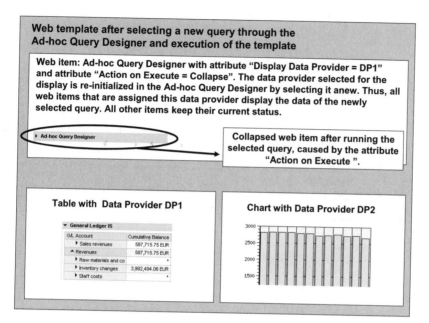

Figure 5.75 The Current Web Template After Running the New Query in the Ad-hoc Query Designer

5.5.15 Example: Sales Analysis with "Query View Selection"

The individual sales organizations of our model company, CubeServ Engines, need a web application that displays the actual sales figures as **Sales Revenues** in tabular form and broken down by different characteristics, as well as displayed in different charts. A dropdown box is supposed to enable the user to toggle between the various data and display types.

Requirements

For this purpose, you must first create different query views based on the sales data provided by the profitability analysis. These query views form the basis for the tables and charts of the web items in the web cockpit. The web items are stored in the different display variants in the web item library. The web item **Query View Selection** is used to enable a simple navigation between the different display variants.

Procedure

▶ Create the views listed in Table 5.6 on the basis of the queries ZECOPAM1Q00002 **Profitability Analysis—Revenue Overview Monthly** (see Section 4.3.3) and ZECOPAM1Q00001 **Profitability Analysis—Revenue Overview** (see Section 4.2.2).

Query View	Row Break-down	Column Breakdown
ZECOPAM1Q00002V0001, Revenue comparison YTD previous year—per company code	Company code	% of total cumulative YTD YTD previous year % YTD deviation compared to previous year
ZECOPAM1Q00002V0002, Revenue YTD—per company code	Company code	Net revenue
ZECOPAM1Q00001V0001, Revenue YTD time series—per company code	Company code	Monthly scenarios January to December
ZECOPAM1Q00001V0002, Revenue YTD time series—per product	Product hierarchy	Monthly scenarios January to December

Table 5.6 Creating Query Views

▶ Store the web items to be used for the display in the web item library (see Table 5.7).

Web Item	Type	Settings
ZEDIACIR001 Chart—pie	Chart	Define chart type, size, header, etc.
ZEDIABAL001 Chart—bars	Chart	Define chart type, size, header, etc.
ZETABLE01 Table—simple	Table	Define scrolling area, size, header, etc.

Table 5.7 Saving Web Items in the Library

▶ Drag the web item into a web template of your choice and then configure all parameters. After that, you can add the web item via the context menu to the web item library. If necessary, you can use the dialog provided there to create a new library (see Figure 5.76, Steps 1 through 5).

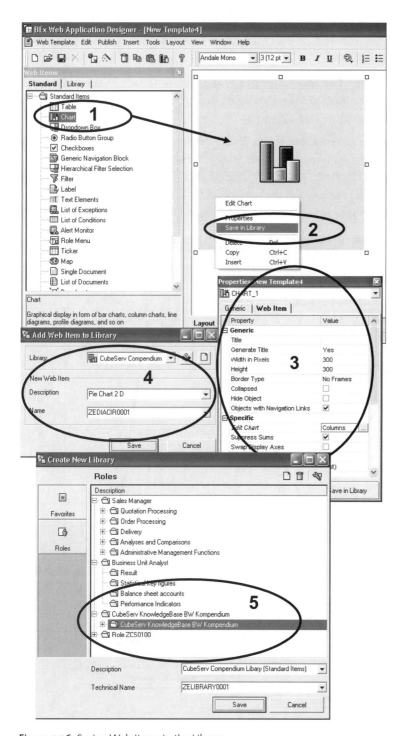

Figure 5.76 Saving Web Items in the Library

▶ Now you must create a new web template in the Web Application
Designer and place the **Query View Selection** web item from the **Web
Items** window in the layout mode (see Figure 5.77, Step 1).

Go to the **Generic** tab in the **Properties** window of the **Query View
Selection** web item and select one of the query views just created as a
data provider (Steps 2 and 3).

▶ Then include the web item **Table—Simple** into the layout mode. This
web item will be used as an assigned display web item for the **Query
View Selection**. Assign the logical name TABLE_1 to the web item
Table and then assign the data provider that you previously assigned to
Query View Selection to the table as well (Steps 4 and 5).

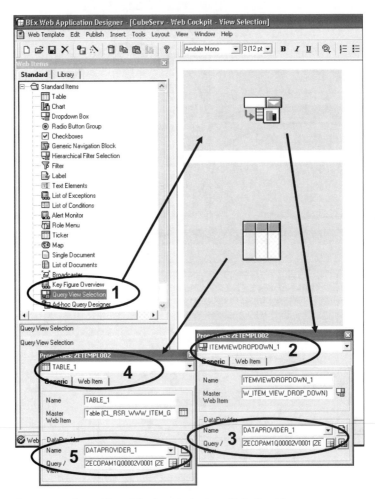

Figure 5.77 Query View Selection: Assigning a Data Provider

Maintaining Attributes

Then you should maintain the **List of Query Views** attributes of the web item **Query View Selection**. Select the web item from the dropdown box in the **Properties** window and then go to the **Web Item** tab. The following steps are necessary:

▶ Create the query and the two query views.

▶ Use the web item **Chart** in the Web Application Designer to create a **Bar chart** and save the chart in a library.

▶ Use the web item **Chart** in the Web Application Designer to create a **Pie chart** and save the chart in a library.

▶ Create a new template in the Web Application Designer and copy the web item **Query View Selection** from the **Web Items** window into the layout mode (see Figure 5.78, Step 1).

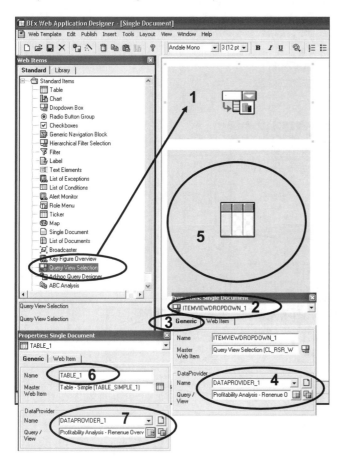

Figure 5.78 Query View Selection: Assigning a Data Provider

▶ Go to the **Generic** tab in the **Properties** window of the **Query View Selection** web item and select the query **Profitability Analysis—Revenue Overview** as a data provider (Steps 2 through 4).

▶ Then include the web item **Table** into the layout mode. This web item will be used as an assigned display web item for **Query View Selection**.

▶ Assign the logical name TABLE_1 to the web item **Table** and then assign the data provider you previously assigned to **Query View Selection** to the table as well (Steps 5 through 7).

▶ Then you should maintain the **List of Query Views** attributes of the web item **Query View Selection**. Select the web item from the drop-down box in the **Properties** window and then go to the **Web Item** tab (see Figure 5.79, Steps 1 and 2).

▶ Enter the logical name of the web item **Table** for the **Affected Web Item** attribute (here: TABLE_1, see Step 3).

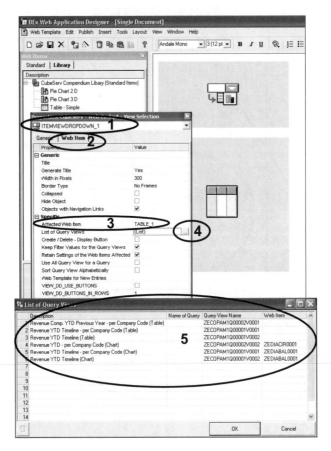

Figure 5.79 Query View Selection: Maintaining the List

▶ Then click on the maintenance button (...) of the relevant attribute to call the **List of Query Views** (Step 4).

▶ After that, you can store the **List of Query Views**. When doing so, you should use the function for assigning query views to web items, as described in Step 5.

▶ Save your web template as ZETEMPL002 **CubeServ—Revenue Cockpit** and launch it in your web browser. You can use the provided drop-down box to select from the list of three items. Depending on your selection, the data is displayed in different ways (see Figure 5.80).

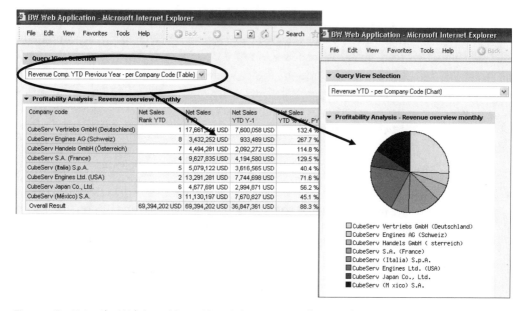

Figure 5.80 Using the Web Item "Query View Selection"—Simple Example

5.5.16 Example: Menu-Controlled Web Cockpit Providing Maps and Hierarchical Filter Selection

The employees at CubeServ Engines are supposed to get role-based access to web reports. This access can be controlled through a menu. To increase the amount of space available for displaying the actual information, it should be possible to hide the menu.

Overall requirements

In addition to the existing reports, another report that will be used for sales and profitability analyses is created. The data that results from this report should be displayed in maps using *geographical reporting*. The revenue is displayed using color shadings, whereas the percentage of the respective contribution margins in the revenue should be displayed as a bar chart. It is possible to filter the company codes on the basis of the company code hierarchy with regional hierarchy levels. Moreover, the report should contain the company logo.

The web item **Map** will be used for geographical reporting. It uses specifically prepared query views as data providers. For the hierarchical selection of the company code, we'll use the web item **Hierarchical Filter Selection**. The report will be called via the role menu. Along with the reports, this menu and the logo form three areas within one frameset. We'll use JavaScript to unhide and hide the role menu.

To use the web item Map, the underlying geographical reporting characteristics must be released (see Figure 5.81). Moreover, the associated maps must be loaded into SAP BW. In the standard version, this has already been done for the characteristics 0COUNTRY (**Country**) and 0REGION (**Region**). These two characteristics and all other characteristics referencing them can be used without a problem as geo-characteristics for displaying key figures in a map. Of course, you can also use navigation attributes such as the country of the customer (0CUSTOMER__ 0COUNTRY) to display the relevant information in a map.

The web item **Map** is composed of the actual map and its properties such as the presentation size or the navigation options, and different layers. A layer represents exactly one data provider. For each layer, you can use the *Map renderer* to choose a type of display. For example, this can be a bar chart or a pie chart.

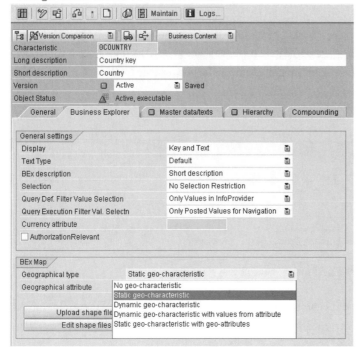

Change Characteristic 0COUNTRY: Detail

⊞ | 🖉 ⛐ | 🔒 | ⇅ | □ | ⊕ 🔲 Maintain | 🔢 Logs...

Ţ₌ | 🔠 Version Comparison | 🔳 | 🔳 | 🔳 | Business Content | 🔳

Characteristic	0COUNTRY
Long description	Country key
Short description	Country
Version	□ Active 🔳 Saved
Object Status	⚠ Active, executable

| General | Business Explorer | □ Master data/texts | □ Hierarchy | Compounding |

General settings

Display	Key and Text
Text Type	Default
BEx description	Short description
Selection	No Selection Restriction
Query Def. Filter Value Selection	Only Values in InfoProvider
Query Execution Filter Val. Selectn	Only Posted Values for Navigation
Currency attribute	
☐ AuthorizationRelevant	

BEx Map

Geographical type	Static geo-characteristic
Geographical attribute	

> No geo-characteristic
> Static geo-characteristic
> Dynamic geo-characteristic
> Dynamic geo-characteristic with values from attribute
> Static geo-characteristic with geo-attributes

Upload shape file
Edit shape files

Figure 5.81 Geographical Reporting: Changing the Characteristic 0COUNTRY

In our example, this means that we must create two map layers and assign a data provider to either layer. Moreover, we'll use two different query views:

Procedure

▶ One query view for the layer containing the formulas for the **Percentage of the contribution margin in the net revenues**, as this layer is to be displayed as a bar chart

▶ One query view for the **Net sales** layer, as this layer is to be displayed as a surface diagram

We don't need any more navigation options in the map for our example, but you can, of course, navigate further in the map.

If you use several layers and data providers in your map, you must maintain the **Affected Data Providers** for each layer in such a way that all data providers that are used for the map are always affected. Otherwise, you would always have to use a filter command for only one level and therefore for only one data provider, for example.

For our requirements, the following minimum steps are necessary:

▶ Provide the country of the company code as a navigation object in the InfoObject 0COMP_CODE to the InfoProvider ZECOPAC1, the Multi-Provider ZECOPAM1, and the query ZECOPAM1Q00003 **Profitability Analysis—Contribution Margin Targeting** (see Section 4.3.4).

▶ Create the two query views listed in Table 5.8 on the basis of that query.

Query View	Row Breakdown	Column Breakdown
ZECOPAM1Q00006V0001, Contribution margin percentage in revenues per company code	Country of the company code	Required formulas for % in net sales
ZECOPAM1Q00006V0002, Net sales per company code	Country of the company code	Net sales

Table 5.8 Query Views for Geographical Reporting

▶ In the local view of the query, you should activate the hierarchy for the company codes in both views and restrict it to the highest node (see Figure 5.82, Steps 1 and 2).

▶ Then you can save them with the names shown in Table 5.8 (Steps 3 and 4).

▶ Create a new web template in which you include the web items **Map**, **Hierarchical Filter Selection**, and **Text Elements**.

The map should have the following properties:

  ▶ Width: 800 pixels, height: 450 pixels

  ▶ To automatically zoom in on only a part of the map for the display area, you must set the **Extent of the Map** property to the value **Data Only**.

  ▶ Since we don't need to navigate through the map, you can disable the **Generate navigation links** property.

This also saves resources for the application server, because it can provide less information here.

  ▶ We don't want the system to determine the height of the map automatically.

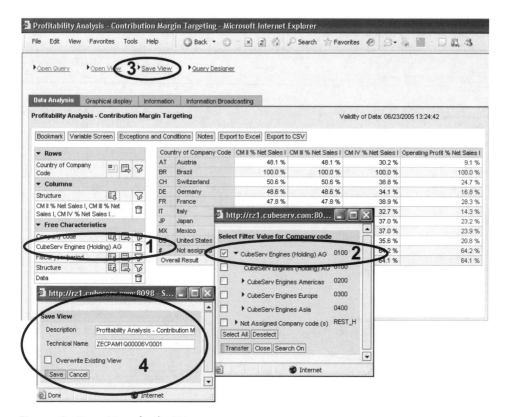

Figure 5.82 Query Views for the Map

This may result in distortions, but if only one country obtains data, the height will be calculated for that country in accordance with the defined width, which means that the country might become rather high (in this case, the user would see only a part of the country and would have to scroll up or down in order to see everything).

▶ We'll use a text element from our ABAP program for the header. In this way, we can enable multiple language support. We'll use the following syntax:

SAP_BW_TEXT?PROGRAM=ZA0TEXTEIMWEB2&KEY=083

▶ Now we must create a new map layer for each report.

▶ New map layers are created in the specific properties of the web item (see Figure 5.83, Steps 1 and 2).

▶ Select map layer 1 via the dropdown menu and go to the **Generic** tab to assign a new data provider to that layer (Step 3).

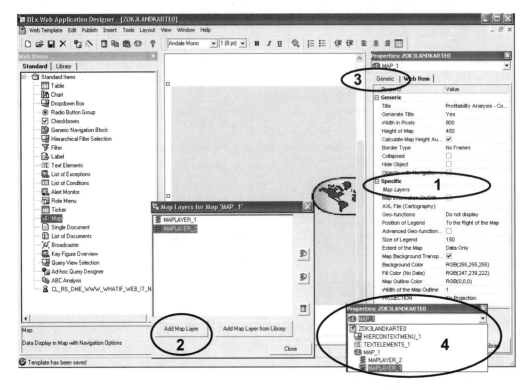

Figure 5.83 Creating a New Map Layer

▶ Click on the **Select View** button to select the view with the **Net Sales** key figure that was previously created (see Figure 5.84, Step 1).

▶ Then go to the **Web Item** tab and select the value **Color Shading** for the **Map Renderer** property (Step 2).

▶ To automatically obtain a finer gradation of the color shadings in the map (i.e., a finer gradation of the class limits based on the data), you should activate the property **Generate Class Limits**.

▶ To display the country names in the map as well, we'll select the value **Text as Label** for the **Label of the Map Layer** property, and we'll do that only for this map layer. The text with the value for the characteristic 0COUNTRY is now displayed in the map.

▶ Repeat these steps for the second map layer. Select **Bar Chart** as a map renderer for layer 2.

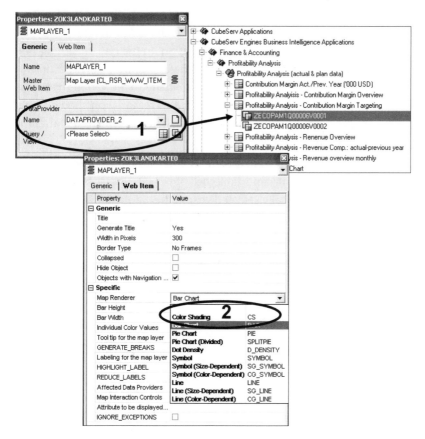

Figure 5.84 Data Providers and Properties of the Map

Creating a Hierarchical Filter Selection and Text Elements

The web items **Hierarchical Filter Selection** and **Text Elements** are to be placed next to each other above the map. We'll use HTML tables, which enables us to define the layout of the web application by ourselves.

► First we must insert a new HTML table into the web template. To do that, go to the **Insert** menu and select the menu item **Insert Table Insert Table** (see Figure 5.85, Step 1).

► The table should consist of one row and two columns (Step 2).

► The Hierarchical Filter Selection is placed above the map in the left-hand table cell (Step 3).

► We don't want to generate any title for the web item **Hierarchical Filter Selection** (Step 4).

- In the next step, we must assign data providers to this web item (Step 5). If a node is selected via the hierarchy, this value should be applied to all data providers of the web application. In the default setting, the command applies only to the stored data provider. However, in our example, we want to apply the filter command to the various data providers of the individual map layers. For this reason, you should select all data providers used in the web template in the **Affected Data Providers** property (Step 6).

- Now place the web item **Text Elements** next to the **Hierarchical Filter Selection** in the right-hand table cell. The text elements are used to display the automatically selected year in the web application (Step 7).

  - The web item **Text Elements** is assigned the same data provider as the web item **Hierarchical Filter Selection**.

  - We don't want to generate a title.

  - Because not all text elements of the assigned data provider are supposed to be displayed, the used variable of the **Fiscal Year** characteristic is entered via the **List of Text Elements** property (Step 8).

- Since query views are used in the web application, the used variables aren't processed again when the web template is called in the browser (provided the entry of variables is optional). Instead, they obtain their values from the query view. Still, you must delete the saved variable values and determine them again to ensure that the system always displays the current year. You can do that via the **Reset Variables to Default Values** property of the web template.

- Then you can save the web template (in our example, it is saved as ZETEMPL003) and run it in the web browser. Figure 5.86 illustrates the functionalities of the map, the hierarchical filter selection, and the text element.

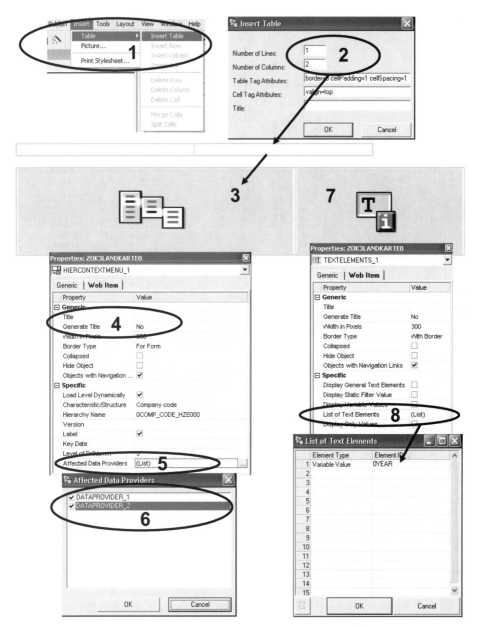

Figure 5.85 Additional Steps for Integrating the Relevant Web Items

Depending on the geo-characteristics used in the underlying data provider, you may be able to carry out very detailed analyses directly in the map. The context menu of the **Map** web item, which enables you to navigate the map on the web, does not yet work with Firefox.

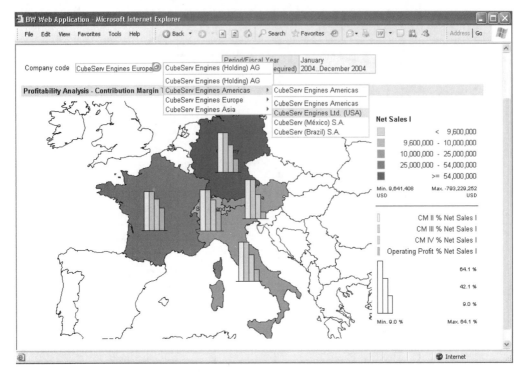

Figure 5.86 Web Application Containing a Map on the Web

Creating a Frameset with Layout and Role Menu

Requirements The role menu is supposed to enable access to all specifically created web templates for reporting on the web. To meet the requirements, we'll use the frame technology. We need a total of four templates:

▶ A web template that contains the defined frameset

▶ A web template that contains the logo and a link for opening and closing the role menu frame

▶ A web template that contains the web item **Role Menu** used for report selection

▶ The previously created web template, which contains the map (here: ZETEMPL003)

Procedure First, you must create the web template that contains the company logo. This frame should also contain a function to expand and collapse the role menu frame. This enables the user to increase the display area and to unhide the report selection menu, if necessary.

This function can be created with JavaScript, which is used to access the frameset definition where the size of the display area can be changed. This requires an interaction between the individual web templates, since JavaScript is used to access objects of other frames via their names. Furthermore, these objects must exist to ensure the proper functionality.

First we'll create the logo:

Creating a logo

▶ Create a new template in the WAD that will be used to display the logo.

▶ Use the menu path **Insert · Table · Insert Table** to insert an HTML table into the template. The table should consist of one row and two columns. Set the table width in the **Table Tag Attributes** field to **100 %**.

▶ In the next step, we'll place the company logo into the web template. Place the cursor into the right table cell, open the menu **Insert · Picture**, and select the logo from the company-specific MIMES. Then mark the logo in the web template and click on the **right-aligned** button in the application toolbar (see Figure 5.87, Step 1).

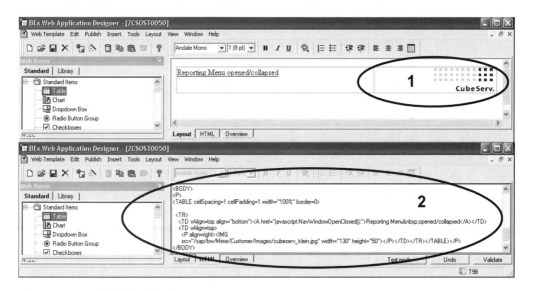

Figure 5.87 Steps to Create the Logo Frame

▶ Now you still need a hyperlink in the left-hand table cell that is used to call the JavaScript function for showing and hiding the role menu. Moreover, you must also insert that JavaScript function in the HTML code. To do that, change to the HTML code of the web template.

▶ Insert the following code inside the ⟨HEAD⟩ and ⟨/HEAD⟩ area:

```
⟨head⟩
. . .
⟨script type="text/javascript"⟩
function NavWindowOpenClosed(){
NavWindow = window.top.frames.document.getElementById
("Navigation");
if(NavWindow.cols=="0,*"){
Nav.Window.cols="250,*";
}
else{ Nav.Window.cols="0,*"; }
} }
⟨/script⟩
. . .
⟨/head⟩
```

▶ The line `NavWindow = window.top.frames.document.getElementById("Navigation");` in this code enables access to the **Navigation** object in the top frame of the window. This object must also be included in the frameset definition.

▶ Then the JavaScript function call must be inserted in the HTML code as well. For this purpose, the following entry must be made in the left-hand table cell (in the code between ⟨td⟩ and ⟨/td⟩, see Figure 5.87, Step 2): `⟨a href="javascript:NavWindowOpenClosed();"⟩⟨SAP_BW_TEXT PROGRAM="ZAOTEXTEIMWEB2" KEY= "102"⟩⟨/a⟩`

▶ The text **Report Menu open/close** has now been integrated as a language-dependent hyperlink including a JavaScript function call into the web template.

▶ Return to the layout mode and save the template (as `ZETEMPL004`).

Note that in the layout mode only a placeholder is displayed, and not the actual language-dependent text.

Creating the role menu

The next template to be created is the one that contains the role menu:

▶ Create a new template in the Web Application Designer.

▶ Drag&Drop the web item **Role Menu** from the **Web Items** window into the layout area (Figure 5.88, Step 1).

- ► The default settings of the role menu won't be changed so that all available role items and favorites are displayed.
- ► Now you must tell the role menu in which frame it should open the individual reports. For this purpose, you must assign the logical name of the target frame to its **Name** of Target Frame attribute. In our example, this will be the **main** frame, and we'll assign this name to the frame in the frameset definition (Step 2).
- ► Save the web template (here ZETEMPL005).

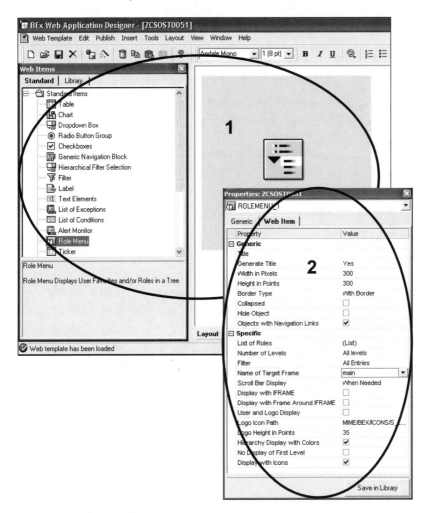

Figure 5.88 Role Menu Frame

The last template we have to create is the definition of the frameset. The Web Application Designer can't handle frameset definitions, which is why

Creating the frameset

SAP integrated the text mode as of Release 3.5. This text mode is used to enter the frameset definition.

▶ Create a new template for the frameset in the Web Application Designer.

▶ Change to the HTML mode and then into the text mode.

A warning dialog displays, which you must confirm as you can't return to the layout mode once you're in the text mode and the template is only available in the text mode from hereon.

▶ Now delete the area within, including the `<BODY>` and `</BODY>` tags, and enter the following frameset definition:

```
<frameset rows="60,*">
<frame name="top" src="<SAP_BW_URL CMD='LDOC' TEMPLATE_
ID='ZETEMPL005'>">
<frameset id="Navigation" cols="250,*">
<frame name="nav" src="<SAP_BW_URL CMD='LDOC' TEMPLATE_
ID='ZETEMPL004'>">
<frame name="main" src="<SAP_BW_
URL CMD='LDOC' TEMPLATE_ID='ZETEMPL003'>">
</frameset>
</frameset>
```

▶ The frameset definition defines three frames. Each frame is assigned a logical name in the **Name** attribute. The template that is to be loaded into a frame is specified using a command URL (see also Section 5.7).

　▶ The template containing the logo is loaded into the upper frame.

　▶ The role menu is loaded into the bottom left-hand frame.

　▶ The previously created web template, which contains the map, is loaded into the bottom right-hand frame.

The frameset for the horizontal separation must still be assigned a unique ID so that the JavaScript function can adjust the width of the role menu from the logo frame. Note that the entries are case-sensitive.

▶ Save the template (here ZETEMPL006) and call it in the web browser. You can integrate this hyperlink into the intranet or portal. The **Report Menu open/close** link enables you to show and hide the role menu.

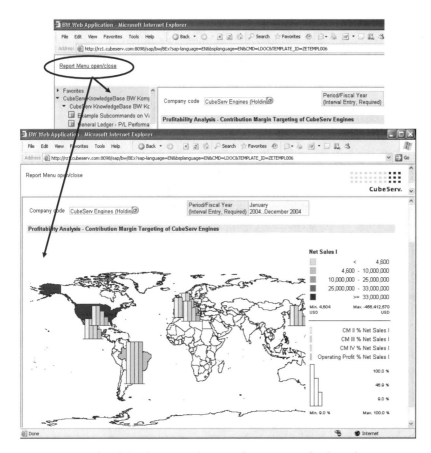

Figure 5.89 Final Web Application with Open/Close Function for the Role Menu

5.5.17 Example: Simple Web Cockpit for Personnel Administration

Our model company, CubeServ Engines, wants to create a cockpit for the HR department that can be used for personnel administration on the web. In the first expansion phase, it should be possible to display a picture of the employee and the corresponding resume.

Requirements

The photograph of the employee is available as a JPG file, while the CV is stored as a PDF file. These files must be loaded into SAP BW as master data documents for the individual characteristic values, and displayed in reporting using the web item **Individual Document**.

In the following example, we'll create two documents for the specific characteristic value 0EMPLOYEE—**Employee** in the Business Document Service of the Administrator Workbench (Transaction RSA1). One of

Procedure

those documents contains a picture of the employee, while the other document shows the employee's profile. The different documents are classified by the **Document Type** attribute:

▶ Picture of the employee, format: .jpg, document type: PICTURE

▶ Profile of the employee, format: .pdf, document type: PROFILE

In the next step, we must create the web application. For our web application, we'll also use the IFrame technology to display the PDF document, which can't be displayed by the web item, in an IFrame. A dropdown box should be provided, from which the user can select the employees of an employee group. If an employee is selected, the stored picture should be displayed by the web item **Individual Document**, and the PDF file should be displayed in an IFrame.

You must perform the following steps when creating the documents:

▶ Go to the document management component of the Administrator Workbench (Transaction RSA1) and select **Master Data** (see Figure 5.90, Steps 1 and 2).

▶ Enter the technical name of the characteristic (here 0EMPLOYEE, Step 3), and click on the **Show me documents from ...** button (Step 4).

▶ Click on the button to import a document (Step 5), select the required document from the **Open** File dialog that pops up, and click on the **Open** button (Steps 6 and 7).

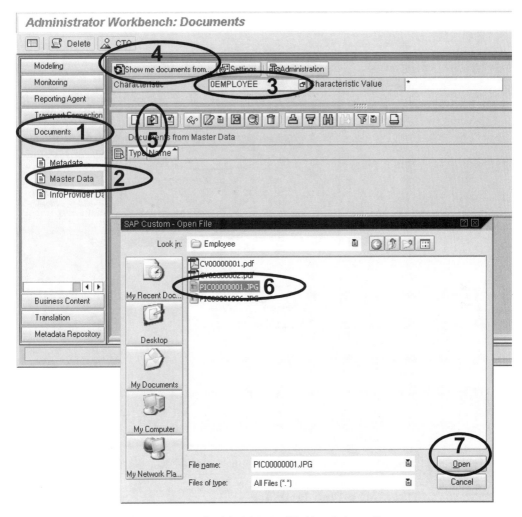

Figure 5.90 Document Management in the Administrator Workbench: Importing Documents

▶ After that, another dialog displays in which you must enter a technical name and a description for your document (see Figure 5.91, Step 1).

▶ Then, open the **Log.Doc.Properties** tab (Step 2).

▶ In this tab, you must define the Characteristic Value to which the document applies. In our example, this is the value 00000001 (Step 3).

▶ Moreover, you must assign the value PICTURE to the **Document Type** attribute. This value is freely selectable (Step 4).

▶ Repeat this process for the PDF document and assign the value PROFILE to the document type attribute.

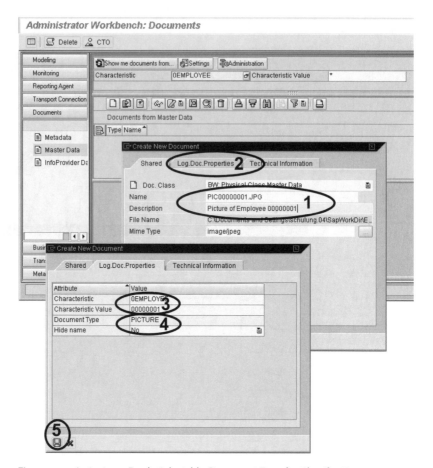

Figure 5.91 Assigning a Freely Selectable Document Type for Classification

Creating a Web Template

Next we'll create a new web template for our application in the Web Application Designer. For that, we'll use the following web items:

▶ **Dropdown Box** (once)

▶ **Individual Document** (twice)

Proceed as follows:

▶ Launch the Web Application Designer and create a new web template.

▶ Drag&Drop the web item **Dropdown Box** once from the **Web Items** window into the layout mode of your template (see Figure 5.92, Steps 1 and 2).

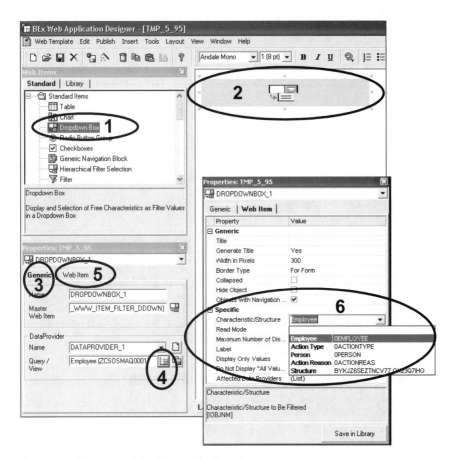

Figure 5.92 Creating and Configuring the Dropdown Box

▶ Then go to the **Generic** tab in the **Properties** window of the web item **Dropdown Box** and select a query that will provide the necessary data to the data provider (Steps 3 and 4).

▶ Then select the **Web Item** tab (Step 5), click on the dropdown box next to the **Characteristic/Structure** attribute and select the relevant characteristic from the list provided (all characteristics and structures of the assigned data provider). In our example, this is the characteristic **Employee** (Step 6).

▶ Then, you must integrate the web item **Individual Document** into your web template. This web item will be used to display the stored picture of the employee. To do that, go to the **Properties** window and select the **Web Item** tab for the **Individual Document** (see Figure 5.93).

Web item "Individual Document"

▶ Then you must assign the values listed in Table 5.9 to the attributes of the web item **Individual Document**.

Attribute	Value
Document Class (DOCUMENT_CLASS)	Master data (='MAST')
Document Type (WWW_DOC_TYPE)	PICTURE (='PICTURE')
Characteristic (IOBJNM)	Employee (='0EMPLOYEE')
Display in the same window (IS_INPLACE)	Yes (='X')
Links for document display (LINK_TO_BOWSER)	No (=' ')
Target Frame (TARGET_FRAME)	Default value of this page (without) (=' ')
Default Picture (DEFAULT_PICTURE_URL)	/sap/bw/MIME/BEX/ICONS/s_n_warn.gif (='/sap/bw/MIME/BEX/ICONS/s_n_warn.gif')

Table 5.9 List of Values for the Individual Attributes of the Web Item "Individual Document"

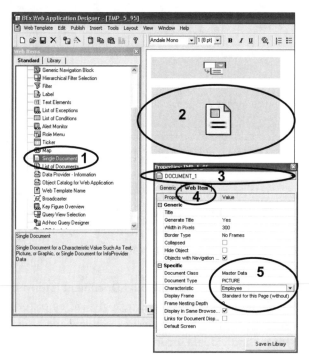

Figure 5.93 Web Item "Individual Document" for Displaying a Picture of the Employee

▶ Now we must integrate another **Individual Document** web item and an IFrame into the web template. This web item will be used to display the stored profile of the employee. Since the profile has been stored as a PDF document, the web item can't display it without any additional input from us in the browser. The reason is that we have to integrate an IFrame into the same web template and communicate the name of the IFrame to the web item by using the **Target Frame** (TARGET_FRAME) attribute.

▶ To integrate an IFrame into the web template, proceed as follows:

▶ In the Web Application Designer, select the HTML mode (see Figure 5.94, Step 1).

▶ Insert the following code for creating the IFrame between the HTML tags <BODY> and </BODY>.

> Note that you must place the IFrame before the second **Individual Document** web item in the HTML code, because the document for the IFrame is called by a JavaScript statement that is generated from the web item (Step 2). If the JavaScript statement is executed prior to the IFrame, this generates an error as at that point in time the IFrame is still unknown to the browser:
>
> ```
> <IFRAME NAME="DOC_PROFIL" SRC="" WIDTH="550" HEIGHT="250" SCROL-
> LING="auto"></IFRAME>
> ```

▶ Return to the Layout mode (Step 3). In the layout mode of the Web Application Designer, the IFrame is displayed as a blue area of the size specified in the code.

▶ Place the second **Individual Document** web item in your web template (Step 4).

▶ Go to the **Properties** window and select the **Web Item** tab for the **Individual Document** (Step 6).

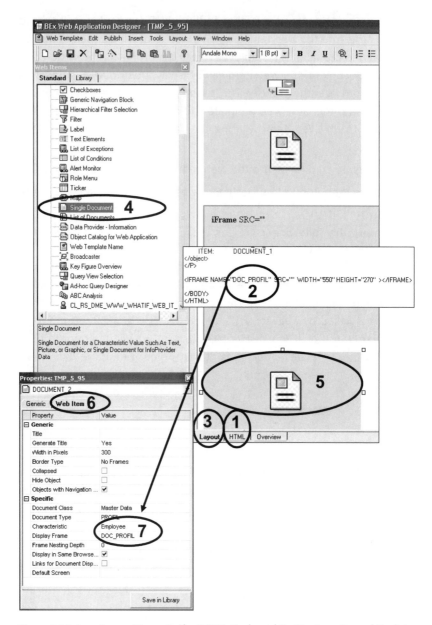

Figure 5.94 Inserting an IFrame in the HTML Mode and Positioning a Second "Individual Document" Web Item for Displaying the Profile Stored as a PDF Document

▶ Then you must assign the values listed in Table 5.10 to the attributes of the web item **Individual Document**.

Attribute	Value
Generate Caption (GENERATE_CAPTION)	No (=' ')
Document Class (DOCUMENT_CLASS)	Master data (='MAST')
Document Type (WWW_DOC_TYPE)	PROFILE (='PROFILE')
Characteristic (IOBJNM)	Employee (='0EMPLOYEE')
Display in the same window (IS_INPLACE)	Yes (='X')
Links for document display (LINK_TO_BOWSER)	No (=' ')
Target Frame (TARGET_FRAME)	DOC_PROFILE (name of the IFrame) (='DOC_PROFILE')
Default Picture (DEFAULT_PICTURE_URL)	/sap/bw/MIME/BEX/ICONS/s_n_warn.gif (='/sap/bw/MIME/BEX/ICONS/s_n_warn.gif')

Table 5.10 List of Values for the Attributes of the Web Item "Individual Document"

▶ Finally, save your web template and call it in a web browser.

Figure 5.95 displays the final web application in the web browser. When the application is called for the first time, the graphic stored for the **Default Picture** attribute is displayed, because the system cannot determine any document for the characteristic value **All** that is provided by the dropdown box. The corresponding documents cannot be determined and displayed until an employee has been selected.

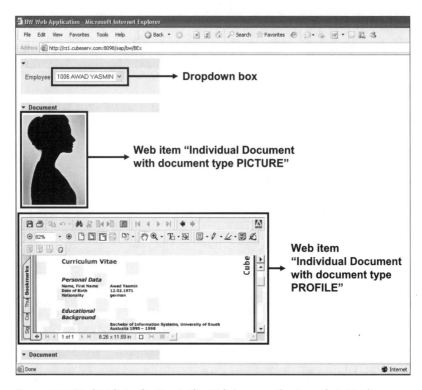

Figure 5.95 Final Web Application in the Web Browser. The Example Is Used to Demonstrate the Functionality Only. For This Reason, the Design Was Kept As Simple As Possible.

Business Add-In (BAdI) For document management purposes, *Business Add-Ins (BAdIs)* are available in SAP BW Customizing. These BAdIs enable you to program your own extensions for the individual document functions.[13] For example, an extension interface is also provided for the **Individual Document** web item in the Implementation Guide of SAP BW (Transaction SPRO). You can use this BAdI to modify the output and functionality of the web item **Individual Document** to meet your specific requirements. For example, you can generate the following functionalities:

▶ Displaying additional properties of the document such as **Last Changed By** or **Last Changed At**

▶ Displaying the contents of the document

▶ Integrating hyperlinks for changing or creating documents into the web application

---

13 Please see OSS Note 598797 for more information.

You can find the Customizing setting for creating a BAdI for the web item Individual Document via the following menu path: **Transaction SPRO · SAP Reference IMG · SAP NetWeaver · SAP Business Information Warehouse · BW Extensions · BAdIs for Document Management · BAdI: Web Item Individual Document**. For these types of extensions, you must know ABAP.

5.6 Web Item Library

A library is a group of web items. To avoid having to enter repetitive settings in web items every time they appear, you can store these web items with their specific settings in a library. You can create and manage any number of libraries according to various criteria. The library is located in the **Library** tab of the **Web Items** window in the Web Application Designer (see Figure 5.96).

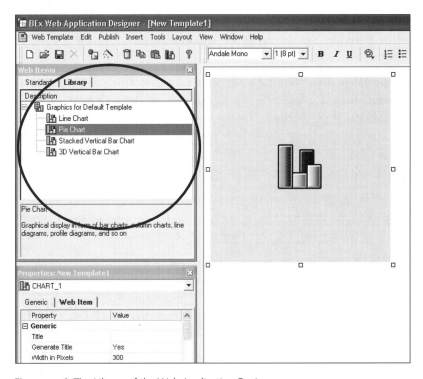

Figure 5.96 The Library of the Web Application Designer

You can create several different libraries in SAP BW that help you structure and organize your own custom web items, which you want to use as templates.

Another benefit of using web items from libraries is the maintainability of web templates and web items. For example, you will probably use the web item **Table** in most of your web templates.

▶ Suppose you have changed the value of the attribute **Number of rows displayed together** in the web item **Table** from the default value 100 to 25. Now you want to apply this setting to all instances of the web item **Table**, because you don't want your web application to contain any scroll bars, which is why the results area of the table should be restricted to 25 rows.

▶ The application now provides buttons that enable the user to scroll through the results rows.

▶ Save your individual web item **Table** in a library and use it as a template for all other web templates.

▶ If, at a later stage, you realize that the display area still allows for more rows without the user having to scroll, you can increase the value of the attribute **Number of rows displayed together** in the web item **Table** from 25 to 27.

Effects of changes

If you change the settings of a web item that is stored in the library, it has a global effect on all web templates that contain this web item. But, you can exclude some of the referencing web items from being affected by the change to the master web item (i.e., the item from the library). If you change the settings of a web item locally, these settings remain unaffected by a change to the master web item.

Furthermore, you can create, edit, and display separate documents for each web item that is stored in a library. In this way, you can document and, if necessary, call the web items that you created.

The use of libraries has become very attractive with the introduction of Release 3.5. The extensive use of the web item **Query View Selection** has made the libraries an indispensable component. Furthermore, since Release 3.5, you can save the attribute **Alternative ABAP OO Class** for tables in libraries as well. This enables you to provide an increased and more sophisticated scope of functionality. For example, you can use individual ABAP-OO classes to extend the functionality of tables to meet your needs. Also, the ability to store these tables in libraries facilitates their reuse and future use dramatically, since you no longer need to add the additional attribute in the HTML code of each web template for the web item **Table**.

Section 5.5.15 contains an example, which includes the use of the library.

In the following sections, we'll demonstrate how you can use, create, edit, and open libraries and also, how you can add, edit, and delete web items from the library.

Creating a Library

To create a new library, proceed as follows:

▶ Select the **Library** tab of the **Web Items** window (see Figure 5.97, Step 1).

▶ Right-click in the **Web Items** window to open the context menu of the library management (Step 2). You can either open an existing library or create a new one. Select **Create New Library**.

▶ The system now displays the Create New Library dialog (Step 3). Here you can save the library that you want to create in one of your personal favorites folders, or as a role. Save the library in a role to provide other web application developers with easy access to your library.

▶ Assign a description and a technical name (you must use unique names within individual libraries) to your new library and click on the **Save** button.

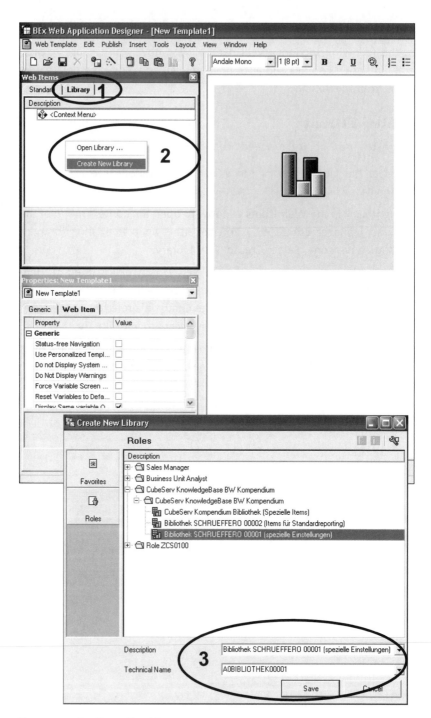

Figure 5.97 Creating a New Library

Once you have saved the library, it is displayed as an empty library in the **Library** tab of the **Web Items** window (see Figure 5.98). The context menu of the library (right-click on the library) provides the following options to process it further:

▶ Open Library ...

▶ Close Library

▶ Create New Library

▶ Delete Library

▶ Change Description

▶ Documents

▶ Publish Library in Role ...

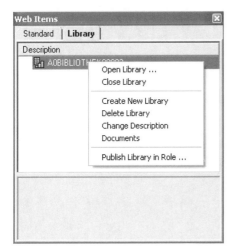

Figure 5.98 Context Menu Providing Options for Using the Library

Saving a Web Item in the Library

As you have integrated a web item in your web template and made the necessary settings in the **Web Items** tab of the **Properties** window, you can now save the web item in a library in the following two different ways:

▶ You can use the **Save in Library** button in the **Properties** window of the web item (see Figure 5.99, 1)

▶ Or, you can use the context menu in the layout area (2)

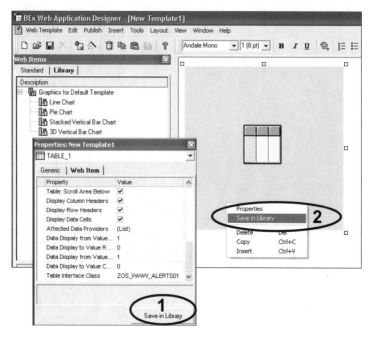

Figure 5.99 Options for Saving a Web Item in a Library

Figure 5.100 "Save" Dialog for Adding Web Items to Libraries

5.7 Command URLs

The BEx Web provides many different functions for a large number of objects such as data providers, web items, the web template, the context menu, the report-report interface, and so forth. Thus, there are different commands available, such as the filter command for data providers, for instance, that can be sent via a hyperlink to the Web Application Server. The BEx Web processing logic processes those commands and sends the newly-generated HTML source code back to the browser, which, in turn, displays the result.

Each command consists of the actual command and its properties. The properties of a command can contain different values, that is, the commands can be parameterized. Now, let's look at the filter command for data providers.

Filtering Data Providers

In a web application, you can select the item **Keep Filter Value** from the context menu of a table cell (see Figure 5.101).

▶ For example, if you right-click in the table cell containing the characteristic value 2000 for the **Company code** characteristic in order to open the context menu, you can select the item **Keep Filter Value**, among others.

▶ If you select this menu item, the data provider assigned to the web item **Table** will be restricted to the value 2000 of the characteristic **Company code**. This functionality is available for almost every table cell, with the exception of the data cells.

▶ If you select the item **Keep Filter Value** from the context menu, a URL containing all the necessary information is generated in the background and sent to the Web Application Server.

▶ The BEx Web processing logic of the Web Application Server then analyzes and executes the URL. A new HTML code is generated and sent back to the browser.

Posting period	Company code		Value Type
Jan	1000	CubeServ Vertriebs GmbH (Deutschland)	Actual
	Keep Filter Value	z)	Actual
	Select Filter Value	rreich)	Actual
	Filter and drilldown according to ▶		Actual
	Drilldown ▶		Actual
	Remove Drilldown		Actual
			Actual
	Sort Company code ▶		Actual
	Goto ▶		Actual

Figure 5.101 Commands in the Context Menu for the Data Provider Assigned to the Web Item "Table"

To send a filter command to the Web Application Server, you need the address of the Web Application Server and the path for the responsible service. Since most system landscapes consist of at least one test system and one production system, which, in most cases, are two physically separate machines, it doesn't make sense to enter a hard-coded address for the Web Application Server (e.g., a hyperlink), because this address

would no longer work once the created web template was transported from the development system to the production system. Therefore, it is preferable to use variables that can be assigned the appropriate values, depending on the system. For the BEx Web, special tags or placeholders are provided in the HTML code of the template, which are replaced by the BEx Web processing logic when a web browser calls a template. For example, the following tag is used as a default placeholder for various BW-specifc commands:
`<SAP_BW_URL>`.

At runtime, the placeholder `<SAP_BW_URL>` is converted into the relevant specifications, such as the path of the corresponding BEx service on the Web Application Server. Typically, the following string is generated for this placeholder:
`/sap/bw/BEx?SAP-LANGUAGE=D&PAGENO=1& REQUEST_NO=2`.

The beginning of the string up to and including the question mark (`/sap/bw/BEx?`) addresses the BEx Web Service on the Web Application Server. After the question mark, there are only attributes (`SAP-LANGUAGE`) with their corresponding values (`=D`); attributes can also be transferred with blank values (example: `FILTER_VALUE=`). Each attribute is followed by the equals sign (=), which, in turn, is followed by the value of the attribute. If another attribute follows, it is added to the URL with an ampersand (**&**). In this way, you can string together a maximum of 2048 characters that can be sent to the Web Application Server.

Please note that you cannot combine all commands simply in a URL; however, there are ways to make this possible. SAP provides the option of using command URLs.[14] Those command URLs enable you to re-initialize several different commands (e.g., a web item) and to simultaneously set a filter for the characteristic **Fiscal Year/Period**. But, the syntax of the command URLs is slightly different from the syntax described here.

Command URL as a Hyperlink in the Web Template

For the filter command, we must now add several attribute-value pairs to the basic placeholder `<SAP_BW_URL>`. It is important that we provide this information in the URL so that the BEx Web knows which data provider

---

14 For more information on command URLs please refer to the SAP Online Documentation.

it has to apply the filter command to. This looks as follows in the place-holder:

```
<SAP_BW_URL DATA_PROVIDER='logical name of the DP'>.
```

The character string generated at runtime would then look as follows: `/sap/bw/BEx?SAP-LANGUAGE=D&PAGENO=1&REQUEST_NO=2&DATA_PROVIDER=DP1`.

Here we have communicated to the BEx Web Service that something needs to be done with the data provider DP1. But, it still needs to know what has to be done. We want to restrict the data provider DP1 to the value 1000 of the **Company code** characteristic. The placeholder in the HTML code of the web template should have the following structure:

```
<a href="<SAP_BW_URL DATA_PROVIDER='DP1' FILTER_
IOBJNM='0COMP_CODE' FILTER_VALUE='1000'>">Filter on com-
pany code 1000</a>.
```

At runtime, the following string is generated in the HTML source text and is included in an HTML anchor (hyperlink):

```
<a href="/sap/bw/BEx?SAP-LANGUAGE=D&PAGENO=1&REQUEST_NO=2&
DATA_PROVIDER=DP1&FILTER_IOBJNM=0COMP_CODE&FILTER_VALUE=
1000">Filter on company code 1000</a>.
```

The text **Filter on Company code 1000** is then displayed as a hyperlink in the web browser. If you click on this hyperlink, the corresponding filter command is sent to the Web Application Server for more processing.

Command URL in the Address Bar of the Browser

In addition to storing the individual commands as hyperlinks in the web template, you can also include them in the initial URL when you launch the web template. For example, you can preassign the variables contained in the data provider when calling the web template. The following URL, which can be started from the role menu or the intranet, would open the web template ZOSBWK3T02 and preassign the value 1000 to the variable COMPCP0.

```
http://rz1.cubeserv.com:8098/sap/bw/BEx?sap-language=
DE&bsplanguage=DE&CMD=LDOC&TEMPLATE_ID=
ZOSBWK3T023&VAR_NAME=COMPCP0&VAR_VALUE_EXT=1000.
```

The BEx Web provides many different commands, including their attributes, that enable you to create very powerful and flexible web applications. Unfortunately, we can't provide a comprehensive and detailed description of the individual BEx Web commands in this volume of the SAP BW Library; however, for additional information, you should refer to the SAP BW online help.

5.8 Web Design API for Tables

The Web Design API for Tables is an interface provided by SAP, or rather a customer or user exit, that enables you to manipulate the output, the contents, the functionality, and the appearance of individual table cells and even of entire web applications. However, the Web Design API for Tables is only available for the web items **Table** and **Generic Navigation Block**. This means that you can only manipulate the output (i.e., the HTML code to be generated) of those two web items. But there are several options available that you can use to query the navigation status, the static and dynamic filter values, and the set variable values. Based on this information, you can include, for instance, specific JavaScript code in the source code of the web application and thus enhance its functionality.

In the SAP BW Release 2.x, the Web Design API for Tables—also referred to as the Table Interface—is the only way to provide a report-to-report interface in web applications, because the standard version doesn't have an interface for tables. Even today, despite the enormous increase in BEx Web options provided by SAP, many requirements couldn't be met without the Table Interface; and if they could, then only with a lot of extra effort due to the complex interaction inherent in using the functionality of web items, HTML, and JavaScript.

As a simple example, let's take a look at the following requirement: You want to create a business intelligence cockpit and output defined exceptions of a data provider as a traffic-light graphic within a table cell, instead of using their actual values. For example, a negative deviation by 10 % of the actual value from the target revenue would generate the alert level 9. Usually, this exception would be displayed with the actual value and red background color in the table cell of the generated table. The Table Interface enables you to query the different alert levels and manipulate the output of the table cell according to your requirements, for instance, by redefining the cell contents even before the HTML code is transferred to the browser. Therefore, you can store the path of a picture that you want to display, for example. At the end of this section, we'll provide step-by-step instructions for this example to show you just how powerful this interface really is.

To use the Web Design API for Tables, you should have experience in ABAP, HTML, and JavaScript. The Table Interface is provided by an ABAP-OO class (object-oriented ABAP) that inherits from the processing superclass. This ABAP-OO class must be assigned to the relevant web items via the attribute **Modified ABAP Class** (MODIFY_CLASS) so that the processing knowledge knows which class is responsible for generating the output of the web item.

Required knowledge

The predefined superclass (CL_RSR_WWW_MODIFY_TABLE) provides many different methods and attributes that include a large number of processing options. When the user-defined class is called by the BEx Web processing logic, all values and descriptions for the individual table cells and the navigation status have already been determined internally. If you're interested in further information on the individual attributes and methods, we'd like to refer you to the SAP BW online help at this stage, as this subject matter is too complex for us to describe it in this volume of the SAP BW Library.

Advanced Formatting Using the Web API

The controlling department of CubeServ Engines has the following requirement: For the overview page of its web cockpit (business intelligence cockpit), which, among other things, displays a table containing active exceptions, a traffic-light graphic should be used instead of the actual exception values. Depending on the alert level of the exception (red, orange, green), different graphics, in other words, different traffic-light colors, should be displayed.

Requirement

In the standard version, you can modify the layout of a cell only by using the styles of a style sheet and integrating a background image into the table cell, which means the cell value is always displayed. For this reason, our model company has decided to implement this requirement using the *Web Design API for Tables*. The following steps are necessary:

Procedure

▶ Log on to your SAP BW system and start the Transaction **Class Builder: Initial Screen** (Transaction code SE24). You must be registered as a developer and have a developer key for this system.

▶ Assign a technical name for the class to be created and click on the **Create** button (see Figure 5.102, Steps 1 and 2).

▶ Select the value **Class** in the subsequent screen and confirm your selection (Steps 3 and 4).

- ▶ The system then prompts you to enter a short description for your class (Step 5).

- ▶ Then, click on the **Create Inheritance** button to assign the superclass (Step 6).

- ▶ An additional input field is now displayed. Here you must enter the technical name of the superclass, CL_RSR_WWW_MODIFY_TABLE and then click on the **Save** button (Steps 7 and 8).

Once you have created the class, the system displays the screen shown in Figure 5.103. It displays all methods that have been adopted from the specified superclass. A separate method that can be used for processing is available for almost every table cell type. For example, if the contents of a characteristic cell are generated (example: company code 1000), the BEx Web processing logic calls the method CHARACTERISTIC_CELL. Various import parameters are available for each method, and these parameters can be queried for further processing.

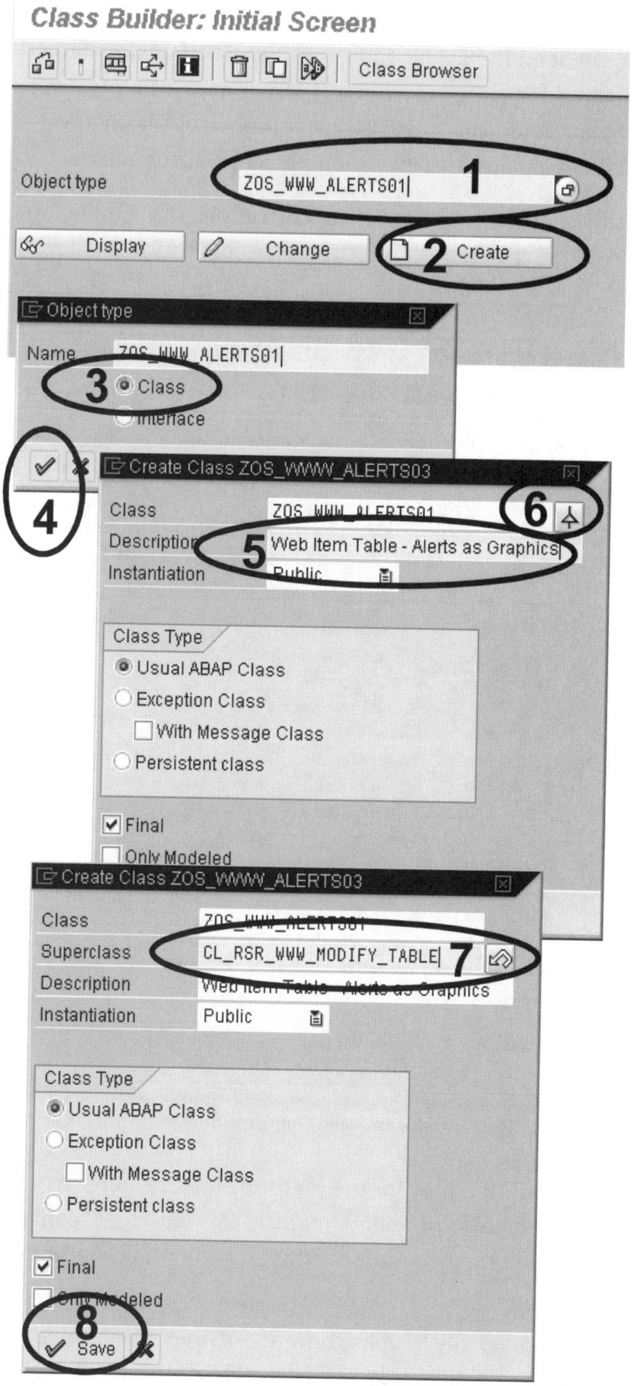

Figure 5.102 Creating an ABAP-OO Class That Inherits from the Superclass CL_RSR_
WWW_MODIFY_TABLE

Defining Methods

For our scenario, we need the DATA_CELL method. The individual methods must be redefined for our class, which means a new local processing logic must be implemented for this method; otherwise, the method of the superclass that we cannot modify would be called automatically.

▶ To redefine the method, position the cursor on the DATA_CELL method and click on the **Redefine** button (see Figure 5.103, Steps 1 and 2).

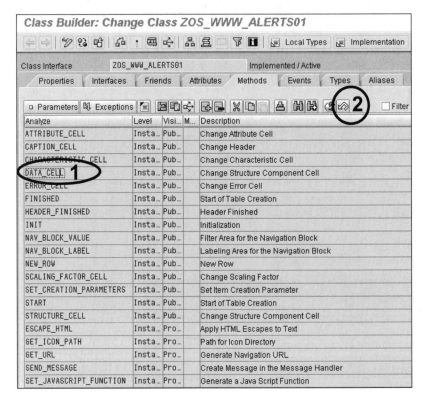

Figure 5.103 The Generated Class for Processing in the Class Builder

▶ You are now in the ABAP Editor for the method. This is where we must implement our logic. Almost every method of our class contains attributes that can be modified, namely the following four methods:

  ▶ **C_CELL_CONTENT**
    This attribute displays the visible contents of the HTML table cell that will display in the web browser. The value of this attribute will be displayed later in the web browser and is thus located between the ⟨TD⟩ and ⟨/TD⟩ tags in the HTML source code.

▶ **C_CELL_STYLE**

This attribute contains the Cascading Style Sheet (CSS) class assigned by the BEx Web processing logic in the standard version. This class contains formatting details and determines the appearance of the table cell contents in the web browser. You can use your own styles here and assign a different formatting to every individual table cell if you like. If you assign a value to this attribute, the following HTML code is generated: `<td class="<My value>">`.

▶ **C_CELL_ID**

Typically, this attribute doesn't contain a value. Here, you can assign an ID to each table cell. The ID must be unique. You can then use JavaScript to address the HTML table cell within the document via the unique ID, and thus perform additional calculations, again by using JavaScript. If you assign a value to this attribute, the following code is generated: `<td id="<My ID>">`.

▶ **C_CELL_TD_EXTEND**

You can assign additional HTML attributes for this attribute, which are output in the `<TD>` tag. For example, you can fill this attribute with the value `WIDTH="50px"`. In that case, the generated HTML code would contain the following text: `<td width="50" nowrap class="SAPBEXstdData">`.

All other attributes that belong to a method are import parameters and cannot be modified. The import parameters provide additional information on the contents of the table cell. For example, the DATA_CELL method contains the import parameter I_ALERTLEVEL, which contains a value every time an exception is active for the current cell. In that case, the import parameter would contain the value of the alert level (0–9).

▶ Now enter the new processing logic in the ABAP Editor for the DATA_CELL method (see Figure 5.104, Step 1).

The following simple code example queries the import parameter I_ALERTLEVEL and, depending on the value, different pictures are transferred via the changing parameter C_CELL_CONTENT to be displayed in the web browser.

```
case i_alertlevel.
  when 1 or 2 or 3.
    move
 '<IMG SRC="MIME/bex/icons/s_s_
```

```
ledg.gif" WIDTH="16" HEIGHT="15">'
   to c_cell_content.
 when 4 or 5 or 6.
    move
'<IMG SRC="MIME/bex/icons/s_s_
ledy.gif" WIDTH="16" HEIGHT="15">'
   to c_cell_content.
 when 7 or 8 or 9.
    move
'<IMG SRC="MIME/bex/icons/s_s_
ledr.gif" WIDTH="16" HEIGHT="15">'
   to c_cell_content.
 when others.
endcase.
```

▶ Then, activate the method (Step 2).

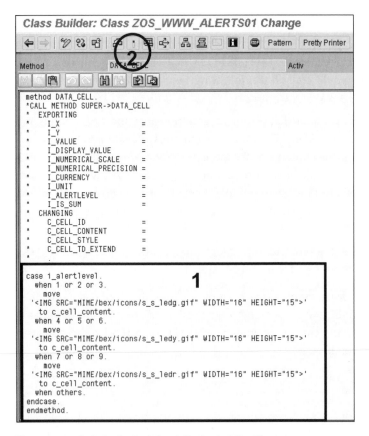

Figure 5.104 Code in the Redefined Method of the Class

Now we must assign the class for the output in our web template, the web item **Table**.

▶ Go to the Web Application Designer and use your existing web template or create a new one.

▶ Change to the layout mode and include the web item **Table** from the list of web items in the **Web Items** window into your template (see Figure 5.105, Step 1).

▶ Go to the **Generic** tab in the **Web Items** window and select your query including exceptions (Steps 2 and 3).

▶ Then, go to the **Web Item** tab in the **Web Items** window and enter the technical name of the created ABAP-OO class in the **Table Interface Class** property (Steps 4 and 5).

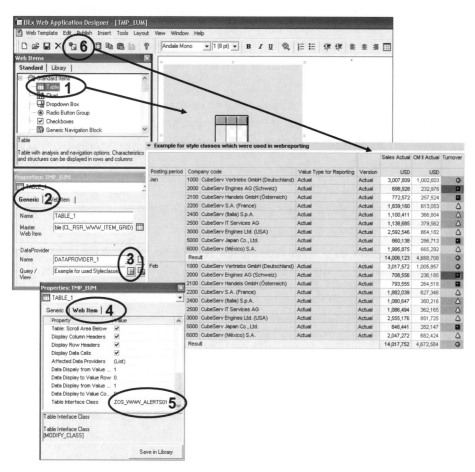

Figure 5.105 Assigning the Table Interface Class to the Corresponding Attribute of the Web Item "Table" Including the Result in the Web Browser

▶ Save the web template and run it in the web browser. As a result, the system now displays different icons per alert-level group in place of the actual values.

5.9 BEx Mobile Intelligence

For the sake of completeness, we'd like to briefly draw your attention to the BEx Web's Mobile Intelligence before concluding this chapter. BEx Mobile Intelligence enables you to receive and use web applications on mobile end devices when you're traveling, without having to modify your web templates.[15]

For example, if you call the URL of a web template from your PDA, the BEx Web automatically recognizes the calling device and generates an HTML source code that supports the respective mobile device. The BEx Web also takes into account the functional scope and display options of such an end device, and therefore generates an optimal code for it. All this occurs automatically and you don't need to perform any changes to your web templates.

Supported end devices Of course, you cannot display all web items without encountering a problem on all devices; but, the scope of functions provided is enormous. The following devices are currently supported:[16]

▶ PDA (Personal Digital Assistant) running Windows CE 3.0 and Pocket Internet Explorer

▶ WAP-enabled mobile phones (e.g., BlackBerry)

▶ i-Mode-enabled mobile phones

▶ Mobile device running the EPOC32 operating system (e.g., Nokia Communicator 9210)

Depending on the web browsers that are installed on the individual systems of the mobile devices, those browsers may also be supported.

Mobile Intelligence provides the following functions:

▶ Device Recognition

▶ Rendering for specific devices (HTML or WML)

▶ Adaptation to the restrictions of devices (size of display area, memory size, number of colors)

---

15 OSS Note 486046 contains a list of supported mobile devices.
16 Please refer to the SAP online documentation and OSS Note 453142 to learn more about using mobile devices.

- Creation of device-specific graphics (e.g., WBMP for WAP)
- Server-based processing of style sheets (for PDAs)
- Adjustment of device-specific user interaction (context menu for PDAs, OLAP navigation for WAP, etc.)

Naturally, you can also create individual templates for all types of devices. To create device-specific web templates, you must use the following naming conventions:

Device-specific web templates

- <Template_ID>_PIE for PDA applications
- <Template_ID>_EPO for EPOC32 applications
- <Template_ID>_WML for WAP applications
- <Template_ID>_IMO for i-Mode applications

If a specific device calls a web template and at the same time a device-specific web template is available for it, the device-specific web template will be automatically used.

6 Information Broadcasting

The distribution of information via Information Broadcasting represents the final step in professional business intelligence solutions. This chapter describes the basic functionality of SAP BW Information Broadcasting and its integration with other SAP NetWeaver components such as SAP Enterprise Portal.

6.1 Problem

Suppose you have a company-wide data warehouse that contains analytical applications for all relevant areas (for instance, financial reporting, cost center reporting, profit center reporting, sales analyses, HR analyses, logistics analyses, production controlling, and so on). In each of these areas, dozens or even hundreds of reports are made available at any time.

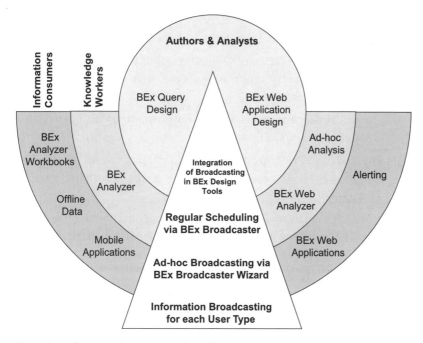

Figure 6.1 Information Broadcasting for Different Target Groups

Consequently, the menu structures—especially those for users who have many authorizations—have become very complex and unclear so that the reports that are relevant for specific individual issues can no longer be found.

This is the point at which SAP BW Information Broadcasting comes into play. The purpose of information broadcasting is to facilitate information access. For this reason, objects containing business intelligence content are made available to end users in a manner that is specifically tailored for the relevant target groups.

According to the particular point of view, you can categorize the information broadcasting functions in the following different ways:

▶ **Type of delivery**

The two main types of delivery are the distribution *via e-mail* and the *publication in SAP Enterprise Portal*. The portal publication can be carried out in various knowledge-management iViews provided by SAP or in customized portal objects.

The information broadcasting components provided by SAP are located in the **Business Explorer** portal role and contain the following elements:

▷ The My Portfolio iView including the stored personal BEx documents (queries, web applications, and so on)

▷ The BEx Portfolio iView including the stored shared BEx documents (queries, web applications, and so on) that can be accessed by authorized users

▷ The BEx Broadcaster iView is used for distributing BEx queries, BEx web templates, and BEx workbooks

▷ The Collaborative BI portal page that contains various knowledge-management iViews and can be used as a storage location for published reports

The **BEx Web Analyzer** iView for analyzing queries, on the other hand, cannot be regarded as a component of information broadcasting as it is actually just a sample web template provided by SAP.

▶ **Status of the information**

All types of delivery can be carried out as *calculated reports* or as *online links* to queries and web applications.

▶ **Triggering the distribution**

The distribution of information can be done manually or automatically. If you trigger the distribution *manually*, the publication of the corresponding BEx application is directly started in the BEx Broadcaster. In the case of an *automatic publication*, the SAP Job Scheduling methods are used to schedule the distribution, which, according to the respective settings, is then carried out either once or several times.

In the following sections, we'll use some sample scenarios to introduce and describe a selection of important information broadcasting functions.

6.2 Sending Reports via Information Broadcasting

6.2.1 Direct Delivery of Offline Reports via E-mail

Upon the month-end closing, the CEO of our model company, CubeServ Engines, expects the delivery of a report that contains the sales figures. Since the data is released by the head of the controlling department, the delivery can be carried out through information broadcasting via e-mail.

Requirements

Calling Information Broadcasting from the Business Explorer Query Designer

A configured and saved Business Explorer query can be directly distributed from the BEx Query Designer.

▶ To do that, click on the **Publish** button in the Query Designer and select the function **BEx Broadcaster...** (see Figure 6.2, Steps 1 and 2).

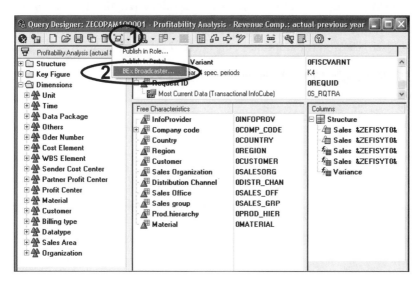

Figure 6.2 Calling the BEx Broadcaster from the Query Designer

▶ An HTML browser window opens in which you can configure the information broadcasting settings (see Figure 6.3).

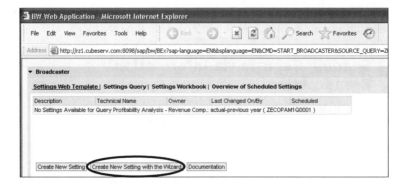

Figure 6.3 Initial Screen for Configuring the BEx Broadcaster

Configuring the BEx Broadcaster Using the Wizard

A wizard supports the configuration of the BEx Broadcaster.

▶ To use the wizard, click on the button **Create New Setting with the Wizard** (see Figure 6.3, circled button). This starts a series of dialogs that prompts you to enter the most important settings.

▶ In the first step, you should select the Distribution Type **Send as E-Mail** and the Output Format **Independent HTML File** (see Figure 6.4, Step 1). Additionally, you should check the **As ZIP File** option.

▶ Then, click on the **Continue** button (Step 2).

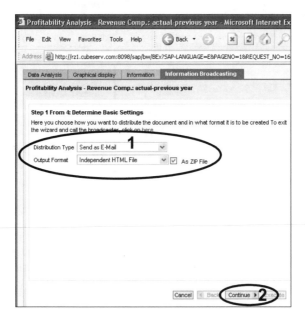

Figure 6.4 BEx Broadcaster Wizard: Distribution via E-Mail

▶ In the next step, enter the recipient's e-mail address, as well as the message subject and text (see Figure 6.5, Steps 1 and 2).

▶ Then, you can already begin publishing by clicking on the **Execute** button (Step 3).

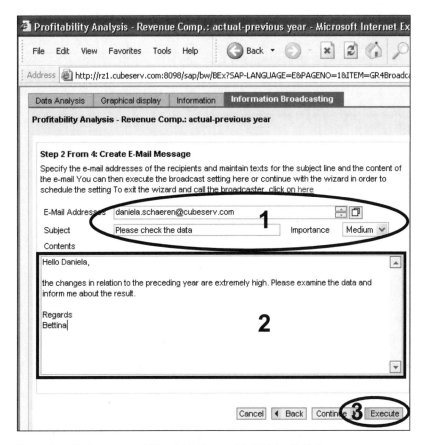

Figure 6.5 BEx Broadcaster Wizard: Writing and Publishing E-Mail

▶ If the publication was successful, the system displays the message **Broadcast setting has been executed** (see Figure 6.6).

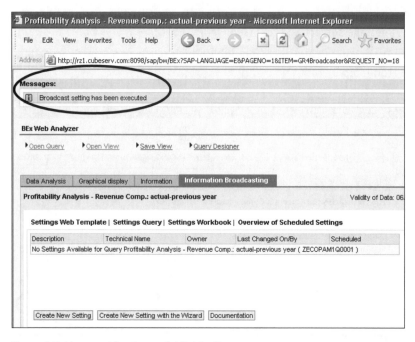

Figure 6.6 Message After Successful Publication

Starting the Offline Report from the E-Mail

Once the e-mail has been downloaded, the document is displayed in the inbox of the current e-mail application in use, where you can open it.

▶ In MS Outlook, which we use in our example, you can do that by double-clicking on the item in the Inbox (see Figure 6.7, Step 1).

▶ In accordance with the format chosen, the published report is displayed as an attachment and can be opened, depending on the respective functionality in the e-mail application used (for MS Outlook: double-click on the attachment, see Figure 6.7, Step 2).

▶ The ZIP file attached to the e-mail in our example contains the report as an independent HTML file (Steps 3 and 4).

▶ When you open the HTML file, the offline report is displayed (Steps 5 and 6).

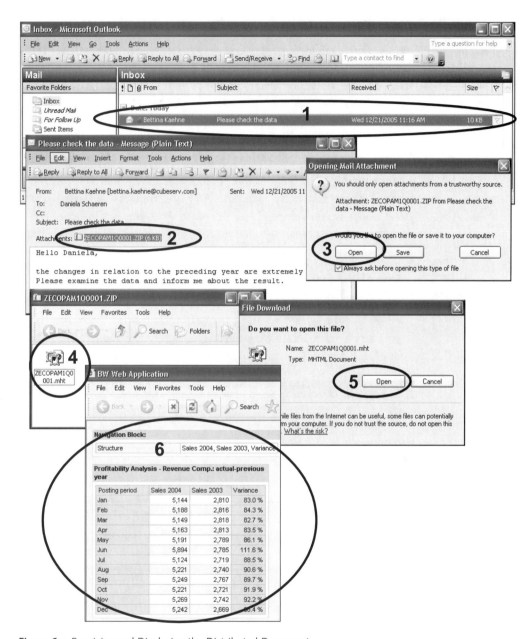

Figure 6.7 Receiving and Displaying the Distributed Document

6.2.2 Periodic Delivery of Offline Reports via E-Mail

Requirements The sales manager of CubeServ Engines AG (Uster, Switzerland), a subsidiary of our model company, CubeServ Engines, (see Sections 3.1.1 and 3.1.2) daily expects the delivery of the current sales order stock with the status of the previous day. The delivery via e-mail is scheduled in the information broadcasting component.

Calling Information Broadcasting from the BEx Web Analyzer

By default, SAP BW 3.5 opens queries in the BEx Web Analyzer, which is a further development of the standard SAP web template that is used in SAP BW 3.0 and higher releases. The BEx Web Analyzer, in turn, contains a dedicated tab providing the functions for calling information broadcasting.

▶ If you click on the **Information Broadcasting** tab (see Figure 6.8, Step 1), the functions are made available (Step 2).

▶ As was the case with the direct delivery (see Section 6.2.1), you can either use the wizard to make the settings, or enter them directly. If you click on the **Create New Setting** button, you can enter the setting directly (Step 3).

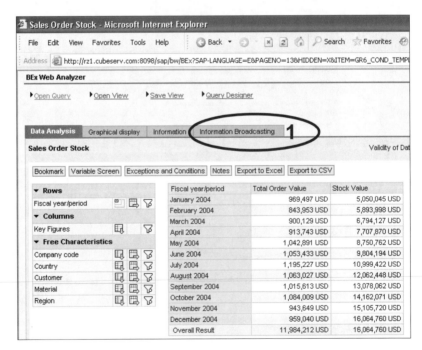

Figure 6.8 Calling Information Broadcasting from the BEx Web Analyzer

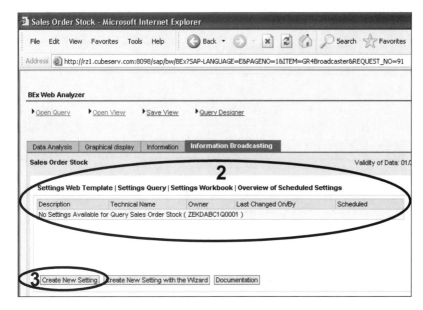

Figure 6.8 Calling Information Broadcasting from the BEx Web Analyzer (Cont'd.)

Direct Configuration of BEx Broadcaster

When you click on the Create New Setting button, a new dialog opens, which provides the possible configuration options. Because we want the setting to be carried out periodically, it must be saved, which is why a description is necessary at this stage.

▶ Enter the description in the input field provided (see Figure 6.9, Step 1).

▶ Corresponding to the settings already made earlier, the default settings (**Send as E-Mail** and **Independent HTML File**) will be adopted here as well (Step 2). You should also check the option **As ZIP File**.

▶ Next, enter one or more addressees (Step 3).

▶ Then, open the **Texts** tab and enter the message **Subject** and the e-mail text (see Figure 6.10, Steps 1 through 3).

▶ Save the setting (Step 4).

▶ Specify a technical name in the **Save Broadcast Setting** popup window (see Step 5).

Technical name for broadcast settings

▶ Click on the **Transfer** button to save the settings (Step 6). If this last step was successful, the system displays the message **Settings ... have been saved successfully**.

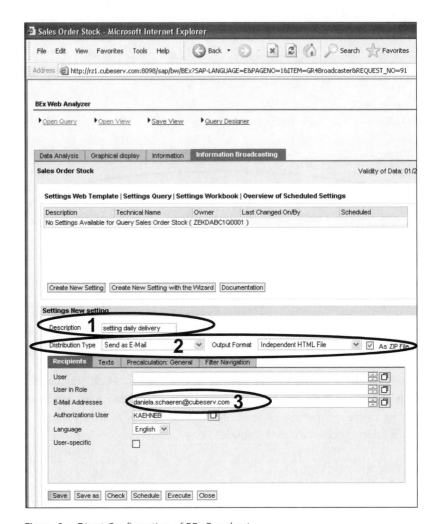

Figure 6.9 Direct Configuration of BEx Broadcaster

Scheduling

▶ Then you can click on the **Schedule** button (see Figure 6.10, Step 7). Doing so opens the **Scheduling setting ...** popup.

▶ In this dialog you must select the option **Create New Scheduling** (see Figure 6.11, Step 1).

▶ According to our requirement, we select the option **Periodic All** (Step 2) **1 Day(s)** (Step 3).

Setting the start date
▶ To define the start date (the default value is always the following calendar day), click into the date field and then select the required start date in the calendar that is displayed (Steps 4 and 5).

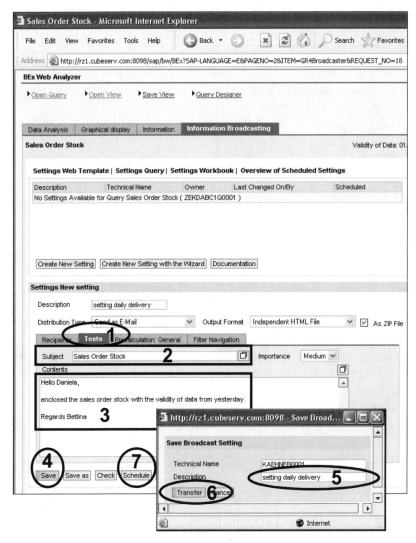

Figure 6.10 Entering the Message Subject and E-Mail Text and Saving the Broadcast Settings

▶ Once you have selected the calendar day, you can enter the start time directly (Step 6).

▶ Click on the **Transfer** button to save the scheduling, which is then displayed in the **Information Broadcasting** tab of the BEx Web Analyzer (Steps 7 and 8).

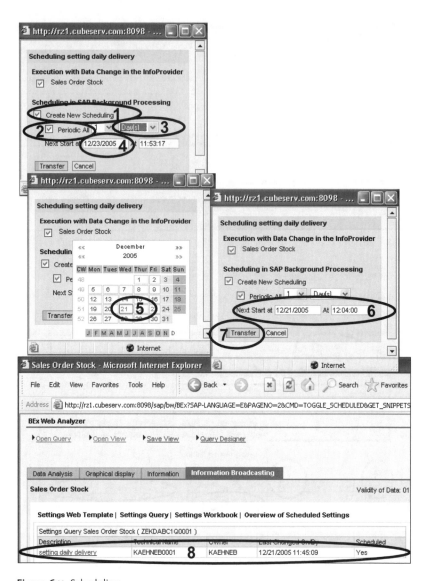

Figure 6.11 Scheduling

Processing the Scheduled Information Broadcasting Settings

At the time of scheduling, the information broadcasting settings are automatically processed as an SAP BW background job. During the course of this process, SAP BW generates an e-mail and sends it to the addressees specified in the respective information broadcasting settings.

Starting the Periodic Offline Report from the E-Mail

When the addressees download their e-mail messages, they will also receive the e-mail that contains the BEx Broadcaster results.

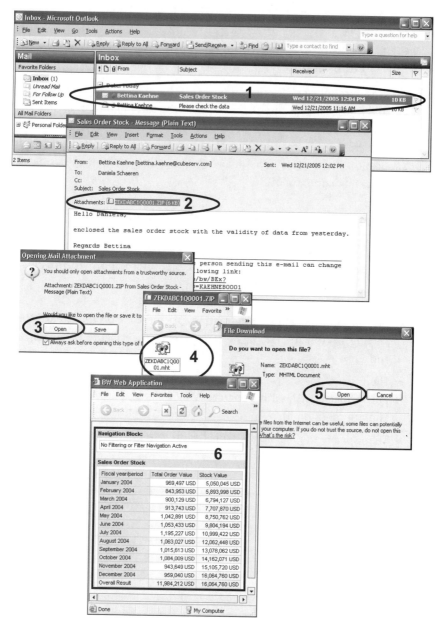

Figure 6.12 Result of the Scheduled BEx Broadcaster Settings Contained in an E-Mail

▶ After opening the e-mail (see Figure 6.12, Step 1) you can open the attachment (Steps 2 through 5) so that the delivered offline report is displayed (Steps 2 through 5).

These settings are executed periodically until you change them.

6.2.3 Sending Offline Reports Containing Filter Navigation via E-Mail

Requirements After each month-end closing, the CFO of our model company wants to be able to use offline reports that contain the sales figures of all the subsidiary companies on his notebook computer. As is the case with online reports, he wants to call each company code from a dropdown list in an application. The delivery via e-mail is carried out through the information broadcasting component.

Configuring Offline Reporting with Filter Navigation

Again, the starting point is the executed query:

▶ Similar to the process shown in Figure 6.8, Information Broadcasting is launched from the BEx Web Analyzer.

HTML
with separate
MIME files

▶ Go to the **Information Broadcasting** tab and click on the **Create New Setting** button to start the setting directly (see Figure 6.13, Steps 1 and 2).

▶ Then, select the distribution type **Send as E-Mail** (Step 3) and the output format **HTML with Separate MIME Files**, and check the **As ZIP File** option (Step 4).

▶ Then specify the recipient's e-mail address in the **Recipients** tab (Steps 5 and 6).

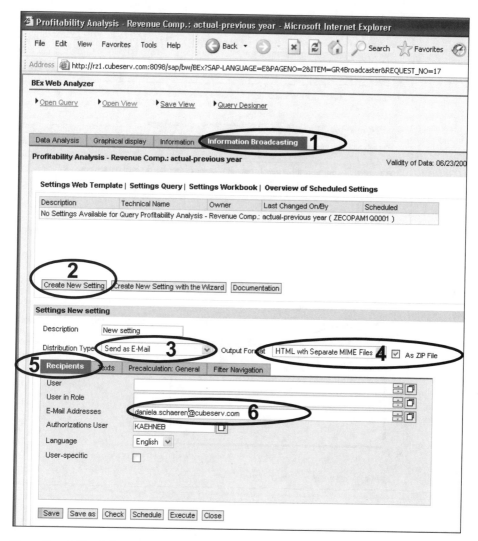

Figure 6.13 Calling Information Broadcasting via E-Mail and HTML with Separate MIME Files

▶ You can enter the message **Subject** and text in the **Texts** tab (see Figure 6.14, Steps 1 through 3).

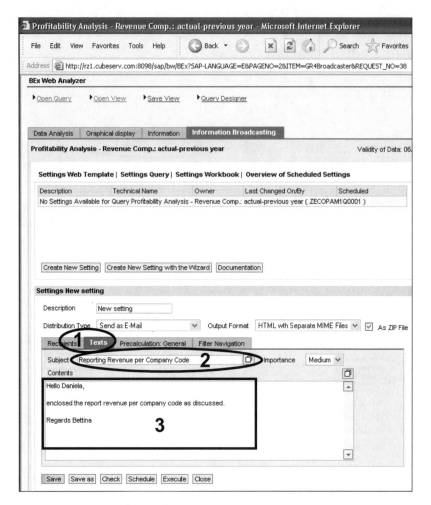

Figure 6.14 Message Subject and Text

▶ Then, go to the **Filter Navigation** tab (see Figure 6.15, Step 1).

▶ Activate the option **Filter by Selected Characteristics** and select the InfoObjects **Company code** and **Country** (Step 2).

▶ Finally, click on the **Execute** button to activate the broadcast settings (Step 3).

▶ The successful creation and dispatch is logged in the **Execution of Broadcast Setting** dialog. Then click on the **Close** button (Step 4).

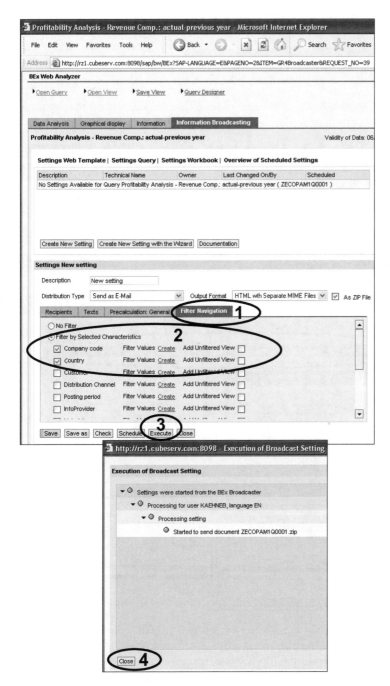

Figure 6.15 Setting the Filter Navigation

Starting the Offline Report with Filter Navigation from the E-Mail

Once the e-mail has been downloaded, the document is displayed in the inbox of the current e-mail application in use, where you can open it.

▶ In MS Outlook, which we use in our example, you can do that by double-clicking on the item in the Inbox (see Figure 6.16, Step 1).

▶ According to the type of attachment selected, a ZIP file is displayed as an attachment that you can now open (for MS Outlook: double-click on the attachment, see Step 2).

▶ The ZIP file contains several documents (Step 3).

▶ Copy those documents into a folder on your machine (Step 4).

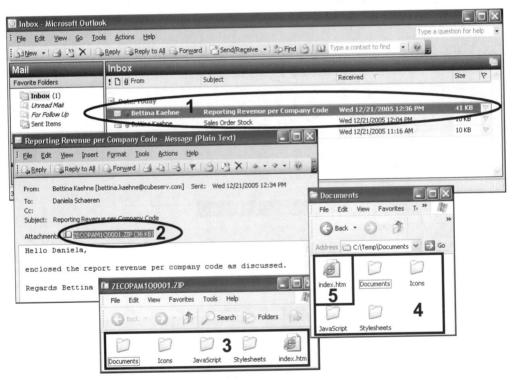

Figure 6.16 E-Mail Containing Offline Reports as HTML with Separate MIME Files

Displaying offline reports

▶ You can then launch the offline report by double-clicking on the **index.htm** item (see Figure 6.16, Step 5).

▶ As the query has been previously calculated for several company codes, an overview page is displayed (see Figure 6.17).

▶ The overview page contains the link **Your precalculated Web template**, which enables you to call the first offline report from the list (here: company code **CubeServ AG**, see Figure 6.17):

Overview page

    ▷ The table **Precalculated Filter Values** provides links to all precalculated pages.

    ▷ Finally, the table **Detailed Information on Precalculation** provides you with the option to call the query that has been delivered as an offline report online (link: **Profitability Analysis—Revenue Comp.: actual-previous year**).

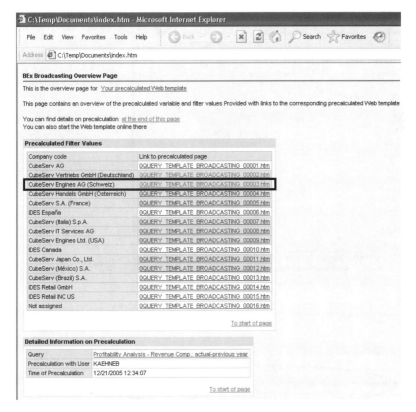

Figure 6.17 Overview Page for Offline Reporting with Filter Navigation in "HTML with Separate MIME Files" Format

▶ If you want to analyze the query results for selected company codes—in our example that's **CubeServ Engines AG (Schweiz)** and then **CubeServ Vertriebs GmbH (Deutschland)**—you can click on a company code first to start it directly (see Figure 6.17, Step 1).

Navigation in offline reporting

This opens the offline report for the company code (see Figure 6.18, Step 1).

▶ To filter another company code, expand the dropdown list and select the entry you want to be displayed, **CubeServ Vertriebs GmbH (Deutschland)** (Step 2), which is then called (Step 3).

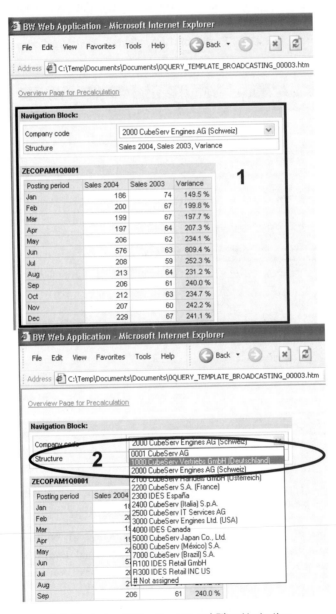

Figure 6.18 Displaying Offline Reports and Filter Navigation

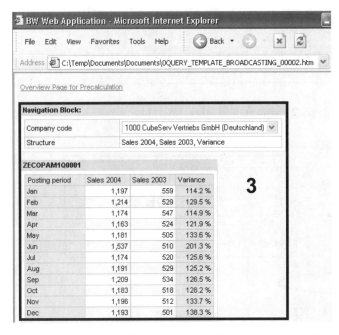

Figure 6.18 Displaying Offline Reports and Filter Navigation (Cont'd.)

6.2.4 Direct Delivery of Navigation Statuses as Online Links

Requirements

The head of the controlling department at CubeServ Engines wants to notify the CFO about a specific situation he encountered during the analysis. So, he sends the specific navigation status as an online link and an additional message in an e-mail to the CFO.

When the CFO clicks on this link, the system displays a specific navigation status that contains the variable assignments (here: fiscal year = 2004), as well as the filter (posting period = December) and drilldown states (vertical drilldown by company code) (see circled sections in Figure 6.19).

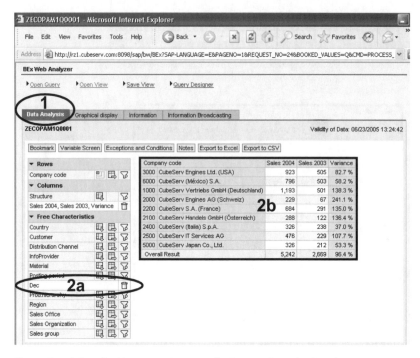

Figure 6.19 A Specific Navigation Status as the Starting Point for Broadcasting an Online Link

Specific Navigation Status of a Query and Distribution via Information Broadcasting

You can use information broadcasting to distribute a specific navigation status via e-mail:

▶ To do that, select the **Information Broadcasting** tab (see Figure 6.20, Step 1).

▶ Select the Distribution Type **Send as E-Mail** (Step 2) and the Output Format **Online Links to Current Data** (Step 3).

▶ Enter the relevant e-mail address in the **Recipients** tab that is displayed by default (Step 4).

▶ Then go to the **Texts** tab (Step 5) and enter the message subject and the e-mail text (Steps 6 and 7).

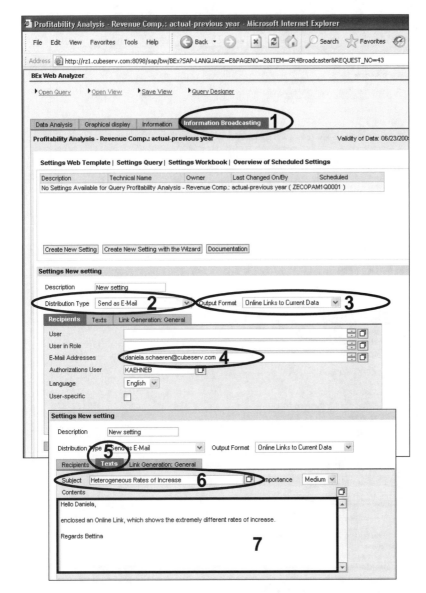

Figure 6.20 Sending an Online Link to a Specific Navigation Status of a Query

▶ To transfer the navigation status, go to the **Link Generation: General** tab (see Figure 6.21, Step 1).

▶ Then click on the **Transfer** Navigation Status link (Step 2).

▶ The option now changes to **Delete** Navigation Status (Step 3).

▶ Then you can start the distribution by clicking on the **Execute** button (Step 4).

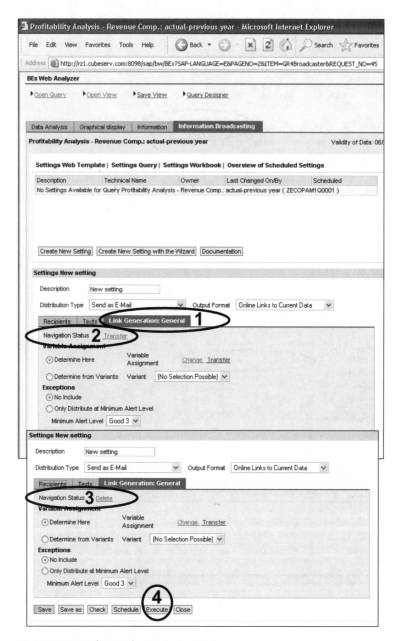

Figure 6.21 Transferring the Navigation Status

Calling the Online Link with a Specific Navigation Status

Once the e-mail has been downloaded, the document is displayed in the inbox of the current e-mail application in use, where you can open it.

- Open the e-mail and click on the online link, which is included in the e-mail text (see Figure 6.22, Steps 1 and 2).

- This starts the query with the transferred navigation status (Step 3).

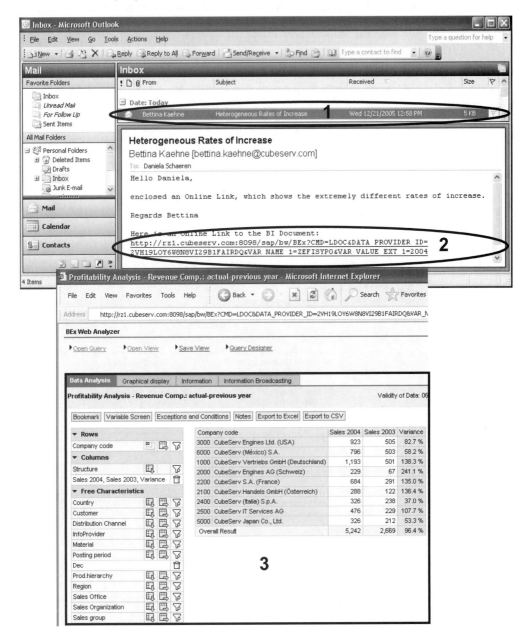

Figure 6.22 E-Mail Containing an Online Link to the Specific Navigation Status of a Query

6.3 Publishing Reports in SAP Enterprise Portal via Information Broadcasting

6.3.1 SAP BW Components and the SAP Enterprise Portal

Due to the information broadcasting functionality in SAP BW 3.5, the SAP Enterprise Portal is becoming increasingly important as it is now possible to publish business intelligence content through SAP Enterprise Portal, in addition to distributing this content via e-mail (see Figure 6.23).

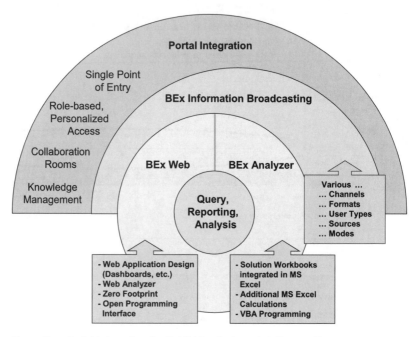

Figure 6.23 Portal Integration for Publishing Business Intelligence Content

The SAP NetWeaver documentation describes the options that are available for integrating SAP BW content in the SAP Enterprise Portal (see Table 6.1).[1]

---

1 SAP NetWeaver '04 Documentation: Overview: Integration and Display Types of BW Content in the Portal, Link: *http://help.sap.com/saphelp_nw04/helpdata/en/9d/24ff4009b8f223e10000000a155106/content.htm*

Display Type	Description
BEx web application as an iView	Web-based BI application that is displayed as an iView in SAP Enteprise Portal (for example, BEx Web Analyzer)
BEx web application as a document in SAP Knowledge Management (SAP KM)	A document containing historical data of a web-based BI application and stored in a SAP KM folder
BEx web application as an online link in SAP KM	Link to a web-based BI application containing current data in a KM folder
BW workbook as an iView	MS Excel workbook containing one or more embedded queries that is displayed as an iView in a separate browser window in SAP Enterprise Portal
BW workbook as a document in SAP KM	MS Excel workbook containing one or more embedded queries that is stored in a SAP KM folder as a document with historical data
BW query as an iView	A query as a web-based BI application in the standard view (Standard web template for the ad-hoc analysis) that is displayed as an iView in SAP Enterprise Portal
BW query as an online link in SAP KM	A link to a query containing current data, which is displayed using the standard web template for the ad-hoc analysis; the link is stored in a SAP KM folder.
BW query as a document in SAP KM	A document containing historical data of a query, which is displayed using the standard web template for the ad-hoc analysis
Single BW document as iView in SAP KM	A single document (for example, documentation on metadata) that has been created in SAP BW and is displayed as an iView in SAP Enterprise Portal
Several BW documents as iView in SAP KM	Several documents or links from a KM folder are displayed using a KM navigation iView. In SAP KM, the documents and links can originate from SAP BW or other sources.
Web interface as an iView	Web-enabled BW-BPS planning application that is displayed as an iView in SAP Enterprise Portal
SAP BW component	Various SAP BW applications and tools such as the Administrator Workbench, the BEx Query Designer, the BEx Web Application Designer, or the BEx Analyzer

Table 6.1 The Capabilities of Information Broadcasting

The portal role Business Explorer provided by SAP Enterprise Portal contains several knowledge management components:

▶ **My Portfolio**
This iView contains stored personal BEx documents.

▶ **BEx Portfolio**
This iView contains stored shared BEx documents that can be accessed by users who have the necessary authorization.

▶ **BEx Web Analyzer**
This iView, which is used for analyzing queries, was originally a sample web template provided by SAP, and therefore, should not be considered as part of information broadcasting.

▶ **BEx Broadcaster**
This iView is used for distributing BEx queries, BEx web templates, and BEx workbooks.

▶ **Collaborative BI**
This portal page contains various knowledge-management iViews and can be used as a storage location for published reports.

▶ **Search function**

As shown in Table 6.1, additional settings are possible; however, in this chapter, we'll focus on the individual components of the portal role Business Explorer listed here.

6.3.2 Publishing Online Reports into the User-Specific "My Portfolio"

Having sent the online link containing the specific navigation status to the CFO, the head of the controlling department of our model company, CubeServ Engines, wants to store this query in his personal BEx Portfolio in order to discuss the information provided with the CFO.

Publishing an Online Link to a Query via Information Broadcasting

You can use the Information Broadcasting component to publish an online link to a query in SAP Enterprise Portal:

▶ To do that, start **Information Broadcasting** (see Figure 6.24, Step 1).

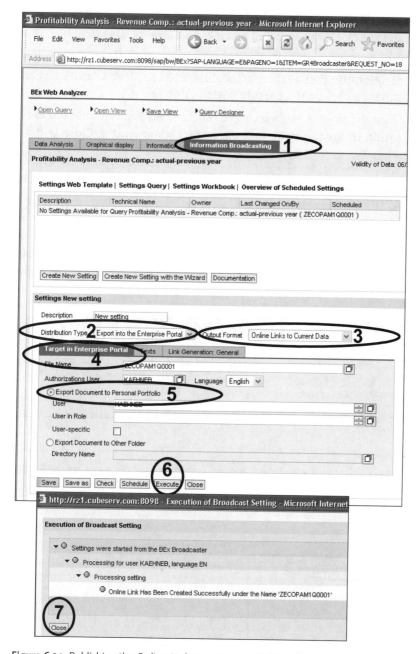

Figure 6.24 Publishing the Online Link to a Query in SAP Enterprise Portal

- Select the Distribution Type **Export into the Enterprise Portal** (Step 2) and the Output Format **Online Links to Current Data** (Step 3).

- Select the option **Export Document to Personal Portfolio** in the **Target in Enterprise Portal** tab, which is displayed by default (Steps 4 and 5), and then click on the **Execute** button (Step 6).

- Once the process has been logged successfully you can close the **Execution of Broadcast Setting** dialog by clicking on the **Close** button (Step 7).

Calling the Online Link in the Personal "My Portfolio"

The published query can then be executed with the saved navigation status in SAP Enterprise Portal:

- When you open the personal **My Portfolio** in SAP Enterprise Portal, the online link to the published query is displayed, including a description and the creation date (see Figure 6.25, Step 1).

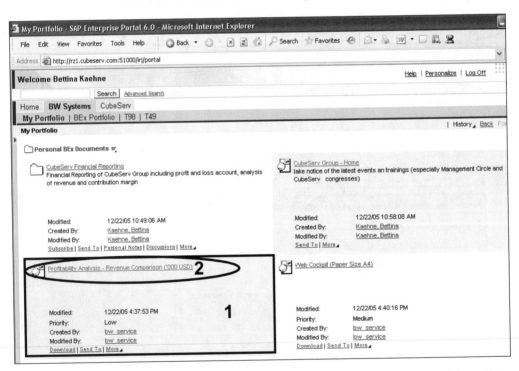

Figure 6.25 Online Link to the Published Query in the Personal BEx Portfolio in SAP Enterprise Portal

▶ Click on the query description **Profitability Analysis—Revenue Comparison ('000 USD)** that is displayed as a hyperlink (see Figure 6.25, Step 2) to launch the query online from SAP Enterprise Portal (see Figure 6.26, Steps 1 and 2).

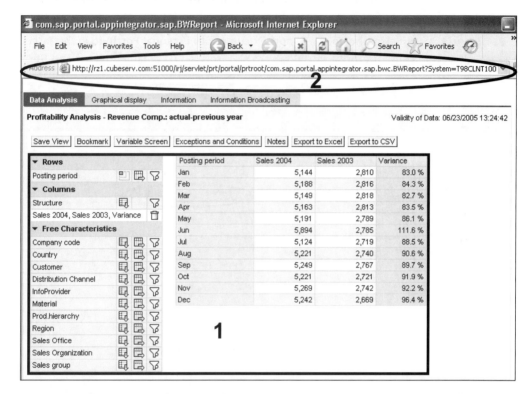

Figure 6.26 Online Execution of the Query from SAP Enterprise Portal

6.3.3 Publishing Offline Reports into the User-Specific "My Portfolio"

In addition to the online link, the head of the controlling department at CubeServ Engines wants to store the report that contains the historical data (i.e., the data that existed before the analysis began) in his personal portfolio.

Requirements

Publishing an Offline Report via Information Broadcasting

You can use the Information Broadcasting component to publish the historical data of a specific navigation status as an offline report in SAP Enterprise Portal:

▶ The starting point for that is a specific navigation status (see Figure 6.19).

▶ Start **Information Broadcasting** (see Figure 6.27, Step 1).

▶ Select the Distribution Type **Export into the Enterprise Portal** (Step 2) and the Output Format **Independent HTML File** (Step 3).

▶ Select the option **Export Document to Personal Portfolio** in the **Target in Enterprise Portal** tab that is displayed by default (Steps 4 and 5).

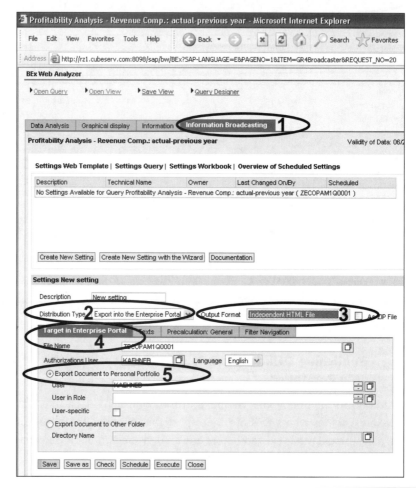

Figure 6.27 Publishing an Offline Report Containing Historical Data in SAP Enterprise Portal

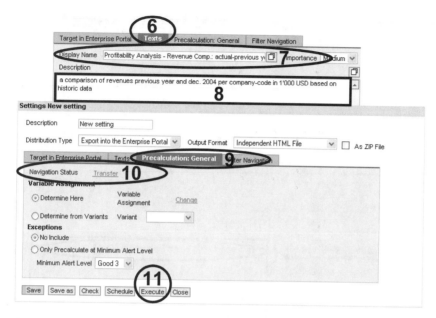

Figure 6.27 Publishing an Offline Report Containing Historical Data in SAP Enterprise Portal (Cont'd.)

▶ Then go to the **Texts** tab (Step 6) and enter the **Display Name** and the **Description** for the offline report (Steps 7 and 8).

▶ To transfer the navigation status, go to the **Precalculation: General** tab (Step 9) and click on the **Navigation Status Transfer** link (Step 10).

▶ Then click on the **Execute** button (Step 11) to process the broadcasting setting and log the processing.

Calling the Offline Report Containing Historical Data in the Personal "My Portfolio"

You can run the published offline report containing the saved navigation status and historical data in SAP Enterprise Portal.

▶ After publication, the offline report is displayed in the personal portfolio of SAP Enterprise Portal with its display name and description (see Figure 6.28, Step 1).

▶ Click on the link **Profitability Analysis—Revenue Comparison ('000 USD)** (see Figure 6.28, Step 2) to display the offline report with its saved selections, the saved navigation status, and the historical data (see Figure 6.29).

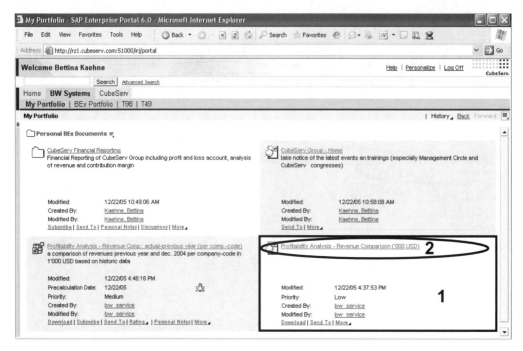

Figure 6.28 Published Offline Report Containing Specific Navigation Status and Historical Data

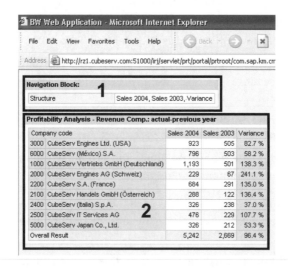

Figure 6.29 Running the Offline Report from SAP Enterprise Portal

6.3.4 Publishing Online Reports in the BEx Portfolio

The sales order stock is to be made available to several executives. There-fore, you must store an online link to the query in the folder CubeServ Financial Reporting (Public) of the BEx Portfolio.

Requirements

Publishing an Online Report in the BEx Portfolio via Information Broadcasting

You can use the Information Broadcasting component to publish an online link to a query in the BEx Portfolio of SAP Enterprise Portal:

▶ To do that, start **Information Broadcasting** (see Figure 6.30, Step 1).

▶ Select the Distribution Type **Export into the Enterprise Portal** (Step 2) and the Output Format **Online Links to Current Data** (Step 3).

▶ Select the option **Export Document to Other Folder** in the **Target in Enterprise Portal** tab that is displayed by default (Steps 4 and 5), and then click on the **Selection** button (Step 6).

▶ Open the folder **CM Repository View** in the **Select a folder** dialog that pops up; then, open the folder **Public Documents** and click on the required folder in the BEx Portfolio (here: **CubeServ Financial Reporting (Public)**, Step 7).

▶ Click on the **Transfer** button to transfer the selection (Step 8). The selected folder is now copied into the **Directory Name** field.

▶ Then click on the **Execute** button (Step 9).

▶ Once the process has been logged successfully you can close the **Execution of Broadcast Setting** dialog by clicking on the corresponding button.

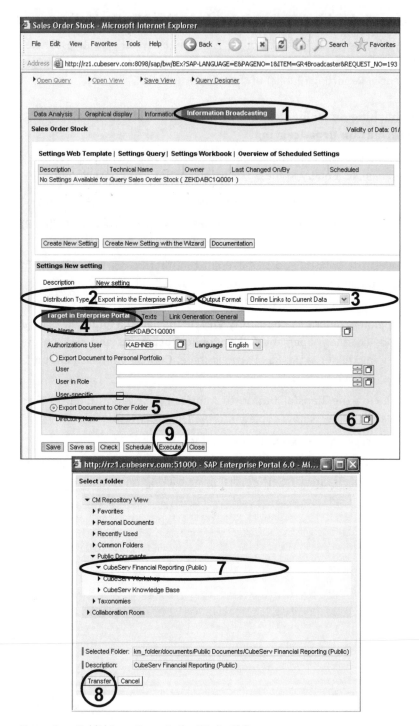

Figure 6.30 Publishing a Query in the BEx Portfolio

Calling the Online Report in the BEx Portfolio

In SAP Enterprise Portal, you can execute the published link to the online report in the corresponding folder of the BEx Portfolio.

▶ To do that, you must first log on to the SAP Enterprise Portal, then click on the **Business Explorer** role (see Figure 6.31, Step 1), and select the **BEx Portfolio** (Step 2).

▶ Then click on the required folder to open it (here: **CubeServ Financial Reporting (Public)**, see Step 3).

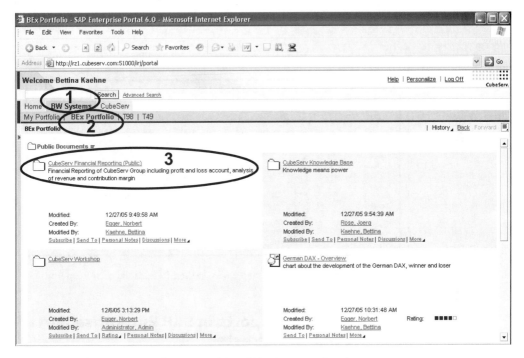

Figure 6.31 Folder Structure in the BEx Portfolio of SAP Enterprise Portal

▶ The system now displays the contents of the folder. In our example, an alternative display is shown (see Figure 6.32): Whereas the BEx Portfolio was displayed in the default tile view (see Figure 6.31), for the selected folder, we chose the Business Explorer and preview view.

▶ If you click on the published report (see Figure 6.32, Step 1), it is displayed in the portal framework (due to the selected view type) (Step 2).

Displaying the report in the BEx Portfolio

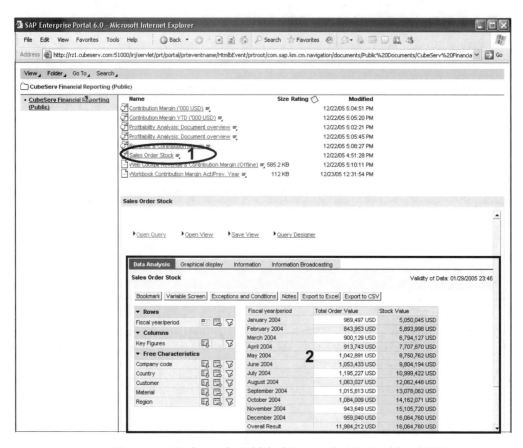

Figure 6.32 Displaying the Published Query in the BEx Portfolio of SAP Enterprise Portal

6.4   Publishing Reports in SAP Enterprise Portal via BEx Broadcaster

6.4.1   The BEx Broadcaster in SAP Enterprise Portal

The BEx Broadcaster is an SAP web item that is contained in SAP BW Business Explorer Web Reporting as of Release 3.5. An iView that contains this standard function is integrated as a knowledge-management iView into the Business Explorer role of the SAP Enterprise Portal. This standard iView enables you to publish reports directly from the portal.

You can use the BEx Broadcaster to publish web templates, queries, and workbooks. The process for publishing queries from the knowledge-management (KM) iView **BEx Broadcaster** is similar to that described above.

In the following sections, we'll describe how you can publish web templates and workbooks from the KM iView **BEx Broadcaster**.

6.4.2 Publishing Web Templates in SAP Enterprise Portal via the BEx Broadcaster

For his analyses, the head of the controlling department wants to use a web template that provides both a tabular and a graphical revenue comparison to the previous year per company code in his personal portfolio. For this reason, an online link to the web template must be stored in his personal portfolio.

Requirements

Publishing a Web Template into the Personal "My Portfolio" in SAP Enterprise Portal via the BEx Broadcaster

▶ Open the KM iView **BEx Broadcaster** in SAP Enterprise Portal (see Figure 6.33, Steps 1 and 2) and click on the **Settings Web Template** link to start the selection process for the web template to be published (Step 3).

▶ The **Choose a Web Template** dialog opens.

▶ Choose the relevant selection from the dropdown list (**History**, **Favorites**, **Roles**) (Step 4), and then select the required web template (Step 5).

▶ Click on the **Transfer** button to transfer the web template selection to the BEx Broadcaster (Step 6).

In the BEx Broadcaster, the settings for the Business Explorer web templates can be entered in the same way as for the Business Explorer queries described above (see Section 6.2). As an example, we will now create an online link according to the requirement described at the beginning of this section:

Settings for BEx web templates

▶ After selecting the web template, click on the **Create New Setting** button (see Figure 6.33, Step 7).

▶ Select the Distribution Type **Export into the Enterprise Portal** and the Output Format **Online Links to Current Data** (Step 8). At this stage, you can keep the default setting **Export Document to Personal Portfolio**.

▶ Click on the **Execute** button to publish the web template (Step 9).

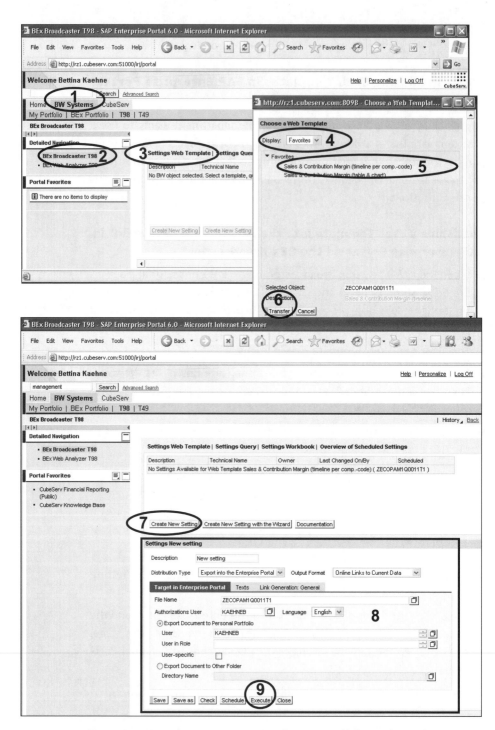

Figure 6.33 Using the KM iView BEx Broadcaster to Publish a Web Template in SAP Enterprise Portal

Executing the Online Link to the Published Web Template from the Personal "My Portfolio" in SAP Enterprise Portal

▶ When you open the personal portfolio in SAP Enterprise Portal (see Figure 6.34, Steps 1 and 2), the web template is displayed as a hyperlink (Step 3).

▶ When you click on the link, the web template opens and is displayed either in a new window or in the portal frame, depending on your settings. In our example, it is displayed in a new window (see Step 4).

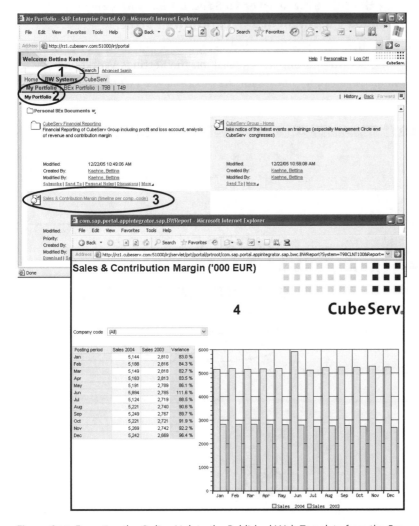

Figure 6.34 Executing the Online Link to the Published Web Template from the Personal Portfolio in SAP Enterprise Portal

6.4.3 Publishing Web Templates in SAP Enterprise Portal via the BEx Broadcaster

Requirements For research purposes, the head of the controlling department at CubeServ Engines wants to publish a Business Explorer (Analyzer) workbook both in the KM iView BEx Portfolio of the portal and via e-mail, so that he and other controllers of the company can commonly access this workbook.

Using the BEx Broadcaster to Send a BEx (Analyzer) Workbook via E-Mail in SAP Enterprise Portal

▶ Open the KM iView **BEx Broadcaster** in SAP Enterprise Portal (see Figure 6.35, Steps 1 and 2) and click on the **Settings Workbook** link to start the selection process for the BEx (Analyzer) workbook to be published (Step 3).

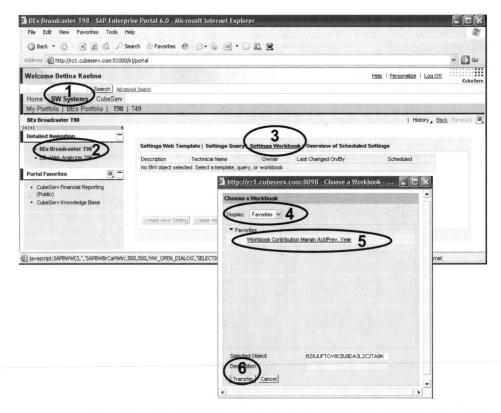

Figure 6.35 Using the BEx Broadcaster to Send a BEx Workbook via E-Mail from SAP Enterprise Portal

- ▶ The **Choose a Workbook** dialog opens. Choose the relevant selection from the dropdown list (**History**, **Favorites**, **Roles**) (Step 4), and then select the required Business Explorer workbook (Step 5).

- ▶ Click on the **Transfer** button to transfer the workbook selection to the BEx Broadcaster (Step 6).

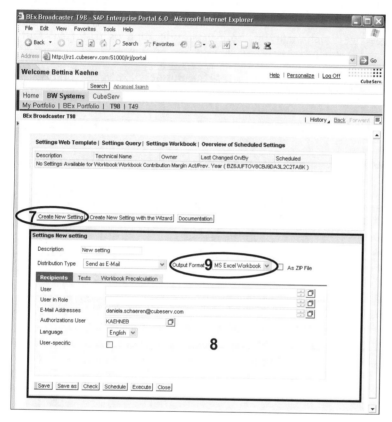

Figure 6.35 Using the BEx Broadcaster to Send a BEx Workbook via E-Mail from SAP Enterprise Portal (Cont'd.)

- ▶ After that you must enter the settings for sending the workbook via e-mail (e.g., recipients and texts). This process is similar to that for sending queries via e-mail described earlier in this chapter (Step 8).

- ▶ The only difference can be found in the output format which is automatically set to the only available option **MS Excel Workbook** (Step 9).

Launching the Business Explorer Workbook from the E-Mail

Once the e-mail has been replicated, the document is displayed in the inbox of the current e-mail application in use, where you can open it.

▶ In our example, we use MS Outlook (see Figure 6.36, Steps 1 and 2).

▶ In accordance with the format chosen, the published report is displayed as an e-mail attachment and can be opened, depending on the respective functionality in the e-mail application used (for MS Outlook: double-click on the attachment, see Step 3).

▶ When you open the attachment, the Business Explorer workbook is displayed (Step 4).

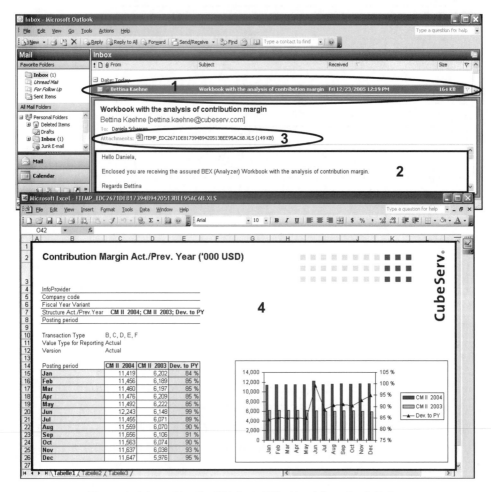

Figure 6.36 Launching the Distributed Workbook from the E-Mail

Using the BEx Broadcaster in SAP Enterprise Portal to Publish a BEx (Analyzer) Workbook in the BEx Portfolio

▶ Regarding the selection process to publish a Business Explorer workbook, you can proceed similar to the above description for the e-mail dispatch (see Figure 6.35, Steps 1 through 6).

▶ Then go to the KM iView **BEx Broadcaster** in SAP Enterprise Portal (see Figure 6.37, Steps 1 through 3) and select the relevant settings (Distribution Type **Export into the Enterprise Portal**, Output Format **MS Excel Workbook**, and the **Export Document to Other Folder** option) (Step 4), in accordance with the various instructions given in the previous sections of this chapter.

▶ To select the folder, click on the **Selection** button, then select the required folder in the **Select a folder** dialog (in our example that's the folder **CubeServ Financial Reporting (Public)**), and confirm your selection by clicking on the **Transfer** button (Steps 5 and 6).

▶ The selection is now transferred into the BEx Broadcaster (Step 7).

▶ Finally, you can start the publication by clicking on the **Execute** button (Step 8).

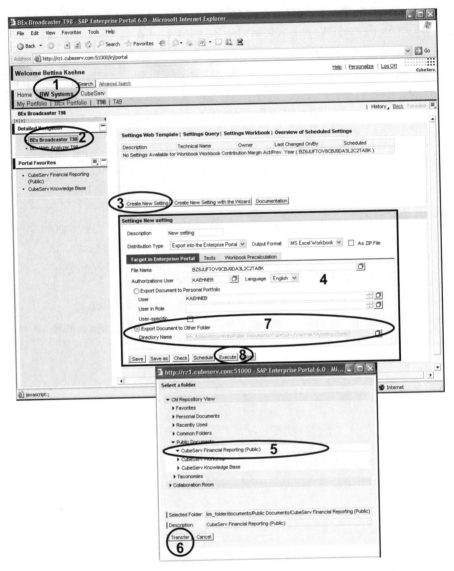

Figure 6.37 Publishing a BEx Workbook in a Collaboration Room in SAP Enterprise Portal

Launching the Business Explorer Workbook from the BEx Portfolio in SAP Enterprise Portal

▶ To execute the workbook stored in the BEx Portfolio, open the SAP KM iView **BEx Portfolio** in SAP Enterprise Portal (see Figure 6.38, Steps 1 and 2).

► Then go to the required folder (here: **CubeServ Financial Reporting (Public)**, see Step 3).

► The display of the selected folder (Step 4) contains the folder name and the workbook entry (Step 4).

► Click on the workbook to open it (Steps 5 and 6).

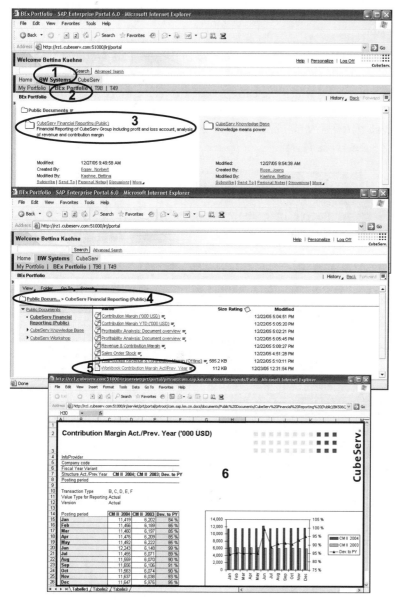

Figure 6.38 Executing the Business Explorer Workbook from the BEx Portfolio in SAP Enterprise Portal

6.5   Finding Content in SAP Enterprise Portal

The Knowledge Management (KM) component of SAP Enterprise Portal provides many useful functions to support your work with business intelligence content (see Figure 6.39). In this brief introduction, we would like to describe the search function used for finding content.

The SAP documentation provides the following description of the search function:

> *The search function helps you find documents in all repositories that you have integrated into Knowledge Management. The system displays only documents for which the current user has read permission in the results list. You can also include the content of websites in your indexes using Web crawlers. This information is then available via the search function in SAP Enterprise Portal.*[2]

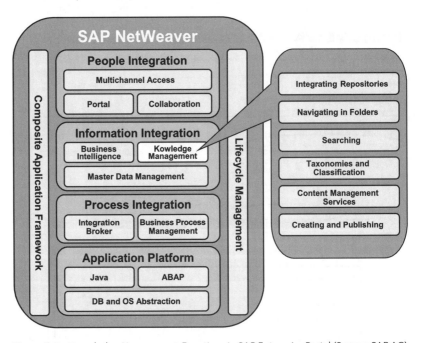

Figure 6.39 Knowledge Management Functions in SAP Enterprise Portal (Source: SAP AG)

2 SAP Online Documentation: Knowledge Management, Link: *http://help.sap.com/ saphelp_nw04/helpdata/en/4c/9d953fc405330ee10000000a114084/content.htm*

Using Search Functions for Business Intelligence Content

If the portal configuration is set up appropriately in the Basis component, you can use the search function without any problem:

▶ For example, if you want to search for a specific sales analysis, you must enter the relevant search term into the input field (see Figure 6.40, Step 1).

▶ You can start the search by clicking on the **Search** button (Step 2). The search result is displayed in a separate window (Step 3).

▶ If you click on one of the items in the results list (Step 4), the corresponding document opens (here: **Profitability Analysis—Revenue Comp.: actual-previous year**, Step 5).

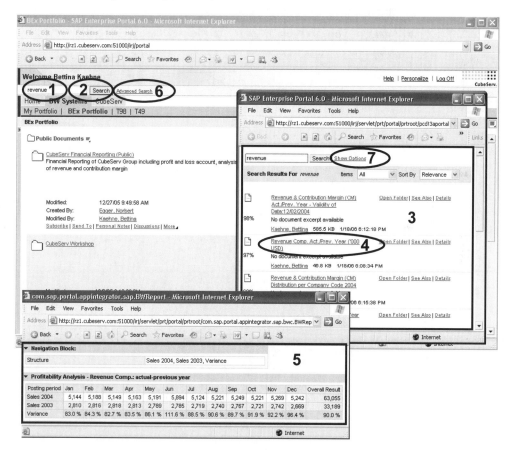

Figure 6.40 Using the Knowledge Management Search Function in SAP Enterprise Portal

Advanced Search Function for Complex Search Criteria

The advanced search function enables you to define complex search criteria.

▶ To do so, you can either click on the **Advanced Search** link when you start the search (see Figure 6.40, Step 6), or you can click on the **Show Options** link in the results list screen (Step 7).

▶ You can use AND-OR combinations (here: **Revenue AND Contribution Margin**, see Figure 6.41, Step 1) or additional selection criteria (here: **Last Modified within the last 3 months**, see Step 2) to define complex search criteria.

▶ You must click on the **Search** button (Step 3) to apply the criteria and obtain a corresponding search result.

▶ Again, if you click on an entry in the results list (Step 4), the corresponding document opens (Step 5).

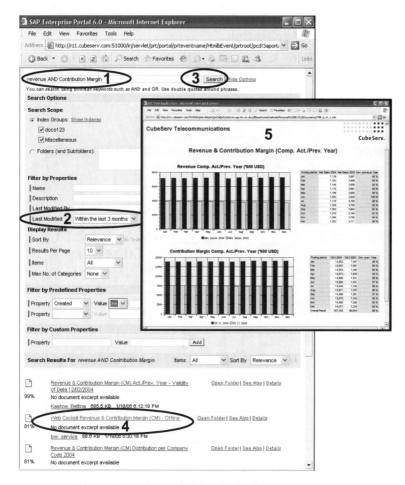

Figure 6.41 Advanced Search in SAP Enterprise Portal

6.6 Information Broadcasting During Report Execution

6.6.1 Publishing Reports Directly from Running Web Applications

While the analyses are being carried out, the head of the controlling department of our model company, CubeServ Engines, learns that although one of the subsidiaries (CubeServ (Mexico) S.A.) developed reasonably well, it didn't meet the growth expectations with regard to exports to Canada. Consequently, he wants to send this information including his comments via e-mail to the person in charge, and store the commented report for future discussions in his personal portfolio.

Requirements

Launching Information Broadcasting from the Context Menu of a Running Web Application

You can call Information Broadcasting from the (standard) context menu of running web applications.

▶ To do that, right-click on any given link in the web application so that the context menu opens (see Figure 6.42, Step 1).

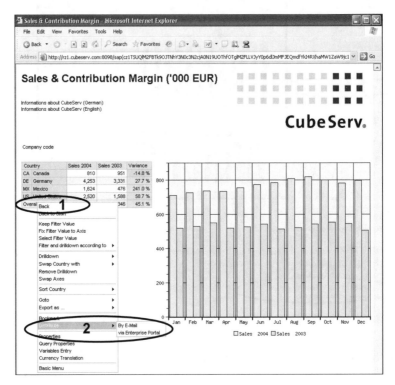

Figure 6.42 Launching Information Broadcasting from the Context Menu of a Web Application

▶ The **Distribute** function provides you with the submenu options **By E-Mail** and **via Enterprise Portal** (Step 2).

Distribution by E-Mail from the Context Menu of a Running Web Application

▶ If you select the **By E-Mail** submenu option (see Figure 6.42, Step 2), the **Broadcaster Wizard for Web Template ...** dialog opens.

▶ Specify the output format and click on the **Continue** button (see Figure 6.43, Steps 1 and 2).

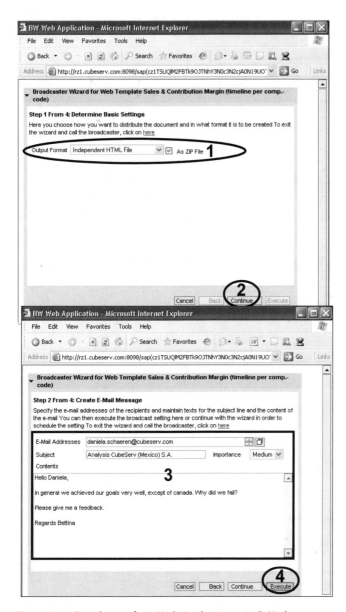

Figure 6.43 Distribution from Web Applications via E-Mail

▶ In the next screen you must specify the e-mail address, as well as the message subject and text (Step 3).

▶ Then click on the **Execute** button (Step 4).

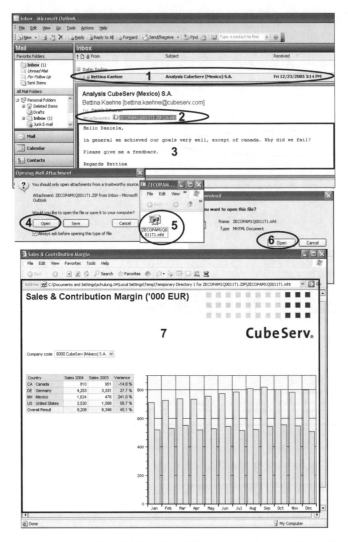

Figure 6.44 Launching the Distributed Web Application from the E-Mail Attachment

Starting the Offline Report from the E-Mail

Once the e-mail has been downloaded, the document is displayed in the inbox of the current e-mail application in use, where you can open it.

▶ In MS Outlook, which we use in our example, you can do that by double-clicking on the item in the Inbox (see Figure 6.44, Step 1).

▶ In accordance with the format chosen, the published report is displayed as an attachment and can be opened (see Figure 6.44, Steps 2 through 7).

Publishing from the Context Menu of a Running Web Application in SAP Enterprise Portal

▶ If you select the **via Enterprise Portal** submenu option (see Figure 6.42, Step 2), the **Broadcaster Wizard for Web Template ...** dialog opens.

▶ Specify the output format and click on the **Continue** button (see Figure 6.45, Steps 1 and 2).

▶ Use the default value **Export Document to Personal Portfolio** in the next screen (Step 3) and click on the **Continue** button once again (Step 4).

▶ In the next dialog, enter the display name and description (Step 5).

▶ Then, click on the **Execute** button (Step 6).

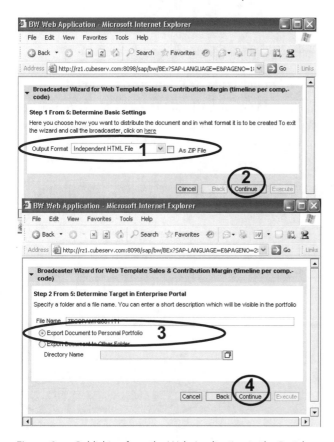

Figure 6.45 Publishing from the Web Application in the Portal

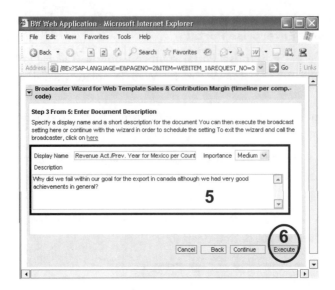

Figure 6.45 Publishing from the Web Application in the Portal (Cont'd.)

Starting the Offline Report from SAP Enterprise Portal

▶ After publication, the offline report is displayed in the personal **My Portfolio** of SAP Enterprise Portal with its display name and description, and you can start it by simply clicking on it (see Figure 6.46, Steps 1 and 2).

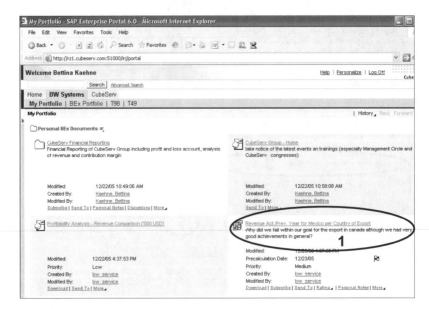

Figure 6.46 Offline Report Including Description in SAP Enterprise Portal

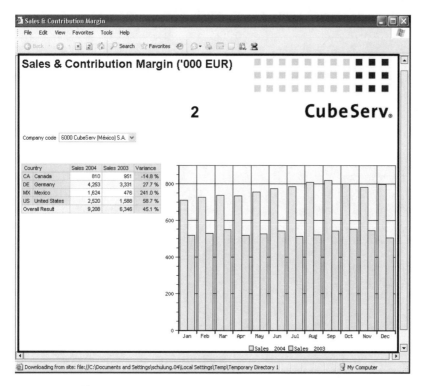

Figure 6.46 Offline Report Including Description in SAP Enterprise Portal (Cont'd.)

7   SAP Business Content

*This chapter describes SAP Business Content—the preconfig-
ured solution that SAP delivers with SAP BW. In particular,
this chapter illustrates the solution's strengths and weaknesses, and recommends ways in which you can leverage
business content for reporting and analysis purposes.*

The SAP Business Content comprises a wide range of predefined analytical solutions that are part of the SAP BW package:

*SAP Business Content is a preconfigured set of role and task-related infor-
mation models based on consistent metadata in the SAP Business Information Warehouse. Business Content provides selected roles within a
company with the information they need to carry out their tasks.[1]*

These predefined solutions greatly help to reduce the time and effort
required to set up and implement SAP BW, because they contain all the
necessary components—from extraction to the data model to reports.
Therefore, as part of a new SAP BW installation, SAP Business Content
means much shorter setup times, even if it is being used only as a template. This makes it possible to implement an application such as Profit
Center Reporting relatively easily and quickly. Needless to say, in order
for this to be possible, the systems in question must have been installed
correctly.

**Benefits of SAP
Business Content**

We are not aware of any other data warehousing product that provides
such comprehensive business content. This is particularly true in cases
where a sufficient amount of data from SAP R/3 is made available in SAP
BW for reporting purposes.

You should also note that the quality of the Business Content is improved
with each new release of SAP BW (and an improvement in the quality of
the existing data is preferable to an increase in the quantity of data).

As we will demonstrate in this section, you should not accept the standard preconfigured solution unquestioningly, even with all its benefits.
This is because the solution does not adequately fulfill the requirements
of the real-world company. You should always check whether you can use

**Problems of SAP
Business Content**

---

1   SAP BW Online Documentation, *http://help.sap.com/saphelp_bw33/helpdata/en/
    37/5fb13cd0500255e10000000a114084/content.htm*

the Business Content directly *as is*, or whether it would make more sense to use it as a template to create your own objects. You should also note that the overall quality of the delivered Business Content can vary widely.

Business Content for reporting In this chapter, we'll focus exclusively on SAP Business Content for reporting and use Business Content Version 3.5.2. For the data modeling and Extraction, Transformation, and Loading (ETL) areas, you should refer to other volumes of the SAP BW Library.[2]

Compared to the data modeling and ETL areas, in everyday practice, the Business Content for reporting has not become the standard solution. While it is used in the ETL area whenever possible, and at least some parts of it are used in the data modeling area, Business Content is only rarely used in reporting. Instead, it is more commonly used as a template or in prototypes.

7.1 Elements of SAP Business Content

SAP Business Content for reporting contains the elements listed below, which will be described in the following sections:

► Roles
► Workbooks
► Web templates
  ► Web items
► Queries
  ► Query views
  ► Query elements (structures, restricted key figures, calculated key figures, variables)
► Currency translation types

7.2 Using SAP Business Content for Reporting

Requirements and problems To use SAP Business Content for reporting, it is imperative that you also use the corresponding InfoProviders for most of the SAP Business Content components.

---

2 See Appendix H, *The SAP BW Library*.

> However, since this is often not the case and customized InfoProviders are used instead, the Business Content can no longer be used.

7.3 SAP Business Content Roles

The roles in SAP BW Business Content are used to summarize jobs of the same type.[3]

SAP provides hundreds of roles with the Business Content. These roles are mainly user menus with groupings of reports (queries, web templates, etc., see Figure 7.2). Thus, the roles represent a relatively comprehensive application landscape.

Scope

> Because the roles contain dedicated queries that are based on Business Content InfoCubes, you cannot employ them in applications that use customized queries or InfoCubes. Unfortunately, this is true for the majority of applications.

Example 1: The Supply Chain Planner Role

Furthermore, some roles in the Business Content contain errors. For example, the **Supply Chain Planner** role (technical name: SAP_BW_0ROLE_0063) contains several menu items that don't have any function:

▶ Opening the role menu (see Figure 7.1, 1)

▶ Selecting a menu item (2)

▶ The menu item detail does not contain the object to be executed (3)

Example 2: The Business Unit Analyst Role

The **Business Unit Analyst role** (SAP_BW_BUSINESS_UNIT_ANALYST) has been available since the release of an early version of SAP BW. It provides several workbooks but no web report (see Figure 7.2). The queries contained in the workbooks are based on the data provided by profit center accounting.

---

3 See SAP Online Documentation.

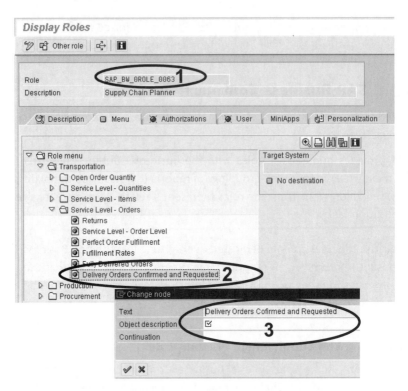

Figure 7.1 "Supply Chain Planner" Role: Example of an Erroneous Role

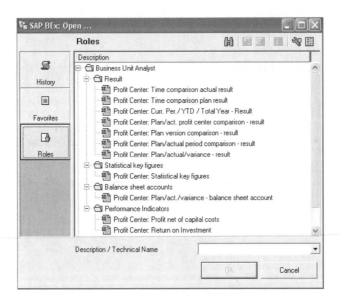

Figure 7.2 Workbooks of the "Business Unit Analyst" Role

A query is integrated in each of the workbooks that are presented without any complex formatting (see Figure 7.3).

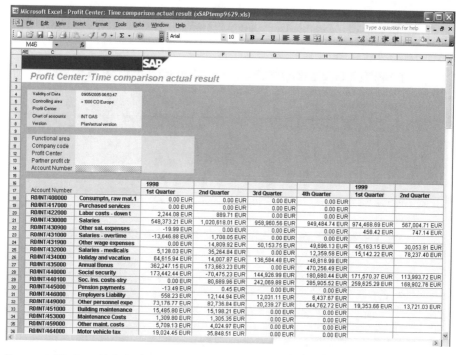

Figure 7.3 "Business Unit Analyst" Role: Example of the Workbook Layout

If you want to use the Business Unit Analyst role, you must consider the following point among others: **Note for usage**

▶ The variable 0P_FVAEX is used for the **Fiscal year variant** characteristic in the queries. This variable is populated with data via an exit from the **Fiscal year variant** attribute for the controlling area.

If the attribute is empty, the system returns an error message that doesn't have a workaround for solving the problem. Help is also missing in the documentation.

▶ The workbooks use variables that are sometimes identical; however, the sort order of the variables in the dialog, which opens for entering the values, seems to have been defined arbitrarily, and it differs with each query. For example, in Query 0PCA_C01_Q0012, the variables for the profit center hierarchy and for the profit center group are listed separately (see Figure 7.5).

It would be very helpful for the user if the sorting was at least identical within a role, which would also make the implementation easier. For example, the time variables should always be located at the beginning or end of a variable (see Figures 7.4 and 7.5).

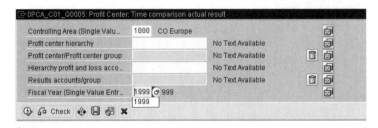

Figure 7.4 Variable Screen of Query 0PCA_C01_Q0005

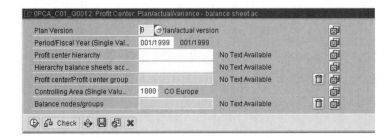

Figure 7.5 Variable Screen of Query 0PCA_C01_Q0012

▶ Although the Statistical key figures workbook does contain variables, these variables don't display during the startup and refreshing of the query.

 Obviously, the workbook contains errors in the standard version.

7.4 SAP Business Explorer Workbooks

Workbooks are the most basic type of specifically formatted queries and have been available in large quantities as part of SAP Business Content since the first versions of SAP BW. They contain one or more queries, and for end users, they represented the only possible way of selecting reports via Role menus before web applications entered the market.

The Business Content roles of earlier SAP BW versions, in particular, contain Business Explorer workbooks (for example, the **Sales manager** role, SAP_BW_0ROLE_0007).

This means that the usage restrictions mentioned in Sections 7.2 and 7.3 also apply to workbooks.

The majority of Business Content workbooks provide only simple presentations of queries and no functions that really require the use of workbooks. Since SAP BW 3.0, this necessity has become obsolete, because you can integrate queries directly into roles. Not having to rely on workbooks—when using web applications with appropriate standard web templates—reduces the maintenance requirements dramatically.

Figure 7.6 displays the Business Explorer workbook **Incoming orders**. The problems that occur here are typical of many Business Content workbooks:

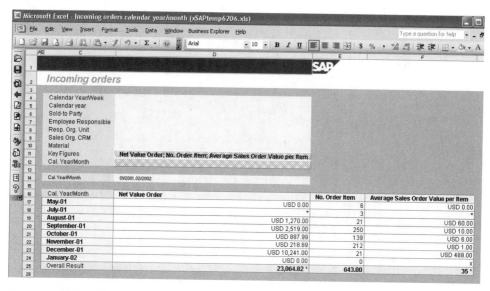

Figure 7.6 BEx Workbook "Incoming Orders"

► There are exactly three Business Content workbooks available with the name **Incoming orders**. This means that the probability of starting the correct workbook when you call it by its name is 33%. One of the workbooks contains the query **Incoming orders (last 12 months)** (0CL_C03_Q0003) with the basic InfoCube **Customer orders** (0CSAL_C03). If the name of the workbook corresponded to the query, it would be much easier to select the right workbook.

Problems

► The workbook mapped is always opened in English, never in the logon language.

7.5   SAP Business Explorer Web Templates

Business Content web templates

Business Content web templates form the basis of the Business Explorer web applications. Since SAP BW 3.0, predominantly BEx web applications are provided in the context of Business Content for reporting.

Standard web template 0ANALYZER

Each query that is run for a specific web template—without an explicit decision in an HTML browser—uses the standard template provided. Many SAP BW customers have left the standard SAP Business Content web template unchanged. Thus, the standard web template (0QUERY_TEMPLATE since SAP BW 3.0; 0ANALYZER since SAP BW 3.5) is one of the most frequently used Business Content components in the reporting area.

Usability of other web templates

In general, web templates represent a specific arrangement of Business Explorer query components (via *web items*, see Section 7.6 and Chapter 5, *The BEx Web*) and other HTML elements. Here too, SAP provides many web templates that cannot be used due to the basic conditions described earlier in this chapter.

Moreover, the use of Business Content web templates is further restricted by other problems:

▶ Some templates contain function errors that, if executed by the user, cause the application to cancel.

▶ Many templates contain useful functions, but what's missing is that "final touch" that users have come to expect. This affects the benefits of the templates, because the finishing represents the major part of the development work.

▶ The restricted informational value of the Business Content queries, which the Business Content web templates are based on—for instance, missing time variables or even performance problems—often make it impossible to use the templates.

Example 1: iView "Customer Plan/Actual Sales"

The iView **Customer plan/actual sales** (0TPL_IVIEW_0SD_C01_Q030) is an example of a Business Content web template that contains various functions and can be displayed both as a table and as a graphic. The basis of the query **Customer: plan/actual sales** (0SD_C01_Q030) on which the web template is based is the InfoCube **Customer** (0SD_C01).

The first and foremost problem for using it in a production system is that the query doesn't contain any variables for the time selection (see Figure 7.7, Step 1). This means that for a given selection, the entire time series of existing data must be read. This can result in unacceptable response times and even non-readability for datasets that span a period of over two years (see Figure 7.7, Step 2). Performance and readability

> Unfortunately, the function **Force variable screen display** has been removed from the context menu so that the selection screen can only be called by manipulating the URL (&VARIABLE_SCREEN=X).

The missing "final touch" becomes obvious with the inappropriate formatting of the names of the axes. **Problems**

▶ The amounts displayed don't contain any thousands separator, and the problem of the "display in 1" is already apparent when we use the data of our sample company, CubeServ Engines. 10000000 only corresponds to 10 million; while revenues of 10 billion would result in an unformatted "monster" of 10000000000!

▶ The display of the time axis when drilling down the detail view is more proof of the absence of a "final touch" (see Figure 7.7, Step 3). Calendar months presented in such a way are simply unacceptable.

▶ Finally, the black-and-white display in the figure emphasizes the poor readability of the graphic, which has a different color in the dialog.

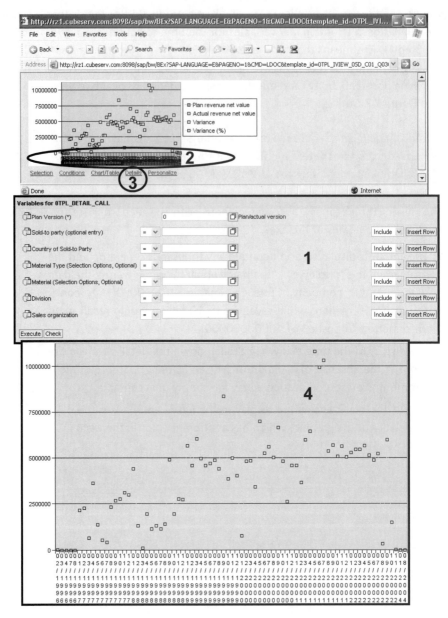

Figure 7.7 Web Template 0TPL_IVIEW_0SD_C01_Q030

Example 2: Web Cockpit "Cockpit Sales Analysis"

The **Cockpit Sales Analysis** (0TPL_COCKPIT_SALES) is a web template that displays data from several sales and distribution InfoCubes in a clear manner (see Figure 7.8). It displays data on the sales figures, the quotation pipeline, as well as sales order and revenue values.

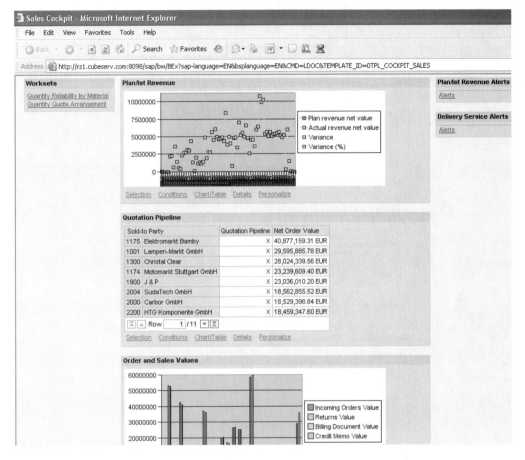

Figure 7.8 Web Cockpit 0TPL_COCKPIT_SALES

If you want to use this cockpit, you should consider the following items: **Problems**

▶ Each of the three cockpit reports contains an option to toggle between a tabular and a graphical display. The selections can be changed via the corresponding link (see Figure 7.9). Because the characteristics for the three reports available in the selections aren't identical, the user can't operate the user interface intuitively.

▶ The left-hand side of the cockpit provides an area where you can call two additional reports. The report **Quantity Reliability per Material** (see Figure 7.10) displays the relevant data in a layout that's similar to that of the web cockpit; however, the web cockpit doesn't contain the **Send** button.

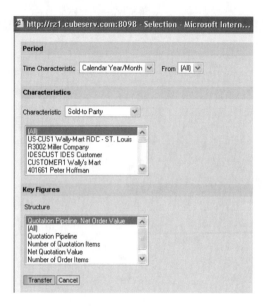

Figure 7.9 Selection in the Web Cockpit

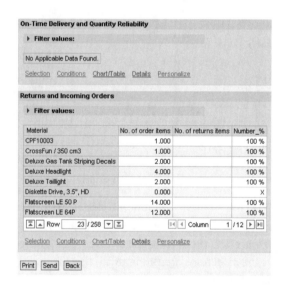

Figure 7.10 Quantity Reliability for the Material (Report)

▶ Moreover, the **Send** button doesn't use the options provided by Information Broadcasting. Instead, it sends a URL via e-mail, which starts the BEx Web Analyzer without a query. This is pretty inefficient.

Due to these deficiencies, you should use the web cockpit only as a template. We also advise you not to use it directly in a prototype intended for end users, because then user friendliness must be your primary concern.

7.5.1 Web Items

Web items are the SAP BW-based components of web templates. Most web items receive data from a data provider and make available the data in HTML format in a web application (see also Chapter 5, *The BEx Web*). SAP Business Content uses many web items such as tables, charts, and so on.

The SAP Business Content web items contain specific settings and are frequently stored in Business Content web item libraries. You can optimize those library objects and use them for your own web templates.

Usability of Business Content web items

Example: Business Content Web Item Library

The **Cockpit Sales Analysis** (0TPL_COCKPIT_SALES), referred to above as an example of a Business Content web template, contains the following web items (see Figure 7.11), which, in turn, are stored in the Business Content web item library **Web items for sales analysis** (0LIB_SALES_ ANALYSIS):

▶ **BarChart 1** (0LIB_CHART_SALESANALYSIS_BAR_1)

▶ **LineChart** (0LIB_CHART_SALESANALYSIS_LINES)

▶ **Table Sales Analysis** (0LIB_TABLE_SALESANALYSIS_1)

Once optimized, these Business Content web items can be used for your own web templates.

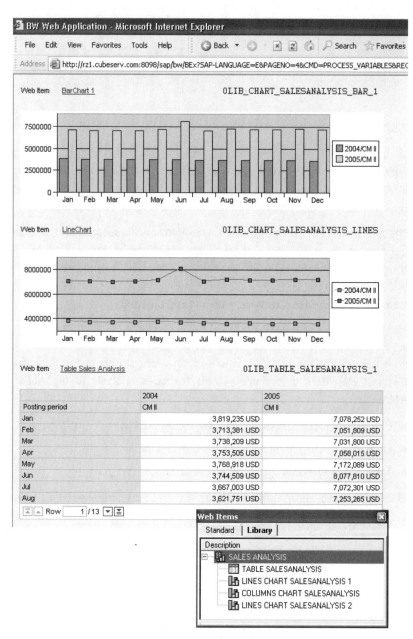

Figure 7.11 Business Content Web Items and Business Content Web Item Library of the Objects Used in the Web Template "Cockpit Sales Analysis" (0TPL_COCKPIT_SALES)

7.6 Queries

Queries are the result of complex requests on InfoProviders and therefore form the core of Business Content objects for reporting. SAP Business Content is provided with many objects that can be used in various areas.

Problems

Of course, the conditions and problems described at the beginning of this chapter directly apply to these Business Content components. Furthermore, you must consider the following additional aspects for some of the Business Content queries:

- **Start drilldown**

  In some of the queries, a line with a characteristic is selected, which typically contains many different values. This results in a large number of output lines, and therefore to a loss in performance (see Figure 7.12).

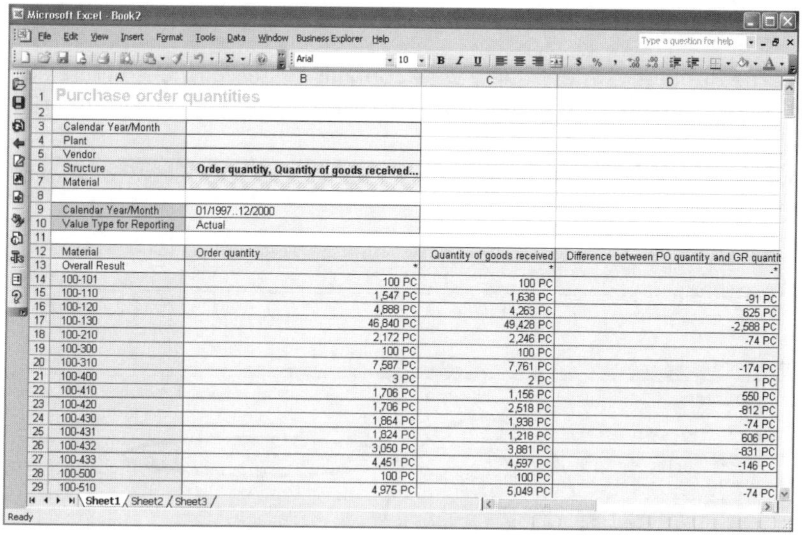

Purchase order quantities

Calendar Year/Month	
Plant	
Vendor	
Structure	Order quantity, Quantity of goods received...
Material	
Calendar Year/Month	01/1997..12/2000
Value Type for Reporting	Actual

Material	Order quantity	Quantity of goods received	Difference between PO quantity and GR quantit
Overall Result	*	*	-*
100-101	100 PC	100 PC	
100-110	1,547 PC	1,638 PC	-91 PC
100-120	4,888 PC	4,263 PC	625 PC
100-130	46,840 PC	49,428 PC	-2,588 PC
100-210	2,172 PC	2,246 PC	-74 PC
100-300	100 PC	100 PC	
100-310	7,587 PC	7,761 PC	-174 PC
100-400	3 PC	2 PC	1 PC
100-410	1,706 PC	1,156 PC	550 PC
100-420	1,706 PC	2,518 PC	-812 PC
100-430	1,864 PC	1,938 PC	-74 PC
100-431	1,824 PC	1,218 PC	606 PC
100-432	3,050 PC	3,881 PC	-831 PC
100-433	4,451 PC	4,597 PC	-146 PC
100-500	100 PC	100 PC	
100-510	4,975 PC	5,049 PC	-74 PC

Figure 7.12 Purchase Order Quantities Query (0PUR_C01_Q0011) with "Material" Drilldown

- **Restrictions**

  The restrictions carried out in the queries; for example, the restrictions to the currency type, are not documented and therefore must be checked in each individual case to ensure that the query displays the expected results.

7.6.1 Query Views

Several Business Content reports (for instance in the form of workbooks or web templates) contain query views, that is, stored navigational states of queries.

Problems   Of course, the aforementioned conditions and problems are already contained in the query views since each Business Content query view is based on a Business Content query. Inappropriate start drilldowns, missing selections, and similar problems complicate the usability of the Business Content query views in productive operation.

Example: Problematic Response Times

In the table displayed in Figure 7.13, the Business Content web template **Cockpit Sales Analysis** (0PTL_COCKPIT_SALES), analyzed earlier in this chapter, displays the Business Content query view **Quotation Pipeline** (0SD_C05_Q0007_V001):

▶ The Business Content query view contains a filter for the structure elements **Quotation Pipeline** and **Net Order Value** (see Figure 7.13, 1).

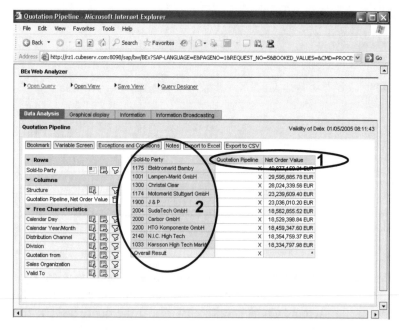

Figure 7.13 Business Content Query View "Quotation Pipeline" (0SD_C05_Q0007_V001) with Underlying Business Content Query "Quotation Pipeline" (0SD_C05_Q0007)

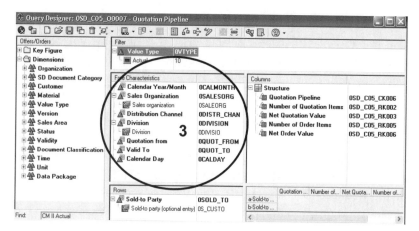

Figure 7.13 Business Content Query View "Quotation Pipeline" (0SD_C05_Q0007_ V001) with underlying Business Content Query "Quotation Pipeline" (0SD_C05_ Q0007) (Cont'd.)

▶ The start drilldown **Sold-to Party**, which can have numerous different values in many companies that use SAP BW, frequently prolongs the response time of the query view (2), and that in itself can be a problem.

▶ Another serious problem is caused by the Business Content query **Quotation Pipeline** (0SD_C05_Q0007), which the Business Content query view is based on. The query doesn't contain any time selection variable (3), which also results in extremely problematic response times.

7.6.2 Query Elements

The Business Content queries contain Business Content query elements such as structures, restricted key figures, and calculated key figures or variables.

Of course, the conditions and problems mentioned so far in this chapter also affect these Business Content components. **Problems**

The Business Content query elements of the "Variable" type represent a special case in this context. Since they are not defined on the InfoProvider but on the InfoObject, and the Business Content InfoObjects are used more frequently in productive SAP BW applications than the Business Content InfoProviders, the Business Content variables are also used more often. **Special case: variables**

If you want to use Business Content variables, note the following: For the exit variables that are available in a large quantity, you should check whether the programming logic that is used to populate the variables with data actually meets the requirements of the project. Because this can be rather time-consuming, we recommend that you use your own exit variables for which you have full control of the code.

Some SAP exit variables however, should and must be used directly. One such variable is the **Latest data (transactional cube)** (0S_RQTRA) variable for the **Request-ID** characteristic. This variable enables you to display data in reporting, even if that data hasn't been closed yet and still has the "yellow" status.

Example: Business Content Structures – Restricted and Calculated Key Figures

The Business Content query **Quotation Pipeline** (0SD_C05_Q0007) already analyzed above contains (global) restricted and calculated key figures, for example, as well as variables:

Calculated key figure
► The (local) structure of the query contains the Business Content query element **Calculated Key Figure "Quotation Pipeline"** (0SD_C05_CK006) as a result of **Net Quotation Value**, **Order probability** and **No. of order items** (see Figure 7.14, Steps 1 through 3).

Restricted key figure
► The formula elements of this calculated key figure consist of, among other things, the Business Content query element of the type **Restricted Key Figure "Net Quotation Value"** (0SD_C05_RK003). This value selects the Document category Q for the key figure **Net value in statistics currency** (Steps 1, 2, and 4).

Variable
► Moreover, several Business Content query elements of the **Variable** type are used (Steps 5 and 6), for instance, the variable **Sales Organization** (0SALESORG).

Unfortunately, the structure is not stored as a global structure—neither with the different basic key figures nor in the restricted and calculated key figures—so it cannot be reused in other Business Content queries, or in customized queries.

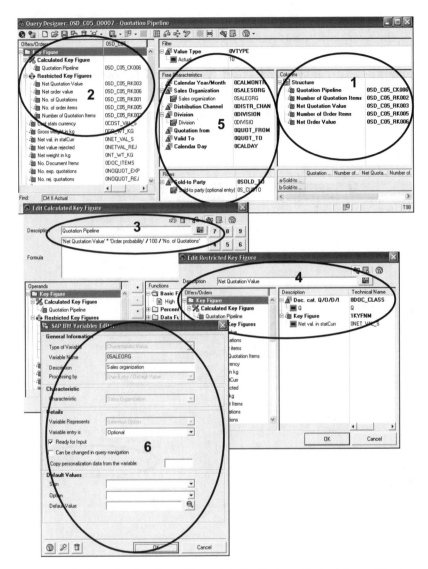

Figure 7.14 Business Content Query Elements in the Business Content Query "Quotation Pipeline" (0SD_C05_Q0007)

7.7 Currency Translation Types

SAP also provides some important *currency translation types* with its Business Content, which can be used directly for reporting purposes.

The currency translation types use the currency settings and exchange rate tables that are also used in SAP R/3. These components can be used

Usability

whenever necessary. This holds true for the definition of key figures, during the query creation as well as for their use at the time the query is run.

Example: Currency Translation Type "Fixed Target Currency, Current Date"

Using the currency translation type **Fixed target currency, current date** (0HRFIXCUR) during the execution of a query (see Figure 7.15, Steps 1 through 4).

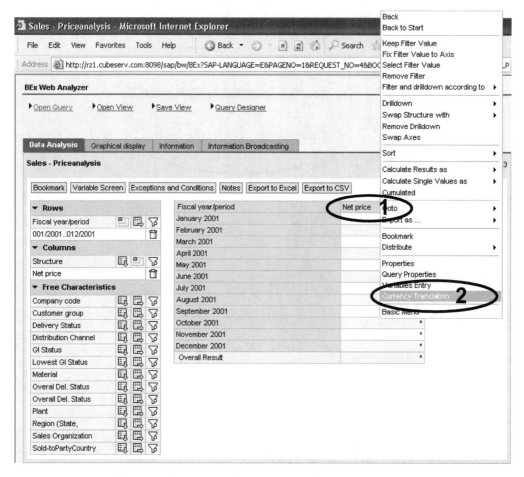

Figure 7.15 Currency Translation Type "Fixed Target Currency, Current Date"

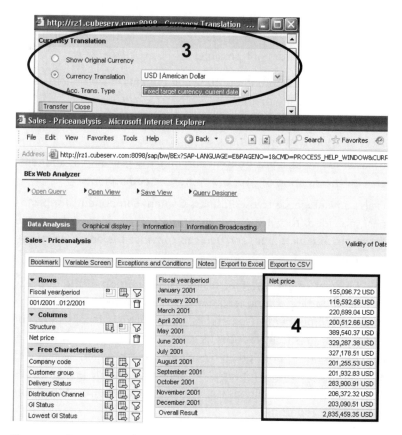

Figure 7.15 Currency Translation Type "Fixed Target Currency, Current Date" (Cont'd.)

7.8   Conclusion

For several reasons, the use of Business Content for reporting plays a minor role:

▶ **Costs**

Activating Business Content for reporting requires a lot of effort and additional objects such as InfoProviders and InfoObjects.

▶ **Logic problems**

Understanding the logic mapped in the queries, variables, and so on is rather time-consuming and the logic frequently doesn't meet the requirements of the actual project that you're currently working on.

Whenever possible, you should utilize the Business Content components for reporting. But, due to the reasons described in this chapter, using these components is often not possible:

▶ To use the Business Content reporting components in a productive system, you must modify them.

▶ Many Business Content reporting components must be optimized or corrected prior to using them.

▶ It is easier to use Business Content components as examples and templates for the creation of your own reporting components.

▶ It is also advantageous to use Business Content components for prototypes, provided the necessary enhancements and corrections are within a reasonable scope, and you can convince the end users of the user friendliness of the components.

It would be great to get a systematically revised version of the Business Content for reporting components from SAP in the near future, as the multitude of components (sometimes contradictory, inconsistent, or even erroneous) drastically reduces its benefit, which, apart from that, is outstanding. To better position an overall excellent product, SAP should revise the Business Content for reporting and try to provide less functionality, but something that still has some of the main benefits of the Business Content for reporting.

A   Abbreviations

ABAP	Advanced Business Application Programming
ADK	Archiving Development Kit
ALE	Application Link Enabling
API	Application Programming Interface
ASCII	American Standard Code for Information Interchange
AWB	Administrator Workbench
BAPI	Business Application Programming Interface
BCT	Business Content
BEx	Business Explorer
BW	Business Information Warehouse
CSV	Comma Separated Values (or Variables)
DDIC	Data Dictionary
DIM ID	Dimension Identification
DWH	Data Warehouse
ETL	Extraction, Transformation, and Loading
IDoc	Intermediate Document
LUW	Logical Unit of Work
ODBO	OLE DB (Object Linking and Embedding Database) for OLAP
ODS	Operational Data Store
OLAP	Online Analytical Processing
OLTP	Online Transaction Processing
RFC	Remote Function Call
RRI	Report-to-Report Interface
SAPI	Service API
SID	Surrogate Identification
SOAP	Simple Object Access Protocol
SQL	Structured Query Language
TCT	Technical Content
TRFC	Transactional RFC

WAD	Web Application Designer
WAS	Web Application Server
XML	Extensible Markup Language
XMLA	XML for Analytics

B   Queries

This appendix contains some documentation samples for various queries used in this book.[1]

The CubeServ BW Documentation Tool is the first professional documentation tool for SAP Business Information Warehouse (SAP BW). It enables you to create online documentation from the SAP BW system "at the push of a button." Several navigation options are available to use the documentation both online and as printed. You can find more information on that at *www.cubeserv.com*. You can also download the documentation of all queries used in this book in its original HTML format from the following URL: *www.bw-forum.com*.

---

1   Other queries are shown in screen captures in Chapter 4, *The BEx Query Designer*.

B.1 Query ZECOPAM1Q00003

Query Details

InfoCube:	ZECOPAM1	Profitability Analysis (actual & plan data)	
Query:	ZECOPAM1000003	Profitability Analsyis - Contribution Margin Overview	

Settings

Result position	Bottom/right		
Format display	false	Suppression of Repitition Texts	True
+/- Sign Display	Plus/minus sign before: -123.45	Zero Suppression	Display Rows and Columns

Filters

InfoObject Description	InfoObject	Restriction
Curency Type	0CURTYPE	B0
Fiscal Year Variant	0FISCVARNT	K4
Valuation view	0VALUATION	#
Version	ZEVERSION	100
Value Type for Reporting	0VTYPE	010

Free Characteristics

InfoObject Description	InfoObject	Restriction
Company code	0COMP_CODE	Company Code (Selection Options, Optional) 0S_COCD
Order	0COORDER	
Country	0CUSTOMER__0COUNTRY	
Region	0CUSTOMER__0REGION	
Distribution Channel	0DISTR_CHAN	
Division	0DIVISION	
Fiscal year/period	0FISCPER	Period/Fiscal Year (Interval Entry, Required) 0I_FPER
Material	0MATERIAL	
Material Group	0MATERIAL__0MATL_GROUP	

Free Characteristics

InfoObject Description	InfoObject	Restriction
ProdHier	OMATERIAL_OPROD_HIER	
Source system ID	OSOURSYSTEM	

Structure

Structure name			
Structure CM Schema			

ElementName	Restriction	Name	Value
Revenue	Keyfigure		▓ 0COPAREVEN
Gross Sales	Keyfigure		▓ ZEBRUMS
Gross Sales	Calculated keyfigure		
CustDiscnt	Keyfigure		▓ 0CUST_DSCNT
MatDiscount	Keyfigure		▓ 0PROD_DSCNT
Revenue reduction	Keyfigure		▓ ZEERLMIND
Net Sales	Calculated keyfigure		
Cash Discount	Keyfigure		▓ 0CASH_DSCNT
Rebate	Keyfigure		▓ 0VOL_REBATE
Sales Commission	Keyfigure		▓ 0SALES_CMSN
Special DC of Sales	Keyfigure		▓ 0SPCDSLS_CS
Accrued Freight	Keyfigure		▓ 0ACCRDFR_CS
Net Profit on Sales	Calculated keyfigure		
Direct Mat. Costs	Keyfigure		▓ 0DIRMAT_CS
Var. Production Cost	Keyfigure		▓ 0VARPROD_CS
Material ovhd.	Keyfigure		▓ 0MATOVHD
Fxd Costs of Product	Keyfigure		▓ 0FIXPROD_CS
Full manuf. costs	Keyfigure		▓ ZEHKVK
CM II	Calculated keyfigure		
Quantity Variance	Keyfigure		▓ 0QUANT_VRNC
Price Var.	Keyfigure		▓ 0PRICE_VRNC
Other Variances	Keyfigure		▓ 0OTHER_VRNC
CM III	Calculated keyfigure		

Structure

Structure name	ElementName	Restriction	Name	Value
Structure CM Schema	Distribution Costs	Keyfigure		▮ 0SALES_CS
	Marketing	Keyfigure		▮ 0MARKETING
	R&D	Keyfigure		▮ 0RSRCH_DEV
	CM IV	Calculated keyfigure		
	Administration	Keyfigure		▮ 0ADMNSTRTN
	Other Overhead	Keyfigure		▮ 0OTHER_OVHD
	Operating Profit	Calculated keyfigure		

Variables

Description	Name	InfoObject	VariableType	ProcessType	Parameter
Company Code (Selection Options, Optional)	0S_COCD	0COMP_CODE	Characteristic value	User entry	Selection option
Period/Fiscal Year (Interval Entry, Required)	0I_FPER	0FISCPER	Characteristic value	User entry	Interval

Calculated Keyfigure

Formula	Content
CM III	(((CM II - Quantity Variance) - Price Var.) - Other Variances)
Net Sales	(((Gross Sales + Revenue reduction) + CustDisont) + MatDiscount)
Net Profit on Sales	(((((Net Sales + Cash Discount) + Rebate) + Sales Commission) + Special DC of Sales) + Accrued Freight)
CM IV	(((CM III - Distribution Costs) - Marketing) - R&D)
Operating Profit	((CM IV - Administration) - Other Overhead)
Gross Sales	(Revenue + Gross Sales)
CM II	(((((Net Profit on Sales - Direct Mat. Costs) - Var. Production Cost) - Material ovhd.) - Fxd Costs of Product) - Full manuf. costs)

B.2 Query ZECOPAM1Q00005

Query Details

InfoCube:	ZECOPAM1	Profitability Analysis (actual & plan data)
Query:	ZECOPAM1Q00005	Profitability Analysis - Contribution Margin cons. and local

Settings

Result position	Top/left	
Format display	false	
+/- Sign Display	Plus/minus sign before: -123.45	

Suppression of Repitition Texts	True	
Zero Suppression	Display Rows and Columns	

Filters

InfoObject Description	InfoObject	Restriction
Currency Type	0CURTYPE	B0
Fiscal Year Variant	0FISCVARNT	K4
Valuation view	0VALUATION	#
Version	ZEVERSION	100
Value Type for Reporting	0VTYPE	010
Fiscal year/period	0FISCPER	Period/Fiscal Year(Interval Entry, Required) 0I_FPER

Free Characteristics

InfoObject Description	InfoObject	Restriction
Company code	0COMP_CODE	Company Code (Selection Options, Optional) 0S_COCD

Structure

Structure name	ElementName	Restriction	Name	Value
Structure CM Schema	Revenue	Keyfigure	0COPAREVEN	
	Gross Sales Plan	Keyfigure	ZEBRUMS	
	Gross Sales	Calculated keyfigure		
	CustDiscnt	Keyfigure	0CUST_DSCNT	

Structure

Structure name	ElementName	Restriction	Name	Value
Structure CM Schema	MatDiscount	Keyfigure		0PROD_DSCNT
	Revenue reduction	Keyfigure		ZEERLMIND
	Net Sales Cons.	0CUSTOMER__0ACCNT_GR	0CUSTOMER__0ACCNT_GRP	PLNT
	Net Sales Cons.	Keyfigure		Net Sales (to be modified)
	Net Sales Local	Calculated keyfigure		
	Net Sales	Calculated keyfigure		
	Cash Discount	Keyfigure		0CASH_DSCNT
	Rebate	Keyfigure		0VOL_REBATE
	Sales Commission	Keyfigure		0SALES_CMSN
	Special DC of Sales	Keyfigure		0SPCDSLS_CS
	Accrued Freight	Keyfigure		0ACCRDFR_CS
	Net Profit on Sales	Calculated keyfigure		
	Direct Mat. Costs	Keyfigure		0DIRMAT_CS
	Var. Production Cost	Keyfigure		0VARPROD_CS
	Material ovhd.	Keyfigure		0MATOVHD
	Fxd Costs of Product	Keyfigure		0FIXPROD_CS
	Full manuf. costs Plan	Keyfigure		ZEHKVK
	Full manuf. costs Cons.	Keyfigure		ZEHKVKK
	Full manuf. costs Local	Calculated keyfigure		
	Full manuf. costs	Calculated keyfigure		
	CM II	Calculated keyfigure		
	Quantity Variance	Keyfigure		0QUANT_VRNC
	Price Var.	Keyfigure		0PRICE_VRNC
	Other Variances	Keyfigure		0OTHER_VRNC
	CM III	Calculated keyfigure		
	Distribution Costs	Keyfigure		0SALES_CS
	Marketing	Keyfigure		0MARKETING
	R&D	Keyfigure		0RSRCH_DEV

Structure

Structure name	ElementName	Restriction	Name	Value
Structure CM Schema	CM IV	Calculated keyfigure		
	Administration	Keyfigure		■ OADMNSTRTN
	Other Overhead	Keyfigure		■ OOTHER_OVHD
	Operating Profit	Calculated keyfigure		

Variables

Description	Name	InfoObject	VariableType	ProcessType	Parameter
Company Code (Selection Options, Optional)	OS_COCD	OCOMP_CODE	Characteristic value	User entry	Selection option
Period/Fiscal Year (Interval Entry, Required)	OI_FPER	OFISCPER	Characteristic value	User entry	Interval

Calculated Keyfigure

Formula	Content
CM II	(Net Profit on Sales - Full manuf. costs)
Operating Profit	((CM IV - Administration) - Other Overhead)
CM IV	(((CM III - Distribution Costs) - Marketing) - R&D)
CM III	(((CM II - Quantity Variance) - Price Var.) - Other Variances)
Net Sales Local	((Gross Sales + Revenue reduction) + CustDisont) + MatDiscount)
Net Sales	((LEAF (Net Sales Local) * Net Sales Local) + ((LEAF (Net Sales Cons.) NOT) * Net Sales Cons.))
Full manuf. costs Local	(((Direct Mat. Costs + Var. Production Cost) + Material ovhd.) + Fxd Costs of Product)
Gross Sales	(Revenue + Gross Sales Plan)
Net Profit on Sales	(((((Net Sales + Cash Discount) + Rebate) + Sales Commission) + Special DC of Sales) + Accrued Freight)
Full manuf. costs	((Full manuf. Costs Plan + (LEAF (Full manuf. Costs Local) * Full manuf. Costs Local)) + ((LEAF (Full manuf. costs Cons.) NOT) * Full manuf. costs Cons.))

B.3 Query ZEKDABC1Q00001

Query Details

InfoCube:	ZEKDABC1	Sales Order Stock
Query:	ZEKDABC1Q00001	Sales Order Stock – Partly Segment Analysis

Settings

Result position	Bottom/right		
Format display	false	Suppression of Repitition Texts	True
+/- Sign Display	Plus/minus sign before: -123.45	Zero Suppression	Display Rows and Columns

Filters

InfoObject Description	InfoObject	Restriction
Fiscal Year Variant	0FISCVARNT	K4
Value Type for Reporting	0VTYPE	010
Version	ZEVERSION	100
Currency Type	0CURTYPE	B0
Valuation view	0VALUATION	#

Free Characteristics

InfoObject Description	InfoObject	Restriction
Company code	0COMP_CODE	
Customer	0CUSTOMER	
Account Group	0CUSTOMER_0ACCNT_GRP	
Country	0CUSTOMER_0COUNTRY	
Industry sector	0CUSTOMER_0INDUSTRY	
Distribution Channel	0DISTR_CHAN	
Fiscal year/period	0FISCPER	Period/Fiscal Year (Interval Entry, Required) 0I_FPER
Sales Employee	0SALESEMPLY	
Sales Organization	0SALESORG	

Free Characteristics

InfoObject Description	InfoObject	Restriction
Sales group	0SALES_GRP	

Structure

Structure name	ElementName	Restriction	Name	Value
Key figures	Total Orders on hand	Keyfigure		
	Segment A1 Orders on hand	0CUSTOMER_OREGION	0CUSTOMER_OREGION	ZEBESTAND
	Segment A1 Orders on hand	Material	0MATERIAL	FL
	Segment A1 Orders on hand	Keyfigure		100-100 - 1300-780
	Segment C3 Orders on hand	0CUSTOMER_OREGION	0CUSTOMER_OREGION	ZEBESTAND
	Segment C3 Orders on hand	Material	0MATERIAL	08
	Segment C3 Orders on hand	Keyfigure		100-100 - 1400-750
	Segment D2 Orders on hand	0CUSTOMER_OREGION	0CUSTOMER_OREGION	ZEBESTAND
	Segment D2 Orders on hand	Material	0MATERIAL	08
	Segment D2 Orders on hand	Keyfigure		100-100 - 1400-750
				ZEBESTAND

Variables

Description	Name	InfoObject	VariableType	ProcessType	Parameter
Period/Fiscal Year(Interval Entry, Required)	0I_FPER	0FISCPER	Characteristic value	User entry	Interval

Query Details

B.4 Query ZECOPAM1Q0001

InfoCube:	ZECOPAM1	Profitability Analysis (actual & plan data)
Query:	ZECOPAM1Q0001	Profitability Analysis - Revenue Comp.: actual-previous year ('000 USD)

Settings

Result position	Bottom/right	
Format display	false	Suppression of Repitition Texts	True
+/- Sign Display	Plus/minus sign before: -123.45	Zero Suppression	Suppress Rows and Columns as in 2.0

Filters

InfoObject Description	InfoObject	Restriction
Version	ZEVERSION	100
Value type	0VTYPE	010
Fiscal Year Variant	0FISCVARNT	K4
Request ID	0REQUID	Most Current Data (Transactional InfoCube)0S_RQTRA

Free Characteristics

InfoObject Description	InfoObject	Restriction
Company code	0COMP_CODE	
Country	0COUNTRY	
Customer	0CUSTOMER	
Distribution Channel	0DISTR_CHAN	
Posting period	0FISCPER3	
InfoProvider	0INFOPROV	
Material	0MATERIAL	
Prod.hierarchy	0PROD_HIER	
Region	0REGION	
Sales Organization	0SALESORG	
Sales group	0SALES_GRP	
Sales Office	0SALES_OFF	

Structure

Structure name: Structure

ElementName: Net Sales &ZEFISYTO&

Restriction	Name	Value
Transaction Type	OREC_TYPE	F
Value type	OVTYPE	010
Keyfigure		Net Sales (to be modified)
Version	ZEVERSION	100
Transaction Type	OREC_TYPE	E
Transaction Type	OREC_TYPE	D
Transaction Type	OREC_TYPE	C
Transaction Type	OREC_TYPE	B

Structure

Structure name: Structure

ElementName: Net Sales &ZEFISYTO&

Restriction	Name	Value
Fiscal year	OFISCYEAR	ZEFISYPO ZEFISYPO
Transaction Type	OREC_TYPE	F
Value type	OVTYPE	010
Keyfigure		Net Sales (to be modified)
Version	ZEVERSION	100
Transaction Type	OREC_TYPE	E
Transaction Type	OREC_TYPE	D
Transaction Type	OREC_TYPE	C
Transaction Type	OREC_TYPE	B
Fiscal year	OFISCYEAR	ZEFISYPO ZEFISYPO 1-

ElementName	Restriction
Transaction Volume &ZEFISYTO&	Calculated keyfigure
Transaction Volume &ZEFISYTO&	Calculated keyfigure
Variance to prev. Year	Calculated keyfigure

Variables

Description	Name	InfoObject	VariableType	ProcessType	Parameter
Fiscal year	ZEFISYPO	OFISCYEAR	Characteristic value	User entry	Single value
Most Current Data (Transactional InfoCube)	OS_RQTRA	OREQUID	Characteristic value	SAP exit	Selection option

Calculated Keyfigure

Formula	Content
Transaction Volume &ZEFISYTO&	(NODIM (Transaction Volume &ZEFISYTO&) / 1000)
Variance to prev. Year	(Transaction Volume &ZEFISYTO& % Transaction Volume &ZEFISYTO&)
Transaction Volume &ZEFISYTO&	(NODIM (Transaction Volume &ZEFISYTO&) / 1000)

B.5 Query ZEC0PAM1Q0003

Query Details

InfoCube:	ZEC0PAM1	Profitability Analysis (actual & plan data)
Query:	ZEC0PAM100003	Contribution Margin Act./Prev. Year ('000 USD)

Settings

Result position	Bottom/right		
Format display	false	Suppression of Repitition Texts	True
+/- Sign Display	Plus/minus sign before: -123.45	Zero Suppression	Suppress Rows and Columns as in 2.0

Filters

InfoObject Description	InfoObject	Restriction
Request ID	OREQUID	Most Current Data (Transactional InfoCube) 0S_RQTRA

Free Characteristics

InfoObject Description	InfoObject	Restriction
Company code	0COMP_CODE	
Posting period	0FISCPER3	
Fiscal Year Variant	0FISCVARNT	
InfoProvider	0INFOPROV	

Structure

Structure name	ElementName	Restriction	Name	Value
Structure	CM II &ZEFISYTO&	Transaction Type	OREC_TYPE	B
		Value type	OVTYPE	010
		Keyfigure		CM II
		Version	ZEVERSION	100
		Transaction Type	OREC_TYPE	C
		Transaction Type	OREC_TYPE	D

Structure

Structure name	ElementName	Restriction	Name	Value
Structure		Transaction Type	OREC_TYPE	E
		Transaction Type	OREC_TYPE	F
		Fiscal year	OFISCYEAR	Fiscal year ZEFISYP0
	CM II &ZEFISYTO&	Transaction Type	OREC_TYPE	B
		Value type	0VTYPE	010
		Keyfigure		CM II
		Version	ZEVERSION	100
		Transaction Type	OREC_TYPE	C
		Transaction Type	OREC_TYPE	D
		Transaction Type	OREC_TYPE	E
		Transaction Type	OREC_TYPE	F
		Fiscal year	OFISCYEAR	Fiscal year ZEFISYP0 1-
	CM II &ZEFISYTO&	Calculated keyfigure		
	CM II &ZEFISYTO&	Calculated keyfigure		
	Deviation to prev. Year	Calculated keyfigure		
	Condition	Calculated keyfigure		
	Dev. % Formula	Calculated keyfigure		

Variables

Description	Name	InfoObject	VariableType	ProcessType	Parameter
Most Current Data (Transactional InfoCube)	0S_RQTRA	OREQUID	Characteristic value	SAP exit	Selection option
Fiscal year	ZEFISYP0	OFISCYEAR	Characteristic value	User entry	Single value

Calculated Keyfigure

Formula	Content
Deviation to prev. Year	((Condition * Dev. % Formula) %A 100)
Dev. % Formula	(CM II &ZEFISYTO& % CM II &ZEFISYTO&)
CM II &ZEFISYTO&	(NODIM (CM II &ZEFISYTO&) / 1000)

Calculated Keyfigure

Formula	Content
CM II &ZEFISYTO&	(NODIM (CM II &ZEFISYTO&) / 1000)
Condition	(CM II &ZEFISYTO& <> 0)

Query Details

B.6 Query ZEKDABC1Q0001

InfoCube:	ZEKDABC1	Sales Order Stock
Query:	ZEKDABC1Q0001	Sales Order Stock

Settings

Result position	Bottom/right	
Format display	false	
+/- Sign Display	Plus/minus sign before: -123.45	
Suppression of Repetition Texts	True	
Zero Suppression	Display Rows and Columns	

Filters

InfoObject Description	InfoObject	Restriction
Fiscal Year Variant	0FISCVARNT	K4
Version	0VERSION	#
Value Type for Reporting	0VTYPE	010
Version	ZEVERSION	100
Currency Type	0CURTYPE	B0
Valuation view	0VALUATION	#
Source system ID	0SOURSYSTEM	R0

Company Code ZDCMPCP0 : EQ 0 - 0

Free Characteristics

InfoObject Description	InfoObject	Restriction
Company code	0COMP_CODE	
Customer	0CUSTOMER	
Country	0CUSTOMER__0COUNTRY	
Region	0CUSTOMER__0REGION	
Fiscal year/period	0FISCPER	
Material	0MATERIAL	

Period/Year From/To ZDFPERIO : EQ 0 - 0

Structure

Structure name	ElementName	Restriction	Name	Value
Key Figures				
	Total Order Value	Keyfigure		☰ ZEBETRAG
	Stock Value	Keyfigure		☰ ZEBESTAND

Variables

Description	Name	InfoObject	VariableType	ProcessType	Parameter
Period/Year From/To	ZDFPERIO	0FISCPER	Characteristic value	User entry	Interval
Company Code	ZDCMPCPO	0COMP_CODE	Characteristic value	User entry	Single value

B.7 Query 0CSAL_C03_Q0003

Query Details

InfoCube:	0CSAL_C03	Sales Order
Query:	0CSAL_C03_Q0003	Incoming Sales Orders (Last 12 Months)

Settings

Result position	Bottom/right
Format display	false
+/- Sign Display	Plus/minus sign before: -123.45
Suppression of Repitition Texts	True
Zero Suppression	

Filters

Restriction

InfoObject Description	InfoObject	
0BP_RESPPER_OUSER_N	0BP_RESPPER_OUSER_NAME	User Name 0P_USER
0BP_RESPPER_OUSER_S	0BP_RESPPER_OUSER_SYST	System of User Name 0P_USSYS

Free Characteristics

Restriction

InfoObject Description	InfoObject	
Employee Responsible	0BP_RESPPER	
Calendar Year/Month	0CALMONTH	Last 12 Months incl. act. Month 0CML12CM : EQ
Cal. Year/Quarter	0CALQUARTER	
Calendar Year/Week	0CALWEEK	
Calendar year	0CALYEAR	
Resp. Org. Unit	0CRMSA_OG_R	Org. Hierarchy Node for User 0CRMOM
Sales Org. CRM	0CRM_SALORG	
Sold-to Party	0CRM_SOLDTO	
Country	0CRM_SOLDTO_0COUNTRY	
Region	0CRM_SOLDTO_0REGION	
Material	0MATERIAL	

Structure

Structure name	ElementName	Restriction	Name	Value
Key Figures	No. of Order Items	Keyfigure		0CRM_NUMOFI
	Net Value Order	Keyfigure		0NETVALORD
	Average Sales Order Value per Item	Keyfigure		Average Sales Order Value per Item

Variables

Description	Name	InfoObject	VariableType	ProcessType	Parameter
Last 12 Months incl. act. Month	0CML12CM	0CALMONTH	Characteristic value	SAP-Exit	Interval
Org. Hierarchy Node for User	0CRMOM	0CRMSA_OG_R	Hierarchy nodes	SAP-Exit	Single value
User Name	0P_USER	0BP_RESPPER_0USER_NAME	Characteristic value	SAP-Exit	Single value
System of User Name	0P_USSYS	0BP_RESPPER_0USER_SYST	Characteristic value	SAP-Exit	Single value

Query Details

B.8 Query 0PCA_C01_Q0005

CubeServ.

InfoCube:	0PCA_C01		PCA: Transaction Data
Query:	0PCA_C01_Q0005		Profit Center: Time comparison actual result

Settings

Result position	Bottom/right		
Format display	false	Suppression of Repitition Texts	True
+/- Sign Display	Plus/minus sign before: -123.45	Zero Suppression	Display Rows and Columns

Filters

InfoObject Description	InfoObject		Restriction
KF Balance Sheet Account	0ACCOUNT__0BAL_FLAG		Account is a P&L Account 0P_PLACC
Fiscal Year Variant	0FISCVARNT		Fiscal year variant (SAP exit) 0P_FVAEX
Value Type for Reporting	0VTYPE		010
Actual Balance	1KYFNM		
Chart of accounts	0CHRT_ACCTS		Chart of acounts (SAP-Exit) 0P_CHAEX
Currency Type	0CURTYPE		Currency type Profit Center Accounting (SAP Exit) 0P_CTPCA
Controlling area	0CO_AREA		Controlling Area (Single Value Entry, Required) 0P_COAR
Version	0VERSION		000

Free Characteristics

InfoObject Description	InfoObject		Restriction
Account Number	0ACCOUNT		Results acounts/group 0N_PLACC
Company code	0COMP_CODE		
Functional area	0FUNC_AREA		
Partner Profit Center	0PART_PRCTR		
Profit Center	0PROFIT_CTR		Profit center/Profit center group 0N_PCTR

Structure

Structure name	ElementName	Restriction	Name	Value
Structure	&OT_FYEAR&	Fiscal year	0FISCYEAR	Fiscal Year (Single Value Entry, Required) OP_FYEAR 1-
	&OT_FYEAR&	Fiscal year	0FISCYEAR	Fiscal Year (Single Value Entry, Required) OP_FYEAR
	1st Quarter	Posting period	0FISCPER3	001 - 003
	2nd Quarter	Posting period	0FISCPER3	004 - 006
	3rd Quarter	Posting period	0FISCPER3	007 - 009
	4th Quarter	Posting period	0FISCPER3	010 - 012

Variables

Description	Name	InfoObject	VariableType	ProcessType	Parameter
Account is a P&L Account	OP_PLACC	0ACCOUNT_OBAL_FLAG	Characteristic value	User entry	Selection option
Fiscal year variant (SAP exit)	OP_FVAEX	0FISCVARNT	Characteristic value	SAP exit	Single value
Chart of acounts (SAP-Exit)	OP_CHAEX	0CHRT_ACCTS	Characteristic value	SAP exit	Single value
Currency type Profit Center Accounting (SAP Exit)	OP_CTPCA	0CURTYPE	Characteristic value	SAP exit	Single value
Controlling Area (Single Value Entry, Required)	OP_COAR	0CO_AREA	Characteristic value	User entry	Single value
Profit center/Profit center group	ON_PCTR	0PROFIT_CTR	Hierarchy nodes	User entry	Single value
Results acounts/group	ON_PLACC	0ACCOUNT	Hierarchy nodes	User entry	Single value
Profit center Hierarchy	ON_PCTR	0PROFIT_CTR	Hierarchy	User entry	Single value
Fiscal Year (Single Value Entry, Required)	OP_FYEAR	0FISCYEAR	Characteristic value	User entry	Single value

B.9 Query 0PCA_C01_Q0012

Query Details

| InfoCube: | 0PCA_C01 | PCA: Transaction Data |
| Query: | 0PCA_C01_Q0012 | Profit Center: Plan/actual/variance - balance sheet accounts |

Settings

Result position	Bottom/right		
Format display	false	Suppression of Repitition Texts	True
+/- Sign Display	Plus/minus sign before: -123.45	Zero Suppression	Display Rows and Columns

Filters

InfoObject Description	InfoObject	Restriction
Fiscal year/period	0FISCPER	Period/Fiscal Year (Single Value Entry, Required) 0P_FPER
KF Balance Sheet Acc	0ACCOUNT__0BAL_FLAG	X
Fiscal Year Variant	0FISCVARNT	Fiscal year variant (SAP exit) 0P_FVAEX
Accumulated Balance	1KYFNM	0BALANCE
Controlling area	0CO_AREA	Controlling Area (Single Value Entry, Required) 0P_COAR
Currency Type	0CURTYPE	Currency type Profit Center Accounting (SAP Exit) 0P_CTPCA
Chart of accounts	0CHRT_ACCTS	Chart of accounts (SAP-Exit) 0P_CHAEX

Free Characteristics

InfoObject Description	InfoObject	Restriction
Account Number	0ACCOUNT	Balance nodes/groups 0N_BSACC
Company code	0COMP_CODE	
Functional area	0FUNC_AREA	
Partner Profit Center	0PART_PRCTR	
Profit Center	0PROFIT_CTR	Profit center/Profit center group 0N_PCTR

CubeServ.

Structure

Structure name	ElementName	Restriction	Name	Value
Structure	Plan	Version	OVERSION	Plan Version OP_VERS
		Value type	OVTYPE	020
	Actual	Version	OVERSION	000
		Value type	OVTYPE	010
	Variance	Calculated keyfigure		
	Variance (%)	Calculated keyfigure		

Variables

Description	Name	InfoObject	VariableType	ProcessType	Parameter
Controlling Area (Single Value Entry, Required)	OP_COAR	OCO_AREA	Characteristic value	User entry	Single value
Profit center/Profit center group	ON_PCTR	OPROFIT_CTR	Hierarchy nodes	User entry	Single value
Chart of accounts (SAP-Exit)	OP_CHAEX	OCHRT_ACCTS	Characteristic value	SAP exit	Single value
Balance nodes/groups	ON_BSACC	OACCOUNT	Hierarchy nodes	User entry	Single value
Plan Version	OP_VERS	OVERSION	Characteristic value	User entry	Single value
Currency type Profit Center Accounting (SAP Exit)	OP_CTPCA	OCURTYPE	Characteristic value	SAP exit	Single value
Period/Fiscal Year (Single Value Entry, Required)	OP_FPER	OFISCPER	Characteristic value	User entry	Single value
Fiscal year variant	OP_FVAEX	OFISCVARNT	Characteristic value	SAP exit	Single value
Profit center Hierarchy	ON_PCTR	OPROFIT_CTR	Hierarchy	User entry	Single value

Calculated Keyfigure

Formula	Content
Variance	(Actual - Plan)
Variance (%)	(Actual % Plan)

B.10 Query 0PUR_C01_Q0011

Query Details

InfoCube:	0PUR_C01	Purchasing Data
Query:	0PUR_C01_Q0011	Purchase order quantities

Settings

Result position	Top/left	
Format display	false	Suppression of Repitition Texts	True
+/- Sign Display	Plus/minus sign before: -123.45	Zero Suppression	Suppress Rows and Columns as in 2.0

Filters

InfoObject Description	InfoObject		Restriction
Value Type for Repor	0VTYPE		010

Free Characteristics

InfoObject Description	InfoObject		Restriction
Calendar Year/Month	0CALMONTH		Calendar Month/Year 0I_CALMO : EQ 0 - 0
Material	0MATERIAL		Material (Selection Options, Optional) 0S_MAT
Plant	0PLANT		Plant (Selection Options, Optional) 0S_PLANT
Vendor	0VENDOR		Vendor number 0S_VEND

Structure

Structure name	ElementName	Restriction	Name	InfoObject	Value
Structure	Order quantity	Keyfigure			0PO_QTY
	Quantity of goods received	Keyfigure			0GR_QTY
	Difference between PO quantity and GR quantity	Keyfigure	0DUTORDERQTY		Difference between PO quantity and GR quantity
	Invoice receipt quantity as at posting date	Keyfigure			0INV_RC_QTY
	GR quantity as proportion of ordered quantity	Keyfigure	0ORDERQTYREC_%		GR quantity as proportion of ordered quantity
	Invoiced quantity as proportion of ordered quantity	Keyfigure	0ORDERQTYINV_%		Invoiced quantity as proportion of ordered quantity

Variables

Description	Name	InfoObject	VariableType	ProcessType	Parameter
Calendar Month/Year	0I_CALMO	0CALMONTH	Characteristic value	User entry	Interval
Plant (Selection Options, Optional)	0S_PLANT	0PLANT	Characteristic value	User entry	Selection option
Material (Selection Options, Optional)	0S_MAT	0MATERIAL	Characteristic value	User entry	Selection option
Vendor number	0S_VEND	0VENDOR	Characteristic value	User entry	Selection option

Query Details

InfoCube:	0SD_C01		Customer
Query:	0SD_C01_Q030		Customer: Plan/Actual Sales

Settings

Result position	Bottom/right	
Format display	false	Suppression of Repitition Texts — True
+/- Sign Display	Plus/minus sign before: -123.45	Zero Suppression — Display Rows and Columns

Free Characteristics

InfoObject Description	InfoObject		Restriction
Calendar Year/Month	0CALMONTH		
Distribution Channel	0DISTR_CHAN		
Division	0DIVISION		Division 0DIVISIO
Material	0MATERIAL		Material (Selection Options, Optional) 0S_MAT
0MATERIAL_0MATL_TYP	0MATERIAL_0MATL_TYPE		Material Type (Selection Options, Optional) 0S_MATTP
Product Hierarchy	0MATERIAL_0PROD_HIER		
Sales Organization	0SALESORG		Sales organization 0SALEORG
Sold-to party	0SOLD_TO		Sold-to party (optional entry) 0S_CUSTO
0SOLD_TO_0COUNTRY	0SOLD_TO_0COUNTRY		Country of Sold-to Party 0S_CSOLD

Structure

Structure name	ElementName	Restriction	Name	Value
Plan/Actual/Variance	Plan revenue net value	Version	0VERSION	Plan Version 0P_VERS
		Value type	0VTYPE	020
		Keyfigure		0INVCD_VAL
	Actual revenue net value	Value type	0VTYPE	010
		Keyfigure		0INVCD_VAL

B.11 Query 0SD_C01_Q030

Structure

Structure name	ElementName	Restriction	Name	Value
Plan/Actual/Variance	Variance	Calculated keyfigure		
	Variance (%)	Calculated keyfigure		

Variables

Description	Name	InfoObject	VariableType	ProcessType	Parameter
Plan Version	OP_VERS	OVERSION	Characteristic value	User entry	Single value
Country of Sold-to Party	OS_CSOLD	OSOLD_TO__OCOUNTRY	Characteristic value	User entry	Selection option
Division	ODIVISIO	ODIVISION	Characteristic value	User entry	Selection option
Sales organization	OSALEORG	OSALESORG	Characteristic value	User entry	Selection option
Material (Selection Options, Optional)	OS_MAT	OMATERIAL	Characteristic value	User entry	Selection option
Material Type (Selection Options, Optional)	OS_MATTP	OMATERIAL__OMATL_TYPE	Characteristic value	User entry	Selection option
Sold-to party (optional entry)	OS_CUSTO	OSOLD_TO	Characteristic value	User entry	Selection option

Calculated Keyfigure

Formula	Content
Variance	(Actual revenue net value - Plan revenue net value)
Variance (%)	(((Actual revenue net value - Plan revenue net value) / Plan revenue net value)* 100)

B.12 Query 0SD_C05_Q0007

Query Details

CubeServ.

InfoCube:	0SD_C05
Query:	0SD_C05_Q0007

Offers/Orders
Quotation Pipeline

Settings

Result position	Bottom/right	
Format display	false	Suppression of Repitition Texts	false
+/- Sign Display	Plus/minus sign before: -123.45	Zero Suppression	Display Rows and Columns

Filters

InfoObject Description	InfoObject	Restriction
Value Type	0VTYPE	010

Free Characteristics

InfoObject Description	InfoObject	Restriction
Calendar Day	0CALDAY	
Calendar Year/Month	0CALMONTH	
Distribution Channel	0DISTR_CHAN	Distribution Channel 0DISCHAN
Division	0DIVISION	Division 0DIVISIO
Quotation from	0QUOT_FROM	
Valid To	0QUOT_TO	
Sales Organization	0SALESORG	Sales organization 0SALEORG
Sold-to party	0SOLD_TO	Sold-to party (optional entry) 0S_CUSTO

Structure

Structure name	ElementName	Restriction	Name	Value
Structure	Quotation Pipeline	Calculated keyfigure		
	Number of Quotation Items	Doc. cat. Q/O/D/I	0DOC_CLASS	= Q
		Keyfigure		= 0DOC_ITEMS
	Net Quotation Value	Doc. cat. Q/O/D/I	0DOC_CLASS	= Q
		Keyfigure		= 0NET_VAL_S
	Number of Order Items	Doc. cat. Q/O/D/I	0DOC_CLASS	= O
		Keyfigure		= 0DOC_ITEMS
	Net Order Value	Doc. cat. Q/O/D/I	0DOC_CLASS	= O
		Keyfigure		= 0NET_VAL_S

Variables

Description	Name	InfoObject	VariableType	ProcessType	Parameter
Division	0DIVISIO	0DIVISION	Characteristic value	User entry	Selection option
Distribution Channel	0DISCHAN	0DISTR_CHAN	Characteristic value	User entry	Selection option
Sales organization	0SALEORG	0SALESORG	Characteristic value	User entry	Selection option
Sold-to party (optional entry)	0S_CUSTO	0SOLD_TO	Characteristic value	User entry	Selection option

Calculated Keyfigure

Formula	Content
Quotation Pipeline	(((Net Quotation Value * Order Profitability) / 100) / No. of Quotations)

C   Formula Operators

C.1   Percentage Operators

C.1.1   Deviation Percentage (%)

Usage
<Operand1> % <Operand2>

Description
Specifies the deviation percentage from Operand1 to Operand2. Is identical to the formula 100 × (<Operand1> – <Operand2>) / abs(<Operand2>), if <Operand2> does not equal zero and DIV0 if <Operand2> equals zero.

Example
"Planned sales % actual sales" specifies the percentage by which the actual sales deviate from the planned sales.

C.1.2   Percentage (%A)

Usage
<Operand1> %A <Operand2>

Description
Specifies the percentage of Operand1 in Operand2. Is identical to the formula 100 × <Operand1> / abs(<Operand2>), if <Operand2> does not equal zero and DIV0 if <Operand2> equals zero.

Example
"Fixed cost %A total cost" specifies the percentage of fixed costs in the total costs.

C.1.3   Percentage in Preliminary Result (%CT)

Usage
%CT <Operand>

Description
Specifies the percentage in relation to the preliminary result. In this context, the preliminary result is the aggregation result at the next higher level.

If a characteristic is drilled down in both the rows and columns, the relationship is not unique, so the system outputs a warning and the "Data doesn't exist" symbol. These symbols can be maintained in the reporting settings in Transaction SPRO.

C.1.4   Percentage in Overall Result (%CT)

Usage
%GT <Operand>

Description
Specifies the percentage in relation to the overall result. In this context, the overall result is the aggregation result at the highest level of the list. The calculation of the

overall result includes the dynamic filters, that is, filters that have not been specified in the query definition.

Example

Month	Country	Revenue	%CT 'revenue'	%GT 'revenue'
January	Germany	50	50	16.7
	Switzerland	50	50	16.7
	(Preliminary) result	100	33.3	33.3
February	Germany	100	50	33.3
	Switzerland	100	50	33.3
	(Preliminary) result	200	66.7	66.7
Overall result		300	100	100

C.1.5 Percentage in Reporting Result (%RT)

Usage
%RT <Operand>

Description
Similar to %GT (see Section C.1.4). In contrast to the overall result, the calculation of the reposting result does not include the dynamic filters. For this reason, a standard unit is used, irrespective of the filter and navigation status.

C.2 Data Functions

C.2.1 COUNT ()

Usage
COUNT (<expression>)

Description
Provides the value 1, if the <expression> does not equal zero; otherwise, the value zero is provided.

Therefore, in the totals line, the number of lines is calculated using a value.

C.2.2 NDIV0 ()

Usage
NDIV0 (<expression>)

Description
Equals zero, if the expression designated by <expression> causes a division by zero during the calculation. Otherwise, the result is the value of the expression. Used to avoid an error message being output, or to continue the calculations using a defined result.

C.2.3 NODIM ()

Usage
NODIM (<expression>)

Description
Provides the pure numeric value of <expression> and suppresses the unit and currency. This function enables you to suppress the output of the "mixed currency" symbol.

C.2.4 NOERR ()

Usage
NOERR (<expression>)

Description
Equals zero, if the <expression> leads to a calculation error during the analysis. Otherwise, the result is the value of the expression. Used to avoid an error message being output or to continue the calculations using a defined result.

C.3 Totals Operators

C.3.1 Subtotal

Usage
SUMCT <Operand>

Description
Provides the preliminary result of the operand in all rows or columns respectively (see %CT, Section C.1.3).

C.3.2 Total

Usage
SUMGT <Operand>

Description
Provides the overall result of the operand (see %GT, Section C.1.4).

C.3.3 Report Total

Usage
SUMRT <Operand>

Description
Provides the reporting result of the operand. See also %GT (Section C.1.4) and %RT (Section C.1.5) regarding the difference between the overall and reporting results.

C.4   Boolean Operators

C.4.1   Relational operators ==, <>, <, >, <=, >=

Usage
<expression1> <operator> <expression2>

Description
Equals 1, if <expression1> and <expression2> are related to each other as designated by <operator> (i.e., <expression1> <operator> <expression2> is true); otherwise, it equals zero. The comparison includes only the numeric values of <expression1> and <expression2>, without considering the units.

C.4.2   Logical And (AND)

Usage
<expression1> AND <expression2>

Description
Equals 1, if <expression1> and <expression2> both does not equal zero; otherwise, it equals zero. The comparison includes only the numeric values of <expression1> and <expression2>, without considering the units.

C.4.3   Logical Or (OR)

Usage
<expression1> OR <expression2>

Description
Equals 1, if <expression1> or <expression2> does not equal zero; otherwise, it equals zero. The comparison includes only the numeric values of <expression1> and <expression2>, without considering the units.

C.4.4   Logical Exclusive Or (XOR)

Usage
<expression1> XOR <expression2>

Description
Equals 1, if either <expression1> or <expression2> does not equal zero; otherwise, it equals zero. The comparison includes only the numeric values of <expression1> and <expression2>, without considering the units.

C.4.5   Logical Not (NOT)

Usage
NOT <expression>

Description
Equals 1, if the <expression> equals zero; otherwise, it equals zero.

Example

A	B	A AND B	A OR B	A XOR B	NOT A
0	0	0	0	0	1
0	1	0	1	1	1
1	0	0	1	1	0
1	1	1	1	0	0

C.4.6 LEAF ()

Usage
LEAF (<expression>)

Description
Equals zero for the result lines or actual (internal) nodes of a hierarchy and equals one for the elementary lines or leaves of a hierarchy.

This operator enables you to carry out different calculations for elementary lines and result lines.

D   Attributes and Values of BEx Web

D.1   CSS Formats

CSS Classes	Purpose
Web Item Containers	
SAPBEXBorderFlexBoxTtl	Header area for web items with frame
SAPBEXBorderlessFlexBoxTtl	Header area for frameless web items and form-like web items
SAPBEXBorderFlexBox	Web items with frame
SAPBEXBorderlessFlexBox	Frameless web items and form-like web items
SAPBEXFlexBoxStdBg	Background
SAPBEXFlexBoxFormBg	Background for form-like web items
Table	
SAPBEXstdData	Numeric values in data cells
SAPBEXstdDataOdd	Even lines when lines alternate
SAPBEXaggData	Aggregated numeric values in data totals cells
SAPBEXstdDataEmph	Emphasized numeric values in data cells
SAPBEXstdDataEmphOdd	Even lines for alternating lines with emphasized numeric values
SAPBEXaggDataEmph	Aggregated emphasized numeric values in data totals cells
SAPBEXstdItem	Structural component, characteristic value, attribute
SAPBEXKeyAttr	Numerical attribute
SAPBEXaggItem	Aggregated structural component, characteristic values total, attributes total
SAPBEXchaText	Header for characteristics and attributes
SAPBEXformats	Format cell (scaling factors)
SAPBEXexcGood1	Exception for priority Good 1
SAPBEXexcGood2	Exception for priority Good 2
SAPBEXexcGood3	Exception for priority Good 3
SAPBEXexcCritical4	Exception for priority Critical 4
SAPBEXexcCritical5	Exception for priority Critical 5

CSS Classes	Purpose
SAPBEXexcCritical6	Exception for priority Critical 6
SAPBEXexcBad7	Exception for priority Bad 7
SAPBEXexcBad8	Exception for priority Bad 8
SAPBEXexcBad9	Exception for priority Bad 9
SAPBEXundefined	Numeric value cannot be defined or is invalid (e.g., for divisions by zero)
SAPBEXTableGrid	Color of gridlines
SAPBEXCellspacing	Gridlines on/off
Navigation block, filters	
SAPBEXNavigatorChaTxt	Labeling of characteristics
SAPBEXNavItem	Characteristic values in the navigation block and filter
SAPBEXNavBlockMargin	Offset between the characteristics in the navigation block
Alert monitor	
SAPBEXAlertItem	Display as list
SAPBEXAlertToolbar	Toolbar
SAPBEXAlertHead	Header
SAPBEXAlertLevel0	Hierarchy level 0
SAPBEXAlertLevel1	Hierarchy level 1
SAPBEXAlertLevel2	Hierarchy level 2
SAPBEXPageDspl	Index for displaying values on several pages
Text Elements	
SAPBEXTElemName	Name of the text element
SAPBEXTElemVal	Value of the text element
Exceptions	
SAPBEXExcName	Name of the exception
SAPBEXExcStatus	Status of the exception (active/inactive)
Conditions	
SAPBEXConName	Name of the condition
SAPBEXConStatus	Status of the condition (active/inactive)

CSS Classes	Purpose
SAPBEXMapLgdHeading1	Legend
SAPBEXMapLgdHeading2	Header
SAPBEXMapLgdLine	Area header
Color legend values	
SAPBEXMapLgdBorder	Formatting of the color legend
SAPBEXMapLgdMinmax	Minimum or maximum
SAPBEXMapLgdLegend	Values for icon legend
Context menu	
SAPBEXCtxtMenuItem	Context menu items
SAPBEXCtxtMenuHeader	Selected context menu item
Calendar	
SAPBEXCalBg	Background
SAPBEXCalBorder	Frame
SAPBEXCalLink	Links
SAPBEXCalSkipMonth	Scrolling within month and year display
SAPBEXCalCurrentDate	Month and year display
SAPBEXCalWeekday	Names of weekdays (Mon, Tue, etc.)
SAPBEXCalDay	Number of the day (1, 2, etc.)
SAPBEXCalDaySelectedNormal	Selected day
SAPBEXCalDaySat	Saturday
SAPBEXCalDaySelectedSat	Selected Saturday
SAPBEXCalDaySun	Sunday
SAPBEXCalDaySelectedSun	Selected Sunday
SAPBEXCalNoDay	Weekday without number
SAPBEXCalWeek	Calendar week
SAPBEXCalMonth	Month in quick navigation
SAPBEXCalCurrentMonth	Selected month in quick navigation
Dialogs	
SAPBEXDialogBorder	Frame
SAPBEXDialogBg	Background

CSS Classes	Purpose
SAPBEXDialogTtl	Header
SAPBEXDialogAreaTtl	Area header
SAPBEXDialogOffset	Horizontal and vertical offsets in dialogs
Menu	
SAPBEXMenuLogo	Header area
SAPBEXTreeLevel0	Tree level 0
SAPBEXTreeLevel1	Tree level 1
SAPBEXTreeLevel2	Tree level 2
SAPBEXTreeLevel3	Tree level 3
Hierarchies	
SAPBEXHLevel0	Hierarchy level 0
SAPBEXHLevel1	Hierarchy level 1
SAPBEXHLevel2	Hierarchy level 2
SAPBEXHLevel3	Hierarchy level 3
Messages	
SAPBEXMessage	Messages
SAPBEXSystemMessage	System messages
SAPBExMsgBarStd	Enterprise Portal messages, ad-hoc web template, and Bex Web Analyzer headers
SAPBExMsgErr	Error messages in Enterprise Portal
SAPBEXTicker	Ticker
Links, text, buttons	
SAPBEXLnk	Standard link
SAPBEXMarked	Hghlighted link
SAPBEXTxtStd	Standard text
SAPBEXTxtStdBold	Standard text bold
SAPBEXBtnStd	Standard button
SAPBEXBtnStdIe4	Standard button (Internet Explorer 4)
SAPBEXBtnStdBorder	Standard and inactive buttons (frame)
SAPBEXBtnEmph	Emphasized button (background)

CSS Classes	Purpose
SAPBEXBtnEmphIe4	Emphasized button (Internet Explorer 4)
SAPBEXBtnEmphBorder	Emphasized button (frame)
SAPBEXBtnStdNextStep	"Next Step" button
SAPBEXBtnStdPrevStep	"Previous Step" button
SAPBEXBtnStdDsbl	Disabled button
SAPBEXBtnEmphDsbl	Emphasized disabled button
SAPBEXBtnStdNextStepDsbl	Disabled "Next Step" button
SAPBEXBtnStdPrevStepDsbl	Disabled "Previous Step" button
Controls and Labels	
SAPBEXDdl	Dropdown box
SAPBEXChb	Checkbox
SAPBEXRb	Radio button
SAPBEXTxtFld	Input field
SAPBEXTxtFldright	Right-aligned input field
SAPBEXTxtFldDsbl	Disabled input field
SAPBEXTextArea	Multi-line input area
SAPBEXTxtLbl	Input field label
SAPBEXWhlOffset	Horizontal and vertical offsets
Loading Pop-Up	
SAPBEXPopUpOuterBorder	3D frame: outer border
SAPBEXPopUpInnerBorder	3D frame: inner border
SAPBEXPopUpBg	Background
SAPBEXPopUpHeader	Header
Navigation Bar (maps, Standard Web Template 3.0)	
SAPBEXNavLine	Navigation bar
SAPBEXNavLineBorder	Navigation bar border
Tree Query Designer	
SAPBEXTreeLevel0Bg	Tree level 0 background
SAPBEXTreeLevel0Ttl	Expandable entries for Tree level 0

CSS Classes	Purpose
SAPBEXTreeLevel0Item	Tree level 0 entries
SAPBEXTreeLevel1Bg	Tree level 1 background
SAPBEXTreeLevel1Ttl	Expandable entries for Tree level 1
SAPBEXTreeLevel1Item	Tree level 1 entries
SAPBEXTreeLevel2Bg	Tree level 2 background
SAPBEXTreeLevel2Ttl	Expandable Entries Tree Level 2
SAPBEXTreeLevel2Item	Tree level 2 entries
SAPBEXTreeLevel3Bg	Tree level 3 background
SAPBEXTreeLevel3Ttl	Expandable entries for Tree level 3
SAPBEXTreeLevel3Item	Tree level 3 entries
SAPBEXTreeBorder	Tree border
Tabstrips	
SAPBEXTbsLnk	Link in selectable tabstrip
SAPBEXTbsTab	Tabstrip to be selected
SAPBEXTbsTabSel	Selected tabstrip
SAPBEXTbsBdyEdg	Border of tabstrip area
SAPBEXTbsBorder	Tabstrip border (Netscape 4.7)
Breadcrumbs Query Designer	
SAPBEXBrdCrBoxContBgColor	Background color of column and line area
SAPBEXBrdCrBoxBorder	Box color of column and line area
SAPBEXBrdCrArea	Formatting of column and line area
SAPBEXBrdCrIna	Labeling of inactive navigation path
SAPBEXBrdCrAct	Labeling of active navigation path
SAPBEXBrdCrDiv	Formatting of navigation path
List Query Designer	
SAPBEXLicWhl	Formatting of the list area
SAPBEXLicTtl	Display area header
SAPBEXLic	Introduction to bullet list
SAPBEXLicBul	Bullet

CSS Classes	Purpose
SAPBEXLicItem	Individual list item
SAPBEXLicItemLnk	Individual list item with link

D.2 Web Items: General Attributes

Description	Attribute	Values
Logical name of a web item	ITEM or NAME	Logical name of the item
Key of a web item	ITEM_ID	Technical name of the web item stored in the library
Class name of the web item class	ITEM_CLASS	Technical name of the associated ABAP Objects class
Logical name of the data provider for the web item	DATA_PROVIDER	Logical name of the defined data provider
Caption	CAPTION	Freely assignable text
Generate caption	GENERATE_CAPTION	'X' = Yes, ' ' = No, 'BORDER' = Only border
Width in pixels	WIDTH	Numeric value, width in pixels
Border style	BORDER_STYLE	'BORDER' = With border 'NO_BORDER' = Without border 'FORM' = For form
Closed	CLOSED	'X' = Yes, ' ' = No
Hide object	HIDDEN	'X' = Yes, ' ' = No
Objects with navigation links	GENERATE_LINKS	'X' = Yes, ' ' = No
Affected data providers	TARGET_DATA_PROVIDER_n (n = unique sequence number)	Logical name of the data provider
Master data read mode	BOOKED_VALUES	M = Master data table D = Dimension table (default) Q = Booked values

D.3 Web Items: Specific Attributes

D.3.1 Table

Description	Attribute	Values
Alternating styles for table rows	ALT_STYLES	'X' = Yes, ' ' = No
Only hierarchy navigation	ONLY_HIERARCHY_NAVIGA-TION	'X' = Yes, ' ' = No
Suppress repetition texts	SUPPRESS_REPETITION_TEXTS	'X' = Yes, ' ' = No
Number of rows displayed together	BLOCK_SIZE	Default setting: 100
Number of columns displayed together	BLOCK_SIZE_COLUMNS	Default setting: 0
Number of rows scrolled per step	BLOCK_STEP_SIZE	Default setting: 0
Number of columns scrolled per step	BLOCK_STEP_SIZE_COLUMNS	Default setting: 0
Top scrolling area	SHOW_PAGING_AREA_TOP	'X' = Yes, ' ' = No (default)
Bottom scrolling area	SHOW_PAGING_AREA_BOTTOM	'X' = Yes (default), ' ' = No
Display column headers	SHOW_COLUMN_HEADER	'X' = Yes (default), ' ' = No
Display row headers	SHOW_ROW_HEADER	'X' = Yes (default), ' ' = No
Display data cells	SHOW_DATA_CELLS	'X' = Yes (default), ' ' = No
Display of data from value row	DATA_ROW_FROM	Presetting: 1
Display of data to value row	DATA_ROW_TO	0 = to the end
Display of data from column	DATA_COLUMN_TO	0 = to the end
Display of data to column	DATA_COLUMN_FROM	Default setting: 1
Alternative ABAP class	MODIFY_CLASS	Technical name of the ABAP OO class

D.3.2 Chart

Description	Attribute	Values
Suppress totals	SUPPRESS_SUMS	'X' = Yes, ' ' = No
Switch axes for display	SWITCHMATRIX	'X' = Yes, ' ' = No
Hide expanded hierarchy nodes	SUPPRESS_OPENHIE-RARCHIENODES	'X' = Yes, ' ' = No
Automatic display of units, currencies, etc.	AUTOMATIC_LABELS	'X' = Yes, ' ' = No
Language-dependent texts in the chart	TITLE	Chart title
	SUBTITLE	Chart subtitle
	TITLE_CATEGORIES	Category axis (X): title
	UNIT_CATEGORIES	Category axis (X): unit
	TITLE_VALUES	Primary value axis (Y): title
	UNIT_VALUES	Primary value axis (Y): unit
	TITLE_SEC_VALUES	Secondary value axis (Y): title
	UNIT_SEC_VALUES	Secondary value axis (Y): unit
	TITLE_SEC_CATEGORIES	Additional axis: title Language-dependent text for the title of an additional axis. This attribute is used for specific chart types only, such as histograms or scatter diagrams.
	UNIT_SEC_CATEGORIES	Additional axis: unit Language-dependent text for the unit of an additional axis. This attribute is used for specific chart types only, such as histograms or scatter diagrams.
Ignore exceptions for the chart display	IGNORE_EXCEPTIONS	
Automatic description of axes for simple charts	AUTOMATIC_DESCRIPTION	'X' = Yes, ' ' = No

D.3.3 Dropdown Box

Description	Attribute	Values
Characteristic/structure	IOBJNM	
Maximum number of characteristic attributes in the dropdown box	MAXVALUES	Default value: 50 0 for "All"
Label	SHOW_LABEL	'X' = Yes, ' ' = No
Display values only	ONLY_VALUES	'X' = Yes, ' ' = No
Don't display "All values" item	NO_REMOVE_FIL-TER	'X' = Don't provide "All values", ' ' = Display "All values" item

D.3.4 Radio Button Group

Description	Attribute	Values
Characteristic/structure	IOBJNM	Technical name of the InfoObject or the characteristic structure or key figure structure
Maximum number of values displayed	MAXVALUES	Default setting: 50
Label	SHOW_LABEL	'X' = Yes, ' ' = No (default)
Items horizontally aligned	HORIZONTAL_ALIGN-MENT	'X' = Yes, ' ' = No (default)
Number of items horizontally or vertically aligned	HORIZONTAL_NUMBER	Number Default setting: 1
Display values only	ONLY_VALUES	'X' = Yes, ' ' = No
Don't display "All values" item	NO_REMOVE_FILTER	'X' = Don't provide "All values", ' ' = Display "All values" item

D.3.5 Checkboxes

Description	Attribute	Values
Characteristic/structure	IOBJNM	Technical name of the characteristic or structure
Maximum number	MAXVALUES	Default setting: 0
Maximum length	MAXLENGTH	No function/obsolete

Description	Attribute	Values
Label	SHOW_LABEL	'X' = Yes (default), ' ' = No
Display size	SIZE	This attribute is obsolete and is only provided for reasons of compatibility.
Items horizontally aligned	HORIZONTAL_ALIGN-MENT	'X' = Yes, ' ' = No (default)
Number of items horizontally or vertically aligned	HORIZONTAL_NUMBER	Default setting: 1

D.3.6 Generic Navigation Block

Description	Attribute	Values
Group axes	SHOW_AXES_GROUPING	'X' = Yes, ' ' = No
Row characteristics collapsed	ROWS_CLOSED	'X' = Yes, ' ' = No
Column characteristics collapsed	COLUMNS_CLOSED	'X' = Yes, ' ' = No
Free characteristics collapsed	FREE_CHARACTERISTICS_CLOSED	'X' = Yes, ' ' = No
Display empty filters	SHOW_EMPTY_SLICER	'X' = Yes, ' ' = No
Limitation between the characteristics	SHOW_MARGIN	'X' = Yes, ' ' = No
Arrange items horizontally	HORIZONTAL_ALIGNMENT	'X' = Yes, ' ' = No
Items horizontally aligned	HORIZONTAL_NUMBER	Default setting: 3
Maximum filter value length	FILTER_VALUE_LENGTH	Default setting: 80
Display row characteristics	SHOW_ROWS	'X' = Yes, ' ' = No
Display column characteristics	SHOW_COLUMNS	'X' = Yes, ' ' = No
Display free characteristics	SHOW_FREE_CHARACTERISTICS	'X' = Yes, ' ' = No
Display navigation icons	SHOW_NAVIGATION_ICONS	
Display filter icons	SHOW_FILTER_ICONS	'X' = Yes, ' ' = No
Frame name for input help	TARGET_HELP_FRAME	Name of the frame

Description	Attribute	Values
Table interface class	MODIFY_CLASS	Technical name of the ABAP OO class that overrides the generated HTML output
List of navigation block items	ITEM_NAV_BLOCK_IOBJNM_n (n = unique sequence number)	Technical name of the characteristic or structure
	BOOKED_VALUES_n (n = unique sequence number)	Read mode of F4 filter values for the corresponding characteristic

D.3.7 Hierarchical Filter Selection

Description	Attribute	Values
Reload level dynamically	DYNAMIC	'X' = Yes (default), ' ' = No
Characteristic/structure	IOBJNM	Technical name of a characteristic of structure with hierarchy
Hierarchy name	HIERARCHY_NAME	Technical name of the hierarchy
Version	HIERARCHY_VER-SION	Version of the hierarchy
Key date	DATE	Key date
Label	SHOW_LABEL	'X' = Yes (default), ' ' = No
Drilldown level	DRILL_LEVEL	Default setting: 3 0 for "All"

D.3.8 Filters

Description	Attribute	Values
Presentation of the filter values	PRESENTATION PRESENTATION_n (n = unique sequence number)	'KEY' = key 'TEXT' = description 'KEY_TEXT' = key and description 'TEXT_KEY' = description and key
Maximum filter value length	FILTER_VALUE_LENGTH	Number Default setting: 0

Description	Attribute	Values
Display values only	ONLY_VALUES	'X' = Yes, ' ' = No
List of characteristics and structures	ITEM_FILTER_ IOBJNM_n (n = unique sequence number)	Technical name of the characteristic or structure

D.3.9 Label

Description	Attribute	Values
Context menu	CONTEXT_MENU	'X' = Yes, ' ' = No
Characteristic/structure	IOBJNM	Technical name of a characteristic or structure
Structural component	STRUCTURE_MEMBER	Technical name of a structural component
Attribute name	ATTRINM	Technical name of the attribute
Display values only	ONLY_VALUES	'X' = Yes, ' ' = No (non-formatted display)

D.3.10 Text Elements

Description	Attribute	Values
Display general text elements	SHOW_COMMON_ ELEMENTS	'X' = Yes, ' ' = No
Display static filter values	SHOW_FILTERS	'X' = Yes, ' ' = No
Display variable values	SHOW_VARIABLES	'X' = Yes, ' ' = No
List of text elements	ELEMENT_NAME_n	REPTNAME = technical name of the query

REPTXTLG = description of the query

INFOCUBE = InfoProvider

SRDATE = key date of the query

ROLLUPTIME = timeliness of the data (date and time) |

Description	Attribute	Values
List of text elements	ELEMENT_NAME_n	AUTHOR = author of the query
		MODTIME = last change of the query (date and time)
		MODUSER = last editor of the query
		SYUSER = current user
		SYUZEIT = last refresh (date and time)
	ELEMENT_TYPE_n	COMMON = common text element
		FILTER = static filter value
		VARIABLE = variable value
		VARIABLE_KEY = key of the variable value
Display values only	ONLY_VALUES	'X' = Yes, ' ' = No

D.3.11 Alert Monitor

Description	Attribute	Values
Query	FILTER_QUERY	Technical name of a query
Display minimum view	MINIMAL_VIEW	'X' = Yes, ' ' = No
Template for the output	TARGET_TEMPLATE_ID	Technical name of the template
List display	LIST_FOCUS_LEVEL	VIEW = navigational state
		CELL = individual cells
		EXCEPTIONS = exceptions
		INFOAREA = InfoArea
		INFOCUBE = InfoCube
		QUERY = query
List of columns with names	COLUMN_NAME_n	TEXT = text
		ACTION = action
		VALUE = values for individual cells
		DOCUMENT = display of documents
		MAX_LEVEL = display highest alert level
		RED = number of red exceptions

Description	Attribute	Values
List of columns with names	COLUMN_NAME_n	YELLOW = number of yellow exceptions
		GREEN = number of green exceptions
		DATE = creation date
		TIME = creation time
	COLUMN_CAPTION_n	Caption
InfoCube	FILTER_INFOCUBE	Technical name of the Info-Provider
InfoArea	FILTER_INFOAREA	Technical name of the InfoArea
Red items	FILTER_RED	'X' = Yes, ' ' = No
Yellow items	FILTER_YELLOW	'X' = Yes, ' ' = No
Green items	FILTER_GREEN	'X' = Yes, ' ' = No
Don't display the number of alerts	SUPPRESS_NUMBERS	'X' = Yes, ' ' = No
Display highest alert level	DISPLAY_MAX_LEVEL	'X' = Yes, ' ' = No
Number of rows in the table	BLOCK_SIZE	Default setting: 10
Display as hierarchy	HIERARCHY	'X' = Yes, ' ' = No
Display column captions	DISPLAY_COLUMN_CAPTION	'X' = Yes, ' ' = No
Display toolbar	DISPLAY_TOOLBAR	'X' = Yes, ' ' = No
Display data provider	DISPLAY_DATA_PRO-VIDER	Logical name of the data provider to which the detail view should be applied
Present in	TARGET_FRAME	Name of the frame for the detail view

D.3.12 Role Menu

Description	Attribute	Values
Role list	ROLE_1, ROLE_2, ROLE_n etc.	Technical name of the role
		SAP_BW__FAVORITES_ for the favorites
Number of levels	LEVEL	0 = all levels

Description	Attribute	Values
Filters	FILTER	'U' = URLs 'P' = web templates 'Y' = queries 'R' = Crystal Reports 'A' = BSP applications
Name of the target frame	TARGET	Name of the target frame
Display the scroll bars	SCROLL_STYLE	▶ Auto ▶ Yes ▶ No
Display with IFrame	IFRAME	'X' = Yes, ' ' = No
Display with box around IFrame	IFRAME_STYLE	'X' = Yes, ' ' = No
Display of user and logo	DISPLAY_USER	'X' = Yes, ' ' = No
Path of logo icon	ICON_LOGO	Path of the image to be displayed
Height of the logo in pixels	HEIGHT_LOGO	
Display of the hierarchy with colors	HIERARCHY_COLOR	'X' = Yes, ' ' = No
No display of the first level	HIDE_FIRST_LEVEL	'X' = Yes, ' ' = No
Display with icons	DIFF_ICONS	'X' = Yes, ' ' = No

D.3.13 Ticker

Description	Attribute	Values
Generate invisible form	ONLY_VALUES	'X' = Yes, ' ' = No
Separator	SEPARATOR	Separator Default setting: +++
Speed in milliseconds	SPEED	Default setting: 200
Width of ticker text in characters	TICKER_SIZE	Default setting: 60
Place caption to the beginning of the ticker text	USE_CAPTION	'X' = Yes (default), ' ' = No
Delay in milliseconds	DELAY	Default setting: 3000

D.3.14 Map

Description	Attribute	Values
Map levels	LAYERS	
AXL file (cartography)	CART_AXL_NAME	Name of the AXL file for cartography description
Cartography information on/off	CART_AXL_VISIBLE	'X' = Yes, ' ' = No (default)
Geographic functions	GEO_FUNCTIONS_POS	▶ Hide (default) ▶ Top ▶ Bottom ▶ Left ▶ Right
Extended geographic toolbar	GEO_FUNCTIONS_ ADVANCED	'X' = Yes, ' ' = No (default)
Legend position	LEGEND_POSITION	▶ Left of map ▶ Right of map (default) ▶ No legend
Legend size	LEGEND_SIZE	Enter in pixels Default setting: 150
Visible map area	MAP_EXTENT	▶ Data with associated geography (default) ▶ Only data ▶ Data and the entire available geography
Transparent map background	CART_COLOR_ TRANSPARENT	'X' = Yes (default), ' ' = No
Background color	CART_BACKGROUND_ COLOR	Color value
Fill color (no data)	CART_FILL_COLOR	Color value
Map outline color	CART_OUTLINE_COLOR	Color value

Description	Attribute	Values
Map outline width	CART_OUTLINE_WIDTH	Enter in pixels Default setting: 1
Projection	PROJECTION	'NONE' = no projection 'FLAT' = flat projection 'MERC' = Mercator projection

D.3.15 Individual Document

Description	Attribute	Values
Document class	DOCUMENT_CLASS	'MAST' = master data (default setting) 'TRAN' = InfoProvider data
Document type	WWW_DOC_TYPE	Document type for classifying documents. The document type can be freely assigned during the creation or modification of a document in the BDS.
Characteristic	IOBJNM	Technical name of the characteristic
Target Frame	TARGET_FRAME	Name of the frame _self _top _blank _parent
Nesting depth of the frame	TARGET_FRAME_LEVEL	Default setting: 0
Display in the same browser window	IS_INPLACE	'X' = Yes, ' ' = No
Links for document display	LINK_TO_BROWSER	'X' = Yes, ' ' = No
Default picture	DEFAULT_PICTURE_URL	Absolute or relative path (and file) of the picture

D.3.16 List of Documents

Description	Attribute	Values
Display properties	SHOW_PROPERTIES	'X' = Yes, ' ' = No
Display selection	SHOW_CONTEXT	' ' = changeable, not displayed initially 'N' = not changeable, displayed initially 'X' = changeable, displayed initially '0' = not changeable, not displayed initially
Number of rows in the table	BLOCK_SIZE	Number of rows default setting: 100
Maximum number of values displayed	MAXVALUES	Default setting: 50
Documents are changeable	DOCUMENTS_ARE_CHANGEABLE	'X' = Yes, ' ' = No
Target Frame	TARGET_FRAME	Name of the frame
Additional properties	PROPERTY_n (n stands for a unique sequence number)	LAST_CHANGED_BY = last person to perform a change LAST_CHANGED_AT = time of change CREATED_BY = creator CREATED_AT = time of creation CHECKOUT_USER = user LANGUAGE = language

D.3.17 Data Provider—Information

Description	Attribute	Values
Output navigational state	NAVIGATIONAL_STATE	'X' = Yes, ' ' = No
Output results data	RESULT_SET	'X' = Yes, ' ' = No

D.3.18 Object Catalog of the Web Application

Description	Attribute	Values
Output web template properties	`PROPERTIES`	`'X'` = Yes, `' '` = No
Output list of data providers	`DATA_PROVIDERS`	`'X'` = Yes, `' '` = No
Output list of web items	`ITEMS`	`'X'` = Yes, `' '` = No

D.3.19 Web Template

Description	Attribute	Values
Only `<body>` tag	`USE_ONLY_BODY`	`'X'` = Yes (default), `' '` = No
Web template	`TEMPLATE_ID`	Technical name of the web template to be embedded
Prefix for the logical names	`NAME_PREFIX`	Prefix for the objects of the embedded web templates, for example, ABC
Overwrite the web item initialization	`SET_ITEM_n` (n is a unique number within the web application)	Logical name of the web item in the web template to be embedded
	`ITEM_ID_n` (n is a unique number within the web application)	Technical name of a web item to be used, which is stored in a library
	`ITEM_CLASS_n` (n is a unique number within the web application)	Technical name of the ABAP OO class, which is responsible for generating the output for the web item. This attribute must be filled with the corresponding value, if a standard web item is to be used.
Overwrite the data provider initialization	`SET_DATA_PROVIDER_n` (n stands for a unique number within the web application)	Logical name of the data provider from the web template to be embedded, which is to be re-initialized
	Attributes, if the new data provider is a query	
	`INFOCUBE`	Technical name of the InfoCube of the query
	`QUERY`	Technical name of the query

Description	Attribute	Values
	VARIANT (optional)	Technical name of the variant, if available and required or desired
	Attributes, if the new data provider is a query view	
	DATA_PROVIDER_ID	Technical name of the query view
	VARIANT (optional)	Technical name of the variant, if available and required or desired

D.3.20 Broadcasters

Description	Attribute	Values
Type of a reporting object	SOURCE_OBJECT_TYPE	'HT' = web template 'QU' = query 'WB' = workbook 'DP' = data provider
Name of the web template	SOURCE_TEMPLATE	Technical name of the web template
Name of the query	SOURCE_QUERY	Technical name of the query
Name of the workbook	SOURCE_WORKBOOK	Technical name of the workbook
Name of the data provider	SOURCE_DATA_PROVIDER	Logical name of the data provider from the web template

D.3.21 Key Figures—Overview

Description	Attribute	Values
Automatic personalization	AUTOMATIC_PERSONALIZATION	'X' = Yes, ' ' = No
Customer web template prefix	CUST_TEMPLATE_PREFIX	
SAP web template prefix	SAP_TEMPLATE_PREFIX	
RFC connection SEM system	SEM_RFC_DEST	

D.3.22 Query View—Selection

Description	Attribute	Values
Affected web item	VIEW_DD_TARGET_ITEM	Logical name of a web item that exists in the web template
List of query views	**Attribute in the object tag** **(n stands for a unique number that refers to the attributes of a row)**	**Description**
	VIEW_DD_DESCRIPTION_n	Freely definable description
	VIEW_DD_QUERY_SELECTION_n	Technical name of the query
	VIEW_DD_DATA_PROVIDER_ID_n	Technical name of the query view
	VIEW_DD_ITEM_ID_n	Technical name of the web item from a library
Display Create/Delete button	VIEW_DD_SHOW_BUTTONS	'X' = Yes, ' ' = No
Maintain filter values for the query views	VIEW_DD_RRI	'X' = Yes, ' ' = No
Maintain settings of affected web item	VIEW_DD_KEEP_SIZE	'X' = Yes, ' ' = No
Use all query views of a query	VIEW_DD_USE_ALL_QUERY_VIEWS	'X' = Yes, ' ' = No
Sort query views in alphabetical order	VIEW_DD_SORT	'X' = Yes, ' ' = No
Web template for the creation of new items for the dropdown box	VIEW_DD_CREATE_TEMPLATE	Technical name of the web template
Generate buttons	VIEW_DD_USE_BUTTONS	'X' = Yes, ' ' = No
Number of buttons per row	VIEW_DD_BUTTONS_IN_ROWS	Default setting: 3

D.3.23 Ad-Hoc Query Designer

Description	Attribute	Values
Technical name of the InfoProvider	INFOCUBE	
Technical name of the query	QUERY	
Template for the output	TARGET_TEMPLATE_ID	Technical name of the template
Frame for outputting the query	TARGET_FRAME	Name of the frame window
Action on execute	ON_EXECUTE	' ' = item not changed 'HIDE' = item hidden 'CLOSE' = item collapses
Action on close	ON_CLOSE	' ' = item not changed 'HIDE' = item hidden 'CLOSE' = item collapses
Display data provider	DISPLAY_DATA_PROVIDER	Logical name of a data provider that exists in the web template

D.3.24 ABC Classification

Description	Attribute	Values
Name of the ABC classification	ABC_NAME	
Display ABC classification	SHOW_ABC_CLASSIFICATION	'X' = Yes, ' ' = No
Display statistics	SHOW_STAT	'X' = Yes, ' ' = No
Display ABC classification chart	SHOW_CHART	'X' = Yes, ' ' = No
Display model names	SHOW_MODEL	'X' = Yes, ' ' = No

D.3.25 Simulation Prediction

Description	Attribute	Values
Name of the mining model	MODEL_NAME	
Name of the service	SERVICE_NAME	
Display model names	DISPLAY_MODEL	'X' = Yes, ' ' = No
Display service names	DISPLAY_SERVICE	'X' = Yes, ' ' = No
Display diagram customizing	DISPLAY_CHART_OPT	'X' = Yes, ' ' = No

D.4 Properties of the Web Template

Description	Attribute	Values
Name of the web template	TEMPLATE_ID	
Use personalized web template, if available	USE_PERSONALIZATION	'X' = Yes, ' ' = No
Path to a style sheet	STYLE_SHEET	Example of a path: /sap/bw/mime/BEx/StyleSheets/Meadow_BWReports.css
Using JavaScript	JAVASCRIPT	'X' = enable, ' ' = disable
Reloading modified page components	SNIPPET_OPERATIONS	'X' = enable, ' ' = disable
Stateless navigation	STATELESS	'X' = Yes, ' ' = No (default)
Automatic session management	USE_PAGE_WRAPPER	'X' = active, ' ' = inactive, 'PING' = prohibit timeout
Open dialogs in new windows	ENABLE_OPEN_WINDOW (optional)	'X' = enable (default), ' ' = disable
Force variable screen display	VARIABLE_SCREEN (optional)	'X' = enable variable screen, ' ' = disable variable screen, if possible
Display identical variables only once	MELT_VARIABLES (optional)	'X' = melt, ' ' = display each query separately
Reset variables to default values	VARIABLES_CLEAR (optional)	'X' = reset variables, ' ' = don't reset variables
Suppress warnings	SUPPRESS_WARNINGS (optional)	'X' = don't display warnings, ' ' = display warnings

Description	Attribute	Values
Suppress system messages	`SUPPRESS_SYSTEM_MESSAGES` (optional)	`'X'` = don't display system messages, `' '` = display system messages
		`'CONDITIONAL'` = display system messages only once per day per user
Read mode for data	`DATA_MODE`	`NEW, STORED, HYBRID, STATIC, STATIC_HYBRID`
Output optimization (device-dependent)	`DEVICE_OPTIMIZATION`	Yes, No
Session encoding in the URL	`NO_SESSION_COOKIE`	`'X'` = session encoding in the URL, `' '` = no session encoding in the URL
Display jump target in	`RRI_DISPLAY_TARGET`	Default setting: `menuebarRRI`

E   Transaction Codes

E.1   Transactions in SAP BW

Transaction	Meaning
BAPI	BAPI Explorer
CMOD	Project Management of SAP Extensions
FILE	Maintenance of Logical File Paths
LISTCUBE	List Viewer for Data Targets (→ BasicCubes, ODS Objects, Characteristic InfoObjects)
LISTSCHEMA	Schema Viewer for BasicCubes (including Aggregates)
PFCG	Role Maintenance
RRC1, RRC2, and RRC3	Create, Modify, and Display Definitions for Currency Conversion
RRMX	Start BEx Analyzer
RS12	Display and Delete Locked Entries (of Tables)
RSA1	Administrator Workbench (→ Modeling)
RSA11	Administrator Workbench (→ InfoProvider)
RSA12	Administrator Workbench (→ InfoSources)
RSA13	Administrator Workbench (→ Source Systems)
RSA14	Administrator Workbench (→ InfoObjects)
RSA3	Extractor Checker SAPI 3.0
RSA5	Transfer DataSources from Business Content
RSA6	Perform Follow-Up Work on DataSources and Application Component Hierarchy
RSA7	Maintenance of Delta Queue
RSA9	Transfer Application Components from Business Content
RSBBS	Maintain Blocked Lines for the Report-to-Report Interface (RRI)
RSCUSTV1	Change Settings for Flat Files (→ Thousands, Decimal, and Field Separators; Field Delimiters)
RSCUSTV6	Change Threshold Values for Data Loading (→ Package Size, Size of a PSA Partition, and IDoc Frequency Status)

Transaction	Meaning
RSCUSTV8	Change Settings for Aggregate Change Run (→ Threshold Value for Restructuring and Block Size)
RSD1, RSD2, and RSD3	Maintenance of InfoObjects: Characteristic/Flag/Unit Types
RSD4 and RSD5	Editing of Technical Characteristics and Time Characteristics
RSDBC	DB Connect: Select Tables and Views
RSDDV	Maintenance of Aggregates
RSDIOBC	Editing InfoObjectCatalogs
RSDMD	Maintenance of Master Data (for one Characteristic)
RSDMPROM	Editing MultiProviders
RSDODS	Editing ODS Objects
RSDV	Maintenance of the Validity Slice (→ BasicCubes with Flag Type of Non-Cumulative Value)
RSFH	Test Tool for Extraction of Transaction Data
RSIMG	SAP BW Customizing Implementation Guide
RSISET	Maintenance of InfoSets
RSKC	Maintenance of Permitted Additional Characters in SAP BW
RSMD	Test Tool for Extraction of Master Data
RSMO	Monitor
RSMON	Administrator Workbench (→ Monitoring)
RSMONCOLOR	Valuation of Requests
RSO2	Maintenance of Generic DataSources
RSO3	Setup of Delta Extraction for Attributes and Texts
RSOR	Administrator Workbench (→ Metadata Repository)
RSORBCT	Administrator Workbench (→ Business Content)
RSPC	Maintenance of Process Chains
RSRT	Query Monitor
RSRTRACE	Query Trace
RSRV	Analysis and Repair of SAP BW Objects
RSSM	Maintenance of Reporting Authorization Objects

Transaction	Meaning
RSU1/RSU2/ RSU3	Create, Modify, and Display Update Rules (→ BasicCubes and ODS Objects)
SARA	Archive Administration
SBIW	Display of Implementation Guide (→ Customizing for Extractors)
SE03	Transport Organizer Tools
SE09	Transport Organizer
SE11	ABAP Dictionary
SE16	ABAP Data Browser
SE37	Function Builder (→ Maintenance of Function Modules)
SE38	ABAP Editor (→ Maintenance of ABAP Programs)
SE80	Object Navigator
SICF	Maintenance of System Internet Communication Framework (ICF)
SM04	User List
SM12	Selection of Blocked Entries
SM21	Online Analysis of System Log
SM37	Job Overview
SM38	Queue (Job) — Definition
SM50	Process Overview
SM59	Maintenance of RFC Connections
SM62	Maintenance of Events
SM66	Global Work Process Overview
SMX	System → Own Jobs
SPRO	Customizing Guidelines
SQ02	Maintenance of SAP Query/InfoSets
SQ10	Assignment of Query/InfoSets to User and Role
ST03	SAP BW Statistics
ST05	Performance Analysis (→ SQL-Trace)
ST22	ABAP Dump Analysis
SU01	Maintenance of Users
SU24	Maintenance of Role Templates

Transaction	Meaning
SU53	Resolve Error Codes (at the Authorization Level)
TRSA	Test Tool for Service API

E.2 SAP R/3 Transactions Relevant to SAP BW

Transaction	Meaning
LBWE	Customizing Cockpit for Logistics Extract Structures
KEB0	Create, Display, and Delete CO-PA DataSource
RSA3	Extractor Checker SAPI 3.0
RSA5	Transfer DataSources from Business Content
RSA6	Perform Follow-Up Work on DataSources and Application Component Hierarchy
RSA7	Maintenance of Delta Queue
RSA9	Transfer Application Components from Business Content
RSO2	Maintenance of Generic DataSources
RSO3	Setup of Delta Extraction for Attributes and Texts
SBIW	Display of Implementation Guide (→ Customizing for Extractors)
SMQ1	qRFC Monitor (Output Queue)
TRSA	Test Tool for Service API

F   Metadata Tables

F.1   InfoObject

Table	Meaning
RSDIOBJ	Directory of all InfoObjects
RSDIOBJT	Texts of InfoObjects
RSDATRNAV	Navigation Attributes
RSDATRNAVT	Navigation Attributes
RSDBCHATR	Master Data Attributes
RSDCHABAS	Basic Characteristics (for Characteristics, Time Characteristics, and Units)
RSDCHA	Characteristics Catalog
RSDDPA	Data Package Characteristic
RSDIOBJCMP	Dependencies of InfoObjects
RSKYF	Key Figures
RSDTIM	Time Characteristics
RSDUNI	Units

F.2   InfoCube

Table	Meaning
RSDCUBE	Directory of InfoCubes
RSDCUBET	Texts on InfoCubes
RSDCUBEIOBJ	Navigation Attributes
RSDDIME	Directory of Dimensions
RSDDIMET	Texts on Dimensions
RSDDIMEIOBJ	InfoObjects for each Dimension (Where-Used List)
RSDCUBEMULTI	InfoCubes Involved in a MultiCube
RSDICMULTIIOBJ	MultiProvider: Selection/Identification of InfoObjects
RSDICHAPRO	Characteristic Properties Specific to an InfoCube

Table	Meaning
RSDIKYFPRO	Flag Properties Specific to an InfoCube
RSDICVALIOBJ	InfoObjects of the Stock Validity Table for the InfoCube

F.3   Aggregate

Table	Meaning
RSDDAGGRDIR	Directory of Aggregates
RSDDAGGRCOMP	Description of Aggregates
RSDDAGGRT	Texts on Aggregates

F.4   ODS Object

Table	Meaning
RSDODSO	Directory of all ODS Objects
RSDODSOT	Texts of ODS Objects
RSDODSOIOBJ	InfoObjects of ODS Objects
RSDODSOATRNAV	Navigation Attribute for ODS Object
RSDODSOTABL	Directory of all ODS Object Tables

F.5   PSA

Table	Meaning
RSTSODS	Directory of all PSA Tables

F.6   DataSource (= OLTP Source)

Table	Meaning
ROOSOURCE	Header Table for SAP BW DataSources (SAP Source System/ BW System
RODELTAM	BW Delta Procedure (SAP Source System)
RSOLTPSOURCE	Replication Table for DataSources in BW

F.7 InfoSource

Table	Meaning
RSIS	Directory of InfoSources with Flexible Update
RSIST	Texts on InfoSources with Flexible Update
RSISFIELD	InfoObjects of an InfoSource

F.8 Communications Structure

Table	Meaning
RSKS	▶ Communications Structure for InfoSources with Flexible Update ▶ Communications Structure (View) for Attributes for an InfoSource with Direct Update
RSKSFIELD	Texts on InfoSources with Flexible Update
RSISFIELD	InfoObjects of an InfoSource with Flexible Update

F.9 Transfer Structure

Table	Meaning
RSTS	Transfer Structure in SAP BW
ROOSGEN	Generated Objects for a DataSource (Transfer Structure, for example) in SAP Source System

F.10 Mapping

Table	Meaning
RSISOSMAP	Mapping Between InfoSources and DataSources (= OLTP Sources)
RSOSFIELDMAP	Mapping Between DataSource Fields and InfoObjects

F.11 SAP BW Statistics

Table	Meaning
RSDDSTAT	Basic Table for InfoCubes/Queries
RSDDSTATAGGR	Detail Table for Aggregate Setup
RSDDSTATAGGRDEF	Detail Table of Navigation for Each InfoCube/Query

G Glossary

Ad-hoc Query Designer

Web item that enables you to create and change ad-hoc queries in a web application. You can use the Ad-hoc Query Designer in the Business Explorer (BEx) Web Application Designer to design web applications in which you can create or change queries.

ADK

see: Archiving Development Kit

Administrator Workbench (AWB)

Central tool for controlling, monitoring, and maintaining all processes involved in data retrieval and processing in SAP BW. The tasks are executed in the following functional areas:

▶ **Modeling** (Transaction RSA1)
This functional area handles the creation and maintenance of metaobjects in SAP BW relevant to the process of retrieving or loading data.

▶ **Monitoring** (Transaction RSMON)
Monitoring enables you to observe and control the data loading process and other data processing activities in SAP BW.

▶ **Reporting Agent** (Transaction RSA1 · Pushbutton **Reporting Agent**)
Tool for scheduling and executing reporting functions in the background (batch). The functions include evaluating exceptions and printing queries.

▶ **Transport connection** (Transaction RSA1 · Pushbutton **Transport connection**)
With the transport connection, you can collect newly created and modified BW objects and use the Change and Transport Organizer (CTO) to transport them into other BW systems.

▶ **Documents** (Transaction RSA1 · Pushbutton **Documents**)
This functional area enables you to link and search one or more documents in various formats, versions, and languages.

▶ **Business Content** (Transaction RSORBCT)
Business Content offers preconfigured roles and task-related information models based on consistent metadata (*see:* Business Content).

▶ **Translation** (Transaction RSA1 · Pushbutton **Translation**)
You can translate short and long texts of BW objects in this functional area.

▶ **Metadata Repository** (Transaction RSOR)
The HTML-based BW Metadata Repository centrally administers all BW metaobjects and their links to each other, which enables a consistent and homogeneous data model across all source systems (*see:* Metadata Repository).

Aggregate

Stores the dataset of a BasicCube redundantly and persistently in a summarized form in the database. Because aggregates use the same form of storage (fact and dimension tables) as BasicCubes, they are often called aggregate cubes. Aggregates enable you to access BasicCubes quickly for reporting. Thus, aggregates help to improve performance. Because a BasicCube can possess several aggregates, the Optimizer of the OLAP processor automatically accesses the most appropriate aggregate during execution of a query. In other words, the decision to use a Basic-Cube or an aggregate for reporting is not transparent to the end user. Information on aggregates, such as technical, content, and status properties, are stored in table RSDDAGGRDIR. Maintenance of aggregates in SAP BW:

▶ Transaction RSDDV

▶ Initial access: **AWB** · **Modeling** · **InfoProvider** · Select **InfoArea** · Select **maintain aggregate** in the context menu of the selected BasicCube.

When building an aggregate from the characteristics and navigation attributes of a BasicCube, you can group the data according to different aggregation levels:

▶ **All characteristic values (*)**
Data is grouped according to all values of the combined characteristics or navigation attributes that define the aggregate.

▶ **Hierarchy level (H)**
The data is grouped according to the nodes of a hierarchy level.

▶ **Fixed value (F)**
The data is filtered and grouped according to an individual value of a characteristic or navigation attribute.

Logical data packages are used to load new data (requests) into an aggregate. When loading data, note the distinction between filling and rolling up. Aggregates enable you to access InfoCube data quickly for reporting. Thus, aggregates help to improve performance.

▶ **Activate and fill**
This function builds the aggregate and fills it for the first time. An active and filled aggregate is used for reporting and can be populated with additional data by rolling up data packages.

▶ **Roll-up**
Loads data packages (requests) that are not yet contained in the aggregates of a BasicCube into all aggregates of the BasicCube. A roll-up is required as soon as the data of the BasicCube has changed to ensure the consistency of data between the aggregate and the BasicCube. After the roll-up, the new data is used in queries.

▶ **Roll-up hierarchy (aggregate hierarchy)**
The roll-up hierarchy displays the dependency of aggregates to a BasicCube and among aggregates in terms of the roll-up. In other words, it displays whether an aggregate is filled by a superior aggregate, or directly by the Basic-Cube during a roll-up. You can use the roll-up hierarchy to identify similar aggregates and then use this information as the basis for manual and targeted optimization of the aggregates.

Additional functionalities:

▶ **On/Off Switch**

If an aggregate is temporarily switched off, it is not used in the execution of a query. When the aggregate is switched back on, it does not have to be reactivated and refilled. This feature allows you to compare the runtime of the query with and without the aggregate to determine whether using the aggregate is beneficial.

▶ **Deactivate**

Deactivation of an aggregate means that all the data of the aggregate is deleted, although the structure of the aggregate remains in place.

▶ **Delete**

Deletion deactivates the aggregate and its structure.

▶ **Compress**

Compression of aggregates corresponds to the compression of BasicCubes, that is, compressed requests can no longer be deleted from the aggregate. You can, however, switch compression off after the roll-up so that the aggregate request remains in place.

▶ **Hierarchy/Attribute Change Run**

If the hierarchy and navigation attributes of characteristics used in aggregates change, structural modifications are required in the aggregates to adjust the data accordingly. A structure modification changes the aggregates of all Basic-Cubes affected by modifications of hierarchies and navigation attributes:

Initial access: **AWB • Tools • Execute Hierarchy/Attribute Modifications for Reporting**

You can use the ABAP program "RSDDS_CHANGE" "RUN_MONITOR" to determine the attributes, hierarchies, and aggregates to be adjusted during the change run. Modifications of master data become effective only if a change run is executed for the master data. When the change run is at a certain size, modification of the aggregates involves more work than rebuilding it. You can set this threshold value yourself:

▶ Transaction RSCUSTV8

▶ Initial access: **BW Customizing Guidelines • Business Information Warehouse • General BW Settings • Parameters for Aggregates**

Aggregation Level

Choice of characteristics and navigation attributes of an InfoCube from which aggregates are constructed. You have the following aggregation options:

▶ **All characteristic values (*)**: Data is grouped by all values of the characteristic or the navigation attribute.

▶ **Hierarchy level (H)**:
The data is grouped according to the nodes of a hierarchy level.

▶ **Fixed value (F)**: Data is filtered according to a single value.

ALE
see: Application Link Enabling

Alert Monitor

A monitoring tool for displaying exceptions whose threshold values have been exceeded or have not been reached. The exceptions that occur are found in background processing with the help of the reporting agent. They are then displayed in the alert monitor as a follow-up action. Exceptions are displayed in the BEx Analyzer, as well as in the reporting agent scheduler of the Administrator Workbench. Exceptions can be displayed as an alert monitor in a Web application.

And Process

Collective process of process chain maintenance. The use of an *And process* in process chain maintenance starts the application process, but only after successful triggers of all events of the preceding processes, including the last of the events for which it waited.

Application Link Enabling (ALE)

ALE supports the configuration and operation of distributed application systems—between SAP systems themselves and between SAP systems and external systems. For communication (data exchange) among distributed application systems, ALE provides tolls and services, such as consistency checks, monitoring of data transfer, error handling, and synchronous and asynchronous connections. Therefore, it guarantees controlled data exchange among the distributed application systems and consistent data storage.

Application Process

A process that is automated in process chain maintenance. Example: a data loading process, or an attribute change run.

Archiving

Data archiving enables you to archive data from BasicCubes and ODS objects (tables with active data). Therefore, you can store the data as a flat structure in a file system and delete it from the BasicCube or ODS object. You archive data for the following reasons:

▶ To lessen the volume or data and therefore save storage space

▶ To improve performance because of the smaller volume of data during analyses, updates, roll-ups, and change runs, for example.

▶ To meet legal requirements for the storage of data

see also: Archiving Development Kit, archiving process, and archiving objects

Archiving Development Kit (ADK)

The ADK of mySAP Technology-Basis is used for archiving. The ADK provides the runtime environment for archiving. It primarily helps read and write data to and from archive files. The ADK guarantees platform and release independence for archived data.

Archiving Objects

All archiving requires archiving objects that describe related business data with a data structure and that are used to define and execute reading, writing, and deleting in the context of the archiving process. They are the link between the ADK and SAP BW objects. Creating an archiving object:

Initial access: **AWB** · **Modeling** · **InfoProvider** · Select **InfoArea** · In the context menu of the selected BasicCube or ODS object, select **Modify** · **Extras·** Archiving.

Archiving Process

The archiving process in SAP BW consists of the following subprocesses:

▶ **Writing data to the archive** (Transaction SARA)

▶ **Deleting the archived data from the BasicCube/ODS Object**
(Transaction SARA)
If you delete archived data from a BasicCube, it is also deleted from the aggregate that belongs to the BasicCube. If you delete data from an ODS object, archiving does not affect the data targets populated with data from the ODS object.

▶ **Restoring archived data in the BW system**
You can restore archived data with the export DataSource of the BasicCube or ODS object from which the data was archived. The ADK provides functions for reading archived data. Later, updates occur with the familiar data loading processes in the BW system.

Attributes

Attributes are InfoObjects (characteristics or key figures) used to describe characteristics in more detail. Example: For the "cost center" characteristic, you can assign the following attributes:

▶ "Cost center manger" (characteristic as attribute)

▶ "Size of the cost center in square meters" (key figure as attribute)

When you maintain an InfoObject for a characteristic, you can also assign attributes with attribute properties to the characteristic:

▶ **Display**
Attributes with this property can be used in reporting only as supplemental information in combination with the characteristic. That means that you cannot navigate in queries. Note the special case that occurs when you define InfoObjects. You can define InfoObjects (characteristics or key figures) as exclusive attributes. You cannot use these attributes as navigation attributes; you can use them only as display attributes.

▶ **Navigation Attribute**
You can define attributes of InfoObject type "characteristic" as navigation attributes. These types of attributes can be used for navigation much like (dimension) characteristics in queries: All navigation functions of (dimension) characteristics in queries also apply to navigation attributes. Unlike (dimension) characteristics, navigation attributes enable current and key-date data views at the query layer (→ Tracking History). To make these attributes available in reporting as navigation attributes, you must also switch them on at the data-target layer. A characteristic used as a navigation attribute can also have its own navigation attributes, which are called transitive attributes (= two-level naviga-

tion attribute). You can also switch on the transitive attributes and make them available for navigation in queries.

▶ **Time Dependency**
You can flag both display and navigation attributes as time-dependent attributes if a validity area is required for each attribute value.

AWB
see: Administrator Workbench

Balanced Scorecard (BSC)
Robert S. Kaplan, professor of management at Harvard Business School, and Dr. David Norton introduced this management instrument in 1992, which began a profound and lasting change in performance management at leading companies. The *Harvard Business Review* calls the concept the most important management idea in the last 75 years.

The core of the theory is that the economic success of a company rests on influencing factors behind the target financial values that causatively determine the ability to reach the financial objective. The BSC usually considers meeting objects from the perspective of finances, processes, customers, and innovation. The evidence of historical key figures is supplemented by the knowledge of future developments.

BAPI (Business Application Programming Interface)
BAPIs are open, standard interfaces defined at the application layer (Transaction: BAPI). These interfaces provided by SAP enable communication between SAP systems and applications developed by third parties. Technically, calling a BAPI calls a function module with RFC or tRFC (*see also:* Staging BAPI).

BasicCube
Creating BasicCubes:

▶ Initial access: **AWB · Modeling · InfoProvider** · Select **InfoArea** · In the context menu of the selected InfoArea, select **Create InfoCube** and select the type of **BasicCube**.

▶ Maintenance of BasicCubes: Transaction RSDCUBE

A BasicCube is a data container; reports and analyses in SAP BW are based on BasicCubes. An InfoCube is a closed, topically related dataset on which queries can be defined. A BasicCube contains two types of data: key figures and characteristics. It is supplied with transaction data relevant to analysis by one or more InfoSources with update rules. A BasicCube is the InfoCube that is relevant for multidimensional modeling, because only objects that contain data are considered for the BW data model.

From a technical viewpoint, a BasicCube is a set of relational tables placed together according to the star schema: a large fact table in the center, surrounded by several dimension tables. The fact table is used to store all key figures at the lowest level of detail. The dimension tables help to store the characteristics required in reporting and during analysis of the key figures. Dimension tables are considered independently of each other. Only the fact table links the dimensions to the key figures. All data is thus stored multidimensionally in the BasicCubes:

▶ **Fact Tables**
A BasicCube consists of two fact tables, each of which stores the key figures.

▷ F table: Normal fact table ($\rightarrow$ partitioned with respect to the request ID)

▷ E table: Compressed fact table ($\rightarrow$ F table without request ID)

A maximum of 233 key figures can be stored. Use of the E table is optional (*see also:* Compression).

▶ **Dimension Tables**
A BasicCube consists of a maximum of 16 dimension tables. Of these, the system automatically generates the time dimension and data package dimension tables. The system generates a unit dimension table only when at least one key figure is of the "amount" or "quantity" type. In this case, you must also supply a fixed or variable currency/unit along with the key figure (*see also:* Key Figures).

▶ **SID Tables/Master Data Tables**
The relationship between the master data tables for a characteristic InfoObject and the dimension tables is created by system-generated INT4 keys, or surrogate identifications (SIDs) of each characteristic InfoObject. Dimension tables store only SIDs of each characteristic InfoObject; they never store characteristic values. A dimension table can contain a maximum of 248 SIDs of each characteristic InfoObject. The relationship between a fact table and the related dimension tables is created with artificially generated INT4 keys, or dimension identifications (DIM IDs).

Administering BasicCubes:

▶ **Selective Deletion (Content tab)**
With this function and a previous selection, you can delete targeted data records that correspond to the selection criteria from a BasicCube. If you use selective deletion to delete erroneous data records from the BasicCube, you can replace the records with correct(ed) data records by using a repair request in the scheduler (**Scheduler · Maintain InfoPackage**).

▶ **Check, Delete, or Repair Indices (Performance tab)**
An index of BasicCubes is created on the fact table for each DIM ID. The indices are required to ensure the optimal finding and selection of data; however, the database system must adjust the indices during write access, which can lead to considerable degradations of performance. The **Delete Indices** function enables you to accelerate write access during the updating of the BasicCubes. After the update ends, you must rebuild the indices with the **Repair Indices** function. You can use the **Check Indices** function to determine whether indices are deleted (red light), rebuilt (yellow light), or active (green light).

▶ **Delete Requests (Requests tab)**
You can use this function to delete selected requests loaded into the Basic Cubes (if they have not been rolled up into aggregates).

▶ **Rebuild Requests (Rebuild tab)**
You can use this function to recreate deleted requests for a BasicCube. You can also use these requests for other BasicCubes. This function works only if the PSA tables store the requests.

▶ **Roll-up Requests (Roll-up tab)**
see: **Aggregate · Roll-up**

▶ **Compress (Compress tab)**
Every BasicCube has a data package dimension table (set by the system) that stores the SID for the 0REQUID (request ID) technical characteristic. Every load process fills this dimension table. Consequently, the fact table stores data with a higher level of detail than is required from a business viewpoint. Depending on the modeling of the BasicCube, the frequency of load processes, and the composition of loaded data, the level of detail can significantly affect the volume of data in the BasicCubes. After the disappearance of the request ID, the data volume can be reduced considerably without having to accept any disadvantages from the perspective of the business. To enable this reduction, each BasicCube consists of two fact tables:

   ▶ F table: Normal fact table

   ▶ E table: Compressed fact table (= F table without request ID)

The **Compress** function fills the E table with data from the F table. The entire F table can be compressed, or only an older portion of the requests can be compressed. New requests are written to the F table and can then be compressed. The compression of aggregates behaves similarly. The disadvantage of the compression function is that it cannot be reversed.

BCT
see: Business Content

BEx
see: Business Explorer

BI Cockpit
see: Business Intelligence Cockpit

BIS
see: Business Intelligence Systems

BSC
see: Balanced Scorecard

Business Application Programming Interface
see: BAPI

Business Content (BCT)
An important advantage of SAP BW over and above other data warehouse solutions is the Business Content (BCT) that SAP delivers with SAP BW. SAP continues the ongoing development of BCT, which requires a comprehensive, predefined information model for the analysis of business processes. It contains the entire definition of all required SAP BW objects, including the following: InfoAreas, InfoObjectCatalogs, roles, workbooks, query elements, InfoCubes, InfoObjects,

ODS objects, update rules, InfoSources, transfer rules, currency conversion types, extractors, and DataSources. Two areas of BCT are distinguished:

▶ BCT for SAP source systems (component hierarchy and DataSources, e.g.)

▶ BCT for the BW system

BCT for SAP source systems (SAP R/3 systems: = Release 3.1 I) is imported with plug-ins. If SAP BW systems are connected to other Business Warehouse systems as a source system, the importing of plug-ins is not required. Before you can use elements of BCT, you must adopt or activate them explicitly. You do so with Transaction SBIW in the source system and Transaction RSORBCT in the BW system.

▶ **Object Versions**

All SAP BW objects are first delivered in the D(elivered) version with BCT. The adoption of these objects from BCT creates an A(ctive) version; the D version remains in place. If the activated objects are modified, a new, M(odified) version is created. You can activate the M version and thus overwrite the older active version. Modifications of BW objects adopted from the BCT are not overwritten by adopting a newer content version.

Business Explorer (BEx)

The BEx is the analysis and reporting tool of SAP Business Information Warehouse. You can use it to evaluate centrally stored data that comes from various sources. The BEx utilizes the following areas:

▶ **Query Design and Application Design**
BEx Query Designer and BEx Web Application Designer

▶ **Analysis and Reporting**
BEx Analyzer, BEx Web Applications, and Mobile Intelligence

▶ **Formatted Reporting**
Crystal Reports integration

▶ **Organization**
BEx Browser

Business Explorer Analyzer (BEx Analyzer)

▶ Transaction RRMX

The BEx Analyzer is the analysis and reporting tool of Business Explorer. It is embedded in Microsoft Excel and can therefore access all Excel functionality. In the Business Explorer Analyzer, you can use navigation to analyze selected Info-Provider data in queries created in the BEx Query Designer and generate various views of the data, namely, query views. BEx Analyzer is used for the following:

▶ To create and modify reports

▶ To analyze reports and navigate within reports

▶ To call and to save reports in roles or as personal favorites

▶ To publish reports for Web reporting

Business Explorer Browser (BEx Browser)

The BEx Browser is a tool used to organize and manage workbooks and documents. You can use it to access all documents in SAP BW that have been assigned to your role and that you have stored in your list of favorites. You can work with the following types of documents in the BEx Browser:

▶ SAP BW workbooks

▶ Documents stored in the Business Document Service (BDS)

▶ Links (references to the file system and shortcuts)

▶ Links to Internet sites (URLs)

▶ SAP transaction calls

▶ Web applications and Web templates

▶ Crystal Reports

Business Explorer Map (BEx Map)

The BEx Map is a Geographical Information System (GIS) of Business Explorer that enables you to display and evaluate data with geographical references (characteristics such as customer, sales region, and country, for example), along with key figures relevant to the business on a map.

Business Explorer Mobile Intelligence (BEx Mobile Intelligence)

BEx Mobile Intelligence is a tool that enables you to use Web applications for mobile devices with an online connection to SAP BW.

Business Explorer Query Designer (BEx Query Designer)

BEx Query Designer is a tool used to define queries based on selected characteristics and key figures (InfoObjects), or reusable structures of an InfoProvider. In BEx Query Designer, you can parameterize queries by defining variables for characteristic values, hierarchies, hierarchy nodes, texts, or formulas. You can limit and refine the selection of InfoObjects by doing the following:

▶ Limiting characteristics and key figures to characteristic values, characteristic value intervals, and hierarchy nodes

▶ Defining calculated and limited key figures for reuse

▶ Defining structures for reuse

▶ Defining exceptions

▶ Defining conditions

▶ Defining exception cells

All queries defined in BEx Query Designer can also be used for OLAP reporting and for flat reporting.

Business Explorer Web Application (BEx Web Application)

Web-based application in Business Explorer for data analysis, reporting, and analytical applications on the web. You can format and display your data in various ways in BEx Web Application Designer with a series of web items (tables, filters, charts, maps, documents, and so on). In this manner, you can create web applications (such as BI cockpits) individually and access them over the Internet or via an enterprise portal.

Business Explorer Web Application Designer (BEx Web Application Designer)
Desktop application for creating websites with SAP BW content. With the BEx Web Application Designer, you can place queries and HTML documents on an intranet, or on the Internet. The BEx Web Application Designer allows you to create an HTML page that contains BW-specific content such as tables, charts, and maps. Such HTML pages serve as the basis for web applications with complex interaction, such as BI cockpits. You can save web applications as a URL, and then access them over an intranet or from mobile end devices. You can also save web applications as an iView and integrate them into an enterprise portal.

Business Explorer Web Application Wizard (BEx Web Application Wizard)
An assistant that supports you in the creation of web pages with SAP BW-specific content. This wizard enables you to use a simplified design procedure with an automated, step-by-step sequence. The BEx Web Application Wizard is integrated into the Web Application Designer.

Business Intelligence Cockpit (BI cockpit)
Synonyms: Web cockpit and information cockpit

Web-based switchboard with business intelligence content. Similar to a cockpit in an airplane, the BI cockpit displays an overview of all relevant business data to a company's management. With the Business Explorer Web Application Designer, you can create individual BI cockpits that display the relevant data in tables, charts, or maps. You can recognize critical data that has exceeded a threshold at a glance with the alert monitor, which is integrated into the BI cockpit. You can also insert additional data, such as documents, sketches, or hyperlinks, into the business data. BI cockpits offer the following options:

▶ Data can be collected from various data sources and displayed in various ways (tables, charts, maps, and so on).

▶ Structured (BI content) and unstructured (documents and so on) information supplement each other

▶ Personalized access: Parameters are automatically filled with user-specific values (references to the cost center, region, and so on)

▶ Role-specific variations: various BI cockpits for various roles

You can get a quick overview of various business news much like you would when reading the front page of a newspaper. You can then perform a detailed query with easy-to-use navigation elements such as hyperlinks, drop-down boxes, buttons, and so on.

Business Intelligence Systems (BIS)
Business Intelligence Systems are a family of IT systems tailored to meet the requirements of a specific user group: knowledge workers. Both observers of the IT industry and analysts differentiate between operational systems and business intelligence systems:

▶ Operational systems help automates routines and makes tasks predictable.

  ▷ They are characterized by a multitude of small transactions whose effects are normally limited and that convert data into a format that can be processed by a computer.

▶ Business Intelligence systems help research, analyze, and present information.

  ▷ They typically involve a relatively small number of queries that are often comprehensive, or that have can have significant ramifications.

  ▷ The type of queries that might arise in the future cannot be predicted. Such systems always involve mining information from the system.

Characteristic

Creating a characteristic InfoObject in the InfoObject tree:

▶ Initial access: **AWB** · **Modeling** · **InfoObjects** · Select **InfoArea** · Select **InfoObjectCatalog** of type characteristic. Select **Create InfoObject** in the context menu of the InfoObjectCatalog

▶ Maintenance of characteristics: Transactions RSD1 through RSD5

Type of InfoObject. Organization term, like company code, product, customer group, fiscal year, period, or region. Characteristic InfoObjects (such as customer or item) are reference objects. They are used to describe, select, and evaluate key figures. In addition, characteristics can carry master data (attributes, texts, and hierarchies) as master data tables:

▶ Attributes
▶ Texts
▶ Hierarchies

Characteristics indicate the classification options of a data set. In general, an InfoCube contains only a subset of the characteristic values from the master data table. The master data comprises the permitted values of a characteristic, the characteristic values. Characteristic values are discrete descriptions. For example, the "region" characteristic has the following properties:

▶ North
▶ Central
▶ South

Characteristics that carry master data can also be used as an InfoSource with direct update for loading master data. (Exception: Reference characteristics, unit InfoObjects, and characteristic 0SOURSYSTEM). Note the following special characteristics:

▶ Units (0CURRENCY (currency key) and 0UNIT (quantity unit), for example)
▶ Time characteristics (0CALYEAR (calendar year), for example)

► Technical characteristics (0REQUID (request ID), for example)

see also: Reference characteristic

Chart

Web item that refers to the data of a query view to create a diagram for a web application. For the diagram, you can select from a variety of display options. You can also navigate and analyze the data displayed in interactive charts.

Cleansing

Cleaning data before posting, checking data for plausibility before posting, or suppressing records with errors.

You can use transfer rules and update rules to homogenize and harmonize data from the source systems in terms of data structure and semantics before posting it to the data targets. You can filter out, cleanse, or correct erroneous information.

Collective Process

In process chain maintenance, a collective process enables you to combine several process strands into one, which makes multiple scheduling of the actual application process unnecessary. Process chain maintenance makes the following collective processes available:

► **And process (last)**
The application process starts only after successful triggers of all events of the preceding processes, including the last of the events for which it waited.

► **Or Process (every)**
The application process starts every time an event of the preceding process is triggered successfully.

► **Exor Process (first)**
The application process starts only when the first event of the preceding process has been triggered successfully.

Common Warehouse Metamodel (CWM)

CWM is a standard recognized by the Object Management Group (OMG); it describes the exchange of metadata in the following areas:

► Data warehousing
► Business intelligence
► Knowledge management
► Portal technologies

CWM uses:

► UML to model metadata
► MOF to access metadata
► XMI to exchange metadata

You can find the specifications for CWM Version 1.0 at *www.omg.org*.

Communications Structure

The communications structure is independent of the source system and depicts the structure of an InfoSource. It contains all the InfoObjects that belong to an InfoSource. Data is updated into InfoCubes from this structure. The system always accesses the active, saved version of the communications structure.

An InfoSource with direct update always contains one communications structure for attributes and one for texts. Both are automatically generated by the system as an InfoSource during the creation of a characteristic. A communications structure for hierarchies is generated only if you select "PSA" as the transfer method.

The technical properties (length and type, for example) of the fields in the communications structure correspond to the InfoObjects of SAP Business Information Warehouse.

Component Hierarchy

▶ **In the SAP source system**

The component hierarchy is an element of the SAP source system Business Content that is imported with the plug-in. You can also maintain the hierarchy manually. The hierarchy helps to organize DataSources. Modify component hierarchy:

▶ Transaction RSA8

▶ Initial access: **Transaction SBIW · Postprocessing of DataSources · Modify Component Hierarchy**

▶ **In the SAP BW system**

The component hierarchy is also an element of SAP BW-Business Content; you can maintain it manually here. It is advantageous to organize the InfoSource tree and PSA tables in the PSA tree.

Compounding

You will frequently need to compound characteristic values to enable the unambiguous assignment of characteristic values. Compounding is implemented in the maintenance of characteristic InfoObjects. You can use multiple characteristics as compounded characteristics. In general, you should use as few compounded characteristics as possible to avoid a negative affect on performance (→ compounded characteristics are elements of the primary key of the corresponding SID and master data tables). Example: Cost center 100 in controlling area 1000 is purchasing and in controlling area 2000, the same cost center is sales: unambiguous evaluation is impossible. Compounding the cost center to the controlling area guarantees no ambiguity.

Condenser

A program that compresses the contents of an InfoCube fact table.

Control Query

An auxiliary query executed in the web template before the queries whose results are used to parameterize the Web template.

CO-PA Updating

Transfer of account assignment data from Contract Accounts Receivable and Payable (FI-CA) into Profitability Analysis (CO-PA).

Crystal Enterprise

Server component for executing reports, scheduling reports, caching reports, and outputting reports to the web. Content and user administration occur over the SAP BW server in the context of integration.

Crystal Report

BW object type. A report definition created with Crystal Reports Designer and stored in SAP BW. Several queries can be embedded in a Crystal Report (similar to an Excel workbook). A Crystal Report does not contain any current data.

Crystal Reports Designer

Design component to create a Crystal Report; it contains the layout (report definition).

CWM

see: Common Warehouse Metamodel

Data Dictionary (DDIC)

▶ Transaction SE11

The (ABAP) Data Dictionary (DDIC) enables central description and management of all the data definitions used in the system. The DDIC is completely integrated into the ABAP Workbench. The DDIC supports the definition of user-defined types (data elements, structures, and table types). You can also define the structure of database objects (tables, indices, and views) in the DDIC. You can use this definition for the automatic creation of the objects in the database.

Data Manager

Part of the OLAP processor: it executes the database accesses that result from the definition of a query. Part of warehouse management: it writes data to the database.

Data Mart Interface

The data mart interface enables the updating of data from one data target into an additional data target. It allows you to update within an SAP BW system (Myself Data Mart/Myself System) and among multiple BW systems. If you use several BW systems, the system that delivers the data is called the source BW; the receiving system is called the target BW. Individual BWs in such a landscape are called data marts.

A transfer of data from one data target into another requires an export DataSource derived from the structure of the source data target. If the source data target is an Operational Data Store (ODS) object, the export DataSource is automatically generated when you activate a newly created ODS object (which differs from the case with a BasicCube).

Data Marts

see: Data Mart Interface

Data Provider

An object that delivers data for one or more web items. A data provider reflects the navigational status of a query at a specific point in time. The star view of a data provider corresponds to a query view. Navigation through the data or parameterization of the call can modify the state of a data provider.

Data Quality
Quality of data in terms of its usefulness for reporting and analysis. *See also:* Cleansing

Data Staging
Formatting process for retrieving data in SAP BW.

Data Warehouse (DWH)
A DWH is a system that stores data that is relevant to decisions made by a company. The functions of a data warehouse are to combine data from sources within a firm and outside of it, to cleanse the data, to consolidate the data, and to make it available consistently with analysis, reporting, and evaluation tools. The knowledge gained in this manner creates the foundation for decision-making that applies to the control of a company. A data warehouse is therefore a system primarily used to support enterprise control.

The integration of OLAP tools in a DWH system is not mandatory. Nevertheless, manufacturers currently offer increasingly more DWH systems with integrated OLAP tools. Such DWH systems are often called OLAP systems or DWH solutions. Accordingly, SAP BW is a DWH solution.

Database Shared Library
see: DB Connect

DataSource
Comprises a quantity of fields in SAP Business Information Warehouse offered in a flat structure, the extract structure, to transfer data. It also describes the properties of the corresponding extractor in terms of transferring data into SAP BW.

A DataSource describes a business unit of master data (material master data, for example) and transaction data (sales data, for example). From the viewpoint of the source system, metainformation (fields and field descriptions of the master and transaction data and programs) belongs to each DataSource; the metainformation describes how the extraction is executed. This information is specific to each source system: a DataSource is dependent on the source system. In SAP source systems, the DataSource information is stored in tables ROOSOURCE and RODELTAM; in SAP BW systems, it is stored in table RSOLTPSOURCE. From a technical point of view, a DataSource distinguishes two types of field structures:

▶ Extract structure

▶ Transfer structure

Note the following types of DataSources:

▶ DataSources for transaction data

▶ DataSources for master data attributes

▶ DataSources for master data hierarchies

The definition of generic DataSources enables you to extract data from any DDIC tables and view, SAP queries and InfoSets, or function modules from SAP source systems. You can therefore extract data from SAP source systems that is not extracted by Business Content (BCT) DataSources (Transaction RSO2). You cannot extract data for external hierarchies with generic DataSources.

Data Granularity
Data granularity describes the level of detail of data. Very detailed data has a low granularity; increasing aggregation produces a higher granularity. Granularity affects disk space, the quantity of information, and read performance. In SAP BW, detailed data for reporting is stored in ODS objects; aggregated data is stored in BasicCubes or aggregates.

Data Requirement
Describes the requirement set on the source system by the scheduler, the quantity of data and information generated in SAP BW and the source system because of the requirement, and the loading procedure.

Data Target
A data target is a BW object into which data can be loaded: it is a physical object. These objects include BasicCubes, ODS objects, and InfoObjects (characteristics with attributes, texts, or hierarchies). Note the distinction between pure data targets, for which queries cannot be created or executed, and data targets, for which queries can be defined. The latter are also called InfoProviders. A data target is a physical object that is relevant during the modeling of the BW data model and when loading the data. Data targets can be the following:

▶ BasicCubes

▶ ODS objects

▶ Characteristic InfoObjects

DB Connect
Enables the connection to various (external) relational database systems and the transfer of data from tables or views from the database system into the SAP Business Information Warehouse.

SAP DB MultiConnect is used to create a connection to the database management system (DBMS) of the external database. Reading metadata and the original data makes it easy to generate the required structures in SAP BW and to load the data. The precondition is that SAP supports the DBMS involved. You can then use Data-Sources to make the data known to SAP BW and to extract it. SAP supports the following database management systems:

▶ SAP DB

▶ Informix

▶ Microsoft SQL Server

▶ Oracle

▶ IBM DB2 390//400/UDB

In addition, you must also install the SAP-specific part of the Database Shared Library (DBSL) interface on the SAP BW application server for each source DBMS.

DBSL (Database Shared Library)
see: DB Connect

DDIC
see: Data Dictionary

Decision-Support System (DSS)
Development of decision-support systems began in the 1970s. Managers wanted query and analysis instruments that were based on flexible database systems, and that allowed them to perform what-if scenarios and ad-hoc analyses. Three main reasons contributed to the failure of this Decision-Support System (DSS) design:

▶ The DSS offered at the time used complex languages and inflexible model structures; they required a great deal of effort to learn and had prohibitively high start-up costs.

▶ To justify the enormous investments in the DSS infrastructure and the high cost of IT specialists, increasingly more lists and reports were created. The sheer quantity and unmanageability of the reports and lists made it impossible to make any reasonable management decisions.

▶ It became apparent that endless lists of numbers for the controller did not determine the success of an enterprise. Success depended on the consistent implementation of strategic goals, coupled with quick decisions.

Delta Process
Extractor feature. It specifies how the data is to be transferred. As a DataSource attribute, it specifies how the DataSource data is to be transmitted to the data target. The user can determine, for example, with which data targets a DataSource is compatible, how the data is to be updated, and how serialization is to take place.

Delta Queue
Data storage in the source system of a BW system. Data records are automatically written to the delta queue in the source system with a posting procedure, or are written after a data request from BW via extraction with a function module. The data is transferred to SAP BW during a delta requirement of the BW scheduler.

Delta Update
A delta update requests that data has been created since the last update. It fills the corresponding data targets with the (new) data. Before you can request a delta update, you must initialize the data process. A delta update is independent of the DataSource. In SAP source systems, the DataSource properties are stored in tables ROOSOURCE and RODELTAM; in SAP BW systems, the DataSource properties are stored in the table RSOLTPSOURCE.

DIM ID
see: Dimension Identification

Dimension

A dimension is the grouping of logically related characteristics into one generic term. A total of 248 characteristics can be combined within one dimension. Technically, a dimension consists of a BasicCube from a dimension table (if it is not a line item dimension, SID tables, and master data tables). During the definition of an InfoCube, characteristics are grouped into dimensions in order to store them in a table of the star schema (dimension table). *See also*: Line Item Dimension

Dimension Identification (DIM ID)

The relationship between a fact table and its dimension tables to a BasicCube is created with a system-generated INT4 key, or DIM ID. During the loading of transaction data into the BasicCube, DIM ID values are assigned unambiguously. Each DIM ID value is explicitly assigned to a combination of SID values of the various characteristics.

Dimension Table

see: BasicCube

Drilldown

Hierarchies can be defined for every dimension. The hierarchies can contain multiple levels. The higher the hierarchy level, the higher the aggregation level of the displayed data. The deeper a user drills down into the hierarchy, the more detailed the information becomes. Drilldown can occur within a dimension (by moving in the product hierarchy from main product groups to product groups, and then to individual products), or by inserting characteristics from other dimensions (*see also*: Hierarchy).

DSS

see: Decision Support System

DWH

see: Data Warehouse

DWH Systems

see: Data Warehouse

E Table

see: BasicCube

EIS

see: Executive Information System

Elementary Test

Component of a test that cannot be split up into subtests. An elementary test checks the consistency of logical objects that belong together.

Error Handling

When loading data with the PSA table, you can use the **Error Handling** function on the **Update Parameters** tab, in the InfoPackage of the scheduler, to control the behavior of SAP BW when data records with errors appear. You then have the following options:

▶ No posting and no reporting (default)

▶ Posting of valid records and no reporting (request is red)

▶ Posting of valid records and reporting is possible (request is green)

You can also determine when (i.e., after how many errors) the loading process aborts. If you don't make any entries, the loading process aborts when the first error occurs.

The request is considered an error when the number of received records does not agree with the number of posted records (key figure: "Aggregation not allowed").

ETL Process
An ETL process consists of the following subprocesses:

▶ Extraction of data from a source system

▶ Transformation of the data (including cleansing and data quality assurance)

▶ Loading the data into the BW system

Event
A signal to background control that a specific state in the SAP system has been reached. Background control then starts all the processes waiting for the event.

Event Collector
An event collector is a set of several, independent, and successfully completed events to which background processing is to react. The event collector corresponds to the "And" process of process chain maintenance. If an application process is scheduled with an event collector, it starts when all the events of the preceding processes have been triggered successfully.

Executive Information System (EIS)
After the era of controllers and the decision-support systems of the 1970s, the evolution of planning systems took an entirely new path in the 1980s. Instead of automatic-decision generators or decision-support systems operated by expensive specialists, developers decided to focus on what they could actually accomplish:

▶ Upper management would be supported by Executive Information Systems (EIS).

▶ If a decision-maker needed information, it was to be available at the push of a button.

▶ Development did not want to be limited to a company's own data, but, to be able to integrate external data instead.

However, the EIS approach failed technologically. It was too expensive and didn't offer optimal performance. The continuing weaknesses of EIS tools, (especially regarding the integration of external data) and a lack of acceptance among upper management also contributed to the failure of this approach. Instead, divisional solutions came into being, such as marketing, sales, and financial and product information systems.

Export DataSource
see: Data Mart Interface

eXtensible Markup Language
see: XML

External Hierarchies
In SAP BW, the term "external hierarchies" is understood as presentation hierarchies that store the properties of a characteristic for structuring in hierarchy tables. In other words, they are triggered by the attributes and texts of a characteristic InfoObject, and can therefore be maintained independently of the attributes and texts of the characteristic InfoObject. When the **With Hierarchy** flag is set, you can also create hierarchies for a characteristic (not reference characteristics) within SAP BW, and load them from the SAP source system or with flat files into SAP BW.

Maintenance of hierarchies for a characteristic:

▶ Transaction RSH1

▶ Initial access: **AWB** · **Modeling** · **InfoObjects** · Select **InfoArea** · Select **Create Hierarchy** in the context menu of the selected characteristic InfoObject

Existing hierarchies for a characteristic are displayed in the InfoObject tree beneath this characteristic and can be edited from the corresponding context menu.

Properties of external hierarchies:

▶ **Version-independence**
External hierarchies can be used in various versions. Version-dependent hierarchies can be used for planning and other reporting tasks similar to simulation. In other words, hierarchy versions can be compared with each other in a query.

▶ **Time-dependence**
Note the following distinctions related to time-dependence:

▷ **Time-dependent whole hierarchy**
The time-dependence refers to the hierarchy root and is therefore transferred to all nodes of the hierarchy. Depending on the key data chosen in the query, you can use various hierarchies.

▷ **Time-dependent hierarchy structure**
The time-dependence refers to the nodes of the hierarchy. Here you can determine the time period a node is supposed to represent at the specified location within the hierarchy.

▶ **Hierarchy interval**
You can append characteristic properties as intervals beneath a hierarchy node. For example, instead of appending the cost element properties to material costs individually in a cost element hierarchy, you can specify cost element properties as cost elements 100 through 1000.

▶ **Plus/minus sign reversal for nodes**
You can use this function to reverse the plus or minus sign of values assigned in a hierarchy node.

External System
An external, non-SAP data source for a BW system used to transfer data and meta-data with staging BAPIs. External systems are non-SAP systems (including SAP R/3 system and SAP R/3 systems with a release level lower than 3.1I) that make data available to SAP BW, and thus act as a source system. The extraction, transformation, and loading (ETL) of this data can occur with staging BAPIs and third-party tools.

Extractor
A program that fills the extract structure of a DataSource with data from the data stored in the SAP source system. Extractors are imported into the SAP source system with the DataSources as a plug-in. An extractor is a program that is used for the following purposes:

▶ To make metadata from an SAP source system available with the extract structure of a DataSource

▶ To process data requests

▶ To perform the extraction

Extract Structure
Transaction in the source system: SBIW

In the extract structure, the data of a DataSource is made available in the source system. You can define, edit, and extend the extract structures of DataSources in the source system.

F Table:
see: BasicCube

Fact Table
A table in the middle of the star schema of an InfoCube. It contains the key fields of the dimension table and the key figures of the InfoCube. The key is built with reference to the entries of the dimensions of the InfoCube. Along with the dimension tables assigned to it, the fact table builds the InfoCube for transaction data (*see also*: BasicCube and InfoCube).

Filter (QD)
A web item that displays the filter values for a query view generated by navigation in a web application, and enables the selection of individual values.

The data container includes a column for a filter flag. You can use this flag to have the data container use several graphic proxies, but access different data sets. This feature makes the creation of a specific data container for every graphic proxy superfluous.

Flat File
Data can be imported into SAP BW with a file interface. Two data formats are supported as source files for SAP BW:

▶ **ASCII (American Standard Code for Information Interchange)**
Files with fixed field lengths

▶ **CSV (Comma Separated Variables)**
Files with variable length: users can define the separator (Transaction RSCUSTV1)

You can use flat files to reduce the number of problems inherent with interfaces; however, you must then maintain the metadata (the transfer structure, for example) manually in SAP BW.

Formatted Reporting
Design for reports with master data, ODS objects, and multidimensional InfoProviders. You can use formatted reporting to make data available for interactive analyses and in formatted print layouts. Formatted reporting is based on the queries defined in the BEx Analyzer. Formatted reporting uses Crystal Reports from Crystal Decision, which is integrated into SAP BW.

Formatted reporting contains all the elements of formatting reports: fonts, font sizes, colors, graphics, and styles. It enables pixel-exact assignment of reporting elements without being limited to a tabular display. It focuses on form-based reports and print output. No analytical functionality: Options for interaction are considered when the report is designed.

Full Update
A full update requests all the data that corresponds to the selection criteria set in **Scheduler · InfoPackage**. Unlike a delta update, every DataSource here supports a full update.

Generation Template
A template from which a program is generated. A generation template is used when the desired program cannot be written generically and therefore must be generated anew and tailored for each new situation.

Granularity
The fineness or level of detail of data.

Hierarchy
A hierarchy usually means an array of objects related to each other. In this sense, SAP BW has hierarchies in the dimension, attribute, and hierarchy tables. In DWH terminology, the term hierarchy is closely related to the term drilldown ($\rightarrow$ predefined drilldown path) (*see also:* External Hierarchies).

Hierarchy Attribute
Attribute that mirrors the properties of the entire hierarchy. The level table type is an example: it indicates the form of the level table.

Homogenization
see: Cleansing

IDoc (Intermediate Document)
An IDoc is data contained for the exchange of data among SAP systems, non-SAP systems, and external systems. It uses ALE technology. An IDoc consists of the following components:

▶ **Header record**
The header contains information on the sender, recipient, and the type of message and IDoc.

▶ **Connected data segments**
Every data segment contains a standard header that consists of a sequential segment number and a description of the segment type, and a 1000 byte field list that describes the data of the segment.

▶ **Status records**
Status records describe the previous processing steps of the IDoc.

These IDocs are used to load data into the SAP BW system if the transfer method PSA was selected during the maintenance of the transfer rules.

InfoArea

InfoAreas help to organize metaobjects in SAP BW. They are the highest organization criterion of InfoProviders and InfoObjects in SAP BW. You can use InfoObjectCatalogs to assign a data target property to InfoObjects; you can also sign them to various InfoAreas.

Every data target is assigned to an InfoArea. The Administrator Workbench (AWB) then displays this hierarchy. The hierarchy organized the objects in appropriate trees:

▶ InfoProvider tree
▶ InfoObject tree

Every InfoProvider must be assigned to exactly one InfoArea in the InfoProvider. You can assign InfoObjects to various InfoAreas in the InfoObject tree with InfoObjectCatalogs. As with other SAP BW objects, you define InfoAreas with a technical name and a description, and create them within the InfoProvider tree or InfoObject tree.

InfoCube

▶ Creating an InfoCube in an InfoProvider tree:
Initial access: **AWB · Modeling · InfoProvider** · Select **InfoArea** · Select **Create InfoCube** in the context menu of the InfoArea.

▶ Editing InfoCubes: Transaction RSDCUBE

InfoCubes are the central objects in SAP BW; multidimensional analyses and reports are based on InfoCubes. From a reporting viewpoint (the viewpoint of the end user of reporting), an InfoCube describes a closed data set of a business report. Queries are defined and executed on an InfoCube. The data set can be evaluated with BEx Query. InfoCubes can function as data targets and InfoProviders.

An InfoCube is a set of relational tables placed together according to the star schema: a large fact table in the center, surrounded by several dimension tables. SAP BW distinguishes among the following types of InfoCubes:

▶ BasicCube
▶ General RemoteCube
▶ SAP RemoteCube
▶ Virtual InfoCube with services

InfoObject

▶ Creating an InfoObject in the InfoObject tree:
Initial access: **AWB** · **Modeling** · **InfoObjects** · Select **InfoArea** · Select **InfoObjectCatalog** · Select **Create InfoObject** in the context menu of the InfoObjectcatalog.

▶ Maintenance of InfoObjects: Transactions RSD1 through RSD5

In SAP BW, business evaluation objects (customers, revenue, and so on) are called InfoObjects. They are therefore the smallest information module (field) that can be identified unambiguously with their technical name. InfoObjects are divided into characteristics, key figures, units, time characteristics, and technical characteristics (such as a request number, for example).

As a component of the Metadata Repository, InfoObjects carry the technical and user information of the master and transaction data in SAP BW. They are used throughout the system to build tables and structures, which allows SAP BW to map the information in a structured form. InfoObjects are subdivided into the following classes, according to their function and task:

▶ **Key figure (revenue and quantity, for example)**
Key figure InfoObjects supply the values that are to be evaluated with characteristics and characteristic combinations.

▶ **Characteristic (material, customer, and source system ID, for example)**
Characteristic InfoObjects are business reference objects used to evaluate the key figures.

▶ **Time characteristic (calendar day or month, for example)**
Time characteristics build the reference framework for many data analyses and evaluations. These characteristics are delivered with Business Content; you can also define your own time characteristics.

　▷ **Unit (currency key or quantity unit, for example)**
　InfoObjects can be entered with the key figures to enable linkage between the values of the key figures and the related units in the evaluations.

　▷ **Technical characteristic**
　These characteristics have an organizational meaning in SAP BW. For example, technical characteristic "0REQUID" supplies the numbers assigned by the system during the loading of requests. Technical characteristic "0CHNGID" supplies the numbers assigned during aggregate change runs.

InfoObjectCatalog

▶ Creating an InfoObjectCatalog in the InfoObject tree:
Initial access: **AWB** · **Modeling** · **InfoObject** · Select **InfoArea** · Select **Create InfoObjectCatalog** in the context menu of the InfoArea.

▶ Editing InfoObjectCatalogs: Transaction RSDIOBC

An InfoObjectCatalog is a grouping of InfoObjects according to application-specific viewpoints. It is used solely for organizational purposes and not for any kind of assessment.

An InfoObjectCatalog is assigned to an InfoArea in the InfoObject tree. The type of InfoObjectCatalog is either "characteristic" or "key figure" and therefore contains a characteristic or key figure, depending on its type.

InfoPackage
An InfoPackage describes which data is to be requested from a source system with a DataSource. The data can be selected with selection parameters, such as only from controlling area 001 in October of 1997. An InfoPackage can request the following types of data:

▶ Transaction data

▶ Attributes of master data

▶ Hierarchies of master data

▶ Master data texts

You can define several InfoPackages for a DataSource. You can define several InfoPackages for a DataSource.

▶ Creating an InfoPackage in the InfoObject tree:

Initial access: **AWB** · **Modeling** · **InfoSources** · Select **InfoSource** · Select **Source System** · Select **Create InfoPackage** (and schedule in the scheduler) in the context menu of the source system)

Existing InfoPackages are displayed in the InfoSource tree beneath the source system and can be edited using the context menu.

InfoPackage Group
Combines logically related InfoPackages.

InfoProvider
An InfoProvider is an SAP BW object you can use to create and execute queries. InfoProviders include objects that physically contain data, for example, data targets like InfoCubes, ODS objects, and InfoObjects (characteristics with attributes, texts, or hierarchies). They also include objects that do not represent physical data storage: RemoteCubes, SAP RemoteCubes, and MultiProviders. InfoProviders are objects or views relevant to reporting. InfoProviders can include the following:

▶ InfoCubes (BasicCubes and virtual cubes)

▶ ODS objects

▶ Characteristic InfoObjects (with attributes or texts)

▶ InfoSets

▶ MultiProviders

Information Cockpit
see: Business Intelligence Cockpit

InfoSet
▶ Creating an InfoSet in an InfoProvider tree:
Initial access: **AWB** · **Modeling** · **InfoProvider** · Select **InfoArea** · Select **Create InfoSet** in the context menu of the InfoArea.

▶ Maintenance of InfoSets: Transaction RSISET

An InfoSet is an InfoProvider that does not contain any data. It consists of a query definition that can usually be read in the BW system with joins of ODS objects or characteristic InfoObjects (with attributes or texts) at the runtime of data analysis. Unlike a traditional InfoSet, this view of the data is specific to SAP BW.

Reporting on master data is a possible use of InfoSets. InfoSets are created and modified in the InfoSet Builder. Based on InfoSets, you can define reports with the Query Designer.

InfoSet Builder
A tool to create and modify InfoSets with SAP BW repository objects (InfoObjects with master data and ODS objects).

InfoSet Query (ISQ)
Corresponds to the InfoSet query (BC-SRV-QUE) familiar in SAP R/3 Basis. The ISQ is a tool used to create lists. The data to be evaluated is combined in InfoSets. SAP List Viewer is the output medium for InfoSet Query.

InfoSource
▶ Creating an InfoSource in the InfoSources tree:
   Initial access: **AWB** · **Modeling** · **InfoSources** · Select **Create InfoSource** in the context menu of an application component · Select **InfoSource type**

A set of all the data available on a business event or a type of business event (such as cost center accounting, for example). An InfoSource is a set of logically related InfoObjects that contain all the information available on a business process (such as cost center accounting, for example). InfoSources can include transaction data and master data (attributes, texts, and hierarchies).

The structure that stores InfoSources is called the communications structure. Unlike the transfer structure, the communications structure is independent of the source system. You can assign several DataSources to an InfoSource; however, you can assign a DataSource to only one InfoSource within a source system. Note the following two types of InfoSources:

▶ **InfoSource with direct update**
   With this type of InfoSource, the master data (attributes and texts) of a characteristic InfoObject is updated directly (one to one with a communications structure) to the corresponding master data tables (exception: a transfer routine is created for a characteristic used as an InfoSource with direct update). The following applies to hierarchies: If you select the "PSA" transfer method, the system generates a communications structure used to load the data into the corresponding hierarchy tables. If you select the "IDoc" transfer method, the system does not generate a communications structure. Instead, the data is updated directly with the transfer structure, and furthermore, you cannot define any (local) transfer rules. (With hierarchies, transfer method "PSA" is independent of DataSources: see table ROOSOURCE.) InfoSources with direct update cannot be used for transaction data.

▶ **InfoSource with flexible update**
With this type of InfoSource, you can use update rules to load attribute, text, and transaction data into data targets (BasicCubes, ODS objects, and characteristic InfoObjects) with a communications structure. You cannot update hierarchies flexibly.

InfoSpoke
Object for data export within Open Hub Services. The following are defined in the InfoSpoke:

▶ The open hub data source from which the data is extracted

▶ The extraction mode in which the data is delivered

▶ The open hub destination into which the data is delivered

Intermediate Document
see: IDoc

Key Figure
▶ Creating a key figure InfoObject in the InfoObject tree:
Initial access: **AWB** · **Modeling** · **InfoObjects** · Select **InfoArea** · Select **InfoObjectCatalog of key figure type** · Select **Create InfoObject** in the context menu of the InfoObjectcatalog.

▶ Maintenance of key figures: Transactions RSD1 through RSD5

Values or quantities. In addition to the key figures stored in the database, you can also define calculated (derived) key figures during query definition in Business Explorer. You can calculate such key figures with a formula from the key figures of the InfoCube.

Examples for key figures:

▶ Revenue, Fixed costs, Sales quantity, Number of employees

Examples for derived key figures:

▶ Revenue per employee, Deviation in percent, Contribution margin

Key figure InfoObjects like revenue and quantity deliver the values to be evaluated with characteristics or combinations of characteristics. SAP BW differentiates among the following types of key figures:

▶ Amount

▶ Quantity

▶ Number

▶ Integer

▶ Date

▶ Time

If you select the amount of quantity type of key figure, you must also enter corresponding units: the key figure is linked to a unit InfoObject or to a fixed value for a unit.

- ▶ **Key figure as cumulative value** (= value that refers to a period of time)
  Values for this key figure must be posted in every time unit for which values are to be calculated for this key figure (revenue, for example).

- ▶ **Key figure as non-cumulative value** (= value that refers to a specific point in time)
  For non-cumulative values, values must be stored for only selected points in time. The values of the other points in time are calculated from the value in a specific point in time and the intermediary balance sheet changes (such as warehouse inventory). You have two options for defining non-cumulative values:

  - ▷ **Non-cumulative with balance sheet changes:** Definition of the non-cumulative values also requires a cumulative value as a key figure InfoObject, a balance sheet change, which agrees with the non-cumulative value to be defined in the definition of the type.

  - ▷ **Non-cumulative with acquisitions and retirements:** Definition of the non-cumulative value requires two cumulative values, "acquisition" and "retirement," which agree with the non-cumulative value to be defined in the definition of the type.

- ▶ **Aggregation of Key Figures**

  - ▷ **Standard Aggregation (SUM/Max/Min):** With standard aggregation, you set how the key is aggregated in the BasicCube in key figure maintenance. This setting plays a role with an ODS object only when you select "addition" (you do not choose "overwrite") as the update type in maintenance of the update rules.

  - ▷ **Exception aggregation (last value, first value, maximum, minimum, and so on):** With exception aggregation, which you set in key figure maintenance, you can perform more complex aggregations of key figures. Example: The "number of employees" key figure is totaled with the "cost center" characteristic (→ Standard-Aggregation). In this case, you could also enter a time characteristic as a reference characteristic for exception aggregation "last value."

- ▶ **Reference key figure**
  You can create a key figure with a reference to another key figure (= reference key figure). You usually need a reference key figure for the elimination of intercompany sales.

Line Item
see: Line Item Dimension
see: Dimension

Line Item Dimension
Characteristics can be defined as line items, which means that no additional characteristics can be assigned to a dimension along with this characteristic. Such a dimension is called a line item dimension (= degenerate dimension). Unlike a typical dimension, a line item dimension does not receive a dimension table. The SID table of the line item is linked directly with the fact table here over a foreign–primary key relationship. This option is used if a characteristic, such as an order num-

ber, has a large quantity of values. Using this option can improve the performance of queries (*see also*: Dimension).

List of Conditions
Web item that lists the existing conditions with their states (active/not active/not applicable/not used) for a query view in a Web application.

List of Exceptions
Web item that lists the existing conditions with their states (active/not active) for a query view in a Web application.

Master Data ID (SID)
Internal key (type INT4) used for characteristics carrying master data to master data, especially for hierarchy nodes and for characteristic names.

Master data IDs and characteristic values are stored in a master data table (SID table). Information on time-independent and time-dependent master data stored in a P or Q table is stored once again in an X or Y table by using SIDs in place of the characteristic values.

MDX
Multidimensional expressions. Query language for queries on data stored in multidimensional cubes.

Metadata
Metadata is data or information about data. Metadata describes the origin, history, and other aspects of the data. Metadata enables the effective use of the information stored in SAP BW for reporting and analysis. Note the following types of metadata:

▶ **Technical metadata**
For example, the storage structure of the data, like the number format of a key figure

▶ **Business metadata and effective metadata**
For example, the person responsible for data and the origin of the data

Metadata Repository
The Metadata Repository contains the various classes of metadata. This type of data storage and presentation results in a consistent and homogeneous data model across all source systems. The Metadata Repository comprises all metaobjects (InfoCubes, InfoObjects, queries, etc.) in SAP BW and their relationships to each other.

▶ Transaction RSOR

▶ Initial access: **AWB · Metadata Repository**

Mobile Application
A web application on a mobile device with an online connection to the SAP BW system. Superordinate term: PDA application and WAP application

MOLAP (Multidimensional OLAP)
Multidimensional online analytical processing. Multidimensional data storage in special data structures based on arrays or cubes. MOLAP is primarily used in comparison with, or as an alternative to, ROLAP (*see also*: OLAP).

MOLAP Aggregate
Aggregate of a MOLAP cube. Like the MOLAP cube itself, the aggregate is stored in MOLAP storage.

MOLAP Cube
A BasicCube whose data is physically stored in MOLAP storage. Superordinate term: MOLAP Storage

MOLAP Storage
see: MOLAP

Monitor
Monitoring tool of the Administrator Workbench. You can use the monitor to observe data requests and processing in SAP BW and within the AWB.

▶ Transactions RSMON (monitoring) and RSMO (monitor)

▶ Initial access: **AWB · Monitoring**

Multidimensional Expressions
see: MDX

Multidimensional OLAP
see: MOLAP

Multidimensional Online Analytical Processing
see: MOLAP

MultiProviders
Initial access: **AWB · Modeling · InfoProvider ·** Select **InfoArea ·** In the context menu of the selected InfoArea, select **Create MultiProvider** and select the **Info-Provider**.

A MultiProvider is a special InfoProvider that merges data from several InfoProviders and makes the data available for reporting. The MultiProvider does not contain any data; its data comes exclusively from the InfoProviders upon which it is based. Like InfoProviders, MultiProviders are objects or views relevant to reporting. A MultiProvider can merge various combinations of InfoProviders:

▶ InfoCubes

▶ ODS objects

▶ Characteristic InfoObjects (with attributes or texts)

▶ InfoSets

Myself Data Mart
see: Myself System

Myself System

A system connected to itself for data extraction over the data mart interface. Such a connection means that data from data targets can be updated to additional data targets (*see also*: Data Mart Interface).

Navigation

Analysis of InfoProvider data by displaying various views of a query's data or of a web application. You can use various navigation functions (such as Set Filter Value and Insert Outline After) to generate various views of the data (query views) that are then presented in the results area of the query or in a web application. Changing views is referred to as navigation.

Navigation Attribute

Attribute in which the query can be selected.

Node Attribute

An attribute at the node level. Every node of the hierarchy has this attribute, for example, date fields DATETO and DATEFROM, if the hierarchy structure is time-dependent.

Nodes

Objects that build a hierarchy. A node can have subnodes. Note the distinction between the following two types of nodes:

▶ Nodes that can be posted to

▶ Nodes that cannot be posted to

ODS Object

An operational data store (ODS) object stores consolidated and cleansed data (transaction or master data) at the document level. An ODS object contains key fields (characteristics) and data fields that can also be key figures and characteristics, which differs from a BasicCube.

An ODS object describes a consolidated data set from one or more InfoSources. You can evaluate the data set with a BEx query. An ODS object contains a key (such as a document number or item) and data fields that can also contain character fields (such as customer) as key figures. The data of an ODS object can be updated with a delta update into InfoCubes or additional ODS objects in the same system or across systems. Unlike multidimensional data storage with InfoCubes, the data of ODS objects is stored in flat database tables. Contrary to BasicCubes, ODS objects consist of three (flat) tables:

▶ **Activation queue (= initial table of ODS objects)**
New data is stored in this table before it is activated. Its structure is similar to that of a PSA table: the key is built from the request, data package, and data record number. After all the requests in the activation queue have been successfully activated, they are deleted from the activation queue.

▶ **Table with the active data**
This table stores the current state of the data. This table has a semantic key (such as order number or item) that the modeler can define. Reporting draws upon this table. If the connected data targets are supplied in the full update

method of updating, the data targets are updated with the active data from this table.

▶ **Change log (= output table for connect data targets)**
During an activation run, the modifications are stored in the change log, which contains all the complete (activation) history of the modifications, because the contents of the change log are not automatically deleted. If the connected data targets are supplied from the ODS object in a delta process, the data targets are updated from the change log. The change log is a PSA table and can be maintained in the PSA tree of the AWB. The change log has a technical key derived from the request, data package, and data record number.

The new state of the data is written in parallel into the change log and into the table with the active data. Note the following types of ODS objects:

▶ **Standard ODS object**

  ▶ Creating a standard ODS object:
    Initial access: **AWB** · **Modeling** · **InfoProvider** · Select **InfoArea** · Select **Create ODS Object** in the context menu of the selected InfoArea.

  ▶ Editing standard ODS objects: Transaction RSDODS

  ▶ Managing a standard ODS object:
    Initial access: **AWB** · **Modeling** · **InfoProvider** · Select **InfoArea** · Select **Manage** in the context menu of the selected ODS object.

This object involves the ODS object (→ three tables) described above. As with BasicCubes, ODS objects are supplied with data from one or more InfoSources with update rules.

The update rules include rules that apply to BasicCubes and an additional option to overwrite data fields.

  ▶ **Selective deletion (Contents** tab): Similar to the situation with a BasicCube, you can selectively delete targeted data records that correspond to the selection criteria from the ODS object. Selective deletion affects only the table with the active data. In other words, only entries in this table are deleted.

If you use selective deletion to delete erroneous data records from the ODS object, you can replace the records with correct(ed) data records by using a repair request in the scheduler (→ **Scheduler** · **Maintain InfoPackage**).

  ▶ **Delete requests (Requests** tab): You can use this function to delete targeted requests that have been loaded into the ODS object, if they have not yet been updated into the connected data targets. Note the following two initial situations:

  ▶ **Non-activated requests**: In this case, the requests are deleted only from the activation queue.

  ▶ **Activated requests**: In this case, the requests are deleted from the table with the active data and from the change log.

  ▶ **Rebuild requests (Rebuild** tab): You can use this function to recover previously deleted requests for an ODS object. The recovered requests are then stored once again in the activation queue. This function works only if the PSA table stored the requests.

- ▶ **Delete change log**: You can use this function to delete requests from the change log, requests that are no longer needed for updates, or to rebuild the connected data targets. We recommend that you delete the change log requests if you don't need the change log.

Management: **Environment · Delete Change Log Data**

▶ **Transactional ODS Object**

- ▶ Creating a transactional ODS object:
  Initial access: **AWB · Modeling · InfoProvider ·** Select **InfoArea ·** Select **Create ODS Object** in the context menu of the selected InfoArea. Select ODS object under the **Type** settings · Select **Modify Type** in the context menu.

- ▶ Editing standard ODS objects: Transaction RSDODS

This type of ODS object has only the table with active data. Therefore, this ODS object cannot be linked to the staging process, because neither the activation queue nor the change log are used. These ODS object types can be filled by APIs and read with a BAPI. They help store data for external applications, such as SAP Strategic Enterprise Management (SAP SEM). Transactional ODS objects are not automatically available for reporting. You must first define an InfoSet with these ODS objects; you can then use the InfoSet to define and execute queries.

OLAP (Online Analytical Processing)
The core of this software technology is multidimensional retrieval of data. Multi-dimensionality allows the creation of very flexible query and analysis tools that then enable rapid, interactive, and flexible access to the relevant information.

▶ **ROLAP (Relational OLAP)**
The task of the ROLAP engine is to format relational data (with the star schema) in a multidimensional structure in order to enable efficient access. SAP BW is an example of a ROLAP system.

▶ **MOLAP (Multidimensional OLAP)**
Data is physically stored here in multidimensional structures (cell and array structures), so that further formatting of the analysis tools is no longer necessary. This approach requires rapid response times for queries and calculations. So far, MOLAP systems are less appropriate than ROLAP systems for large sets of data.

OLAP Reporting
Reporting based on multidimensional data sources. OLAP reporting enables simultaneous analysis of multiple dimensions (such as time, location, product, and so on). The goal of OLAP reporting is the analysis of key figures, such as a revenue analysis of a specific product over a specific period. The business question is formulated in a query that contains key figures and characteristics; the query is required for analysis and a response to the question. The data displayed in the

form of a table serves as the starting point for detailed analysis that can address many questions.

Several interaction options such as sorting, filtering, exchanging characteristics, and recalculating values enable the flexible navigation in the data at runtime. In SAP BW, the data in the Business Explorer can be analyzed in the following areas:

▶ In BEx analyzer in the form of queries
▶ In BEx web applications

Unlike table-based reporting, the number of columns is dynamic here. Data analysis is the primary concern. The layout, formatting, and printing of the reports is secondary.

Synonyms: analytical reporting and multidimensional reporting

OLAP Systems
see: Data Warehouse

OLAP Tools
see: Data Warehouse

OLTP (Online Transaction Processing)
The core of this software technology is the relational retrieval of data for processing and the documentation of business processes (billing and inventory management, for example). However, the required standardization ($\rightarrow$ as a rule, the third standard form $\rightarrow$ ensures data consistency and referential integrity) makes the queries increasingly more complex, because many tables must be read. (The traditional SAP R/3 system is an example of an OLTP system.)

Online Analytical Processing
see: OLAP

Online Transaction Processing
see: OLTP

Open Hub Service
A service that enables the sharing of data from an SAP BW system with non-SAP data marts, analytical applications, and other applications. The open hub service ensures the controlled distribution and consistency of data across several systems.

Operational Data Store Object
see: ODS Object

Or Process
Collective process of process chain maintenance. When you use or process in process chain maintenance, the application process starts each time that an event of the preceding process was triggered successfully.

Original Source System
Source system from which newly created or modified objects are transported into another system, the target source system. In the context of a system landscape consisting of OLTP and BW systems, an original source system is an OLTP development system. The target source system is the OLTP system linked to the BW tar-

get system. To be able to transport objects specific to a source system (such as transfer structure), you must enter the logical system name for the source system into a mapping table in the BW target system before and after the transport.

PDA Application
Web application on a PDA device with Pocket IE.

P Table
Master data table for time-independent master data. This table includes the following fields:

▶ The characteristic that carries master data itself

▶ The characteristics associated with this characteristic ("superordinate characteristics")

▶ All time-independent attributes

CHANGED (D: record to delete; I: insert record; space: no modification; modifications are evaluated only with activation)

OBJEVERS (A: active version; M: modified and therefore not the active version)

These fields build the key.

Persistent Staging Area (PSA)
The persistent staging area (PSA) represents the initial view into SAP BW architecture. The PSA consists of transparent database tables (PSA tables) that can be used for (temporary) storage of unmodified data from the source system. One PSA is created for each DataSource and source system. The basic structure of PSA tables corresponds to the transfer structure. To be precise, it consists of the following: key fields of the PSA plus fields of the transfer structure. The key consists of the request, data package, and data record number. The system generates PSA tables (technical name: /BIC/B000*) for each DataSource at activation of the transfer rules only if you selected "PSA" as the transfer method in maintenance of the transfer rules.

When loading data into data targets (characteristic InfoObject, BasicCube, and ODS object), you can select from the following posting types in the scheduler:

▶ **PSA followed by data target (by package)**
This type of posting first extracts a data package of a request from the source system and writes it to the PSA table. Posting of the data to the data targets begins as soon as the data package has been completely transferred into the PSA table. Extraction of the next data package begins at the same time as the posting, so that extraction and posting are executed concurrently.

▶ **PSA followed by data targets in parallel (by package)**
Parallel posting to the data targets begins at the same time as writing the data packages to the PSA table.

▶ **Only PSA followed by updating to the data targets**
This type of posting first posts all the data packages of a request to the PSA table and then posts them to the data targets. Posting and extraction do not occur in parallel here.

▶ **Only PSA**

This posting type enables you to store all the extracted data packages of a request in a PSA table, without updating them to the data targets. You can trigger follow-up posting at a later time.

▶ **Only data target**

The data packages of a request are posted directly to the data targets. The data packages are not stored temporarily in a PSA table.

Process

A procedure within or external to an SAP system. A process has a defined beginning and end.

Process Chain

Maintenance of Process Chains: Transaction RSPC

A process chain is a series of processes that are scheduled in the background (= batch) and are waiting for an event. Some of the processes trigger their own event, which can then start other processes. You can use process chains for the following:

▶ To automate complex flows (like the loading process) in SAP BW with event-driven processing

▶ To display flows with the use of network graphics

▶ To control and monitor the running of the processes centrally

Process Instance

A property of a process. The process instance contains the most important information that the process might want to communicate to subsequent processes. During a loading process, for example, this information would be the name of the request. The instance is determined by the process itself at runtime. The logs for the process are stored beneath the process instance.

Process Type

The type of process, such as the load process. The process type determines the tasks that a process has and what properties it has in maintenance.

Process Variant

Name of the process. A process can have various variants. For example, with the loading process, the name of the InfoPackage represents the variant of the process. Users define a variant at scheduling.

PSA

see: Persistent Staging Area

PSA Table

see: Persistent Staging Area

Q Table

Master data table for time-dependent master data. In terms of its fields, the Q table corresponds to the P table.

Query
A combination of characteristics and key figures (InfoObjects) to analyze the data of an InfoProvider. You can use a query to combine characteristics and key figure InfoObjects in the BEx Query Designer to analyze the data of an InfoProvider. A query always refers to one InfoProvider, but any number of queries can be defined for an InfoProvider.

A query is defined in BEx query by selecting InfoObjects or reusable structures of an InfoProvider, and setting a view of the data (query view) by distributing filters, rows, columns, and free characteristics. You can save the defined starting view of the query in the BEx Query Designer among your favorites or roles. You use the saved query view as the basis for data analysis and reporting in BEx Analyzer, BEx web applications, BEx Mobile Intelligence, or formatted reporting.

Query Designer
see: Business Explorer Query Designer

Query View
Saved navigational view of a query.

Record
In a relational database table: a set of related values. A record is stored in the relational database management system (DBMS) as a line.

Reference Characteristic
You can use reference characteristics to reuse defined characteristic InfoObjects. Reference characteristics deliver technical properties to another characteristic. You can maintain these properties only with a reference characteristic. Technical properties include master data tables (attributes, texts, and hierarchies), data type, length, number and type of compounded characteristics, lowercase letters, and conversion routines (*see also*: Characteristic).

Referential Integrity
A check of referential integrity can occur only for transaction and master data updated flexibly (→ InfoSource with flexible update). The check determines the valid values of the InfoObject. The check occurs after filling the communications structure, but before application of the update rules. The check occurs against the SID table of a characteristic or against an ODS object highlighted in maintenance of a characteristic InfoObject. To be able to use the check for referential integrity, you must always select the option to post data, even if no master data for the data exists, in the Update table of the scheduler (Maintain InfoPackage). You must also flag the characteristic InfoObjects that are to be checked against SID tables and ODS objects in the Referential Integrity column in InfoSource maintenance.

Relational OLAP
see: ROLAP

Relational Online Analytical Processing
see: ROLAP

RemoteCube

An InfoCube whose transaction data is managed externally rather than in SAP Business Information Warehouse. Only the structure of the RemoteCube is defined in SAP BW. The data is read with a BAPI from another system for reporting.

Remote Function Call (RFC)

You can use Remote Function Call (RFC) to transfer data reliably between SAP systems and programs that you have developed. RFC can be used to call a function module in another SAP system, BW system, a program you have developed, or within an SAP system. The data is transmitted with TCP/IP or X.400 as a byte stream. If the call is asynchronous, it is referred to as transactional RFC (tRFC).

Reporting Agent

A tool that you can use to schedule reporting functions in the background. You can execute the following functions:

▶ Evaluation of exceptions

▶ Printing of queries

▶ Precalculation of web templates

Results Area

In the Business Explorer (BEx) Analyzer, the results area is the portion of the worksheet that shows the results of a query. The results area corresponds to the web item table in web applications.

Reusable Structure

A component of a query stored for reuse in an InfoCube. You define a query template when you want to use parts of a query definition in other queries. For example, you can save structures as query templates. Structures are freely defined evaluations that consist of combinations of characteristics and basic key figures (e.g., as calculated or limited key figures) of the InfoCube. For example, a structure can be a plan-actual comparison or a contribution margin scheme.

RFC

see: Remote Function Call

ROLAP

Relational Online Analytical Processing. The storage of multidimensional data in a relational database: in tables organized in a star schema. Opposite model: MOLAP (*see also:* OLAP).

SAP Exit

A type of processing for variables delivered with SAP BW Business Content. The variables are processed by automatic substitution in a default substitution path (SAP Exit).

SAP RemoteCube

Access to transaction data in other SAP systems, based on an InfoSource with flexible update. The objects in SAP BW that do not store data include: InfoSets, RemoteCubes, SAP RemoteCubes, virtual InfoCubes with services, and MultiProviders (*see also:* InfoProviders).

SAPI (Service API)

The (BW) SAPI is the interface imported with the plug-in. SAPI is used for communication and data exchange among SAP systems (SAP SEM, SAP CRM, SAP APO, and SAP R/3) and the SAP BW system, between XML files and the SAP BW system, and between SAP BW systems. The SAPI is based exclusively on SAP technology and is available for SAP system as of Basis Release 3.1I. SAP BW service API technology is used in various places within the architecture of SAP BW:

▶ To transfer data and metadata from SAP systems

▶ To transfer data between SAP BW data targets within an SAP BW system

▶ (Data mart Myself interface) or into another SAP BW system (data mart interface)

▶ To transfer data from XML files

Scheduler

You use the scheduler to determine which data (transaction data, master data, texts, or hierarchies) is requested and updated from which InfoSource, DataSource, and source system and at which point in time.

Scheduling Package

Logical combination of multiple reporting agent settings for background processing.

see: SAPI

SID

see: Surrogate Identification

SID Table

see: Master Data Tables

Source SAP Business Information Warehouse

see: Source SAP BW

Source SAP BW (Source SAP Business Information Warehouse)

SAP Business Information Warehouse that serves as the source system for additional BW servers. (*see also:* Data Mart Interface)

Source System

System available to SAP Business Information Warehouse for data extraction. Source systems are instances that deliver data to SAP BW.

▶ External Systems (Non-SAP Systems, SAP R/2 Systems, and SAP R/3 Systems prior to 3.1I)

▶ SAP systems

▶ BW systems (data marts)

▶ Databases (DB connect)

▶ Flat files (CSV and ASCII files)

▶ Flat files for external market data (from Dun & Bradstreet (D&B), for example)

▶ XML file

Staging
The process of retrieving data in a data warehouse.

Staging BAPI
You can use staging BAPIs to transfer data (metadata, master data, and transaction data) from external systems in SAP BW (*see also*: BAPI).

Star Schema
The classic star schema is intended for relational database systems at the physical design level. A drawing of the start schema looks like a star in which multidimensional data structures are mapped in two types of tables (*see also* BasicCube):

▶ **In a single fact table**
The table contains the key figures and a combined key with an element for each dimension.

▶ **In dimension tables (one per dimension)**
These tables are completely non-normalized and contain a composed primary key from all the attributes required for non-ambiguity, the hierarchical structure of the related dimension, and a level attribute that displays all the individual entries on affiliation for a hierarchy level.

Start Process
Defines the start of a process chain.

Surrogate Identification (SID)
SIDs are system-generated INT4 keys. An SID key is generated for each characteristic. This assignment is implemented in an SID table for each characteristic. The characteristic is the primary key of the SID table. The SID table is linked to the related master data tables (if present) with the characteristic key. If a characteristic is assigned to a BasicCube when it is created, the SID table of the characteristic is linked to the corresponding dimension table after activations of the BasicCube. SID values are generated during the loading of master data or transaction data, and then written to the appropriate SID tables. For transaction data, the values are also written to the dimension tables to set up the DIM ID. Use of INT4 keys (SID and DIM ID keys) enables faster access to the data than do long alphanumeric keys. The SID technique in the SAP BW star schema also enables use of master data across BasicCubes.

Surrogate Index
A special SAP BW index of all key figures of a fact table. The surrogate index is created on a fact table in place of the primary index. Unlike the primary index, the surrogate index does not have a UNIQUE limitation.

Reporting is based on one-dimensional tables: analysis is limited to one dimension with its attributes. Contrary to OLAP reporting, you can assign columns however you want during the design of a query in tabular editing mode of BEx Query Designer. For example, you can place a characteristics column between two key figure columns. The column presentation is fixed and is set at the time of design.

Target BW
A BW system connected to another BW system as a source system and into which data can be loaded with export DataSources (*see also*: Data Mart Interface).

TCT
see: Technical Content

Technical Content (TCT)
Technical Content (TCT) makes the required SAP BW objects and tools available for the use of SAP BW Statistics. SAP BW Statistics is a tool for the analysis and optimization of processes, such as access time to data with queries and loading times. The data of SAP BW Statistics is stored in SAP BW and is based on a Multi-Provider that is founded on several SAP BW BasicCubes. TCT is transferred in the same manner as Business Content (BCT).

To use SAP BW Statistics, you must activate it ahead of time for selected Info-Providers. (Initial access: **AWB · Tools · BW Statistics for InfoProviders**).

Temporal Join
A join that contains at least one time-dependent characteristic. The time dependencies are evaluated to determine the set of results. Each record of the set of results is assigned a time interval that is valid for that record (valid time interval).

Test
A check for the consistency of internal information with SAP BW objects. A repair is offered in some circumstances. A test consists of a series of elementary tests. To avoid performing unnecessary checks, you can select elementary tests individually. *Synonym:* Analysis

Test Package
A sequence of elementary tests as the result of a selection of specific tests or elementary tests. You can save a test package and schedule it for a later run.

Text
Texts (such as the description of a cost center) belong to master data in SAP BW, as do attributes and hierarchies. In maintenance of a characteristic Info Object (→ Master Data/Texts tab), you can determine whether the characteristic should have texts. If so, you must select at least one text: short, medium, and long text (20, 40, and 60 characters). You can also determine whether the texts are time- or language-dependent. Texts are stored in a master data table for texts related to the characteristic.

T-Logo Object
Logical transport object. A T-logo object consists of the total of several table entries that are transported together. Example: The T-logo object "InfoObject" consists of table entries of the InfoObject table, the characteristics table, the text table, and the basic characteristics table.

Traditional InfoSet
Corresponds to the InfoSet familiar in SAP R/3 Basis: Element of an SAP query. An InfoSet determines the tables or table fields to which a query refers. InfoSets are primarily created with table joins or logical databases.

Transaction BasicCube

Transaction BasicCubes are typically used with SAP Strategic Enterprise Management (SAP SEM). Data of such a BasicCube is accessed in a transactional manner: Data is written to the BasicCube (sometimes by several users simultaneously) and might be read immediately. Standard BasicCubes are not appropriate for such use. You should use standard BasicCubes for read-only access.

Transaction Data

The transaction data of a system has a dynamic character.

Transfer Routine

In maintenance of a characteristic InfoObject, you can create a (global) transfer routine (ABAP routine/no formula editor). Contrary to a local transfer rule, you can use a global transfer routine across all source systems. The transfer routine is employed only if the characteristic is used as an InfoSource with direct update. If both a local and a global transfer routine are used, the local transfer routine runs first, followed by the global transfer routine.

Transfer Rule

▶ Editing transfer rules:

Initial access: **AWB** · **Modeling** · **InfoSources** · Select **Application Component** · Select **InfoSource** · Select **Source System** · Select **Modify/Delete Transfer Rules**

The transfer rules determine how source data is transferred to the communications structure over the SAP BW transfer structure, that is, transfer rules apply to the data from only one source system. Therefore, one usually speaks of local transfer rules. Note the differentiation of the following transfer rules:

▶ Data is updated 1:1.

▶ Supply with a constant: During the load process, the fields of the communication structure can be supplied with fixed values: the fields are not supplied via the transfer structure.

▶ You can use ABAP routines and the formula editor to design transfer rules.

See also: Cleansing

Transfer Structure

The structure in which data from the source system is transferred into SAP Business Information Warehouse. The transfer structure helps BW retrieve all the metadata of an SAP source system on a business process or a business unit. The structure represents the selection of the fields of an extract structure of the SAP source system. In the maintenance of the transfer structure in SAP BW, you assign the DataSource and InfoSource to determine which fields should be used for the load process. When you activate the transfer rules, the transfer structure is generated in the SAP BW system and in the SAP source system. The transfer structure in the SAP BW system is stored in table RSTS; in the SAP source system, it is stored in table ROOSGEN. The data is copied 1:1 from the transfer structure of the SAP source system into the transfer structure of SAP BW and then transmitted to the communications structure of SAP with the transfer rules. If the source system is a file system, the metadata is maintained in SAP BW, so that the transfer structure must also be defined manually in SAP BW. The structure of the transfer structure must describe the structure of the file (*see also*: InfoSource).

UML
Unified Modeling Language (UML) is the standard recognized by the Object Management Group (OMG) for semantic analysis of objects and for the design of object-oriented models with graphic tools. The UML standard is integrated in XMI. You can find the specifications for UML at *www.omg.org*.

Unified Modeling Language
see: UML

Update Rules
Via the communications structure of an InfoSource with flexible updating, the master data and transaction data are transferred into the data targets (BasicCubes, ODS objects, and characteristic InfoObjects with attributes or texts) based on the logic defined in the update rules.

Update rules are not specific to a source system, but to a data target, which is how they differ from transfer rules; however, you can copy the update rules of one data target for use with another data target. These rules help you supply the data targets of one or more InfoSources. They help post data in the data targets and with modifications and enhancements of the data.

▶ Definition of update rules:
Initial access: **AWB · Modeling · InfoProvider** · Select **InfoArea** · Select **Create Update Rules** in the context menu of the selected data target.

Examples of update rules include the following:

▶ Reading master data attributes

▶ Filling fields in the data target with constants

▶ Using a routing (ABAP coding) or a formula (transformation library) to supply the fields of a data target

▶ Currency conversion

With an update, you must select one of the following update types:

▶ **Addition/Maximum/Minimum**
The standard aggregation behavior of a key figure is set in the maintenance of key figures and offered in the update rules for this key figure as addition, maximum, or minimum. In particular, addition is an option for data fields of ODS objects, as long as the ODS objects have a numeric data type. This update type is invalid for characteristic InfoObjects as a data target.

▶ **Overwrite**
This type of update is not available for BasicCubes; it is only available for ODS objects and characteristic InfoObjects.

▶ **No update**
If you select this type of update, no value is calculated for the affected key figure. In addition, no calculation is performed for the corresponding characteristics and key fields.

See also: Cleansing

Update Types
see: Update Rules

Variables
Parameters of a query created in BEx Query Designer. The parameters are filled with values only when the query is inserted into a workbook. Variables function as placeholders for characteristic values, hierarchies, hierarchy nodes, texts, and formula elements. They can be processed in various ways. Variables in SAP Business Information Warehouse are global variables: They are defined unambiguously and are available for the definition of all queries.

Virtual Cube
Virtual cubes are special InfoCubes in SAP BW. A virtual cube represents a logical view. Unlike BasicCubes, however, virtual cubes do not physically store any data. The data is retrieved from the source systems during the execution of queries. In terms of data collection, note the following types of virtual cubes:

▶ **SAP RemoteCube**
An SAP RemoteCube allows the definition of queries with direct access to the transaction data in other SAP systems. Requirements for the use of SAP Remote Cubes:

▷ The functionality of BW SAPI is installed (contained in the plug-in of the SAP source system).

▷ The release level of the source system is at least 4.0B.

▷ DataSources from the source system are assigned to the InfoSource of the RemoteCube. The DataSources are released for direct access and no transfer rules are active for this combination. To determine whether a DataSource supports direct access, view table ROOSOURCE: Direct access is supported if field VITCUBE is populated with a 1 or a 2.

▶ **General RemoteCube**
A general RemoteCube enables reporting on data from non-SAP systems. The external system uses BAPIs to transfer the requested data to the OLAP processor. The data must be delivered in the source system, because it is required for analysis. You cannot define any transfer rules in the SAP BW system.

▶ **Virtual InfoCube with services**
This type of virtual cube enables you to analyze the data with a self-developed function module. It is used for complex calculations that queries with formulas and exception aggregations cannot perform, such as those involved in Strategic Enterprise Management (SEM).

WAP

Wireless Application Protocol. A transmission protocol optimized for compression transfer of the Wireless Markup Language (WML) content in mobile networks.

Web Application

see: Business Explorer Web Application

Web Application Designer

see: Business Explorer Web Application Designer

Web Application Wizard

see: Business Explorer Web Application Wizard

Web Cockpit

see: Business Intelligence Cockpit

Web Item

An object that refers to the data of a Data Provider and makes it available in HTML in a web application. Examples include generic navigation blocks, tables, filters, text elements, alert monitors, maps, and charts.

Web Item Paging

A mechanism to distribute the web items of a web template across several pages that are linked to an overview page that is generated automatically.

Web Template

An HTML document that helps to set the structure of a web application. It contains placeholders for web items, Data Providers, and SAP BW URLs. Web template is a superordinate term of Master Web template, standard Web template, and device-specific Web template.

Wireless Application Protocol

see: WAP

Wireless Markup Language

see: WML

WML

Wireless Markup Language. An Internet language standard used to describe pages for mobile WAP devices.

Workbook

A file with several worksheets (an expression from Microsoft Excel terminology). You insert one or more queries in the workbook in order to display them in the Business Explorer Analyzer. You can save the workbook in your Favorites or in your rolls.XMI (XML Metadata Interchange).

A standard, XML-based format to exchange metadata between UML-based modeling tools and MOF-based metadata repositories in distributed, heterogeneous development environments. The exchange occurs with data flows or files.

In addition to UML and MOF, SMI forms the core of the Metadata Repository architecture of the Object Management Group (OMG). You can find the specifications for XMI at *www.omg.org*.

XML (eXtensible Markup Language)

A descriptive markup language that can be enhanced. XML is a subset of the Standard Generalized Markup Language (SGML) developed for users on the World Wide Web. XML documents consist of entities that contain parsed or unparsed data. A parsed entity contains text: a sequence of characters. Note the following types of characters:

► Character data

► Markup (smart tags, end tags, tags for empty elements, entity references, character references, comments, limits for CDATA sections, document-type declarations, and processing instructions)

The XML 1.0 specification was designed by the Word Wide Web Consortium (W3C) and accepted by the W3C as a recommendation in 1998. You can view the specification at *www.w3.org*.

Several standards (XLink, Xpointer, XSL, XSLT, and DOM, for example) have been developed based on XML. More standards are still being developed.

XML for Analysis

A protocol specified by Microsoft to exchange analytical data between client applications and servers via HTTP and SOAP as a service on the Web. XML for Analysis is not limited to a specific platform, application, or development language.

You can view the specification for XML for Analysis at *www.msdn.microsoft. com/library*: **Web Development · XML and Web Services · XML (General) · XML for Analysis Spec**. The use of XML for Analysis in SAP Business Information Warehouse enables direct communication between a third-party reporting tool connect to SAP BW and the online analytical processing (OLAP) processor.

XML Integration

Data exchange with XML is based on standards defined by the Object Management Group (OMG), which aims to develop industry standards for data exchange among various systems. In SAP BW, such transfer methods for the integration of data are implemented with XML. Transfer of XML data into SAP BW occurs with the Simple Object Access Protocol (SOAP) and the use of the Hypertext Transfer Protocol (HTTP). The data is described in XML format. The data is first written to the delta queue and then updated over a DataSource for the Myself source system into the desired data targets. Do not use this transfer method for mass data; use the flat file interface for large data sets.

XML Metadata Interchange

see: XMI

X Table

Attribute SID table for time-independent master data. This table includes the following fields:

► The SID of the characteristic

► OBJVERS (object version); both fields build the key

- ▶ The values of the superordinate characteristics
- ▶ The value of the characteristic itself carries master data
- ▶ CHANGED
- ▶ SIDs of the time-independent attributes

For more information on OBJEVERS and CHANGED,
see: P Table

Y Table

Attribute SID table for time-dependent master data. In terms of its fields, the Y table corresponds to the X table.

H   Literature

Balanced Scorecard Institute: *http://www.balancedscorecard.org*.

Codd, Edgar Frank: A Relational Model of Data For Large Shared Data Banks, Communications of the ACM 26, No. 1, January 1983.

Codd, Edgar Frank et al.: Providing OLAP (Online Analytical Processing) to User-Analysts: An IT Mandate, 1993. See also: *http://www. fpm.com/refer/codd.html*.

Egger, Norbert: SAP BW Professional, SAP PRESS, 2004.

Egger, Norbert; Fiechter, Jean-Marie R.; Rohlf, Jens: SAP BW Data Modeling, SAP PRESS, 2005.

Egger, Norbert et al.: SAP BW Data Retrieval, SAP PRESS, 2006.

Fischer, Roland: Business Planning with SAP SEM, SAP PRESS, 2004.

Imhoff, Claudia; Galemmo, Nicholas; Geiger, Jonathan G.: Mastering Data Warehouse Design: Relational and Dimensional Techniques, John Wiley, 2003.

Inmon, Claudia; Galemno, Nicholas; Geiger, Jonathan G.: Mastering Data Warehouse Design: Relational and Dimensional Techniques, John Wiley, 2003.

Inmon, William H.: Building the Data Warehouse, John Wiley, 3. Edition 2002.

Inmon, William H.; Imhoff, Claudia, Sousa, Ryan: Corporate Information Factory, John Wiley, 2. Edition 2000.

Kaiser, Bernd-Ulrich: Corporate Information with SAP-EIS: Building a Data Warehouse and a MIS-Application with Insight. Academic Press, 1998.

Kaplan, Robert S.; Norton, David P.: The Balanced Scorecard. Translating Strategy Into Action, 1996.

Kimball, Ralph; Merz, Richard: The Data Warehouse Toolkit: Building the Web-Enabled Data Warehouse, John Wiley, 2000.

Kimball, Ralph; Reeves, Laura; Ross, Margy; Thornthwaite, W.: The Data Warehouse Lifecycle Toolkit: Expert Methods for Designing, Developing, and Deploying Data Warehouses, John Wiley, 1998.

Kimball, Ralph; Ross, Margy: The Data Warehouse Toolkit: The Complete Guide to Dimensional Modeling, John Wiley, 2. Edition 2002.

Pendse, Nigel: The OLAP Report. What is OLAP? An analysis of what the increasingly misused OLAP term is supposed to mean, *http://www.ola-preport.com.*

Rafanelli, Maurizio: Multidimensional Databases: Problems and Solutions, Idea Group Publishing, 2003.

Thomsen, Erik: OLAP Solutions: Building Multidimensional Information Systems, John Wiley, 2. Edition 2002.

Totok, Andreas: Modellierung von OLAP- und Data-Warehouse-Systemen, Deutscher Universitäts-Verlag, 2000.

The SAP BW Library

With this special edition, SAP PRESS offers you valuable, expert knowledge on every aspect of SAP BW. All volumes share the same, practical approach. Step by step and with easily understood sample cases, you'll learn how to master all the important topical areas in SAP BW. All authors are SAP BW specialists of the CubeServ Group. This ensures profound, expert knowledge and a uniform, application-oriented conception of all the books.

Egger, Fiechter, Rohlf
SAP BW Data Modeling
This book delivers all the essential information needed for successful data modeling using SAP BW. In a practice-oriented approach, you'll learn how to prepare, store, and manage your data efficiently. Essential topics such as data warehousing concepts and the architecture of SAP BW are examined in detail. You'll learn, step-by-step, all there is to know about InfoObjects, InfoProviders, and SAP Business Content, all based on Release SAP BW 3.5.
ISBN 1–59229–043–4

Egger, Fiechter, Salzmann, Sawicki, Thielen
SAP BW Data Retrieval
The correct approach to data retrieval from the very beginning. This book offers fundamental advice on how to set up, execute, and optimize data retrieval in SAP BW. It takes you through all important areas of data retrieval step by step and introduces you to working with master data, transaction data, and SAP Business Content. You'll learn how to master a successful extraction, transformation, and loading (ETL) process with perfect interaction among these three factors. This book is based on the current Release SAP BW 3.5.
ISBN 1–59229–044–2

I   The Authors

The authors are all acknowledged SAP Business Information Warehouse (SAP BW) specialists of the CubeServ Group (*www.cubeserv.com*). The CubeServ Group (CubeServ AG, CubeServ GmbH, and CubeServ Technologies AG) specializes in Business Intelligence (BI) solutions and has practical experience with SAP BW dating back to 1998. It has already worked on hundreds of projects with SAP BW and SAP Strategic Enterprise Management (SAP SEM).

Meet the Experts! Would you like to speak with the authors of this book and submit additional questions? An Internet forum is available for this purpose. Stop by for a visit to exchange ideas with the business intelligence community: *www.bw-forum.com*.

Contact the authors: bw-forum.com

Norbert Egger is the Managing Director of the CubeServ Group, which specializes in BI solutions. In 1996, he established the world's first data warehouse based on SAP. Since then, he has implemented hundreds of projects with SAP BW and SAP SEM. He has many years of experience working on SAP-based BI solutions.

Norbert Egger (*n.egger@cubeserv.com*) is the author of Chapter 3, *Sample Scenario*, Chapter 6, *Information Broadcasting*, and Chapter 7, *SAP Business Content*.

Jean-Marie R. Fiechter has worked as a data-warehousing consultant at CubeServ AG (Jona, Switzerland) since 2003 and is a certified SAP NetWeaver '04 Business Intelligence consultant. He has international, practical experience in the areas of data warehousing, business intelligence, massively parallel processing, and management information systems (MIS). For the past several years, he has taught data warehousing at various universities and colleges.

Jean-Marie Fiechter (*j-m.fiechter@cubeserv.com*) is the author of Chapter 1, *Data Warehousing and SAP BW*, and of Chapter 2, *Data Retrieval Concepts and Their Implementation in SAP BW*.

Jens Rohlf is the Managing Director of CubeServ GmbH, which specializes in business intelligence solutions and is headquartered in Flörsheim am Main, Germany. After studying business administration, he first worked in production controlling at Linotype-Hell AG in Kiel, Germany, and then established the SAP Business Intelligence area of autinform in Wiesbaden, Germany. He also served as the area's director. He has many years of experience with SAP R/3, SAP BW, and SAP SEM (with a focus on planning and the Balanced Scorecard), and has directed numerous projects in various industries.

Jens Rohlf (*j.rohlf@cubeserv.com*) wrote Chapter 7, *SAP Business Content*.

Jörg Rose manages the competence area of business intelligence and performance management solutions consulting at CubeServ GmbH in Flörsheim, Germany. After studying European Business Administration in Cambridge and Berlin he graduated with a B.A. and MBA. For several years, Jörg Rose has been realizing business intelligence applications based on the SAP BW and SAP SEM technologies in global projects. One of his main areas of occupation is the identification of business requirements, the implementation of data, planning, and Balanced Scorecard models, as well as web-based and automated reporting solutions.

Jörg Rose (*j.rose@cubeserv.com*) is the author of Chapter 3, *Sample Scenario*, Chapter 4, *The SAP Business Explorer Query Designer*, and Chapter 5, *The BEx Web*.

Oliver Schrüffer has worked for CubeServ AG (Jona, Switzerland), which specializes in business intelligence solutions, since 2001. He is a Senior Consultant for business intelligence solutions and a certified application consultant for SAP Business Information Warehouse (SAP BW) systems. Oliver Schrüffer has managed and successfully implemented numerous SAP BW projects. In addition, he has many years of experience in Internet-based B-to-C solutions.

Oliver Schrüffer (*o.schrueffer@cubeserv.com*) is the author of Chapter 5, *The BEx Web*.

 **Wiebke Hübner** joined the CubeServ Group in 2004 as Project Manager for SAP publications. She has many years of experience in the preparation and communication of specialized topics. After graduating with a degree in Liberal Arts, she worked in project management for a cross-regional museum. In 2001, she became editor at Galileo Press (Bonn, Germany) for business-oriented SAP literature.

Index

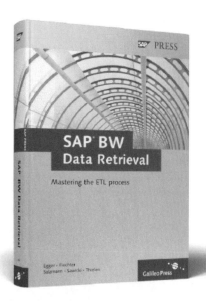

SAP BW
Data Retrieval

www.sap-press.com

How to succeed with InfoObjects, InfoProviders, and SAP Business Content

Step-by-step instruction to optimize your daily work

All new and up-to-date for SAP BW 3.5

437 pp., 2005, US$ 69,95
ISBN 1-59229-043-4

SAP BW Data Modeling

www.sap-press.com

N. Egger, J.-M. Fiechter, J. Rohlf

SAP BW Data Modeling

This book delivers all the essential information needed for successful data modeling using SAP BW. In a practice-oriented approach, you'll learn how to prepare, store, and manage your data efficiently. Essential topics such as data warehousing concepts and the architecture of SAP BW are examined in detail. You'll learn, step-by-step, all there is to know about InfoObjects, InfoProviders, and SAP Business Content, all based on the newly released SAP BW 3.5.

Comprehensive overview of the functions of SAP BI

Extensive descriptions of all new features

Includes details on Visual Composer and High Performance Analytics

approx. 600 pp.,US$ 69,95
ISBN 1-59229-082-6, Dec 2006

SAP Business Intelligence

www.sap-press.com

N. Egger, J.-M. Fiechter, R.P. Sawicki, S. Weber

SAP Business Intelligence

This book provides information on all the important new BI features of the SAP NetWeaver 2004s Release. Essential subjects like data modeling, ETL, web reporting, and planning and covered along with all of the newest functions making this book an unparalleled companion for your daily work. Real-life examples and numerous illustrations help you hit the ground running with the new release. Plus, useful step-by-step instructions enable the instant use of new features like Visual Composer, and many more.

**Tips and tricks for dealing
with SAP Business
Information Warehouse**

450 pp., 2004, US$ 69,95
ISBN 1-59229-017-5

SAP BW Professional

www.sap-press.com

N. Egger

SAP BW Professional

Tips and tricks for dealing with SAP Business
Information Warehouse

Learn the ins and outs of SAP Business Information
Warehouse (BW), and gain the knowledge to leverage the full potential of this key technology. Whether
it's in terms of project management, data modeling
or reporting, you'll benefit from volumes of basic and
advanced information. All content is presented in an
easy-tofollow format, illustrated by proven examples,
sample solutions and clear graphics and screen shots.

Provides basics as well as practical guidance for analysis and tuning of SAP BW 3.5

Contains in-depth description of BW data model, sizing, system load analysis, and DB indices

452 pp., 2006, 69,95 Euro / US$
ISBN 1-59229-080-9

SAP BW Performance Optimization Guide

www.sap-press.com

T. Schröder

SAP BW Performance Optimization Guide

Finally, a detailed reference that gives administrators expert instruction to analyze and optimize performance in SAP BW. All the BW basics are covered such as architecture and data modelling, plus the ins and outs of systematic performance analysis, as well as volumes of valuable data design tips. Readers get an in-depth introduction to SAP BW indices, statistics, and database optimizers and learn about the key aspects of reporting performance.

**A highly detailed overview of
BEx tools and functionalities**

**Understand exactly how BEx
works and how it impacts business**

**Learn from proven report design
strategies, tips, tricks and more**

71 pp., 2006, 68,– Euro / US$ 85,–
ISBN 1-59229-086-8

Peter Scott

Peter Scott

SAP Business
Explorer (BEx) Tools

www.sap-hefte.de

Peter Scott

SAP Business Explorer (BEx) Tools

SAP PRESS Essentials 18

Learn how to effectively use BEx. This guide helps
BW professionals efficiently use BEx Browser, BEx
Query Designer, Web Applications and BEx Analyzer.
It also covers OLAP functionality and other key
aspects.

Integrated Business Planning: Concepts and Realization

Project-Oriented Application of SAP SEM-BPS

Includes a Chapter on SAP BW

403 pp., 2005, US$ 69,95
ISBN 1-59229-033-7

Business Planning with SAP SEM

R. Fischer

Business Planning with SAP SEM

Operational and Strategic Planning with SEM-BPS

This book focuses on the functions of SEM-BPS (Release 3.2) as well as potential processes and scenarios. First, discover the basics of business planning; then, develop the know-how and learn the key techniques required for a successful implementation. You'll quickly gain an in-depth understanding of SEM's project-oriented applications. Whether you are looking for guidance to apply SEM-BPS in your company in order to maximize the interrelation of operative and strategic planning, or to fully leverage interaction with SAP BW, this reference book is where you'll get competent and reliable answers to your most pressing questions.

Modeling and designing intuitive business applications with SAP NetWeaver Visual Composer

Practical expert advice on the various aspects of the Development Lifecycle

approx. 450 pp., US$ 69,95
ISBN 1-59229-099-X, Oct 2006

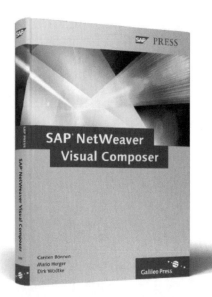

SAP NetWeaver Visual Composer

www.sap-press.com

C. Bönnen, M. Herger, D. Wodtke

SAP NetWeaver Visual Composer

Instead of conventional programming and implementation, SAP NetWeaver Visual Composer (VC) enables you to model your processes graphically via drag & drop—potentially without ever having to write a single line of code. This book not only shows you how, but also serves as a comprehensive reference, providing you with complete details on all aspects of VC. You learn the ins and outs of the VC architecture—including details on all components and concepts, as well as essential information on model-based development and on the preparation of different types of applications. Readers quickly broaden their knowledge by tapping into practical expert advice on the various aspects of the Development Lifecycle as well as on selected applications, which have been modeled with the VC and are currently delivered by SAP as standard applications.

Comprehensive details on the new capabilities of mySAP ERP

Expert insights and best practices to ensure a successful upgrade

In-depth analysis of the technical infrastructure of SAP NetWeaver and ESA

293 pp., 2006, US$ 59,95
ISBN 1-59229-071-X

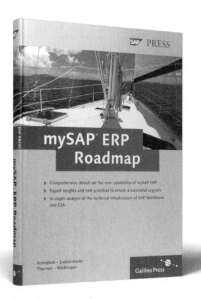

mySAP ERP Roadmap

www.sap-press.com

F. Forndron, T. Liebermann, M. Thurner, P. Widmayer

mySAP ERP Roadmap

Business Processes, Capabilities, and Complete Upgrade Strategy

Finally, a book that delivers detailed coverage of the functionality and technology of mySAP ERP, and provides you with a clear, simple and comprehensive path to your upgrade. This book introduces you to the business processes supported by mySAP ERP and helps you understand the evolution from SAP R/3 to mySAP ERP. You get exclusive insights into the technical infrastructure of SAP NetWeaver and the Enterprise Services Architecture, all designed to help you hit the ground running. Through clear decision criteria, practical examples, and Transition Road-maps, readers will uncover the optimal path from SAP R/3 to mySAP ERP. This book is an invaluable resource to support your upgrade decision.

An integrated approach to analyzing liquidity

How to perform successful cash accounting in SAP R/3

In-depth details on exact cash flow planning using SAP BW and SAP SEM

88 pp., 2006
68,00 Euro, 85,00 US$
ISBN 1-59229-070-1

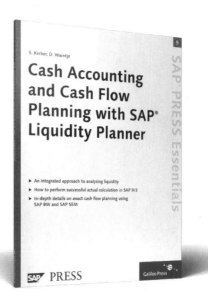

Cash Accounting and Cash Flow Planning with SAP Liquidity Planner

S. Kerber, D. Warntje

▶ An integrated approach to analyzing liquidity
▶ How to perform successful actual calculation in SAP R/3
▶ In-depth details on exact cash flow planning using SAP BW and SAP SEM

SAP PRESS · Galileo Press

Cash Accounting and Cash Flow Planning with SAP Liquidity Planner

www.sap-press.com

S. Kerber, D. Warntje

Cash Accounting and Cash Flow Planning with SAP Liquidity Planner

SAP PRESS Essentials 9

This SAP PRESS Essentials guide teaches you how to optimize your use of SAP for liquidity calculation and planning. SAP Liquidity Planner consists of SAP Actual Calculation (cash accounting) and SAP BW/ SEM. The first part of the book describes how you can successfully implement cash accounting in SAP R/3. Each relevant area of SAP Actual Calculation, from the technical settings (via customization) through to the liquidity analysis processes is described in great detail. The subsequent sections provide you with a fundamental introduction to reporting and planning using SAP BW/SEM. The last chapter concludes with details of an exclusive workaround that enables you to perform liquidity planning and reporting without SAP BW/SEM.

Interested in reading more?

Please visit our Web site for all
new book releases from SAP PRESS.

www.sap-press.com